PA
4167
.D56
1989

Dimock, George.

The unity of the
Odyssey

$30

PA
4167
.D56
1989

Dimock, George.

The unity of the
Odyssey

$30.00

DATE	BORROWER'S NAME	

LITERATURE & LANGUAGE DIVISION

© THE BAKER & TAYLOR CO.

THE UNITY OF THE *Odyssey*

THE UNITY OF THE

Odyssey

George E. Dimock

The University of Massachusetts Press

Amherst, 1989

Copyright © 1989 by
The University of Massachusetts Press
All rights reserved
Printed in the United States of America
LC 88-14824
ISBN 0-87023-643-1
Designed by Edith Kearney
Set in Linotron Electra by Keystone Typesetting, Inc.
Printed by Thomson-Shore, Inc.
and bound by John H. Dekker & Sons, Inc.

Library of Congress Cataloging-in-Publication Data

Dimock, George.
The unity of the Odyssey / George E. Dimock.
p.   cm.
Bibliography: p.
Includes index.
ISBN 0–87023–643–1 (alk. paper)
1. Homer. Odyssey. I. Title.
PA4167.D56 1989
883'.01—dc19   88–14824
CIP

British Library Cataloguing in Publication data are available.

This publication has been supported by the
National Endowment for the Humanities, a federal agency which
supports the study of such fields as
history, philosophy, literature, and language.

To Mary

Contents

ACKNOWLEDGMENTS   ix

NOTE ON SPELLING AND PRONUNCIATION   xi

INTRODUCTION   3

BOOK 1: *The Image of Odysseus*   5

BOOK 2: *Right and Wrong*   25

BOOK 3: *Nestor the Home-Goer*   38

BOOK 4: *The Waiting of Menelaos; Penelope and the Suitors*   46

BOOK 5: *Odysseus Unveiled*   63

BOOK 6: *The Maiden Unmastered*   76

BOOK 7: *The Happy City*   83

BOOK 8: *The City Sacker*   94

BOOK 9: *The Kyklops*   107

BOOK 10: *Kirke*   119

BOOK 11: *The Dead*   133

BOOK 12: *Helios*   162

BOOK 13: *Athena and Odysseus*   175

BOOK 14: *Eumaios, the Faithful Slave*   189

BOOK 15: *The Return of Telemachos*   199

BOOK 16: *Father and Son*   207

BOOK 17: *Beggar on the Threshold*   216

BOOK 18: *Afternoon to Evening*   232

BOOK 19: *The Man of Pain*   246

BOOK 20: *A "Sweet" Dinner*   264

BOOK 21: *Odysseus Strings His Bow*   277

BOOK 22: *Justice*   295

{ CONTENTS }

BOOK 23: *Penelope*   316

BOOK 24: *Peace*   323

WORKS CITED   337

INDEX   339

Acknowledgments

I would first like to thank my father, George E. Dimock, for persuading me by his example to study Latin and Greek. Of my many good teachers I must confine myself to mentioning here only Harriet Budd and Otho L. Vars of the Pingry School, then in Elizabeth, New Jersey, Allen Rogers ("Zeus") Benner of Andover who introduced me to Homer, and Professor Harry M. Hubbell of Yale, my father's companion and my superlative Mentor.

Of the many students whose special interest demanded the best answer I could give to the question, "What is so good about the Classics," I will name three who are no longer with us: Gertrude Simer, Catherine Campbell Rhorer, and Elizabeth Bynum. Among my colleagues, Louise Adams Holland's combination of scholarship and humanity has been an inspiration and her friendship a source of strength for more years than I care to think. Justina Gregory and Andrew Ford have helped hugely not only by "being there" but also by devoting much time and thought to the early stages of the MS. Of others who, like them, have provided much-needed advice and support, I must name at least Howard Porter, C. L. Barber, Helen Bacon, Bernard Knox, and Ronald Macdonald. Without the aid and forbearance of friends and of wife and sons and daughter I would never have finished this book. I thank them each and all for their great patience.

Let me thank here as well the American Council of Learned Societies and the Simon Guggenheim Memorial Foundation for freedom to spend 1960–61 and 1964–65 writing and traveling in Greece. I am also grateful to the Ministry of Culture of the Hellenic Republic for the reproduction on the jacket of the Blinding of Polyphemos from the Eleusis amphora.

Finally, I owe more than I can say to Leone Stein and, after her retirement, to Richard Martin, both of the University of Massachusetts Press, for their interest and encouragement. From them and their able assistants I have experienced nothing but the greatest kindness and cooperation. Nor must I close these acknowledgments before thanking Ellen Dibble not only for her cheerful wizardry on the word processor and her editorial expertise but also for her elucidation of Homer's text on pages 233–34 of this book.

Note on Spelling and Pronunciation

In spelling and pronunciation of Greek names, this book follows H. J. Rose's *Handbook of Greek Mythology* in essentially transliterating the Greek. It should be remembered that all syllables are pronounced. The names Antinoos and Alkinoos have four syllables, *oo* being a disyllable in Greek. Other disyllables are *ae*, *ie*, and *oe*, as in Laertes, Scherie, and Noemon. On the other hand, *eu* is a diphthong, so that Proteus has two syllables, Odysseus three.

Consonants in Greek are pronounced as they are in English, with the exception that pronunciation of the combinations *kh*, *ph*, and *th* is like the sound of the corresponding letters in *back home*, *up here*, and *at home* respectively. Greek vowels have a pronunciation similar to the corresponding vowels in the words below.

Greek	Example
a	father
ai	aisle
au	sauerkraut
e	pet
ē	me*a*sure; (French) fête
ei	eight
eu	eulogy
i	hit *or* machine
o	potato
ō	score
oi	oil
ou	soup
u	(French) rue

In proper names I follow Rose in transliterating simple upsilon as *y* and chi as *ch*, although in other Greek words I write *u* and *kh* respectively. On occasion

I have represented Greek zeta as *zd* to remind readers that it is pronounced like the *sd* of *wisdom*.

Rose excepts the following from strict transliteration: Achaians (instead of Achaioi), Achilles (Achilleus), Aeschylus (Aischylos), Crete (Krētē), Helen (Helenē), Mycenae (Mykēnai), Phoenicia (Phoinikē), Trojans (Trōes), and Troy (Troia). I write the Latin Ithaca instead of his Ithake. I have allowed myself also the Latinate Phaeacians, Aegean, Argives, Danaans, Cythera, and Sirens (instead of Phaiakes, Aigaian, Argeioi, Danaoi, Kythera, and Seirenes).

THE UNITY OF THE *Odyssey*

Introduction

The "intentional fallacy" dies hard. There is no way to prevent the common reader from hearing Homer as the voice of a single human being consciously manipulating narrative material for artistic effect (Finnegan, 273; de Romilly). Although it may be true that we can never be absolutely certain what Homer means to imply in any particular case, readers guess right often enough to enjoy what he has to say. Otherwise we would not be reading him. My purpose in writing this book is to pass along what I take some of Homer's implications to be. It has seemed to me that guesses at implications confirm themselves by suggesting further guesses elsewhere in the poem consistent with the original ones and pointing toward the poem's unity. May it seem the same to my reader, who will then continue the process!

Readers may find the next paragraphs somewhat technical. They seem necessary in order to show that Aristotle chose Odysseus's boar hunt on Parnassos in the *Odyssey*'s nineteenth book as his test of the poem's unity. Arguments both here and in the following chapter from Aristotle's and Homer's original language may suggest why people continue to study Greek.

Concerning the unity of Homer's *Odyssey*, Aristotle in his *Poetics* has something to say that has not yet been generally understood. He substantiates his famous remark that Homer knew better than the other epic poets what a literary unity is with the following words: "For when he composed a poem about Odysseus, he did not put in everything that happened to him, as for instance, on the one hand, his being wounded on Parnassos, and, on the other, his pretending to have gone mad at the time of the gathering of the host, events neither of which rendered the other necessary or likely; but rather he made his *Odyssey* concern a unified action as we call it, just as he did his *Iliad*" (1451a). This passage used to be read (with insufficient attention to the Greek *men . . . de*, "on the one hand . . . on the other") as though Aristotle meant that neither of the episodes mentioned was included in the *Odyssey*. Such a reading was

3

embarrassing, since the story of how Odysseus was wounded by a boar on Parnassos, told as part of Eurykleia's recognition of him in Book 19, is included in every relevant manuscript which has come down to us.

In 1962, a Yugoslav scholar, K. Gantar, solved the problem. In a note published in *Ziva Antika*, he demonstrates that Aristotle means that the boar hunt is included in Homer's *Odyssey*, while the incident in which Odysseus pretends to be insane is purposely omitted. These two incidents have such conflicting tendencies that no poem about Odysseus could include both and maintain its literary unity. In the boar hunt Odysseus shows himself to be a hero; in pretending to be insane when the army was gathering for Troy, a story that was also told of him but not in the *Odyssey*, he appears a coward. It is as simple as that; I phrase the antithesis as Gantar phrases it. Aristotle, then, far from implying that the boar hunt was not in his text of the *Odyssey*, is using it as his touchstone for the *Odyssey*'s literary unity: according to him nothing inconsistent with the spirit of that episode belongs in the poem.

By looking more closely at the boar hunt, we can hope to see better wherein the unity of the *Odyssey* lies, both for Aristotle and for ourselves. As Homer tells the story, the adventure on Parnassos is the earliest occasion in Odysseus's life on which he shows his essential character. He does so by enacting the meaning of his name in the presence of the grandfather who gave it to him. For the grandfather, as we shall see, the name Odysseus means "man of pain," and Odysseus, given the name at birth, proves his right to it in young manhood by both killing the boar and being wounded by it. Moreover, since in spite of his wound he and everyone else rejoice in the happening, the paradox of his grandfather's giving him such a name is at once explained: there are times when to injure and suffer is counted as glorious. Depicting Odysseus earning his name in this glorious adventure of his youth, the boar hunt makes a fundamental statement about what it is to be Odysseus. With this statement, Aristotle implies, everything else in the poem agrees. Proceeding through the *Odyssey* book by book, we shall find, I think, that this is indeed the case.

The Image of Odysseus

> The man sing, Muse, the shifty man, so
> buffeted abroad after he sacked the holy citadel of Troy.

So begins Homer's *Odyssey*. Who or what is this Muse?

Belief in the Muses depends on the notion that the gods put ideas into people's minds. At the beginning of the *Iliad*, for example, Hera puts it into Achilles' mind to call an assembly of the army in order to do something about the plague (1.55). Not everything people think of comes from the gods, however, as we see in book 3 of the *Odyssey*. There, when Telemachos asks Athena, disguised as his father's old friend Mentor, how he can possibly find words to address someone as venerable as King Nestor, the goddess replies,

> Telemachos, some things you will think of for yourself,
> others divine agency will suggest, for I do not think
> that you were born and reared without the gods' favor.
> (3.26–28)

Clearly the gods may inspire words as well as actions. They may also inspire information pure and simple. In book 1 of the *Odyssey* Athena, this time disguised as Mentes, another old friend, tells Telemachos that he may get news of his father from either man or god.

> Either some mortal may tell you, or better yet
> you may hear a rumor from Zeus. (1.282–83)

Rationalists that we are, we see nothing supernatural about rumors; but the attitude in antiquity was that news without a readily identifiable human source comes ultimately from heaven. How could mere mortal agency, for example,

account for the speed with which some things become known? The historian
Herodotus, three hundred years after Homer, was in many ways a skeptic, but
he believed implicitly that the rumor of the Greek victory at Plataia reached the
Greek fleet all the way across the Aegean at Mykale on the same day that it
occurred, and he expressly attributed this phenomenon to the gods (*History*
9.100). If the gods convey information which seems impossibly far removed in
space, they can do the same in respect to time, and here we find the Muses
explicitly mentioned. In book 2 of the *Iliad* Homer, about to sing the "Catalogue of Ships," calls for their help in the following words:

> Tell me now, you Muses, who have your homes on Olympos—
> for you are goddesses, you are present, and you know everything,
> while we hear only the fame of things, and know nothing at all—
> who were the lords of the Greeks, who led them to battle?
>
> (2.484–87)

Here the ordinary human's general notion of what happened at Troy long,
long ago is contrasted with what we would regard as the poet's passionate
reconstruction in imagination of the very words, gestures, and feelings of the
heroes, or, in this case, of the name, home, and number of ships of every
leader present. The general notion, the poet implies, is human tradition; the
detail can come only from the Muses. For them, to be is to know, as the
alliteration of the passage's second line suggests.

> humeis gar theai *este*, par*este* te, *iste* te panta.
> for *you are* goddesses, *you are* present, and *you know* everything.

As divine knowledge of the truth they "are present" at all times and places, both
at the scene of the action in the past and within the mind of the poet in the
present (cf. Detienne, 15). Through them he has direct access to everything
just as it happened, whereas human tradition is indirect, scant, and fast fading,
a mere nothing in comparison. That the Muses were thought to tell the truth is
indicated also by Alkinoos's remark at *Odyssey* 11.368 that Odysseus's tale
seems no falsehood but, on the contrary, like what a bard might sing, and by
the revision of Hesiod's Muses of what must have been the prevalent notion.

> Oh you shepherds who sleep in the open, contemptible, bellies merely;
> we can and do tell many lies that sound reliable;
> but we also can, when we wish, utter perfect truth.
>
> (*Theogony* 26–28)

That the Muses in fact know more than any human voice has the physical endurance to utter is implied in the lines immediately following those quoted from the *Iliad* above.

> The multitude I could not recite, I do not name them;
> not even if I had ten tongues, ten mouths;
> not if my voice never broke, and the heart in me were bronze.
> Only the Muses of Olympos, Zeus's daughters, could
> make mention of every one of those who came beneath Ilion.
> The leaders of the fleet I tell, and all the ships.

Obvious though it may be to us that what Homer does find himself able to sing comes from human tradition, the poet himself thinks that the lines which contain the names of the leaders come to his mind not from a singer or singers he happens to have heard but from the Muses (Burkert, 111). The reasons are not far to seek. Given the idea that the remarkable in human life, including brilliant or crucial or otherwise impressive knowledge or speech, often comes from the gods, it is utterly natural that a culture like the Greeks' should hypostatize the Muses or some similar divine agent as the source both of the power and of the content of its poetry. As such a culture develops a poetic language to celebrate the impressive in its experience (Dimock, 42–44), the enthusiasm felt and communicated by poets will be ascribed not to their human predecessors but to divinity, "the gods," and so will the ease with which verses come even unbidden to the poet's lips. Fired by his subject and guided by what other singers have more or less unconsciously established as the proper language for the remarkable, the good singer's imagination will tell him instantly, and in poetry, what his hero must look like, say, or do. It does not matter whether he has heard the words that come to him sung before or whether he himself has formed them unconsciously by analogy; they will be for him the voice of the Muse singing through him. He will not fear to innovate or to contradict what others have sung. Are not these others often palpably wrong? Do they not contradict each other and, on occasion, even sing obvious nonsense?

How much better it is to take god rather than man for one's poetic source is suggested by Odysseus's household bard Phemios as he pleads for his life at the end of the poem.

> I am self-taught, and the god implants in me
> songs of all sorts. Be sure I shall sing for you
> as for a god. . . . (22.347–49)

Phemios implies that ordinary poets do indeed copy one another, but that the best practitioners of the art are "self-taught": they listen only to the god within them and thus receive the truth at first hand. How greatly human tradition could in fact be thought to err, and how willing the gods were to correct it, is shown by the story of Stesichoros, whom the gods struck blind for singing that Helen went to Troy with Paris. When he composed a recantation, his famous *Palinode*, his sight was restored (Plato *Phaedrus* 243A). The Muse, then, far from forcing traditions on Homer which do not fit his conception, impels him to discard whatever does not fit. His own feeling as artist for what is true and right, regardless of what others say or sing, is for him the voice of the Muse within him, and not to be disobeyed.

We must conclude, then, that what Homer feels as the Muse is what we would call his own imagination, engaged passionately and responsibly in re-creating the past on the basis of, but not blindly following, what he has heard from others. If the re-creation includes some history, that is only to be expected. If it contains folk motifs and narrative patterns, these are simply forms established by the culture as proper to the remarkable. If the largest part of the re-creation is, from our point of view, unhistorical, it is nonetheless what a great mind—Homer's—passionately believes to have happened, controlled by his sense of the way the world actually works. If in the course of this book I sometimes speak of the poet as though he were inventing his material, this is because the Muse, in our terms, sets him free to compose fiction; but we must not forget that both he and his audience considered this fiction to proceed from the very mouth of Truth.

We have seen that for Homer the Muse has objective reality. She "is present" and can be talked to. In this conviction, he identifies for her in the first nine lines of the *Odyssey* the particular story which he wishes her to put, words and all, into his mind. Some have thought that this particular "invocation of the Muse" identifies the story so badly that it can never have been meant for the poem as we now have it. Homer asks her to sing of "the shifty man," driven astray after he sacked Troy; he mentions his seeing the towns of many men on his way home and his sufferings on the sea; he states that he lost his companions because they foolishly ate the cattle of the sun-god. That seems to be all. No Telemachos, no Penelope, no suitors—in fact nothing that could be construed as indicating directly either the first four books of the poem or the last twelve. Can the few details which Homer does mention really be meant to suggest to the Muse the song which she ends by singing?

Here is a case where, because the sense has seemed to fail us, we can see particularly clearly the contribution which the sound and physical arrangement of Homer's Greek make to the unity of the poem. The primarily auditory elements of the nine lines of the invocation combine with their sense to inform us that we have here not a synopsis of the plot of the poem but a pair of contrasted images. As we observe the extent to which word order, phrasing, sound, and meaning are here coordinated, it will become obvious that Homeric poetry is capable of the highest degree of organization. The following literal translation shows us the effect achieved by the physical arrangement of the grammatical members:

> The man sing, Muse, crafty-shifty, who very much
> *was-buffeted-abroad*, after of Troy the holy citadel he sacked:
> many men he saw the towns of, and the mind knew;
> many on the sea were the woes he suffered in his heart,
> trying to win his own life and the homecoming of his companions.
> But not even so his companions did he save, eager though he was;
> of their own recklessness they perished,
> childishly innocent, who did the cattle of Hyperion's son the Sun
> *eat-up*; and he from them took away their homecoming day.

The contrasted images here are "the man . . . , crafty-shifty, who . . . *was-buffeted-abroad*" and "his companions . . . , childishly innocent, who did . . . *eat-up*." The first two lines of this invocation match the last two in that each pair applies an epithet to its respective member of the contrast ("the man . . . , crafty-shifty" and "his companions . . . , childishly innocent") and then adds to the epithet a *who* clause which ends with an important-sounding verb at the beginning of the second line of the pair. These verbs thus receive, metrically and grammatically speaking, the chief emphasis of their respective halves of the passage. In the Greek, both these verbs (corresponding to "was-buffeted-abroad" and "eat-up" in the translation) end within the first metrical foot, so that the clauses which follow them and complete the second line of the pair are necessarily of almost identical length. The similarity of length and position of these following clauses in turn reinforces a certain balance of meaning in that the first of these two clauses tells what led up to "was-buffeted-abroad," whereas the second tells what happened as a result of "eat-up." This completes our account of lines 1–2 and 8–9.

Lines 3 and 4, in turn, balance lines 6 and 7 in that each pair of lines consists of two statements about its member of the comparison, each statement being exactly one line long. In lines 3 and 4, the statements begin with forms of the same Greek word (*pollōn* and *polla*); in lines 6 and 7, they begin with a similar sound (*all* and *au*). Lines 3 and 4 state the consequences of the emphatic verb of lines 1 and 2; "was-buffeted-abroad" is as close as I can come in English to its meaning, which combines the notions of wandering and being beaten. Line 3 conveys the experience which comes with the wandering; line 4, the suffering which comes from being beaten. Lines 6 and 7 state the consequences of the emphatic verb of lines 8 and 9, "did . . . eat-up": with respect to "the man," the companions' eating caused his failure to save them (line 6); with respect to the companions, this eating caused them to perish through their own foolish willfulness (line 7). Line 5, in the center of this composition, in its first half ("trying to win his own life") essentially finishes with the first member of the comparison, the man, and in its second half ("and the homecoming of his companions") introduces the second member, his companions. At the center of this central line, the word *psukhēn* ("ghost," here implying "life") is the pivot of the whole passage, both as the center of the ring composition and because it is what the man may still achieve and what his companions eventually lost.

In Homer, when a man dies, his visual image as a living person parts company with his body and flies away to the underworld, as we see on many occasions in the *Iliad*. He quite literally "gives up the ghost," and that explains how he can appear to people in dreams and otherwise after he is dead. One thinks immediately of Patroklos's psukhē appearing to Achilles in *Iliad* 23.65–68. Thus to "win one's ghost" in Homer is the opposite of "giving up the ghost" in our parlance. In Homeric Greek, the expression for "risking one's life" is *psukhas parthemenoi*, "setting up one's ghost as a prize to be fought for" (*Odyssey* 3.74). As opposed to his companions, Odysseus in the first instance won his ghost by staying alive when they perished. Not inappropriately, a completed reading of the poem suggests that psukhē, conceived of as the image one creates by living, is the central theme of the *Odyssey*. Odysseus's psukhē will live in human memory in a sense in which his companions' will not.

The physical arrangement, then, of the Greek words in the invocation helps to show what kind of an introduction this is. We have here a pair to be compared: the man, crafty-shifty, who "was-buffeted-abroad" in the effort to win his life (or ghost); and the companions, childishly innocent, who "did . . . eat-up" the cattle of the Sun and as a result disappeared from view before they got home.

From what has been said, I think it is evident how the emphatic verbs "was-buffeted-abroad" (*plankhthē*) and "did . . . eat-up" (*ēsthion*) focus the meaning of their respective halves of the proem. To a remarkable degree they also focus the sounds of each half. Notice the Greek of the first half.

Andra moi ennepe, Mousa, polutropon, hos mala polla
plankhthē, epei Troiēs hieron ptoliethron epersen;
pollōn d'anthrōpōn iden astea kai noon egnō,
polla d'ho g' en pontōi pathen algea hon kata thumon,
arnumenos hēn te psukhēn . . .

We can hear how the succession *an am en em pol pon pol* prepares for the
sound *plankhthē;* how phrases like *hieron ptoliethron, pollōn d'anthrōpōn, kai
noon egnō,* and *polla d'ho g'en pontōi* keep it ringing; and how *pathen algea
hon kata thumon* expands it (*pa . . . al . . . on ka . . . thu*). P, the first
consonant of *plankhthē,* occurs fourteen times in this half of the passage and
only five times in the other, the *ēsthion* half. *Plankhthē,* then, focuses the
sounds as well as the meaning of the first half.

In the second half, *s,* the first consonant of *ēsthion,* occurs fourteen times,
while the *plankhthē* half has only seven s-sounds. In the *ēsthion* half, if we read
it aloud, we shall hear how, in lines 5, 6, 7, and 8, the ten s-sounds following
down-beat vowels lead up to *ēsthion* in line 9; how the vowel sequence of
nēpioi, in the same metrical position in the previous line, prepares for *ēsthion;*
and how the two down-beat s's following *ēsthion* maintain its effect.

. . . kai noston hetairōn.
All' oud' hōs hetarous, errusato, hiemenos per;
autōn gar spheterēisin atasthaliēisin olonto,
nēpioi, hoi kata bous Huperionos Ēelioio
ēsthion; autar ho toisin apheileto nostimon ēmar.

Perhaps merely pointing out the succession *spheterēisin atasthaliēisin . . ./
nēpioi . . . Eelioio / ēsthion* would be enough to make the point that *ēsthion*
focuses the sounds of the second half.

The reader may well wonder how such an elaborate pattern could be more
than fortuitous, given the limits of what Milman Parry, among others, has
shown us was essentially a formulaic, extemporaneous technique of poetic
composition (Finnegan, 59). The answer is that, whatever limits the technique
may seem to impose, it does not prevent a skillful poet from choosing from
among a large number of possibilities that one which is most adequate to his
purpose. Within the limits of the technique inherited by Homer, a great—
perhaps infinite—variety of openings for such a poem as the *Odyssey* is
possible; therefore that a poet of genius should hit upon a peculiarly happy one
is not to be wondered at. Nor need we assume that the invocation we have is

our poet's first attempt. Homer may have cast and recast an opening for an "Odyssey" many times, either in performance or by himself, practicing as we know that singers in similar extemporaneous traditions do (Lord, 24). The passage before us is undeniably complex, and as far as I can see, the only conclusion to be drawn is that Homer's poetry can compare in degree of organization with anything in the literary traditions of later times.

The physical organization of the *Odyssey*'s first nine lines has brought the following statements into the clearest possible opposition: the man was clever and was driven about the world; he sacked Troy, saw, and knew; he endured pain and privation; we may suppose that he won his life (so to translate *psukhēn* for the moment). His companions were pathetically foolish; unwilling or unable to restrain themselves, they ate what they knew was forbidden, and so they fell from sight and mind. Far from winning their lives, they could not be saved by another's efforts. He experienced the world and endured pain (*plankhthē*); they ate (*ēsthion*). This contrast, I believe, is the way Homer defines the topic of all twenty-four books of his *Odyssey*, the same *Odyssey* we know and admire today.

Having identified his topic in this fashion, Homer explicitly leaves it to the Muse to begin the story at whatever point she chooses, thus calling special attention to the poem's opening. Its chief effect is a kind of paradox. We discover the Great Sufferer caught in a suffering which does not seem to be one.

> Beginning anywhere, Goddess, daughter of Zeus, tell us too this story.
>
> By then all the others, all who had escaped sheer destruction,
> were at home, safe from war and the sea;
> that man alone, deprived of home and wife,
> a queenly nymph held prisoner, Kalypso, divine goddess,
> in her hollow caves, urging him to be her husband.
>
> (1.10–15)

Kalypso means "she who conceals." The nymph's name and her "hollow caves" suggest that Odysseus is hidden somewhere, no one knows where. One may well feel also that being hidden is a seductive thing, since a "queenly nymph" is "urging him to be her husband"; Odysseus hardly seems to need the wife he is said to be deprived of. Furthermore, as the poet makes us see it, what "the others" have gained by getting home is escape from war and the sea, which Odysseus too has achieved. We may be tempted to ask why this Kalypso is not at least as good as home.

Without deigning to satisfy us on this point, the Muse moves ahead to portray Odysseus's captivity as an instance of a world out of joint.

> But when the year came round in which,
> in the weaving of the gods, his homecoming to Ithaca
> was determined, not even then was he free from his struggles [*aethlōn*]
> and safe with his loved ones. All the gods pitied him
> except Poseidon: he raged inveterately against
> good-as-a-god Odysseus, until he should reach his homeland.
>
> (1.16–21)

Poseidon is interfering with "the weaving of the gods." Captivity to Kalypso may seem comfortable, but it is presented here as a struggle, for which the hero, now named for the first time, receives the pity of all the gods but one. Revealed in the context of Poseidon's hostility, Odysseus's name not only satisfies our awakened curiosity but shows a peculiar appropriateness: the epic verb *odussasthai* means "to will pain to," and Poseidon wills pain to Odysseus. This suggestion in turn heightens the meaning of the epithet *antitheos*, "good as a god," here conjoined with Odysseus's name. *Anti* basically means "facing; opposite." *Antitheos* suggests a person who can be compared with, be matched with, stand in for, even oppose on equal terms, a god (*theos*). If, as the passage hints, Odysseus can survive Poseidon's hostility and come home safely, he will richly deserve his epithet. If, on the other hand, he cannot, the gods' purpose will be defeated, and there will be a rift in the universe. The Muse's deceptively gentle opening thus makes the poem actually a test of whether the world is essentially out of control and hostile to man, or not.

Homer proceeds at once to put matters partially, at least, to rights. He shows us Zeus on Olympos, defending the justice of the gods. Men blame the gods for their troubles, he says, and yet through their own recklessness, they suffer more than would otherwise be their lot. His example is Aigisthos, who, "though he knew it would be fatal" (1.37), took Klytaimnestra to wife and murdered Agamemnon. Hermes had advised him not to, pointing out that, if he did, vengeance would come from Orestes, but Aigisthos would not listen and paid the price. Athena agrees heartily that Aigisthos deserved what happened to him: "So perish whoever else does likewise!" she exclaims. "But," she says in effect, "what about Odysseus?" Here is a mortal who suffers more than most and yet, she implies, cannot be convicted of recklessness. Did his sacrifices at Troy somehow not find favor in Zeus's sight? Using the verb *odussasthai*, which we have already mentioned as audible in Odysseus's name, she asks, "Why did you so will his pain, Zeus [*ti nu hoi toson ōdysao, Zeu*]?" (1.62).

Zeus exonerates Odysseus, both from recklessness and from failure to propitiate the gods. No man has better sense, he says, and no man has sacrificed more (1.66–67). Thus if Odysseus's case lends itself to generalizing, as Aigisthos's has already done, Zeus is in a position to answer the question of undeserved suffering in the world as he has that of deserved suffering and thus to solve the philosophical problem of evil. But Zeus refrains from generalizing (1.68–79). Odysseus is kept absent from home, he says, because Odysseus has angered Poseidon by blinding Poseidon's son, the Kyklops Polyphemos. Apparently no blame attaches to Odysseus for this, for otherwise Athena would have understood—or Zeus would have explained to her—that Odysseus, like Aigisthos, brought his suffering on himself. But no word suggesting such a thing is uttered by either divinity. Quite the contrary, Zeus is at pains to point out that Poseidon does not kill Odysseus but merely beats (*plazei*, present active of *plankhthē*) him off from his native land, as though to say that the ultimate effect of Poseidon's treatment is not yet clear. Better still, he invites the other gods to arrange for Odysseus's return, adding that Poseidon will give up his wrath, not being able to oppose the will of all the rest. In short, Zeus is well on the way to healing any rift in the universe as far as Odysseus's homecoming is concerned; unfortunately or fortunately, however, by her punning question on Odysseus's name, Athena has meantime raised an even graver problem: is it really fair that Odysseus should suffer so much as he has done already and still is likely to do? Why should Zeus so countenance his pain? We may expect to discover more when we get to the affair of the Kyklops, but so far we are in the dark.

Meanwhile, in the course of raising her question about Odysseus's suffering, Athena has given us a start toward understanding what is wrong with Kalypso. Kalypso's name means "she who conceals, veils, shrouds, enfolds, engulfs, covers." She protects Odysseus, but she also hides him. It is as though Homer, meditating on the ten years between Troy and Ithaca, when Odysseus was out of sight and out of mind, conceived of him as detained by the very spirit of sea-enshrouded obscurity (Woodhouse, 215–17). In 1.50–59, Athena describes Kalypso as inhabiting "a wave-washed island at the sea's exact center . . . covered with trees." The "baneful mind" of her father, Atlas, comprehends "all the sea's depths," although he also "keeps the tall pillars which hold earth and heaven apart." One cannot pronounce this passage aloud in Greek without sensing with one's tongue the sea's liquidity: *hothi t' omphalos esti thalassēs* ("at the sea's exact center"), *nēsos dendrēessa* ("island covered with trees"), *hos te thalassēs pasēs benthea oiden* ("who knows all the sea's depths"). This liquidity, in turn, is what Kalypso seems to use not only to hide Odysseus from his world but to hide his world from him.

> aiei de malakoisi kai haimulioisi logoisi
> thelgei hopōs Ithakēs epilēsetai. . . .

> and always in soft dissembling syllables she seeks
> to soothe him from remembering Ithaca. . . .

As a result, "yearning to see were it but the smoke rising/from his native land, he longs to die." In spite, or even because, of Kalypso's charms, it is not difficult to assent to so passionate a yearning for home. The interesting thing is the way Homer makes us feel it as a yearning for definition. Odysseus and his home alike seem almost dissolved, and it is even a little disconcerting to be reminded by all these sibilants of the fate that overtook Odysseus's companions in the poem's invocation. Can this be the man whose endurance in contrast to his friends' fecklessness had the solidity to be "battered abroad"?

Kalypso's father, Atlas, is relevant to this contrast. His name suggests both endurance and the lack of it (cf. the verb *tlan*, "endure"); and, sea filled though his mind may be, he also solidly maintains the separation of earth and sky. Painful definition or dissolution? Together Kalypso and her father suggest an ultimate choice reminiscent of the poem's initial contrast between Odysseus's firmness and his companions' fecklessness. The gods' decision to set Odysseus free from Kalypso therefore seems appropriate in these terms as well as in those of simple justice.

By choosing to begin her story with the image of Odysseus's captivity to Kalypso, the Muse identifies obscurity as Odysseus's prime enemy. She further has the consummate tact to show us next not his escape from obscurity but rather the havoc which that obscurity causes at home in Ithaca, havoc which makes Odysseus's reemergence into the light, when it finally comes, that much more crucial. Accordingly, she essentially devotes the first four books of the poem to Athena's rousing of Telemachos. In the course of this rousing we are shown, first, how uncertainty about whether Odysseus will return has caused a horde of suitors to fasten upon Odysseus's wife and, second, how his son attempts to clear up the uncertainty. Although Telemachos fails in his main object, much else is brought into clearer focus: Telemachos's own situation as he perceives that he must take a stand against the suitors and proceeds to do so (book 1); the suitors' situation as they are compelled by his opposition to reveal that their claim rests on force alone (book 2); Penelope's predicament as she comes to recognize that her suitors will destroy her son (book 4); and the character of Odysseus himself as Telemachos experiences the difference between his father and the worthies from whom he seeks news of him (books 3 and 4). Once this further clarity has been obtained, we are truly ready to experience the homecoming of Odysseus.

Our conception of the nature of Homer's Muse implies that the gods do not so much add a further, miraculous dimension to human life as embody the remarkable within it, the "remarkable" in the Muse's case being the magic of poetry. Athena's rousing of Telemachos bears this implication out. In book 1, she takes the form of one Mentes, an old friend of the family, whose name suggests the "spirit" (*menos*) which she intends to inspire in her protégé (1.89). She drops in for a visit, listens to Telemachos's troubles, gives him some good advice, and then departs. Though she leaves with uncanny suddenness, it is clearly the effect of her words—ordinary words such as a human might use— which suggests to Telemachos that he has been talking to a god.

> So speaking, gray-eyed Athena departed.
> Like a bird she vanished upward, and in his heart
> put spirit [*menos*] and daring, making him imagine his father
> more clearly than before. Conscious of this, he
> marveled; for he felt it was a god.
> At once he approached the suitors, a man equal to a god [*isotheos phōs*].
> (1.319–24)

Athena's departure was sudden and no doubt miraculous. For our benefit, the poet reports that she vanished into thin air; but that is not what revealed her presence to Telemachos. The suitor Eurymachos also saw her leave and yet suspected nothing supernatural (1.405–11). The words "conscious of this" (*phresin hēisi noēsas*) and their position show that Telemachos noticed the change within himself, his new feeling of confidence, and his more vivid sense of his father which helped produce it. What can make us sure of this interpretation is the fact that the "old friend's" words prove exactly calculated to produce this effect. In other words, from a skeptic's point of view there was no need of a goddess at all; the old friend would have done as well. But Homer is not a skeptic. He (and his culture) are unwilling to regard as mere random chance an experience so powerfully felt by Telemachos and so deeply affecting the life not only of Telemachos but of Penelope, the suitors, Odysseus, and eventually all Ithaca. Athena then it was, made unmistakable for us by her miraculous departure, who heartened Telemachos, and not the Taphian Mentes. At the same time, the passage shows us that we may expect Athena and the other gods to provide no help, or very little, that goes beyond what we ourselves might experience in our own lives. In this respect the *Odyssey's* world proves to be essentially the one we regard as real, but with the gods assumed to be present wherever events seem more significant than mere chance would allow.

The presence of the goddess in human guise gives Homer occasion for a splendid irony. Here Athena, disguised as Mentes, assures Telemachos that his father is probably held captive by "wild savages." She ventures to prophesy that Odysseus will soon be home,

> just as the gods
> put it into my heart and as I think will happen,
> being no prophet and knowing little of bird signs.
>
> (1.200–202)

Could the fact that we humans are condemned to imperfect knowledge be more wittily presented? Athena tells Telemachos not what we know she knows but only such things as a real Mentes might guess.

Nevertheless, Mentes' words are clearly sufficient to set Telemachos on his way. By asking about the high-handed feasting of the suitors, Athena makes Telemachos admit to himself as well as to her that not only his livelihood but his life is in danger (1.224–51). By responding to this information with such indignation as a Mentes might show, she focuses the perturbation which we have been told Telemachos was experiencing before she arrived (1.114–17). Indignation is even made to seem to be Athena's middle name.

> ton d' *epalastēsasa* prosēuda *Pallas* Athēnē.
> Him *in indignation* addressed *Pallas* Athena. (1.252)

Speaking as Mentes, she calls up for him a vision of his father as the ideal answer to his problem,

> standing in the doorway
> with helmet, shield, and two spears,
> just as he was when I saw him first
> drinking and feasting in our house
> returning from Ephyra from Ilos Mermerides'—
> Odysseus had gone there too on his fast ship
> looking for a deadly poison

to smear his arrows with. Ilos
wouldn't give it: he feared the eternal gods;
but my father gave him some, so much he loved him—
if as he was then Odysseus should join the suitors,
short would be the life, sorry the wedding, for them all.

(1.255–66)

Even if, as Telemachos supposes, the living Odysseus is lost beyond recall, here is the model he needs to save his own situation and wreak on the suitors the vengeance they deserve. As that great student of Greek poetry Howard Porter used to enjoy pointing out, the arrow poison is important: squeamishness is not appropriate when the odds are as uneven as they are in Telemachos's case, and Athena's words about her father's gift suggest to us, who know who her true father is, that the gods are not so fastidious as Ilos Mermerides supposes. Long since, Athena announced that she intended to put menos, or spirit, into Telemachos's mind, and here is the very image of it.

Telemachos is well prepared to embrace this image of Odysseus. We remember that, at the moment Athena arrived, he was picturing his father chasing the suitors about his halls, though with no real hope that he might still return (1.114–17); now, however, that Mentes has made him voice his own peril, has exhibited the proper emotional response to it, and above all has emphasized Telemachos's resemblance to his father (1.208–11), he is ready for the thought that, if his father could and would kill the suitors, why should not he? Mentes tells him the correct steps to take (1.272–92): call a public assembly and declare before god and man that the suitors are in his house against his will; declare further that, if Penelope wishes to remarry, she can go to her father's house for the wooing. These declarations will remove any ambiguity about where the suitors stand. No shadow of an excuse is to remain for their presence in Telemachos's house. As for Telemachos himself, Athena advises him to sail to Pylos and Sparta to find out whether his father is "alive and coming home" or dead. If alive, Telemachos may "continue to endure the wastage" for as long as a year, preparing to play whatever part in punishing the suitors his father determines when he arrives; if he is dead, Telemachos should come home, celebrate his father's funeral with proper lavishness, and "give his mother to a husband"; that is, he can then, with proof of his father's death, inherit the property and take full charge in the difficult question of his mother's remarriage. Athena concludes her advice as follows:

When you have done all this,
take thought in your mind and heart

how you may kill the suitors in your halls
by trick or openly. Why submit
to a childishness you have outgrown?
Have you not heard what glory noble Orestes got
in all men's eyes when he killed the father killer,
devious Aigisthos, who slew his famous sire?
You, too, friend, big and handsome as I see you,
be brave, that men to come may speak well of you.

(1.293–302)

Of course, Athena is not telling Telemachos to kill the suitors "in his halls" after he has already married off his mother. We are meant to understand more largely. We have already responded to the image of Telemachos sitting helpless among the suitors (1.114–17), watching as they order his father's servants about and kill his cattle (1.106–12). We too would like to see them dead. Athena's image of an avenging Odysseus, when it comes, should strike us as utterly appropriate. But Athena understands that, when wrongs are to be righted, it is well to add objective confirmation to subjective certainty. Therefore, even though we all know that the suitors are already guilty, she advises Telemachos to offer them publicly the chance to leave his halls and to cease to do him violence; then she advises him to go to Pylos and Sparta to determine, if possible, whether Odysseus has survived to play the main role in the vengeance or whether he himself has inherited it. Only when he has "done all this" can he act, and be seen by others to act, with the clearset possible justification. Theoretically the suitors might yield to his more-than-just demands; theoretically he might celebrate his father's funeral and marry off his mother; in either case the revenge might theoretically be obviated. But what we have already seen of the suitors makes it morally and aesthetically certain that they will not leave his halls willingly or recognize his rights vis-à-vis his property or his mother. Accordingly, Athena advises him to consider not how he might "remove" but how he might "drive" (apōseai, 1.270) the suitors from his halls; and, as we have seen, she ends with the certainty that they must be killed. In short, the purpose of Athena's instructions is not for Telemachos to persuade the suitors to leave, which she knows they will not do, but rather to make their crime and Telemachos's need to avenge it absolutely clear before god and man.

Tomorrow call the heroic Achaians to assembly.
Speak before all, and call the gods to witness. (1.272–73)

For an ancient audience the suitors' crime is more than enough to justify Athena's eagerness to see them dead. Her comparing it to Aigisthos's murder of

Agamemnon may startle us at first; after all, they never do actually murder anybody; nevertheless, we should eventually be able to recognize that the comparison is apt.

Athena's help to Telemachos is not miraculous but only such as human life as we know it affords. Words of advice in a chance conversation can, as Athena's do here, lead a receptive mind from despair to resolution. Nor is Telemachos's response forced upon him by her divine power. We can easily imagine some other young man recoiling in horror from Mentes' suggestion. Homer thus maintains our commonsense feeling that human will is free, and Telemachos gets full credit for his courage.

To the possible question, actually asked of Athena by Odysseus at 13.417, why she does not simply appear to Telemachos in convincingly divine form and tell him that his father will soon be home to take care of things, we have already provided one answer: life is not like that. But the poem more emphatically suggests another reason: thus reassured, Telemachos would have less occasion to exercise his courage and thereby win the honor Athena intends for him (1.95). Thus already the answer to Athena's question to Zeus concerning undeserved suffering begins to emerge: the gods allow virtuous humans to suffer troubles so that, by taking arms against them, they may both show and know, as they otherwise could not, their own worth. Such knowledge, of course, Kalypso absolutely prevents.

In this first book of the poem, Telemachos indeed shows his virtue. By its end he has taken charge in his own house and declared open war on the suitors. In all this nothing is more remarkable than the way his father's image is seen to contribute to that result. Telemachos accepts the connection of Odysseus's image with himself only gradually. At first, in a famous speech, he claims not to know whether he is Odysseus's own child.

> My mother says he begot me, but I myself don't know,
> for nobody ever yet was sure of his own begetting.
> Would that I were son of some happy man
> whom old age caught in the midst of his possessions!
> As it is, the one man in the world whose fate is most obscure,
> his they say I am, since that is what you ask me.
>
> (1.215–20)

Somewhat later Telemachos regrets that Odysseus did not die at Troy and thereby win *kleos* ("repute") for his son among the living (1.236–40). We have seen that, in Mentes' opinion at least, public knowledge that Odysseus was dead would establish Telemachos's right to control his estate (1.289–92). As it is, Odysseus seems to have disappeared, leaving no image at all. As Telemachos puts it,

> The Harpies have snatched him away *kleos*-less;
> he is gone unseen, unheard of, and to me has left
> pain and lamentation [*odunas te goous te*]. (1.241–43)

In other words, Odysseus is held captive by Kalypso the Veiler, out of sight and out of mind. Only after Athena has evoked Odysseus at his most "painful" in the active sense, poisoned arrows and all, does Telemachos find in the image of his father the help he needs. We may remember how, at the end of the scene, he marveled and felt that his visitor "was a god," whereupon he "approached the suitors, a man equal to a god" (1.324).

It has often been pointed out that the first four books of the *Odyssey* concern, among other things, the coming of age of Telemachos. His experiences in Pylos and Sparta are usually, and rightly, thought to contribute much to this end. But as we watch him immediately after Athena's departure gain the moral advantage in his house, we see that the essential part of his maturing has already occurred under the influence of his father's image. Telemachos begins to assert himself by assuming authority over his mother (to her acquiescent surprise), declaring that, from now on, he intends to be master in the house (1.359). Very soon he will show that he is not afraid even of becoming king of Ithaca (1.386–93). He sends his mother upstairs, and when the suitors break into ribald prayer concerning her (1.366), he immediately and with startling audacity bids them be silent. Telling them that he will call an assembly the next day to order them out of the house, he threatens to pray the gods for requital if they refuse to leave (1.378–79). Such is the menos with which he has been inspired by the image of the father he has come so close to rejecting.

That image works as strongly on Penelope, but in the opposite way, to inhibit. Part of Telemachos's problem is, as he says, that his mother "neither refuses the marriage she loathes, nor can she/go through with it (1.249–50). These words imply that, if Penelope had said no to the suitors in the first place or should now do so, the situation Telemachos now faces would not exist. In Telemachos's opinion at least, Penelope thinks of marrying again. Since he himself is practically certain that Odysseus will not return (1.160–62, 166–68), it would seem that she has waited long enough, and to assume that Penelope means to remain faithful to Odysseus forever, dead or alive, seems a romantic prejudice, especially when we must then suppose that she acquiesces in the wooing in order to control wooers who need not have been there in the first place. No; Penelope is naturally and properly unwilling to foreclose the possibility of marrying, even though she loathes the prospect of selecting any particular suitor any time soon. The reasons for this loathing are not far to seek: for one thing, there is always a faint chance that Odysseus might return; for another, there is Odysseus's image. When Penelope overhears Odysseus's bard Phemios sing for the suitors the song of the Achaians' disastrous return from Troy, she enters the hall and begs him to cease.

> Stop this song, this bitter song,
> which ever in my breast wrings
> my heart, for to me above all comes the unforgettable pain:
> such is the face I long for, remembering always,
> my husband, famed throughout Hellas and Middle Argos.
>
> (1.340–44)

Clearly Penelope wants to be reminded of Odysseus as little as possible. Remembering him hurts too much. Yet, just as clearly, even after twenty years she is no nearer to forgetting him than she was when he left. This always-remembered image of Odysseus must be the reason she cannot go through with the marriage, which might in time assuage the pain. The contrast between her memory of him and her perception of the suitors, who are scarcely "famed throughout Hellas and Middle Argos," is too great.

In just this matter of the image of Odysseus, Telemachos seeks to school his mother. The bard, he says, should be allowed his song, since it pleases; Penelope must get used to it; Odysseus is not the only man who was lost because of Troy (1.346–55). It seems reasonable to infer that Telemachos can bear the idea that Odysseus is dead because he has found in Athena's timeless image of him the strength to take arms against the suitors on his own. A similar timeless image, we are aware, is binding Penelope in helpless indecision. Even so, since we know that Zeus desires Odysseus's return, we want that indecision to continue and therefore approve Telemachos's insistence that the bard be allowed to keep Penelope's pain alive. Here, too, as well as in the case of Poseidon's persecution or Telemachos's troubles, we are given the opportunity to see the pain implicit in Odysseus's name and image in a positive light.

In contrast, a definite image of Odysseus is the last thing the suitors desire. We have seen that, by right and usage, definite news of Odysseus's death at Troy would, at least arguably, give Telemachos control over both the house and his mother's marriage; alternatively, definite evidence that Odysseus will return would of course remove all excuse for the wooing. The beauty of the suitors' position lies precisely in the fact that, as long as nothing is known about Odysseus, they can woo his wife as though he were dead, while ignoring Telemachos's rights as though Odysseus were alive. When we first see them, they have already taken over Odysseus's house and property. Telemachos sees that they will destroy his patrimony and with it his proper self, whether or not he survives physically.

> Bit by bit they devour
> my house. Soon they'll break me to bits as well.
> (1.250–51)

Although the suitors as a group feel a certain shame when Telemachos threatens them with vengeance (1.381–82), Antinoos's prayer that Telemachos never become king in Ithaca (1.386–87) shows the direction which things will take. Eurymachos feigns shock at the thought that anyone would deprive Telemachos of his property (1.403–4), but his words, coming as they do from one who is depriving him of it already, only inspire mistrust. In effect, the suitors are treating Odysseus and Telemachos as nonentities; they aim to fill their places as though they were vacant. The names of the leaders emphasize this. Antinoos (Hostile Minded) and Eurymachos (Wide Fighter) match Odysseus (Man of Pain) and Telemachos (Far Fighter). The possibility of substitution is clear. If the suitors have their way, they will blot out the images of Odysseus and Telemachos completely. This is the real murder, much worse than mere killing, which Telemachos proposes to avenge.

Even as the suitors' criminal behavior threatens Odysseus and Telemachos with the annihilation by obscuring which Kalypso embodies, the incidental actions of Telemachos and the suitors suggest that they, rather than he, are ripe for obliteration. Telemachos is "far the first" to see the stranger, Athena, at the gate, and only he feels chagrin that she might be kept waiting there. He arranges that he and the stranger eat apart from the suitors,

> that his guest not lose
> his pleasure in the meal, amid such riot,
> and he in secret question him about his father.
> (1.133–35)

The result is that the two meals, described one after the other at almost equal length, are implicitly compared. Despite their formulaic verbal similarity, they could not be more different in their atmosphere. Telemachos's and Athena's meal is full of purpose and circumspection; the suitors', on the other hand, is, as Telemachos says, "easy, absorbed in the sound of song and the harp, since/scot-free they consume another's substance" (1.159–60)—this while Telemachos and Athena are plotting to kill them. Without too great strain such a contrast may remind us of the man who sacked Troy and knew and suffered, compared with his unthinking crew, who merely ate and died.

As with eating, so with going to bed. At the end of the book the suitors scatter to undistinguished couches, but Telemachos is attended by his old nurse Eurykleia, whose name means "wide fame." She carries torches. Surely it is permissible to be reminded of the kleos which Athena plans for Telemachos as the result of his newfound menos (1.89, 95). As the book ends, we see him locked in (1.442) and covered up (*kekalummenos*, 1.443), Kalypso'ed (it is the same verb) like his father; but his chamber is off by itself in a high, conspicuous place (1.426), and Telemachos does not sleep; instead, "all night long, covered in a sheep's great fleece,/he pondered in his heart the journey which Athena proposed" (1.443–44). Indefiniteness and passive surrender to impulse are here eschewed in favor of active, aggressive purpose. Telemachos, like his father, is about to emerge into the world.

In the course of this account we are told a curious fact about Eurykleia. Odysseus's father, Laertes, gave twenty oxen for her in her girlhood and showed her the same regard that he did his legal wife; "but he never slept with her, for fear of his wife's anger" (1.433). This is the Eurykleia who, old now, puts Telemachos to bed at the end of the book. Under the circumstances it is difficult not to contrast Laertes, who, to avoid unpleasantness, denied himself the embrace of Wide Kleos, with the "far fighter" Telemachos, who has just taken on the suitors as his enemies. Although they do not take him seriously enough to endanger him quite yet, if, when the time comes, he manages to overcome them, with or without his father, he will win a kleos granted to few.

Right and Wrong

The *Odyssey* is a poem about right and wrong, in a sense that the *Iliad* is not. In the *Iliad* Homer defines the only terms on which, given the *Iliad's* assumptions, human life can have meaning in the face of the terrible fact of death. Questions of right and wrong fade into insignificance by comparison. The *Odyssey*, on the other hand, unabashedly exhibits the triumph of life over death in terms of the triumph of good over evil: quite simply, it suggests that Odysseus vindicated justice so strikingly that his name will never die.

In book 2, the theme of right and wrong as such first comes strongly to the fore. Telemachos confronts the suitors in the assembly with all the spirit and adroitness Athena could wish, and yet the suitors manage to cow the Ithacans into overlooking their depredations. The suitors make it clear that they will physically resist any attempt to stop them and, furthermore, that anyone who helps Telemachos obtain a ship and crew to seek news of his father will have them to deal with. Telemachos's initiative seems thwarted almost before it has begun. Only after Athena shows him how the justice of his cause will help him, even though it has failed in the assembly, is he able to carry on.

In the *Odyssey* recognition of right and wrong begins with *nemesis*, which in Homer means an individual's feeling of moral repugnance, weak or strong, at some act or situation. In the first book Telemachos "felt nemesis" that the stranger (Athena) might be kept waiting at the gate (1.119); he also hoped that the stranger would not feel nemesis at his referring to his own troubles before he asked the stranger about himself (1.158). In the second book he predicts that, if he forces his mother to go back to her father's house, as the suitors suggest, she will call down the Furies upon him and he will incur the nemesis of mankind (2.135–37). He implies that the suitors themselves ought to feel nemesis for putting him in such a position (2.138). In his earlier speech he urges the people of Ithaca to feel nemesis themselves at the behavior of their sons and brothers, the suitors; second, to feel shame before the people of the neighboring communities; and, finally, to "fear the wrath of the gods,/that they may turn the tables in their repugnance [*agassamenoi*] for evil deeds" (2.64–67). Here is a clear implication that what people themselves feel to be wrong, or would be ashamed to have others know about, is in fact wrong and liable to incur the anger and punishment of the gods, however secure the wrongdoers may seem at the time.

We have seen that in Homer the gods on occasion inspire humans to act, or suggest words and ideas to them. It is abundantly clear that they also inspire moral force, the menos which Mentes gave Telemachos in book 1 and with which gods frequently inspire the combatants in the *Iliad*. Strong feeling evidently implies the operation of divinity, as sexual passion, for example, implies the operation of Aphrodite. Indignation too, therefore, may often come from the gods, who are seen as sharing the humans' anger and as aiding and abetting its expression in revenge and punishment. We may recall here how, "feeling indignation [*epalastēsasa*]," "Pallas" Athena proclaimed her sympathy with Telemachos and urged him to kill the suitors (1.252). Thus the punishment of wrong tends to be thought of as both human and divine.

Furthermore, divine punishment as it is presented in the *Odyssey* is no random occurrence but part of a plan which is knowable, if imperfectly, even by humans. We are told in book 1, for example, that the gods have "spun" Odysseus's return for the year in which the action before us is taking place (1.17). In the assembly in book 2, no sooner does Telemachos call upon Zeus to grant the suitors' destruction if they continue to prey upon him than Zeus sends the omen of the eagles, which is immediately interpreted by a professional soothsayer to mean that Odysseus is near, "planting death and doom" for the suitors (2.165). The soothsayer goes on to proclaim that the omen confirms a prophecy he made to the Ithacans when the fleet left twenty years before, that Odysseus, "having suffered much and lost all his companions," would come home "in the twentieth year unrecognized by anyone" (2.174–76). Events are thus seen to be not isolated but part of a fabric designed by the gods and known, in part at least, to humans of superior understanding. We see too that, as the full context emerges, events can change their aspect. Odysseus will return, it now appears, not as the victim of the gods' hostility, which he seemed in the soothsayer's earlier prophecy and in Phemios's song of the "disastrous return" (1.326–27), but as their agent in an act of justice. It is further evidence of design that the man whose name means "man of pain" should be "planting death and doom" for the suitors with Zeus's sanction, a design seen too in the symmetry of turning the tables on the suitors that is referred to twice by Telemachos.

> But if you think it better and fairer
> that one man's livelihood be ruined, and nothing to pay,
> crop away; I shall cry to the everlasting gods
> for Zeus to grant requital: then you
> would be ruined within my halls, and nothing to pay.
> (1.376–80 = 2.141–45)

In Homer's world such predictability, such apparently significant correspondences, and such symmetries so strongly suggest a conscious, divine ordering of events that symmetry itself can lead Telemachos to hope he will in fact be able to kill the suitors with impunity. Still further patterning is suggested when he alludes to the mildness of Odysseus's rule.

> Stop this, my friends, and leave me alone to nurse
> my grief, unless good Odysseus, my father,
> out of hatred [*dysmeneōn*] injured the Achaians,
> in return for which, in your hatred [*dysmeneontes*], you injure me,
> urging the suitors on. (2.70–74)

Here of course a possible symmetry and its correspondence with the sound and meaning of Odysseus's name is pointed to in order to deny its existence: in spite of his name, Odysseus has been a notably gentle king (2.46–47, 233–34). Nevertheless, this too is evidence that in Homer human events are naturally assumed to conform to a pattern over which the gods preside.

At the same time, we see that not all potential patterns are realized. Humans are free to choose. In spite of the meaning of his name, Odysseus chose to be a gentle king. Men are also free to err. In the words of Zeus, men suffer not only according to their lot but, by their own willfulness, beyond it (*huper moron*, 1.34). This state of affairs implies that, at any given moment, a number of possible patterns exists. Aigisthos, although he contributed to the pattern which involved Orestes' revenge, was not compelled to do so, any more than Odysseus was compelled by his name to be cruel to his subjects. In the patterns that are fulfilled, however, the gods are often seen as contributing substantially to the evidently more-than-random design. For example, Athena evidently both shares in Telemachos's desire to punish the suitors and helps him to do so. In fact, it is almost always so clear how circumstances (that is, the gods) might have prevented any given event, that the whole fabric of events as it unrolls is thought of as essentially the product of their will, or Zeus's will (which comes to the same thing), even while it is admitted that human will is free.

The chief difficulty in accepting such a view comes from predictions which seem to imply that everything that happens has been determined from the beginning of time, like Halitherses' prophecy that Odysseus would return in the twentieth year, or Homer's and the Muse's statement that this was the year the gods had destined for Odysseus's homecoming. This seems, for example, as though it might give Odysseus no freedom of choice when the question of leaving Kalypso comes up. The solution is contained in a phrase which I owe to Bernard Knox (Knox, 39): prediction is not predestination. Gods, soothsayers, and oracles may know in advance what a given person's free choice is going to be, without making it any less free. Thus in book 5, Odysseus is still free to choose not to come home, even though this is the year the gods have designated for his return. The point is that, at the time of the poem's composition, the poet and the Muse know that he did in fact choose to return in the twentieth year and succeeded in doing so. They also assume that, although much happens contrary to human desire and expectation, nothing happens against the gods' general will. Therefore Odysseus's free choice is at the same time part of the pattern "spun" (1.17) by the gods. Once a thing happens, the design is clear, but the design does not determine the events; they, rather, freely produce it.

The fact that the epic poet necessarily sees as past what from his characters' point of view is future may account for the historical Greeks' tendency to see the future as in some sense already determined. They asked the god Apollo at Delphi not "What ought I to do?" but "What will happen if I do so-and-so?" Thus actions which humans regard with indignation are at the same time felt to be bad not so much in themselves as for their results. Doubtless it was wicked of Aigisthos to entertain thoughts of seducing Klytaimnestra and murdering his cousin the king. Nevertheless, the gods show little or no indignation; Hermes merely points out, "in kindness," that the murder will entail Orestes' revenge (1.35–43). Indeed, the thought of future revenge mitigates the indignation called forth by the act itself, as Mentor suggests in the assembly.

> I do not think it too much that the proud suitors
> commit this violence in their feebleness of wit.
> They risk their own heads when they violently consume
> Odysseus's store, not believing he'll return. (2.235–38)

This confidence that the future, like a good story, will make moral sense, actually contributes to that freedom from censoriousness which we find so refreshing in Homer and Greek literature generally.

We have seen that the feeling that an action is wrong (the feeling of nemesis) leads to the feeling that the gods too disapprove, which in turn suggests that the action will have unhappy consequences. These unhappy consequences then become by far the simplest and most obvious explanation why the action was wrong in the first place, and evildoing becomes a matter of folly rather than of moral turpitude. For their part, victims of such folly will do well not to rely blindly on their unassisted superior rectitude to save them but rather will search for and try to abet the gods' particular design in the given case.

This is the meaning of Athena's rather curiously phrased encouragement of Telemachos in book 2. Apparently prevented by the suitors' hostility from getting a ship and crew in order to search for news of his father, Telemachos prays for help to a being whom he knows only as "the god who appeared yesterday." To Telemachos's eyes it is Odysseus's friend Mentor who appears in answer to this prayer, but the Muse tells us that it is really Athena. We note that again Athena impersonates someone whose name suggests menos. Mentor's advice is worth some study.

> Telemachos, in the end you'll not prove bad or foolish
> if, as is true, your father's good menos is instilled in you,
> the force he had to make good word and deed:
> your journey, then, won't fail.
> If you are not his child and Penelope's,
> I have no hope you'll do what you intend.
> Few children equal their fathers:
> most fall short, and only a few are better.
> But since in the end you'll not prove bad or foolish,
> nor has Odysseus's resource completely deserted you,
> there's hope you'll achieve your task.
> Disregard the suitors' purpose;
> in no way are they wise or just at all,
> oblivious of death and black extinction
> so close to them, to die all on one day.
> You won't wait long for the journey you desire:
> I'm friend enough of your father's
> to find a boat and accompany you myself. (2.270–87)

What is strangest about this speech is that Athena, in Mentor's gruff and negative way, does not say, "You will succeed because you are good and wise," but rather, "You will succeed because you *will turn out to be* good and wise," and here we can see the advantages of regarding the future as though it were past. Virtue in Homer is not something one possesses from the beginning, nor is wisdom anything apart from its exercise; both are rather the hard-to-win accolade for completing a well-conducted and successful life. Telemachos will not be handed his success by the gods simply because he is the innocent victim of the suitors' aggression; he will have to win it or else "prove bad or foolish" in his failure to vindicate his honor. As we can see, Athena's "looking to the end" in this way, as Solon was later to recommend, is advantageous in the first place because it summons Telemachos to vigorous and circumspect action, where mere consciousness of innocence might have invited repose. Second, it takes the gods' larger pattern of events into account, transcending the immediate present, in which the suitors' threats seem to have prevented Telemachos's journey. Even without omens and prophecy, the future is more or less predictable. That Telemachos has inherited Odysseus's virtues seems already confirmed. In his determination to kill the suitors, he has already shown his father's menos, and in his dealings with them he has shown his father's *mētis* ("resource"), even though the assembly has ended in apparent impasse. If he is like his father to this degree, he should eventually prove at least not bad or foolish; therefore he will probably succeed in making his trip.

The suitors too are part of the pattern. If Telemachos will turn out to have been wise in deciding to oppose them, they are indeed, as Athena says, not wise in pursuing their present unjust course, which incurs his nemesis and makes him wish to destroy them. In the assembly Telemachos's prayer to Zeus for their destruction was answered by the omen of the two eagles, interpreted in Telemachos's favor by Halitherses, and the true Mentor recognized that the suitors were indeed risking their necks. In the scene before us Athena, posing as Mentor and keeping his character, names as the height of their folly their ignoring the "death and black extinction" which awaits them. She refers, of course, to their rejection of the omen and the prophecies and thus of the pattern of events as a whole. According to Athena, their disregard of the pattern of events will lead to their failure, just as Telemachos's acceptance of it will lead to his success. He has only to move ahead along the line he has planned, even if, for the moment, it seems to him impossible that anyone should lend him the boat he needs.

Thus in this matter of right and wrong, the pattern is all-important, and unquestionably it is provided by the gods. It is they, for example, who cause men called Mentes and Mentor to be involved in it in such a way that Athena can use their personae to awaken Telemachos's menos. The gods are manifest in symmetries of all sorts, including, of course, the symmetry of punishment answering to crime. They, we might say, make sense of experience by providing it with aesthetic shape, and this operation of theirs gives rise to the alternative notion of nemesis as the personified wrath of the gods which wrongdoers must fear.

On the other hand, it is human events that the gods organize, and since human will is free, the human contribution to the pattern is as essential as the divine. When Athena takes her part in these events disguised as Mentes and Mentor, we can see the two contributions merging. Mentes' encouragement of Telemachos is elaborately and recognizably human, even if Athena does depart by vanishing into thin air; and even if Mentor finally turns into a vulture in the presence of upward of four thousand people and, as the vulture flies away, is hailed as Athena by King Nestor (3.371–78), the divine assistance to Telemachos consists not in that fact but in the quite human words Mentor speaks to him before the transformation, before Telemachos has any idea that the goddess is present. Thus even events which are obviously divine keep within an essentially human compass.

Divinity never obviates human choice. The divine pattern which involves the suitors' destruction can be forestalled at any point, as it would be (probably) if Telemachos should find the situation too much for his nerve or if the suitors should take warning in time. When Mentor and the soothsayer beg the Ithacans to call a halt to what is developing, or when the suitors try to cajole Telemachos from his wrath, we accept theoretically, at least, that either of these possibilities might occur. The omen of the eagles itself, to judge from a similar omen in Sophokles' *Antigone*, shows that affairs are terribly out of joint, but not irrevocably so.

> So spoke Telemachos, and far-seeing Zeus made fly for him
> two eagles from the high peak of the mountain.
> At first they rode the blast of the wind
> side by side on outstretched wings; then,
> dead over the loud assembly,
> they turned violently flapping,
> [and flew in the faces of all, and looked death;]
> and tearing cheeks and necks with their talons
> flew off to the right through the houses of the town.
>
> (2.146–54)

First of all, it must be understood that the lame line, "and flew in the faces of all, and looked death," has been interpolated by someone who thought that the two eagles represented Odysseus and Telemachos and therefore ought not to tear each other. But for the eagles to tear the "cheeks and necks" of the crowd is manifestly worse, and we escape this alternative as soon as we realize that one of the eagles represents the suitors. In fact, the passage quoted introduces a series of omens extending through the poem, in which Odysseus and Telemachos, represented by an eagle or hawk, carry off or kill weaker and tamer birds, such as geese or doves, representing the suitors. In the first omen, the suitors contend on such equal terms that they are represented by one of the eagles, and it takes the soothsayer's eye to see that the conflict will be fatal for them if they pursue it.

The omen in Sophokles' *Antigone* (998–1004) is enough like the one we are discussing to have been influenced by it. In Sophokles' play, a whole flock is seen and heard clawing each other murderously with screams and whirring wings. Teiresias explains that Kreon's fate is poised on a razor's edge (996), and we realize that the conflict between Kreon and Antigone has reached a degree of intensity where Kreon must yield at once or ruin them both forever. In the event, he repents too late. Similarly in the *Odyssey* the conflict between Odysseus's party and the suitors is now joined as a result of Telemachos's initiative, and the suitors must yield or face the consequences. That the eagles fly off to the right through the town means that the outcome will favor Telemachos and Ithaca as a whole. In both Homer and Sophokles the violence between birds of the same or related species conveys the unnatural horror of strife within the body politic, and in both cases there is still a chance that it may be healed.

In the *Odyssey* Halitherses takes the eagles as meaning that the threat of Odysseus is close (2.165) but not yet actually present and accomplished. He is able to specify that the eagles' strife portends Odysseus's revenge because he knows that this is the year for Odysseus's return. Had the suitors at this point believed Halitherses and accepted the omen as significant, they could theoretically have avoided their fate; but because Odysseus's return seems impossible and Telemachos's power hopelessly weak and because the suitors have no regard for nemesis, they refuse to believe. Therefore not predetermined fate but the suitors' own blindness justifies Athena's words above,

> oblivious of death and black extinction
> so close to them, to die all on one day. (2.283–84)

Human will is free. The gods provide the potential pattern, but free human choice elects whether or not to fulfill it. Zeus announced as much at the beginning of the poem when he said,

> How strange it is that humans give us the blame
> and say that troubles come from us, when they too
> by their own recklessness suffer beyond their lot.
>
> (1.32–34)

Much suffering is inevitable, and Odysseus is an example of that fact; but much, too, is self-inflicted. Neither Odysseus's own companions, adduced in the invocation, nor the suitors were compelled to die as ignominiously as they did.

Nor, of course, is Telemachos compelled to succeed. Mentor's advice may be paraphrased as follows: "Look at the degree to which you have inherited your parents' good qualities, and you will see that you will turn out well; look at the suitors' contempt for your just anger, and be confident that they will be destroyed." These words presuppose a world that makes sense and, within that world, define justice as respect for nemesis. Nevertheless, since the words seem to come from a human source, Telemachos can deny them now as easily as Ithacans and suitors alike denied the implications of the events in the assembly. Even the eagles, as Eurymachos insists, may have been mere accident (2.181–82). Telemachos can succeed only if he has the courage to accept Mentor's words. It therefore ultimately depends on Telemachos's *menos* whether justice will be done in the present instance and the world be seen to make as much sense as in general it does.

Not that Telemachos must uphold the justice of the world single-handed. Good men like Mentor as well as goddesses like Athena are moved by injustice, and so we feel no inappropriateness when, in the guise of Mentor, Athena proposes to find Telemachos a ship and crew and accompany him on his journey in spite of the suitors' opposition. Nor should we be surprised that, when the time comes, Athena borrows the boat and collects the crew not in Mentor's form but in Telemachos's own. Homer is showing unequivocally that sympathy for Telemachos and not simply respect for Mentor produces this support. Later in the poem the boat's owner Noemon answers the suitors' indignant questions as follows:

> I gave it freely: what would anyone do
> when a man like Telemachos, troubled as he is,
> asks? To refuse would be hard indeed. (4.649–51)

In providing him with a boat, Athena has clearly done no more for Telemachos than he could have done for himself. Nevertheless, her help is never redundant. It always calls attention to something providential in the external world; here, to the sympathy which injustice itself occasions for its victims. We need not doubt that Noemon and those who consented to man the boat would have responded as they did to a human Telemachos; all the same, there is something divine about the fact that they did so.

With all Athena's help, great scope remains for Telemachos's courage. With Mentes he had felt the divine presence in the visitor who evoked his father's image; from Mentor he receives only what he takes to be a human calculation based on his own heredity and the suitors' injustice. He embarks therefore on Athena's plan much perturbed (*philon tetiēmenos ētor*, 2.298). In the circumstances, for him to be able to refuse the suitors' proffered friendship, as we now see him do, is even more impressive than his defiance on the previous day.

> "Antinoos, how can I feast with you and rest
> my heart at ease amid your outrage?
> Is it not enough that until now you fleeced me
> of all that wealth, and I too young to know?
> Now that I'm big, when others talk,
> I understand. Rage swells in me.
> If I can I'll put you all to an ugly death,
> whether I go to Pylos or stay here.
> But I shall go—you'll see—
> a passenger, without ship of my own or oarsmen
> since you will have it so."
> He spoke, and lightly from Antinoos's hand
> drew his. (2.310–22)

However tempting it might be to yield to Antinoos's sudden friendliness and to trust his assurance that the suitors will arrange for his journey, Telemachos's newfound menos prevents his falling into such a trap. Hitherto he has told the suitors first in private and then in public that, if they continue to consume his livelihood, he will pray the gods for Zeus to grant an unspecified requital; now, however, that in the assembly the suitors have declared that they will continue their depradations, he makes it unmistakable that he personally will bring about their deaths if he can. Nor is this courage foolhardy: again, as he had on the previous evening, he conceals how much support he really has. On that occasion he hid his feeling that Mentes was more than he seemed; this time he deliberately denies that Mentor, or anyone, has offered to get him a boat. Here certainly is his father's resource at work, seen once more in alliance with his father's equally famous menos.

Even as it shows Telemachos finding new grounds to trust in the justice of his cause, book 2 shows how the suitors are driven to rely more and more on mere force. When Antinoos proposes in the assembly that Telemachos send Penelope home to her father, Telemachos's reason for refusing is clearly sufficient: to drive his mother from her own home against her will would incur the greatest nemesis from both gods and men. When this refusal is backed by Zeus's eagles and Halitherses' interpretation of them, Eurymachos, whom we have come to know as the more circumspect of the suitors' two leaders, can only threaten the soothsayer and his family with violence (2.178–79) and an unjust fine (2.192) and then suggest once more that Telemachos send his mother back to her father. When Mentor expresses his shock that the Ithacans do not bring the wooing to an end by shouting the suitors down, the suitor Leokritos in reply makes no claim to any kind of justice; he merely suggests that it is "a hard thing/even for a majority to fight about a dinner" (2.244–45). The situation is now clear: if the Ithacans want to remove the suitors from Odysseus's hall, even though they are a majority, they will have to fight to do it; words in the assembly are not enough. To convince the Ithacans that this is so, Leokritos adds with grisly wit that the suitors would kill even Odysseus if he should return and try to stop them, Odysseus in that case being in the minority. Leokritos is counting on the Ithacans' not risking injury or death to save a situation which, after all, Penelope herself presumably can save either by marrying or by going home to her father's house. As we have already seen, Leokritos's estimate is quite correct.

The suitors' confidence in their own violence shows clearly also in the scene discussed above in which Telemachos refuses their feigned friendship. With crude irony they joke about how Telemachos may bring back from his proposed voyage avengers from Pylos or Sparta, or even poison "from Ephyra" to put in their wine (2.326–30). Actually, of course, they think no one will dare to help him with a ship and crew. Furthermore, they announce in his presence what they mean to do if by any chance he should die abroad.

> Who knows he won't himself, going in the hollow ship,
> be lost like Odysseus wandering far from his friends?
> That way he'd add still more to our toil, when we
> divide all the property and donate the house
> to his mother and him who wins her. (2.332–36)

They affect to divine from Telemachos's name that he will die "far from his friends" (*tēle philōn*), just as, in their opinion, the wandering Man of Pain has done. They do not say that they will kill Telemachos themselves—one doubts that they have thought things through to such a point—but now that they have made it plain that they respect nothing except force, we can no longer doubt that they have the will, as well as the motive, to murder both the son and the father. As they see it, Telemachos's life is all that stands between them and complete control of the property.

In these hypothetical imaginings the suitors give voice to the violence both Telemachos (1.251) and Eurykleia (2.368) know they will eventually have recourse to, even before, perhaps, they realize it themselves. Telemachos, now definitely in the right and, thanks to Mentor's words, trusting to it, resolutely takes upon himself the responsibility of vengeance; the suitors, on the other hand, now definitely in the wrong because they have set force above justice, begin to submit to the fatal implications of a situation which to them seems merely comfortable. The book ends with two images it is difficult not to compare in this light. First, Athena drives the suitors drunk to bed.

> Then gray-eyed Athena thought of something else:
> off she went to the house of godlike Odysseus;
> there upon the suitors she poured sweet sleep,
> fuddled them as they drank, knocked the cups from their hands.
> They hurried home to bed through the town nor long
> stayed, once sleep had fallen upon their eyelids.
>
> (2.393–98)

Then, in deliberate detail, we hear how Athena, taking the form of Mentor, conducts Telemachos to his ship and crew on the shore; how under Telemachos's leadership they fetch the previously prepared provisions from the palace and load the ship; how all embark, Athena and Telemachos sitting in the stern sheets; and how they set sail, a wind provided by Athena blowing behind and a purple wave gurgling loud beneath the bow. Finally,

> making all fast on the swift black ship
> they broke out the bowls and filled them with wine,
> then poured libations to the gods who live forever,
> all, but most to Athena, Zeus's gray-eyed daughter.
>
> (2.430–33)

As book 2 develops the conflict between Telemachos and the suitors, it also complicates our perception of Penelope. Although there is no reason to accept the suitors' implication that she keeps them dangling for the sake of the fame she gains thereby (2.125–26), we need not doubt that she actually did keep them at bay for three years by the trick of weaving Laertes' shroud by day and unraveling it at night (2.89–110). The point, I take it, is that she did this not for the sake of being known to be courted for so long by so many but rather to postpone the necessity of accepting a husband inferior to Odysseus, as I have suggested above. The image of weaving and unraveling well conveys her painful indecision. Thus there is no fundamental dishonesty in her behavior toward the suitors which could justify, as they claim, the wasting of Telemachos's property. Nor is there any question of her loyalty to Telemachos, although he finds himself unable to confide in her. His reason for not doing so is that, the more she loves him, the more she is likely to ruin his plan to control the suitors. When he makes Eurykleia swear not to tell his mother of his departure for Pylos (2.372–77), Eurykleia's own protest against his "exposing himself to wandering and danger on the barren sea" like his father (2.370) shows how violent Penelope's reaction would be if she knew, and there is no telling what she might not do, advertently or inadvertently, to stop him. Telemachos's suggestion that he wishes to save her good looks from the ravages of grief (2.376) is not exactly irony, but its understated sangfroid loudly calls attention to the much more serious possibility that her outcry will inform the suitors of his departure, which we know they are concerned to prevent. Even so, they may seize the opportunity of his trip to kill him, as Eurykleia has just pointed out (2.367–68). When, in the assembly, the other Ithacans failed to oppose the suitors, they gave them tacit permission to put virtually any sort of pressure they liked on Penelope. If before long she should turn up married, Telemachos having somehow disappeared in the meantime, we cannot believe that very many Ithacans would be seriously concerned. To Telemachos it must seem that the only hope for the future of the House of Odysseus is for him personally to find out whether Odysseus is alive or dead. That means exposing himself, as his father has done before him, to wandering and danger on the sea; and, our poem suggests, this is a necessity which Penelope, whose husband has apparently been lost at Troy, cannot be counted on to understand.

Nestor the Home-Goer

Ēelios d' anorouse, lipōn perikallea limnēn,
ouranon es polukhalkon, hin' athanatoisi phaeinoi
kai thnētoisi brotoisi epi zeidōron arouran.

The sun leapt up, leaving the beautiful calm surface of the sea,
into the brazen heaven to give light to gods
and mortal men upon the fruitful earth. (3.1–3)

With this magnificent impetus, Telemachos's adventures in foreign parts begin. He and the disguised Athena run their ship ashore at Pylos to find themselves in the midst of a great session of sacrifice and feasting in honor of Poseidon. No less than 4,500 people are present, and eighty-one bulls are being slaughtered (3.5–8). As it turns out, this impressive ceremony is appropriate to what follows, for this book much concerns the gods. In the presence of Athena, disguised as Mentor, Nestor intimates that the goddess herself has brought about Odysseus's loss, and the rest of the episode is chiefly concerned with refuting this view.

According to Nestor, after the fall of Troy, Zeus and Athena became angered at the Argives because "some were not at all wise or righteous" (3.130–35). Zeus therefore "willed the bitter return" (3.132), of which we have already heard Phemios sing (1.326–27). It began when Athena "set strife" (3.136) between Menelaos, who was for returning home immediately, and Agamemnon, who wished to remain and perform hecatombs in the hope of propitiating the goddess. As a result, Agamemnon and Menelaos submitted their disagreement to a most ill-advised assembly late in the afternoon when everybody was drunk (3.137–40).

By his very name, Nestor has to be of the faction of Menelaos. "Return," as a noun, is *nostos*; the verb is *neesthai*; and the agent noun "home-goer," for

Homer's purposes at least, is *nestōr*. Nestor, then, by name is a home-goer.
Temperament, too, inclines him to this choice. The mention of Odysseus's
name reminds him, as it does so many others in the poem, of pain—in this
case, the pain they all suffered together at Troy (3.103–4)—and the word he
uses for this pain, *oïzdus*, just as typically echoes Odysseus's painful name. In
the grip of these memories he begins his answer to Telemachos by dwelling at
length on the miseries of the Trojan War (3.103–17). Clearly, for Nestor, Troy
was a place to get away from as quickly as possible, just as the pain associated
with Odysseus's name was something to be avoided.

As for Agamemnon's plan to stay and try to propitiate the goddess, Nestor
does not hesitate to tell Telemachos and Mentor what he thinks of that.

> Fool, little did he know that he would not persuade her:
> the mind of the gods, who are forever, does not change so lightly.
>
> (3.146–47)

The rest of his account is designed to prove that Agamemnon and Odysseus
were wrong to stay and that he and Menelaos were right to depart at once.
Therefore he tells how the gods "made the sea smooth" for his party's journey
from Troy to Tenedos (3.158), how with a remnant of that party he "fled" from
there because he "knew that the gods had evil in store" (3.166), and how on
Lesbos the gods themselves directed them to take the dangerous, open-sea
route to Euboia so that they "might escape evil the quickest way" (3.175). He
tells what a splendid run that was and how gratefully they sacrificed to Poseidon
when they came ashore. Indeed, Nestor seems to be repeating that sacrifice on
the present occasion. In the end, Diomedes, the third leader in their party,
reached Argos from Troy in four days, while Nestor, continuing on, had a fair
wind all the way to Pylos (3.180–83). Obviously Nestor is implying that the
Greeks would have escaped the effects of the wrath of Athena if they had only
all left Troy as soon as he did. The fatal thing was that "the god scattered the
Achaians" (3.131); that is, separated them, beginning when Athena "set strife
between the two sons of Atreus" (3.136). As he sees it, not following Menelaos
was the immediate cause, as the wickedness of a few was the general one, why
"many met an evil doom/because of the terrible wrath of the gray-eyed one,
Zeus's daughter" (3.134–35).

Very few, however, were of Nestor's opinion at the time. He tells us that half
the army accompanied him and Menelaos to Tenedos (3.157) but that there
strife broke out again, "since Zeus did not yet mean us to get home" (3.160).
The sacrifices (3.159) apparently were unfavorable. Everyone except Diome-

des "followed Odysseus" back again "to bear favor to Agamemnon" (3.163–66). Menelaos himself, the original home-goer, evidently wavered, for we are expressly told that he caught up with Nestor and Diomedes, "late," in Lesbos (3.168–69). This large-scale rejection of his opinion must have rankled with Nestor. As a result, when Telemachos asks him about "the death" of Odysseus (3.93), he cannot resist emphasizing that his great rival as adviser to the Achaians evidently ended by making a serious mistake about the gods. Therefore he stresses the fact that he and Odysseus never disagreed about "what was best for the Argives" until the "bitter return" (3.126–36). Concerning that return, he and Odysseus finally disagreed, and Odysseus is now lost. What better proof can there be that he was right and Odysseus wrong? To be sure, he came home too soon to know anything certain about Odysseus's end, as he admits (3.184–85), and therefore he says no more about him; but is not the fate of Agamemnon a sufficient indication of what must have happened, even though many in that group too came home safely (3.188–94)? The inescapable implication is that Odysseus is lost because he did not run fast enough from the wrath of Athena.

Though Nestor thinks that his wisdom has proved superior, he does not mean to gloat, and he tries to be comforting. To be sure, Agamemnon was killed, but did not Orestes avenge him? Nestor suggests that Telemachos is now in a position to win similar honor (3.195–200). Telemachos replies with praise of Orestes and a poignant wish that the gods would give him too such power. He cannot believe, however, that the gods have granted such happiness either to him or to his father; he can only endure the suitors' outrage (3.202–9). In a word, Telemachos refuses to be comforted. Although it would suit the prudence of his character to conceal his reasons for confidence (we may remember how he concealed from the suitors both Mentes' and Mentor's aid), and although he may be angling for help from Nestor (we may remember the suitors' ironic remarks about his bringing back "avengers from Pylos," 2.326), ostensibly at least he has changed from the youth who set sail so boldly, telling Eurykleia that his venture was "not without the gods" (2.372). Certainly he was not then in a mood simply to endure, the course he now proposes.

Nestor's account of the returns from Troy might well cause this change. It implies that a man should fear the gods' anger rather than trust in their help, and Telemachos seems to have taken the hint. Especially now that the death of his father seems even more certain than it did, he appears simply unable to believe that the gods will give him strength enough to kill so many suitors, whatever Orestes may have accomplished. This impression is strengthened by what follows. Nestor continues, not very convincingly, to try to be encouraging: Has Telemachos applied to the Ithacans, or are they against him because they have listened to some god? Or perhaps Odysseus will come home after all, with or without his fleet. Would that Athena might support Telemachos as openly as she once supported Odysseus (3.214–24)! None of this is very helpful—neither the gratuitous thought that the gods are behind Telemachos's lack of public support nor the reminder that Athena, in Nestor's view, favored Odysseus only to abandon him later. It is not surprising that Telemachos replies,

> Venerable sir, I do not think this will ever come to pass:
> You have said a thing too great. Awe holds me. I could never
> hope for a thing like that, not even if the gods should will it.
> (3.226–28)

Having learned from Nestor to fear the gods, Telemachos seems overawed. On coming ashore, Mentor tells him that he must put awe (*aidōs*) behind him (3.14) and face Nestor boldly. Telemachos duly takes Mentor's advice; but cheerfully to expect help from the dread gods whom Nestor has now evoked is another matter. No wonder that Athena now takes a hand. Still disguised as Mentor, she rebukes Telemachos's lack of faith.

> Telemachos, what a thing to say: with ease
> a god, if he wills, can save a man no matter how distant.
> (3.230–31)

So much for Nestor's pessimism about Odysseus's return. And perhaps Athena has not been so unkind to him as everyone supposes.

> I myself would choose, though toiling through many woes,
> to come home to my house at last and see my homecoming day,
> rather than come and die at my hearth as Agamemnon
> died by the treachery of Aigisthos and his own wife.
> (3.232–35)

Nor is death necessarily evidence of the gods' hostility; Agamemnon's (or Odysseus's) end may not be a punishment at all.

> But of course death comes to all, and the gods themselves
> cannot keep it off even from one they love, when the time has come
> for horrid death to seize him and lay him low.
> (3.236–38)

In this way Athena tries by ordinary common sense to free Telemachos from excessive fear of the gods; but under the influence of Nestor's demonstration, he refuses to be convinced.

Telemachos unwittingly (and ironically) prefers Nestor's wisdom to that of the wise goddess herself. He declares himself sure that the gods have contrived Odysseus's "death and dark fate" (3.241–42) and turns from Mentor to Nestor with the following words:

> For Nestor knows beyond all others what is right to do;
> they say he has kept his kingship through three generations of men,
> and so I look upon him as I would on an immortal.

> (3.244–46)

Nestor, not Athena, becomes for the moment the possessor of divine wisdom.

Such a state of affairs cannot be allowed to continue, of course. To our relief, Telemachos removes the cause of his own discouragement by asking Nestor what are in essence two simple questions (3.248–52): "How did Agamemnon die, and where was Menelaos? What technique did Aigisthos use to kill a better fighter than himself, and was Menelaos somewhere outside Greece, that Aigisthos took courage and slew Agamemnon?" Discouraged Telemachos may be, but he has the wit to notice that Nestor has not yet said that Menelaos came home safely. He also recognizes that what protects great chieftains from emulous assassination is the inevitability of revenge at the hands of their powerful connections. Finally, the question of how a worse man may prevail over a better is of interest from the points of view of both expediency and justice, especially for a young man with his mother's suitors on his hands.

As often in Homer, the questions are answered in reverse order. Nestor assures Telemachos that he is absolutely right. I paraphrase 3.254–312: Of course revenge was to be expected from Menelaos, and of the extremest sort. Aigisthos was in effect out of his mind to risk it. He might well have accepted Klytaimnestra's refusal and let matters rest there, had "the fate of the gods" (3.269) not bound him to his destruction by inducing him to murder her poet-guardian, win her consent thereby at last, and take her to his own house. From then on, his death was only a question of time. He never expected to be able even to kill the returning Agamemnon and so sacrificed greatly to the gods when that happened (3.273–75; cf. Sophokles' Elektra 277–81). How did he manage to kill the stronger man, contrary to his own expectation? It seems the gods had a hand in that, too. Menelaos would have been in Greece in time to protect his brother if Apollo had not brought quick death to Menelaos's helmsman on the way home. Menelaos naturally stayed behind to bury him, with the result that a storm blew him to Crete; he eventually remained abroad for seven years (3.276–312). Revenge therefore had to wait for Orestes. The lost helmsman's name, Phrontis Onetorides (Thought Son of Helpful), shows how irrational these things sometimes are. Menelaos or Nestor did not lack wisdom in their choice of the quick run home; the gods simply made that wisdom ineffective for Menelaos.

All Homer's audiences from the first have been aware how unsatisfactory this answer of Nestor's is. We all know that the true reason Aigisthos was able to kill a better man was that he set a watch and ambushed Agamemnon at a feast (4.512–37). Only Nestor's preoccupation with the success of his quick run home could keep him from realizing that what Agamemnon needed was more swords to support him at the banquet. In a more general sense, Nestor seems aware that it was unfortunate that the Achaians were scattered, but he does not notice that he himself is as responsible as anyone for the scattering. Without his influence Menelaos and Agamemnon might well have reached Mycenae together, with an entirely different result.

More generally still, in his first account of Troy's aftermath, Nestor had assumed that mortals can avoid such things as "the bitter return" by the free exercise of rational choice. Accordingly, before Telemachos asks his questions, he tells of many such choices: the choice at Troy, to leave at once or to wait; the one on Tenedos, to go on or back to Agamemnon; the one on Lesbos, to go inside Chios or across the open sea. His account of the misfortunes of Menelaos, by contrast, is full of alternatives where, at least as Nestor sees it, there is no room for choice at all: first, Menelaos is forced to wait at Sounion to bury his helmsman while Nestor and Diomedes go on; then part of Menelaos's fleet is driven ashore in northwest Crete while the rest are blown south past the western end of the island; finally, part of these vessels are caught on Cape Lithinion while the five remaining craft weather it and are blown ultimately to Egypt. For this last disaster Homer, or the Muse, provides an image which irresistibly suggests how small a thing may make a great difference.

> There is a smooth rock dropping steep to the water
> on the point beyond Gortyn in the hazy passage,
> where the Southwind drives the big billows against its leftward surface
> into Phaistos, and a small stone beats back the big billows.
> The remaining ships came there, happy to escape destruction—
> the men, that is; the ships were smashed on the ledges

by the waves, all but five; those, with their blue prows,
wind and water carried onward until they reached Egypt.

(3.293–300)

The "small stone" not only deflects the big seas; it also divides the fates of
Menelaos's ships and men. In Nestor's first account we see a fleet divided and
scattered by human choice; in his second, by death, wind, and sea. It is as
though he were being forced to admit that, while rational decision often
determines a good or bad outcome, just as often it has nothing to do with it.
Odysseus's fate, for example, may not be the result of his having made a foolish
choice in going back to Agamemnon at all.

We may note as well that the embarrassment of having to admit that the
quick run home did not work for Menelaos has apparently caused Nestor to do
what Zeus has accused mortals in general of doing, namely, to blame the gods
for what is the mortals' own fault. By making "the fate of the gods" responsible
for Aigisthos's reckless act, he may try to diminish the importance of Menelaos's absence, but he certainly contradicts Zeus's own statement that Aigisthos, not the gods, was to blame (1.32–37).

So Telemachos need not be discouraged. It is by no means as certain as
Nestor originally thought that the wrath of Athena against others brought
about Agamemnon's death, let alone Odysseus's, nor is it necessary to believe
that, when Athena is angry, the only thing to do is to run for home; it may even
be that her help can still be hoped for. We shall see this same point reinforced
when we consider book 4.

Nestor himself is less the home-goer by the end of his second speech than he
seemed at the beginning. To be sure, Menelaos's arrival in Mycenae too late to
assist in the revenge occurs to him as an example of how unwise it is to stay
abroad too long, and he warns Telemachos against it; nevertheless, he does
recommend that he visit Menelaos and profit from what knowledge he may
have acquired in his long travels (3.309–22). We see therefore that his propen-
sities do not prevent him from giving Telemachos the proper advice in the end.

Thus Athena triumphs in Nestor's mind as well as in Telemachos's. After an
initial check her view can now prevail, the view that Telemachos may look to
her with hope. Accordingly, she first makes elaborate farewells as Mentor and
then departs in the shape of a large vulture, revealing her divine nature. Nestor
recognizes her at once as Athena and congratulates Telemachos on his good
fortune in enjoying the gods' escort, especially at his age. Nestor's generous
enthusiasm brings with it a touch of pathos, for we realize almost with regret
that the gods have not attended him so readily. He fears them perhaps too

much. Telemachos, on the other hand, may now be sure that his efforts are "not without a god" (2.372). Nestor vows to sacrifice on the morrow a yearling heifer to Athena, wrapping its horns in gold foil, and in the sequel we are privileged to watch this sacrifice in all its graceful detail. It makes an ending to match the huge sacrifice to Poseidon with which the book began and, by contrast with it, signals the change in attitude toward heaven, from fear to hope, which the narrative has implied is justified.

At the end of the book Homer expresses Athena's triumph and Nestor's joyous acceptance of it through this splendid festivity, but he has alluded to it earlier in a piece of wit. At the close of Nestor's conversation with Telemachos on the previous day, Athena, still disguised as Mentor, twits Nestor on his garrulity.

> Venerable sir, all this of yours has been fitly said;
> but come, now let us *cut the tongues* and mix the wine,
> so that to Poseidon and the other gods
> we may make offering and think of bed, for it is time;
> the light goes down now into dark, and it is not good
> to sit long at the gods' banquet, but *to go home.*
>
> (3.331–36)

Here at least is a case where Nestor may properly follow the implications of his name.

The Waiting of Menelaos;
Penelope and the Suitors

Telemachos's encounter with Menelaos follows the same pattern as his visit to Nestor: a first stage in which the great man's view of life threatens to shake Telemachos's purpose is followed by a second in which this view is found wanting and Telemachos continues on his way in a manner more in keeping with the spirit of his father. At the same time, the two episodes are contrasted at almost every point. If Nestor's name suggests going home, the first two syllables of Menelaos's name just as obviously mean "wait." Where Nestor hurries home to avoid the presumed hostility of the gods, Menelaos, although he was the original proponent of the quick return, ends by delaying too long in foreign parts, waiting for his problems to go away.

This major contrast is supported by a whole series of others. Telemachos travels to Pylos by ship at night and arrives in the morning, but he journeys to Sparta overland by chariot in the daytime and arrives in the evening. As far as Pylos he has Athena, disguised as Mentor, to guide him, but at Sparta, with only Nestor's son Peisistratos for company, he is essentially on his own. His interview with Nestor takes place on a sandy beach (3.5), recalling Pylos's stock epithet, whereas Sparta is introduced as a fertile plain (3.495). Nestor's establishment is so modest and informal that he relies on his children to wait on his visitors (3.354–55), and his daughter gives Telemachos his bath (3.464–65); Menelaos's palace, on the other hand, makes Telemachos think of the palace of Zeus himself (4.71–74), and servants attend the guests at every turn. Finally, while we first see Nestor well pleased with himself, Menelaos, in spite of all his wealth and power and the possession of the most beautiful wife in the world, is full of grief.

Menelaos is simply waiting for Zeus to put an end to his pain. When his herald hesitates to admit his new guests, Menelaos cries out,

> Great was the hospitality we enjoyed
> in other men's houses on our way here,
> so may Zeus one day end our pain. (4.33–35)

He then repeats the act which caused his woe in the first place by insisting that the guests be admitted.

The idea that the herald holds back because he remembers the abduction of Helen is at least as old as the ancient commentaries on the text. The only difference is that this time Menelaos invites not one handsome young man into his palace but two (4.20–36). Telemachos and Peisistratos do not reenact Paris's crime, but their visit is the occasion for something that can be regarded as even worse: the demonstration that recovering Helen has done Menelaos no good. This is the pain for the end of which Menelaos is still waiting. From the moment he sees Telemachos and Peisistratos, he envies them because their families, unlike his, have a hope of continuing. His first words to them are,

> Fall to, and welcome. After dinner
> we shall ask who you are. In your case, at least,
> the line has not died out; you come
> of Zeus-nurtured kings, scepter holders;
> no commoner fathers' sons like you. (4.60–64)

As we have just been told (4.12–14), Helen has not been able to give Menelaos a son, and the son he has had by a slave woman is, evidently, no consolation, since he has named him Megapenthes (Great Grief, 4.11). Even the one child he has had by Helen, the beautiful Hermione, he is about to lose. When Telemachos and Peisistratos arrive at his palace, he is in the act of sending her off to Thessaly to marry Achilles' son, Neoptolemos. This too is, in a sense, Helen's fault inasmuch as the betrothal was made at Troy, presumably in return for Neoptolemos's participation in the war (4.6). No wonder Menelaos hails with such emphasis Nestor's happiness in marriage and the birth of sons (4.207–11)!

Menelaos also regrets all those who died because of Troy. First, there is his brother, Agamemnon, murdered after the war while Menelaos wandered in foreign parts. As a result Menelaos takes no joy, he says, in the incomparable wealth he amassed as a guest on his wanderings (4.90–93). Nor was the property he lost when Helen and Paris absconded worth the lives of those who died trying to recover it; he wishes that he "were living at home with only a third as much," and that "those who died at Troy, far from the pastures of Argos" were alive and well (4.94–99). Worse than all is the loss of Odysseus, which takes from him the joys of food and sleep. Odysseus is a source of such pain because, although he was the chief architect of the victory, now no one even knows whether he is alive or dead (4.104–10). Even the victory at Troy has only added to Menelaos's misery.

There remains, of course, Helen. Even though she has failed to carry on Menelaos's line, may such beauty as hers not compensate for everything? Telemachos's experiences in Sparta allow us no such illusion. Helen bursts on the scene like a vision of Artemis (4.121–22), attended with all the luxury that her travels with Menelaos in Egypt and elsewhere can bestow, but she arrives only to shatter the decorum that should obtain between host and guest. Telemachos has made it almost certain who he is by weeping when Menelaos evokes Odysseus's loss, and Menelaos is debating whether to ask him tactfully who his parents are or wait for him to speak (4.117–19), when Helen enters and gives the whole secret away.

> Do we know, Zeus-cherished Menelaos, who
> these new guests of ours claim to be?
> Shall I pretend, or not? My heart bids me be frank.
> Never did I see anyone so like,
> man or woman—awe holds me as I look—
> as this youth here is like Odysseus's son,
> Telemachos. . . . (4.138–44)

To be sure, Menelaos does not object to this indiscretion, remarking only that he too had suspected that their guest might be Telemachos; as we shall see, he has a habit of not presuming to criticize the overpowering daughter of Zeus. Nevertheless, the passage points clearly to the central fact about Helen: she betrays men, either directly, as here, or by making them give themselves away.

Ensuing events make unmistakable just how dangerous Helen is. The characteristics of the drug with which she alleviates everybody's sorrow for Odysseus's loss are described as follows. It

> banished grief and rage, blotted out every evil.
> Whoever swallowed it, once it was mixed with the wine,
> for that whole day would shed no tear,
> not even if mother and father should die,
> not even if before his face his brother or his son

> men should slay with the sword, and his own eyes see it.
> Such ingenious medicines the daughter of Zeus possessed,
> good ones. . . . (4.221–28)

Helen is truly the daughter of Zeus, and no doubt it is in a sense good to be spared grief and rage, but surely not in the situations named? Who would choose to be unaffected by the death of a mother or the murder of a son? We cannot help feeling that the state Helen has induced in the company is not an entirely desirable one, however in keeping it may be with Peisistratos's wish not to "weep after supper" (4.193–94). What happens next proves us right. Helen proceeds to tell the story of how she saw through Odysseus's disguise when he came to spy on the Trojans, and how he admitted who he was after she swore not to betray him before he returned safely to the ships (4.235–64). She rejoiced at the success of his raid, she says, because she had already regretted her infatuation for Paris, far preferred Menelaos, and wished only for the Greeks to win the war and take her home. In other words, she suggests that, whatever she may have been or done in the past, her repentance now makes her a wife whom Menelaos can trust.

Homer, however, proceeds to make us doubt her steadfastness, for Menelaos counters with a story which suggests that her repentance did not last (4.266–89). He tells how, when he, Odysseus, Diomedes, and the others were shut inside the wooden horse, Helen came and, stroking its hollow sides, called out the names of the Greek chiefs inside in tones which reminded them of their wives. All, including the stalwart Diomedes, would have betrayed themselves by answering if Odysseus had not prevented them. This incident occurred, of course, later than Helen's alleged change of heart. We even know how, at this later date, she knew what was inside the horse, for her own story mentions the fact that Odysseus told her "all the intent of the Achaians" (4.256). In short, Menelaos makes clear that, far from repenting, she nearly secured victory for the Trojans. She was ambivalent enough and feared her oath to Odysseus enough not to betray the Greeks outright, but she did her best to make them give themselves away. As for her yearning for her former husband, Menelaos knows all about that too. As he indicates, after Paris's death Helen attached herself to Deïphobos. On the evidence, she is not somebody Menelaos can trust very far.

Taken together, these two stories suggest that, drug or no drug, Helen has not succeeded in winning Menelaos's confidence even ten years after their marriage was resumed. We now see why Menelaos avoided discussing Telemachos's business in front of her (4.214–15): just conceivably she might make as dangerous use of what she might hear from Telemachos as she did of what she heard from Odysseus. Nevertheless, her untrustworthiness provokes from Menelaos no great show of anger or distress. Of her attempt to make the chiefs in the horse give themselves away, he says merely,

> You must have been inspired
> by a god who wished glory for the Trojans;
> and Deïphobos was with you. (4.274–76)

Helen's drug allows him to contemplate with a certain equanimity the disloyalty of his wife, just as it allows fathers to see their sons cut down before their own eyes, oblivious of the pain of what is going on.

By this time it should be clear that Helen's so-powerful drug has the same effect as her beauty: both make men forget who and where they are and what is most important to them. Even though the Greek chiefs inside the horse could not see her, when she stroked its sides and called to them "in a voice like the voice of the wives of all the Argives" (4.279), all but Odysseus would have answered, as we have seen. Because it makes men forget themselves, it is basically her sexual attractiveness, not some flaw in her character, that makes her dangerous. For this reason, I think, we forgive her and forgive Menelaos for forgiving her. When she blurts Telemachos's name, exhibits her joy in uncovering Odysseus's disguise, takes up with Deïphobos, and tempts the chiefs in the horse, not to mention when she elopes with Paris, we can feel these things essentially as extensions of her triumphant sexual appeal. Nevertheless, we are by now aware of her drug as only ambiguously a good one, and we probably would not change places with Menelaos. Drugged by Helen's beauty, he is even unhappier than he knows, for the recovery of Helen seems, finally, not to have been worth it. He is still waiting for an end to pain.

Unfortunately, Odysseus's ability to resist her seems to be of no use either. Helen and Menelaos both hail Odysseus for his unsurpassed strength of mind. Helen introduces her story in these words:

> I could never tell nor describe
> all Odysseus's laborious feats;
> but what a deed that was he did and endured, strong man,
> in the land of Troy, where you Achaians suffered!
>
> (4.240–43)

Menelaos begins his tale as follows:

> By now I have come to know
> many a hero, and traveled much of the earth;
> but never yet have my eyes seen a heart
> like the heart in laborious Odysseus.
> What a deed that too was he did and endured, strong man,
> in the wooden horse, where all the best of us sat,
> the Argives, bringing death and doom to the Trojans!
>
> (4.267–73)

Helen tells how Odysseus had the hardihood even to have himself whipped before he went spying into Troy, to improve his disguise; and Menelaos, as we have seen, shows how Odysseus alone of all the Greek heroes could resist Helen's sexual appeal. Here truly is the Odysseus, full of menos, whose image gave Telemachos the courage to act in book 1. Yet at Menelaos's court all Odysseus's strength of heart begins to seem futile. Menelaos has already said that no one even knows whether he is alive or dead and that he alone of the Argives, by heaven's will, is "without return" (4.181–82). We know, of course, that he will return, but Telemachos and Menelaos do not. Furthermore, Telemachos's expedition already seems to have ended in failure: evidently Menelaos can give him neither proof of his father's death nor hope that he will return. He is exactly where he was before he set out. No wonder, then, that Helen's and Menelaos's praise of his father's strength of mind only makes him cry out,

> All the worse, since it did not prevent his terrible loss,
> not though the heart within him was strong as iron.
>
> (4.292–93)

Here is a discouragement which could prevent Telemachos from trying to exact justice from the suitors, particularly considering how little Menelaos seems to have gained by avenging himself on Paris.

From one point of view, the tale of Proteus, which Menelaos tells to Telemachos on the following day, adds nothing to the discouraging picture we have been contemplating. For Telemachos's immediate purposes it is simply a virtuoso's cadenza on the theme "We do not know whether Odysseus is alive or dead, but after all this time he surely will not come home." Nevertheless, in the course of the tale Menelaos proves, by contrast, the value of a spirit like Odysseus's, whether he is coming home or not.

Menelaos is charming, but his heart is definitely not "as strong as iron." His enthusiasms flare up quickly, only to wane almost at once. His response to Telemachos's problem is a good example. I paraphrase 4.333–588:

That's certainly a strong-minded man whose bed those suitors are trying to fill! They might as well be fawns whose mother has left them in a lion's den. It's terrible to think what he will do to them when he comes back. Zeus, Athena, and Apollo grant that he come upon them as he was when he threw the wrestler Philomeleides, and all the Achaians rejoiced! Then their lives would be short and their wedding a sorry one, I assure you. But let me tell you what the Old Man of the Sea told me: he saw Odysseus weeping on an island, captive to the nymph Kalypso. He can't get home, since he has no ship or crew to carry him over the sea. Why don't you wait here with me for a week or two?

Characteristically, Menelaos begins by seeing the punishment of the suitors as certain, only to end by suggesting that Telemachos may all but put it from his mind, it is so unlikely.

Menelaos is a do-nothing, even though he is perhaps not only the richest but also the most powerful man in the world. He says that, if Odysseus had returned, he would have sacked one of his own cities and installed Odysseus, his son, and his whole people there so that he might spend the rest of his days entertaining Odysseus in Sparta (4.171–80). Even if Odysseus is not coming home, a king who can do this can certainly help Telemachos against the suitors, as Peisistratos hints that he might (4.161–67). Nevertheless, Menelaos does not think of doing anything to help his friend's son. Apparently, retrieving his honor and property does not strike him as worth the effort. We remember in this connection his disillusion with the Trojan War in his own case. Not only have we heard him say that the property he regained was not worth the lives that were lost, but Nestor has told us that, although Menelaos was presumably the first to advocate the war, he was also the first to urge going home without even attempting to secure Athena's pardon for its crimes (3.141–47). Nor does this passion to hurry home last long: his helmsman's death and the unlucky storm are enough to make him exchange it for a seven years' sojourn collecting hospitality abroad (3.301–12). When this, too, is over, his resolution is yet again called into question when the nymph Eidothea castigates him for his fecklessness as a traveler. After he has spent twenty days on the island of Pharos waiting for a fair wind to bring him home from Egypt, she appears to him and says:

Are you so great a fool and trifler, stranger,
or do you purposely waste time, enjoying what you suffer?
Here you are stuck on this island, and no skill
to find a remedy, while your men's heart grows weaker.

(4.371–74)

Divinities in Homer, it is true, often take an unfairly superior tone with mortals, whether to emphasize the helplessness of the human condition or for other reasons; but in this case Eidothea seems to have a more particular reason for her scorn. Menelaos has told us that Pharos is a day's sail from Egypt. He is in despair because, while he waits there for his wind, the food is giving out. Why does he not, then, return to Egypt where he has been so well entertained? At worst his men will have to row the equivalent of a day's sail, and there can be no question of a head wind, since such a wind would be the very wind for Greece for which they have been waiting.

As though to make Menelaos act out his propensity to submit to circumstance and wait passively for a solution to his problems, Eidothea enjoins upon him his elaborate lying in wait for her father, Proteus, the Old Man of the Sea, and, when he is caught, the task of enduring his shape-shifting until he reveals "which one of the immortals" (4.380) bars his return. The answer turns out to be very like what we suggested Menelaos might have thought of for himself: go back to Egypt and sacrifice to Zeus and the other gods. Menelaos is predictably dismayed at this news; nevertheless, when the time comes, the voyage is performed without difficulty. To say the least, Menelaos has not the strong-mindedness of an Odysseus.

We have seen that Telemachos despairs of the value of Odysseus's strong-minded approach to life. We have seen Menelaos hail the strong-minded revenge that Odysseus would undoubtedly take on the suitors, only to counter that image with what Proteus has said of Odysseus's inability to get home. Shall Telemachos carry on with his project, or abandon it? Menelaos's story constitutes, as it were, a vote against carrying on, since it shows Menelaos himself as virtually having decided not to take part in the punishment of Aigisthos and Klytaimnestra. As usual, he has changed his mind.

When Proteus tells him of Agamemnon's murder, his grief at first is such as we might expect of someone who knows that the death was in large part his own fault; some relief, however, comes from Proteus's suggestion that, if he hurries, he may arrive home in time to kill Aigisthos before Orestes does, or at least to take part in the funeral (4.543–47). From this point on we naturally look for Menelaos to carry out as quickly as he can the requirement that he return to

Egypt and sacrifice to all the gods. But at this point also, Proteus tells him, as his final piece of news, that, because he possesses Helen, the gods will take him, as Zeus's son-in-law, to Elysion and make him immortal (4.561–69). As a result of this further news, apparently, Menelaos, "much troubled in mind" (4.572), takes his time returning from the scene of Proteus's ambush, has supper, sleeps, and only on the next day sets out for Egypt. Once there, he propitiates the gods and then proceeds to raise a cenotaph to Agamemnon's memory; whereupon, as he tells the story to Telemachos, he simply goes home. There is not a word of Orestes' vengeance on Aigisthos and Klytaimnestra or of Menelaos's attending their funeral feast, even though Nestor and Proteus have both mentioned these events and we are expecting them. It certainly looks as though Menelaos means to substitute the cenotaph for the punishment of Aigisthos he would have been in time to exact if he had not built it; furthermore, it looks as though the prospect of immortality has brought about this change of heart. Why should he, Menelaos seems to ask, covet the fame Orestes will win by performing a notable act of justice, if he can win a less painful and more substantial immortality as kinsman of Zeus? Here at last, in his immortality, is the end to pain we have known Menelaos to be waiting for ever since he first appeared in the poem.

By announcing Menelaos's coming immortality immediately after describing Odysseus's captivity to Kalypso, Proteus implicitly compares the two fates, and Menelaos evidently sees his own as the better. As Menelaos understands Proteus's words, Odysseus will die while still on Kalypso's island, if indeed he is not dead already (note the words *ēe thanōn*, " or else dead," at 4.553), whereas he, Menelaos, will live forever. Nevertheless, his very insistence that, in his earlier phrase, no one knows any longer whether Odysseus is alive or dead and that he very well may have died since Proteus saw him (*ēe thanōn* above) shows where Menelaos is wrong. Captivity to Kalypso, whatever he may think, is not tantamount to ignominious death. The story is not yet over. A man as enterprising as Odysseus, as long as he is alive, may still escape, ship and crew or no ship and crew, and we know from book 1 that he will indeed escape. As for Menelaos, once he reaches his painless Elysion, his story is closed, however alive he may be in other ways. To have missed this chance to punish Aigisthos is simply not worth such an immortality. Divorced from the pursuit of justice, his life loses its meaning, and his story (or his image; it comes to the same thing) is a sorry one compared to Orestes' (in Homer's version), not to mention to such a story as Telemachos's and Odysseus's promises to be.

Menelaos's greatest feat, lying in wait for Proteus and forcing from him the secret of his future immortality, in spite of the charm with which it is told, ruthlessly reveals what his life is really like. It is difficult to dissociate the idea of Menelaos and his companions waiting beneath their sealskins, whose stench they endure only by virtue of the ambrosia with which Eidothea has smeared their nostrils, from the idea of Menelaos dragging out a life made bearable only by Helen's beauty as he waits for Elysion. In the context, his enduring Proteus's shape-shifting looks too passive to be real fortitude. If it also suggests getting at the reality beneath appearances, Menelaos mistakes the reality: where Proteus assumes revenge, Menelaos in effect decides against it. Clearly, Menelaos would have won more of a Greek audience's admiration if he had defended his own honor and Agamemnon's and gone to Hades' house than he does as Zeus's immortal son-in-law in Elysion. We shall soon see Odysseus make the choice in the opposite sense: he will prefer his mortal pains to immortality with Kalypso. Similarly, Telemachos, once he has heard Menelaos's story of Proteus, knows which decision is the right one.

Only in the most delicate way, however, does Telemachos show Menelaos that he is of his father's mind rather than of his host's. I paraphrase 4.594–608: "No, thank you, I must not linger much longer. I could listen to your stories for a year, and never tire; but I am concerned about my crew, back in Pylos. And another thing: I can't accept the chariot and team you offer me as guest present. They are a splendid adornment for you here in spacious, grassy Sparta, whereas Ithaca is steep and rocky, better for goats than horses; but lovely, for all that. Make my present something handier." This is the tone of a son no longer despairing of the value of his father's iron heart or rugged life. He has not given up on Ithaca, in spite of his desperate situation there, and he is careful of the ship that will bring him home.

The fact that Ithaca can be reached only by ship is emphasized by the questions Telemachos asks Athena.

> On what ship did you arrive? How did it happen that sailors
> brought you to Ithaca? Who do they claim to be?
> I can't believe you came here on foot. (1.171–73)

Eumaios makes the identical query of Odysseus at 14.188–90, Telemachos a similar one of Eumaios concerning Odysseus at 16.57–59, and, finally, Telemachos of his father at 16.222–24. Nestor makes it clear that "on foot" includes by chariot.

> Now go [to Sparta] with your ship and your companions;
> or if you wish to go on foot, here are chariot and horses.
>
> (3.323–24)

On his way to Sparta Telemachos experiences first sailing and then charioteering and repeats that experience in reverse order on his return. It is as though he has made trial of the horse-taming world of the great palaces, of Menelaos's godlike wealth and power, and found it wanting. It is as though he knew that the future would belong to smaller, less hierarchical communities and to ships. At any rate, from this point on the *Odyssey* is a seafaring rather than a charioteering poem.

Menelaos's heart may not be steady, but it is in the right place. He applauds Telemachos's decision.

> Your words show your good blood, dear child;
> it's no trouble to change your gift. (4.611–12)

Like Nestor, Menelaos ends by admitting that his young guest is right.

One further feature of Proteus's story must be remarked on. Proteus silences once and for all the thought that Odysseus's troubles are the result of Athena's anger. By itself, his statement that "two only of the leaders . . ./ were lost in the return" (4.496–97) mitigates considerably our conception of the goddess's anger, but there is more. Of the two who were lost, even Aias, son of Oïleus, "though suffering under Athena's wrath," got safely to shore and "would have escaped death" if he had not boasted that he was saved "in spite of the gods" (4.499–504). Since Aias was notoriously guilty of raping Kassandra at Athena's altar when Troy was sacked, this reservation is mitigation indeed. Clearly, for Homer's Muse, the only truly deadly sin is setting oneself above the gods. If, then, Athena's anger at what happened at Troy did not cause Aias's death, the same must be true of the other Achaian who was "lost on the return," who is, of course, Agamemnon. Proteus tells us that the goddess Hera herself saved him from the sea (4.513). The reason for his eventual death at his wife's and Aigisthos's hands was quite simply that the time had come for him to die (3.234–38). As for Odysseus, Proteus's third case of an unfortunate return, Telemachos may be sure that, if he has died, it will not be because of Athena's wrath for what happened at Troy.

Thus Telemachos will return home confident that, at least, his father has not forfeited heaven's favor and that he himself enjoys it. By returning he will also demonstrate that, in contrast to Menelaos, he regards his life as something more than waiting for Zeus to end his pain. His journey has not informed him whether his father is alive or dead, but it seems to have ensured that his father's example lives on in him.

Now that Telemachos's experience in foreign parts is complete, Homer turns, not yet to Odysseus as we might expect, but to Ithaca to show us how the mere discovery of Telemachos's departure affects, first, the suitors, and then Penelope. One result of this change of scene is a sudden increase in our sense of Telemachos's importance; another is that we see more clearly where both the suitors and Penelope stand.

The manner in which the transition from Sparta to Ithaca is made is itself remarkable. Just as Menelaos is pronouncing his approval of Telemachos, feasters arrive at his palace, and they bring their own dinner (4.620–24). This feast is appropriate as a continuation of the wedding festivities which Telemachos and Peisistratos encounter when they arrive, and it makes a frame for the episode as a whole. Nevertheless, some have felt it odd that the guests should need to supplement a hospitality as lavish as Menelaos's clearly is. This difficulty comes from regarding only verisimilitude, when we should be looking for poetic function as well. In the very next line Homer turns his narrative to the suitors as, "in their insolence" (4.627), they take their pleasure in front of Odysseus's palace, and their reappearance is much enhanced when, stimulated by the contrast, we reflect that they are certainly not the sort of guests to contribute to their own entertainment. We remember Athena's remark concerning them, "This certainly is no contribution feast" (1.226). With Menelaos's self-supplied feasters the transition to the suitors is made closer, smoother, and more interesting.

The careless arrogance of the suitors is at once demonstrated as Noemon inadvertently discloses the fact of Telemachos's departure. They had no idea Telemachos could begin his trip (4.638–40), and their surprise and rage are gratifying. Antinoos now takes Telemachos seriously.

> Incredible, the presumption of Telemachos to bring off
> this journey! We never thought he'd do it.
> From the midst of us all, this youngster, gone, like that,
> launches a ship, with the pick of the best men in town.
> He begins to be a menace. (4.663–67)

When the suitors predict that Telemachos will become a menace (*kakon*, "evil") to them, we note yet again the number of ways in which, in the *Odyssey*, that which seems hostile can be good. The more Telemachos becomes an evil in the suitors' eyes, the more he will win our admiration. Even among the suitors we see the beginning of what looks like respect.

They are becoming aware of Telemachos's importance, but they are not nearly aware enough. Noemon's innocent news contains a clear, if unconscious, warning: Mentor went along as captain—"Mentor or a god," Noemon adds, since, as he explains, he has seen the true Mentor in Ithaca since Telemachos's ship departed (4.653–56). This sign that the gods are helping Telemachos should give the suitors pause, but like Aias, son of Oïleus, they feel themselves exempt from the operation of the divine in human affairs and so do not make the connection. No more did they heed the omen in the assembly. Evidently Telemachos hardly needed to disguise from them his consciousness of Athena's presence in the shape of Mentes on the previous day (1.417–20). Of a piece with this willful blindness is the callousness with which Antinoos calls for Telemachos's death.

> He begins to be a menace. So, then,
> Zeus cut his life off before he gets his full strength!
> Give me a fast ship and twenty companions,
> and we'll set an ambush for his return
> in the passage between Ithaca and rugged Samos.
> Let's spoil his junketing to seek his father. (4.667–72)

The speed with which the suitors have turned Telemachos's death from the joke it was in book 2 to a matter of cold reality shows, as Odysseus will one day say, that they have never really respected anyone, god or man, king or beggar (22.39–40, 414–15). For this reason they are now ripe for Odysseus's revenge and the gods' justice.

To this point in the poem we have had no indication of the degree to which Penelope is concerned about the destruction of her son's estate. Now, at the end of book 4, we discover that she has indeed noticed what is happening to Telemachos's property and authority and has indeed considered telling the suitors to give up their suit and go elsewhere. In fact, their arrogance has reached such a pitch that sending them away no longer seems a sufficient alternative; she would like to see them dead.

> Herald, why have the noble suitors sent you?
> To order Odysseus's serving maids
> to leave their work and get dinner for them?
> May they neither woo me, nor go elsewhere;
> instead may this be the last dinner they ever eat!
> —all you who come every day and consume our store,
> wise Telemachos's property. (4.681–87)

Far from ignoring the suitors' depredations, Penelope has come to regard them as intolerable and is willing to give up her marriage if doing so will help her son.

Why did it not occur to Penelope earlier that she might take some action? First, it is easiest to imagine the suitors' killing of Odysseus's cattle as a gradual development. From Penelope's point of view there can have been no reason to forbid the suitors when they first arrived or to refuse them hospitality. In his speech in the assembly Telemachos speaks of their actions as *no longer* endurable and their wasting of his property as *no longer* fair (2.63–64). By the time they had outstayed their welcome and had begun to order the servants about, it was difficult for either Telemachos or Penelope to speak out. The first overt move in this direction was doubtless Telemachos's defying them in book 1. Although it was more Penelope's place, both as mistress of the house and as object of the wooing, to tell the suitors to be gone, for her the question of their presence was bound up with her chance of marriage; besides, she truly meant to solve Telemachos's problem in a less offensive way by choosing a husband. Her weaving and unweaving the shroud expressed a real ambivalence: both the general desirability of marriage and Telemachos's interest counseled finishing it, but the power of Odysseus's image made her undo at night what she wove by day. Once she was forced to finish it, dismissing the suitors was even more difficult, since she had agreed to choose a husband when it was done. Under the circumstances, it is not so remarkable that, prior to Telemachos's departure, she took no active step.

By the time Penelope reaches the state of exasperation which we see in book 4, the action—or rather, inaction—of the assembly has supervened. The suitors now have tacit permission to continue to waste Telemachos's goods until she chooses one of them. If she tries to refuse the marriage now, the Ithacans will attribute it to her duplicity, as suggested by the suitors in book 2, rather than to her real attitude, since previously she has seemed willing enough. Thus any idea that she might dismiss the suitors at this point is as unrealistic as her wish that today should see the last dinner of their lives; both are an expression of her sense of frustration and helplessness rather than a statement of purpose. Nevertheless, we can now be sure where her heart lies, as we could not be at the end of book 2. These words, uttered even before she hears, almost in one breath, that her son has gone to seek news of his father and that her suitors have planned to ambush him on his return, prove that Penelope has come to realize, like Mentes and Telemachos, that the suitors deserve to die.

Once the secret of the suitors' plot is out, of course, and Penelope can see

unmistakably how far the suitors are willing to go, there is no longer even in
her mind any question of telling them to leave. They would only laugh. For
them the scheme now is, as we have seen, kill Telemachos, make Penelope
choose a husband, and divide the property. If Penelope refuses to choose, they
can choose for her. Even if Laertes or Mentor should dare to oppose them, it is
not likely that the Ithacans, as we have come to know them, will intervene.
Penelope herself knows how little can be expected from the Ithacans: referring,
doubtless, to their earlier failure to act, she speaks of them as wishing to bring
Laertes' line to an end (4.739–41). Nonetheless, to her they seem the only
hope of saving Telemachos, and once she has recovered sufficiently from her
shock and horror at the herald's news, she asks that Laertes be urged to appeal
to their pity (4.735–41).

Eurykleia has a better idea.

> Take a bath, put on clean clothes,
> go upstairs with all your serving women
> and pray to Athena, daughter of Zeus-who-wears-the-aegis;
> she can save Telemachos when the time comes, even from death.
> Don't grieve the old man, broken by grief already; for I think
> Arkeisios's son's race is not utterly hated
> by the immortal gods; one scion will still remain
> to hold the high-roofed house and the fat, far-spreading fields.
>
> (4.750–57)

If there is any truth in what we have said in chapter 2, this advice means, in
effect, "Trust the plan of the gods and your own son's strength."

We see how these two women who love Telemachos are contrasted. Penelope demonstrates that to be gentle and kind is not enough. She complains
bitterly that the suitors show no gratitude for Odysseus's good treatment of them
(4.687–95), and we have seen how little she can expect from an appeal to the
people to save Telemachos. She would have died to prevent her son's journey
(4.732–34), seeing in it, instead of the glory which Athena plans, only the
extinction of her son's name.

> Herald, why is my son gone? What need has he
> to embark on the fast-faring ships, men's horses
> on the sea as they cross the big water: does he
> wish not even his name to be left among mankind?
>
> (4.707–10)

We must not forget that Telemachos's name means *"far fighter."* Evidently Penelope would not have approved when, about to leave Menelaos, he showed his preference for ships, and she is as mistaken about the way in which names are preserved, as she is about how to oppose violence. This is natural enough in a mother, of course, as are her fears for Telemachos's youth and inexperience (4.817–23), but we cannot help but applaud Eurykleia's attitude rather than hers. It was she, Wide Fame, who ended by assisting Telemachos's venture (2.371–80).

Nevertheless, to Penelope's credit let it be said that she immediately does as Eurykleia proposes; and here we begin to see that, gentle as Penelope's instincts are, she is at the same time deadly. Homer expresses this when he compares her, in her motherly anxiety for her son, to a lion surrounded by hunters. The comparison occurs after she has already prayed to Athena to "ward off" the suitors and strengthened the prayer by a ritual shout. The suitors hear and conclude that she is already preparing to marry one of them, "not knowing at all that murder is in store for her son." Homer adds, "So they said, but they did not know the truth of the matter" (4.772). Doubling the irony in this way so brings out the peril of the suitors that, when the simile of the lion occurs nineteen lines later, we almost feel sorry for them: we see that Penelope is the bait in the trap the gods have set to catch their hubris. Although for the moment Penelope is like a frightened lion (4.791–92), when Odysseus returns, if Menelaos is right, the suitors will be like fawns in a lion's den. We now see that Odysseus is not the only lion: Penelope, too, would be glad to see the suitors dead.

The insufficiency of the peaceful-happy without the painful-hostile is shown in a different way as the book ends. As though to confirm Eurykleia's advice, Athena sends Penelope, "sweetly slumbering in the gates of dreams" (4.809), a vision in which Penelope's sister tells her that the gods "who live at ease" will not let her weep and grieve and that her son will return, "since he has never offended the gods" (4.805–7). But Penelope can see beyond the immediate sweetness of her sensations and the simple trust in rectitude proposed to her.

> Why, my sister, . . .
> do you bid me cease from pain and sorrow [*oïzduos ēd' odunaōn*],
>
> . . . .
>
> me, who have lost my goodly husband with the lion heart,
> distinguished for all virtue among the Danaans,
> goodly, whose fame spread wide through Hellas and Middle Argos;
> and now my beloved child is gone in the hollow ship,

a novice, not well skilled in action or speech—
for him I sorrow still more than for the other,
for him I shiver and dread what will happen to him,
either in the land he has gone to, or else on the sea—
for many are they who wish him ill and plot against him,
eager to kill him before he comes back to the land of his fathers.

(4.810–23)

Even in the midst of sweet sleep, Penelope does not forget her true situation, and the simple assurance that her child has done no wrong does little to relieve her mind. Her dream sister tries again.

Take courage; surrender not entirely to the fear in your heart.
Your son has an escort whom others too
have prayed to stand by them—such is her power—
Pallas Athena, who pities you in your pain.
It is she who but now sent me to tell you this.

(4.825–29)

This second version, with its mixture of hope and anxiety and its emphasis on power, is a good deal more like life. Like life, too, is the dream's explicit refusal to tell Penelope, although she asks, whether her husband is alive or dead. None of this excludes the truth of the first version, that Telemachos will come home safely, not having offended the gods; but we can understand that the second is necessary to heal Penelope's heart (4.840).

Book 4 closes with the grim particulars of the ambush.

There is a rocky island in the midst of the water
between Ithaca and rugged Samos,
Asteris, not large, with hiding places for ships,
one on each side; there the Achaians awaited him.

(4.844–47)

To say the least, these words add urgency to the narrative of Odysseus's return from Kalypso's island to Ithaca, occupying the next eight books.

Odysseus Unveiled

The *Odyssey*'s idea of the world is seen at its simplest in book 5, for there Odysseus faces the world alone, without the complications introduced by other human wills. In coming home, Odysseus moves from being hidden to being revealed. His struggle against Poseidon and Kalypso is thus a struggle to be known, to emerge into the light.

By the end of book 4, Telemachos has found out all he can from Nestor and Menelaos, and we have seen how the suitors and Penelope have reacted to Telemachos's departure. Homer now returns to Odysseus. At the council of the gods at the beginning of the poem, Athena has suggested that Hermes be sent to tell Kalypso to let Odysseus go. Shall Homer now commence an extended narrative in the pluperfect tense to mark the fact that, while Athena was visiting Telemachos, Zeus had sent Hermes to Kalypso? Homer could have made Hermes' mission contemporary with Athena's, but he did not see fit to do so, and one may guess why. At the beginning of the poem Odysseus's release was presented to us as overdue.

> But when the year came round
> in which the gods had decreed that he should go home
> to Ithaca, not even then was he safe from his toils
> and among his friends. . . . (1.16–19)

The result is that, at the end of the conversation between Athena and Zeus in the first "council of the gods," we should be left feeling that Odysseus does not deserve his long captivity with Kalypso, that it is only due to Poseidon's wrath, and that the world is perhaps not quite so well ordered as Zeus has just made it out to be in citing the case of Aigisthos.

Since that scene on Olympos two new seeming injustices have been added to the count: Odysseus is not only wise and respectful of the gods (1.66–67), but he has been an excellently kind and just king, as both Mentor and Penelope have insisted (2.230–34; 4.689–93); second, Telemachos, who has done no wrong (4.807), is now in mortal danger, as Medon says at 4.697–702, and Penelope at 4.727–28 and 817–23. The characters' feeling of the unfairness of it all easily becomes our own. By showing Athena as carrying these new complaints to Zeus in much the same words as those in which the characters voiced them, the poet allows us, as it were, to make our continuing objections known to the ruler of the universe and at the same time keeps alive the tension that we met in the first book between Zeus's tone of insistence that everything is really all right and Athena's tone of reasonable objection. Here in book 5.7–20, she objects (in summary), "Why should kings be just, when no one remembers Odysseus? He can't get home, and now they want to kill his child"; to which Zeus replies, "What a thing to say! Didn't you yourself make this plan, that Odysseus should return and take revenge? Take care of Telemachos yourself, as I well know you can" (5.22–27, again in summary). Zeus then turns to Hermes and sends him to release Odysseus with the same air of "Of course I was going to do it all the time" with which he suggested his release in the first book. In this way we may well be left anxious as to whether all really is right with the world, or whether Zeus is just bluffing; in fact, I believe that this is exactly the state in which the poet wishes to put us. That Zeus should seem to need to be reminded in the fifth book of what he had said in the first is thus not a defect in the poem, as some have alleged, but a happy and intended stroke. If it is at the same time the simplest way of reminding the audience of that earlier scene, of recapitulating events and of marking how far matters have progressed from the Olympian (and the audience's) point of view, so much the better. The second council on Olympos reflects no naïve inability or reluctance to portray simultaneous happenings, but rather intensifies our awareness of the problem of evil.

This second scene on Olympos has still other uses: the hero, now that he is to enter the action at last, deserves an impressive sponsorship at least as much as Telemachos did. Accordingly he gets a personal endorsement from Zeus himself (5.29–42), and that endorsement makes two vital points: Zeus decrees that Odysseus is to make his own boat and to cross the sea in sorrow with no help from gods or men (for this is a do-it-yourself world); but once he has reached the Phaeacians, who are near to the gods, Odysseus will be escorted home with more wealth and honor than he won at Troy (for this is after all a world where the deserving do, on occasion, succeed). There are of course other possible implications of Zeus's prescriptive prediction ("prescriptive" because the will of Zeus is, from the Greek point of view, what ought to happen), but those mentioned seem the implications most consistent with the rest of the poem. We shall note further evidence for them as we go along.

First, however, we must face another seeming anomaly when, in the scene between Hermes and Kalypso, Homer seems quite definitely to make the goddess correct the god about what happened to Odysseus after Troy. Hermes says, speaking of Odysseus as one of the Achaians,

> On the way home they offended *Athena*
> who roused against them bitter winds and a heavy sea.
> Then all his goodly companions perished,
> and the winds and waves carried him to your shore.
>
> (5.108–11)

In the course of her reply, Kalypso contradicts this account, or seems to.

> I saved him, as he bestrode his own keel
> all alone, for *Zeus* with his blazing bolt
> had smashed his swift ship in the midst of the wine-dark sea.
> Then all his goodly companions perished,
> and the winds and waves carried him to my shore.
>
> (5.130–34)

There are indications that Hermes' version, not Kalypso's, is the traditional one. We have heard Phemios sing of "the return of the Achaians,/that grim return, which Pallas put upon them after Troy" (1.326–27). Nestor and Proteus both speak of Athena's anger, and Proteus knows of a storm resulting from it which wrecked Aias, son of Oïleus (3.135; 4.499–502). Later writers like Aeschylus and Euripides have much to say of this storm also. The traditional version, then, is that Athena in anger wrecked many of the Greeks on their way home, including Odysseus and his men, and Hermes' words strongly suggest the same thing.

In the *Odyssey*, however, Athena clearly has no fault to find with Odysseus. Homer makes this point not only in the debate on Olympos but also when Athena in person rebuts Nestor's attempt to demonstrate her hostility to Agamemnon and Odysseus. Even against the other Greeks, her anger is portrayed as not so fatal as the tradition assumes. Nestor himself admits that most of the Greeks came home well (3.188–92), and as we have seen, Proteus remarks pointedly that *on the return* only two of the chiefs were lost, and one of those, Agamemnon, not at sea (4.496–97, 512–13). That leaves only Aias, and he too, Proteus says, would have escaped, "though in the bad graces of Athena," if he had not made one final boastful speech (5.502–3). As a result, when we hear Hermes in the fifth book voicing the old conception of a grim return caused by Athena's wrath and storm, we are sensible of how inadequate it is. Ever since the poem's invocation we have known that Odysseus's shipmates were doomed by Helios's anger rather than by Athena's, as Hermes seems to imply. Kalypso's correction—adding, as it does, still another element, Zeus's thunderbolt—comes as a welcome corroboration of our feeling that Hermes' account is incomplete and prepares us for the still fuller version we shall meet in the course of Odysseus's own tale.

Notoriously, war is harder on the good than on the scoundrels; in the *Odyssey* Odysseus, presented by Athena as the paradigm of undeserved suffering (1.62), comes home latest of all. We have already seen, also, good reason to regard his captivity to a beautiful nymph on a desert island as no slight evil. Oblivion is oblivion. Nevertheless, it remains to consider the beauty of the nymph more closely. In discussing book 1, I hinted that it was somehow worse for Odysseus to be seduced from his memory of Ithaca than for him simply to forget it. Those at home, at any rate, must think so, and the beauty of Kalypso in Homer's conception must owe something to this feeling. Thinking along these lines in his concrete way, Homer would then see in Kalypso not only hiding and revelation, perceiving and not perceiving, but also pleasure (the desirable Kalypso) and pain (the struggle to get home). Out of these two oppositions—knowledge and ignorance, and pleasure versus pain—we should remember, the poem is made: was Odysseus not announced in the invocation as the man who *knew*, and *suffered*, much?

Kalypso and her surroundings are certainly pleasant: even the citified Hermes (5.100–102) finds them so (5.73–76). Odysseus too liked them at first, but later

> his eyes were
> never dry of tears; his sweet life ebbed away, drop by drop,
> as he mourned for his homecoming, once the nymph no longer pleased him.
> The fact was that he spent his nights perforce
> in the hollow cave, reluctant lover, ardent mistress.
>
> (5.151–55)

Pleasure and pain. What is more painful than unwanted pleasure? But first, why does Odysseus not want it? Kalypso asks, in effect, what Penelope has that she does not (5.203–13). Odysseus can only say that he wants to see his home again (5.219–20). But why? Is he simply homesick and a fundamentally faithful husband? It does not seem so. In book 5, Homer gives us good, selfish reasons for such faithfulness.

Goddesses have loved mortals before, as Kalypso observes (5.118–29), and it has not worked out very well. In fact, it usually means death for the human. The gods, Kalypso complains, seem to begrudge goddesses such happiness. To Kalypso this restriction seems unfair, yet Athena and Zeus in book 1 have led us to expect a modicum of justice from the gods. Can it be that it is somehow not right that a mortal should enjoy favors so divine? Something is wrong about loving Kalypso; and though, as Odysseus says, no fault is to be found with her looks, other words and acts of his will show us what is wrong.

Our first sight of him has been peculiar enough, sitting on the shore with the tears streaming down; his first words are perhaps even more peculiar. When Kalypso suggests that he build a boat and offers to help him escape, he shudders with fear and replies that he would not undertake so dangerous a trip unless Kalypso should swear that she meant no evil. Strangely again, this speech elicits only admiration. Kalypso smiles, caresses him, and says, "Only a smart old sinner like you/would think of saying what you did" (5.182–83), where-upon she proceeds to swear as Odysseus requested. To our original question, why does Odysseus not love Kalypso? this exchange surely adds a second: why does he expect evil from a nymph who loves him? We shall discover that it is his nature to be suspicious and that this is the kind of man whom the gods allow to achieve his victory. He refuses to be seduced, whether by the goddess herself or by her sudden offer to gratify his dearest wish—to go home. That is our first direct experience of him, and we may with profit remember his resistance to Helen's blandishments, reported by Menelaos in book 4. Kalypso, after all, is no more to be trusted than any other being: she may swear that, in this instance, she wishes for Odysseus only what she would wish for herself (5.188), but we already know from the scene with Hermes that Kalypso thinks of Kalypso first (5.135–40) and that her offer is not so spontaneous as she tries to make it seem. As the Hider, her essential purpose is to make Odysseus "forget Ithaca"; she is not, then, to be blindly trusted any more than any other seeming object of desire.

What is wrong with her is not just untrustworthiness, however; she dimin-ishes Odysseus. "Poor fellow," she calls him when she comes to him with her offer of escape (5.160); but once he has made her swear and his separation from her has emerged as a real possibility—once he has declared his indepen-dence—"Zeus-sprung son of Laertes, ingenious Odysseus," she begins, giving him for the first time in the poem his full hexameter line of epithets, so often to be repeated hereafter whenever the hero achieves recognition of his full stature, as he does, for example, from Kirke. I quote the rest of this speech in which Kalypso stakes what is hers to offer against Odysseus's own fate.

> So do you really wish to go home to your own country,
> now, right away? May you fare well, then.
> But if you pictured in your heart how many griefs
> it is your lot to live through before you get to that country,
> you would stay here with me and keep this house
> and be immortal, much though you yearn to see
> your wife. . . . (5.204–10)

When Odysseus answers that, less beautiful though Penelope may be, he would still like to go home and see the day of his return; that, even if some god should wreck him on the sea, he can stand that too; war and the waves he has often known; this would only be more of the same—when he replies in this way, he seems very fine. I can imagine how every instinct of Homer's original hearers might cry out that this is far, far better than enjoying and being enjoyed by a goddess, even for all eternity. In the world that Homer creates, how do pleasure and pain look now? Odysseus, we may well feel, was made, and so is any mortal, to fight and struggle and come home at last; not to be eternally safe and satisfied, free of ills. If this is what was in Homer's mind, Odysseus returns to Penelope because that way he can best fulfill himself as a man—that is the basis of his faithfulness. We can feel, after our initial puzzlement, that he has made the right choice and that we now know what is really wrong with Kalypso. Even if she meant no harm, life with her would diminish him to the vanishing point. Odysseus was "the man," according to the invocation, who experienced and suffered so much "in the struggle to save his life and bring his comrades home." Now we see that "saving one's life" is more than a matter of physical survival. Kalypso offered an eternity of that. Is it too much to say that what Odysseus is saving and has had to save from her is his integrity, his identity? Well may Kalypso address him by name when, and only when, he has rejected eternity with her.

The best thing to do with Kalypso is to leave her. As soon as Odysseus has announced his decision to depart and brave the sea, his feelings about her change.

> So he spoke; the sun set and darkness fell.
> The two then went and in the recess of the hollow cave
> took their joy of love as they lay side by side. (5.225–27)

Is there an inconsistency with the line about the reluctant lover and the ardent mistress? Of course not. Once Kalypso's oblivion is resisted, once a man can act like a man again, sex with her becomes again a delight.

Gods may bask at ease; mortals must have something to do. Odysseus builds a boat, the boat which means that he is rejoining the mortal world, and for this reason every detail of its construction becomes more interesting. How refreshing after seven years of inactivity is all this cutting and doweling and fitting! Human art and skill, useless in Kalypso's paradise, now come into their own. Tools "fit the hand," all is done "expertly." And now it makes sense to count the days.

> It was the fourth day, and he had everything finished.
> The fifth came, and Kalypso sent him off from her island.
>
> (5.262–63)

Time matters now! And so, "In joy Odysseus set his sail to the following wind" (5.269).

Men have always wondered why the world is not a more comfortable place, when paradise would seem so simple a matter for heaven to arrange. The author of the account in Genesis realizes that to live in paradise would mean having to do without the knowledge of good and evil but seems to consider such ignorance an advantage. Homer disagrees. He can see no real happiness in a world free of danger and hardship and work and a final end in death. To be hidden in the midst of the sea with Kalypso might well mean to be free of these things; Homer made it mean that. But could a man really enjoy such freedom? Homer's narrative makes us feel more strongly than any argument that one could not enjoy this paradise, this freedom from mortality, without losing what is most precious about being human.

To be human is to accept "evil," all those things one calls bad, as one's lot, and that is what Odysseus is doing as he leaves Kalypso to cross the dangerous sea. This evil, Poseidon is only too happy to provide. Catching sight of Odysseus as he sails, he says:

> Well! so the gods have changed their minds
> about Odysseus. . . .
> . . . .
> Still, I think I can give him all the evil his heart desires.
>
> (5.286–90)

Then, having smashed his boat and nearly drowned him, he bids him farewell as follows:

> Go ahead, now; suffer your evils as you stray on the sea,
> until you find yourself among men Zeus cherishes;
> even then you won't, I think, find fault with your suffering.
>
> (5.377–79)

Could anything make clearer than these speeches Homer's awareness that his subject is not merely what happened to Odysseus but the nature and meaning of evil? Narrative is a way of thinking about life. Throughout the poem we have been thinking of evil as the result of wickedness and folly; Aigisthos's comeuppance gives us hope that the suitors too will receive theirs; but we have also been told, and it is abundantly clear, that Odysseus's trouble is not from this source. Gods (or a god) are against him for other reasons. He, not Aigisthos, embodies the real problem of evil. Now we begin to understand his kind of evil more clearly. In order to be himself instead of a "well-pleased pleaser," in Conrad's phrase, Odysseus deliberately courts evil; if he is to escape Kalypso he must brave the sea, risk shipwreck, defy Poseidon. There is no alternative. We should remember here that Homer's age is the age of Greek maritime colonization. In any case, as we read we can heartily agree that Odysseus has made the right choice. The risk of pain in these circumstances is to be preferred to Kalypso's offer of pleasure and comfort. So Odysseus takes on Poseidon, the god of the sea, as his adversary.

Strangely enough, Poseidon turns out to have something in common with Kalypso. Poseidon and the sea, like Kalypso, are out to cover Odysseus, to obscure him, to engulf him, even to make him forget Ithaca itself. Poseidon opens his attack on Odysseus with a wave which knocked him far from his boat and

> kept him under water a long time . . .
>
> . . . .
>
> for the clothes that Kalypso gave him weighed him down.
> Finally he came up and spat from his mouth the salt water,
> bitter, which streamed copiously from his head.
> Still, hard pressed though he was, he did not forget his boat;
> He turned about in the water, swam back and seized it;
> in its center he sat, avoiding his final end. (5.319–26)

This passage, and others like it, makes us at some level (subliminal or not) think of Odysseus as one whose characteristic effort is to emerge from obscurity, whether it is the obscurity of Kalypso's arms, where he can neither know himself nor be known, or whether it is the annihilation with which a hostile environment threatens him.

Poseidon's hostility is not scanted; the world is not painted as an easier place than it really is. Yet human tenacity is not slighted either: the poem goes on to describe Odysseus and his dismasted craft blown about the sea like a ball of thistledown, "and close together the wisps of it stick" (5.329). The immense force of the storm is powerless against a bit of thistle. Poseidon's hostility is not scanted, but there is such a thing as pity in the world, too. We may remember how Noemon's sympathy and pity got Telemachos his ship when he was hard pressed (4.649). Homer seems to recognize such sympathy with the underdog in the natural world as well. Ino, once a much-suffering human but now a sea-nymph, takes pity on Odysseus. She suggests that he leave the comparative security of his wrecked boat and, stripping off Kalypso's clothes, swim for the land which he had glimpsed at the beginning of the storm. To this advice she adds a bit of magic.

> Here, tie this headband around your waist.
> It is immortal, and you need fear neither hurt nor destruction.
>
> (5.346–47)

This is magic. From our point of view it is supernatural, and yet it is not arbitrary. It ought to happen to Odysseus, and at precisely this juncture, for by surviving Poseidon's wave, he has just demonstrated that, as Zeus assured Athena at book 1.75, Poseidon's hostility is not necessarily fatal, in spite of the negative connotations of Odysseus's name. Realization that it is not fatal is in itself a great encouragement. Such is the burden of Ino's opening remarks.

> Poor man, why is Poseidon the Earthshaker
> so violently hostile to you, planting for you so many evils?
> Yet assuredly he will not kill you, much as he would like to.
> Do, then, as I suggest. (5.339–42)

At the beginning Odysseus feared that the storm came from Zeus and meant his end (5.299–305); now the nymph says it is from Poseidon and will not be fatal. If this is true he can risk still bolder measures than any he has taken to leave Kalypso. But so much is the magical world of Homer the same as the world with which we ourselves are familiar that Odysseus behaves at first as we would in such a situation: he prefers not to trust the goddess immediately (5.356–64). He treats her proposition exactly as we in a similar situation might treat the dawning idea that we were not due to die this time after all, and that perhaps we might even save ourselves by swimming. "Time enough for swimming," he thinks, "when I have no other alternative." In this poem good ideas come from goddesses, which is as good an explanation as any. When they involve taking a particularly long chance, the goddess provides a charm. Fair enough: men like Odysseus do not gamble until they need to; but when it is necessary they take the long chance undismayed and often bring it off, as though they had some special talisman. We should note, however, that the talisman is used sparingly and is only now and then given: Ino asks for her headband back (5.348–50). In Homer's narrative the luck of the resolute and their confidence that they will survive take the form of a nymph's sympathetic assistance—in fact who can deny that people like Odysseus seem to have the help of the gods?

But Odysseus is not the type to trust to luck so soon. Poseidon must leave him no choice.

> While Odysseus was thinking these thoughts,
> Poseidon the Earthshaker raised against him a great wave,
> savage and terrible, arching over, and struck him.
>
> (5.365–67)

The boat which earlier had held together like thistledown now is scattered like a heap of chaff in a blast of wind (5.368–70). But Odysseus

> bestrode a single timber, as though riding a racehorse,
> and took off the clothes which divine Kalypso gave him.
> Quickly he tied the headband around his waist,
> then dove into the water, stretching out his arms,
> eager to swim. (5.370–75)

In this condition Poseidon, bidding farewell, leaves him (5.377–79). Not everyone, I think, would have been "eager to swim" at this juncture, whether or not they had decided to leave the last bit of security, probably false, which the remaining timber seemed to provide. Odysseus, when he has to, embraces danger with a will. Ino, in sum, provides that extra something which every so often the bold need, and so often seem to get.

The narrative thinking continues: Poseidon has departed "for his halls at Aigai," Athena takes over (5.382), and peculiarly enough, the worst is still to come. Though Athena calms the sea and after two days in the water Odysseus is permitted to see the land close up, "from the top of a great wave" (5.393), waves and rocks now come closest to killing him. Why is Poseidon expressly absent from this event? It is as though his function is primarily to strip Odysseus of all the protection against nature's hostility, all the obscuring security, which human skill and forethought ordinarily provide. He dismasts and then wrecks his boat, and then he drives Odysseus to abandon not only its last timbers but the very clothes Kalypso gave him. From here on the test is whether Odysseus, stripped of all assistance, can survive. This is what Zeus meant when he said that Odysseus will get home "without escort from gods or men" (5.32) and that Poseidon "keeps him from his home but does not kill him" (1.75). It is indeed a do-it-yourself world.

Naked, utterly exposed except for the headband tied around his waist (which means that Poseidon will not kill him), Odysseus surveys a savage coast. When she gave him the headband, Ino not only said that Poseidon would not kill him but implied that Odysseus was related to Poseidon's hostility in some very special way.

> Kammore, tipte toi hōde Poseidaōn enosikhthōn
> ōdusat' ekpaglōs, hoti toi kaka polla phuteuei?
>
> Poor man, why is Poseidon the Earthshaker
> so violently hostile to you, planting for you so many evils?
>
> (5.339–40)

These lines repeat the pun on Odysseus's name which we have already heard from Athena at 1.62. *Pun* is a modern term which in cases like this is apt to mislead. To Homer's audience, or for that matter Pindar's, a pun is certainly not funny or even witty. Personal names are expected to mean something, and their owners are expected to be aware of their significance. It is an ominous thing to be named Odysseus, and the owner of such a name might well be concerned to know the source of the hostility he is named for. Athena asked why Odysseus was Zeus's enemy; now Ino says he is Poseidon's enemy, with the distinction that Poseidon's hostility will not kill him. At the beginning of the storm Odysseus thought that Zeus raised it and that all was over. Now, leaving his boat and finally his single timber on the chance that the enemy is not Zeus but a less-than-fatal Poseidon, he accepts Ino's explication of his name. Surveying the savage coast, he says that, although Zeus has given him to see the land so unexpectedly and although he has crossed such a gulf of waters, there seems no way to come ashore: reefs, cliffs, and breakers straight ahead, "no way to stand firm on both feet and escape evil" (5.413–14). But if he swims along the coast,

> I fear the storm will seize me again
> and again bear me moaning and groaning over the fishy sea,
> or else heaven will send against me some great fish
> from the salt water, such as Amphitrite breeds in plenty:
> for I know how *I am the* famous earthshaker's *enemy.*
>
> (5.419–23)

Oida gar hōs moi odōdustai [perfect tense of *odyssasthai*] klutos ennosigaios is the Greek of the last line, repeating Athena's and Ino's pun. Odysseus now knows for certain that he is named for Poseidon's enmity, not Zeus's.

He knows he is named for Poseidon's enmity, and we have seen in his leaving Kalypso that it is an enmity he must deliberately face. Now the poem is about to demonstrate another aspect of evil, as the book's third and greatest wave hurls Odysseus upon the rocky coast. Poseidon is now out of it, departed, so that his particular grievance is no longer in question. Stripped of his raft and Kalypso's clothes, of every last shred of cover, Odysseus faces the world at its simplest, the world that, as Homer sees it, fundamentally presents itself to all of us. First, the promise of security seems to come flooding back. In Homer's simile (5.394–98), the sight of the Phaeacians' island Scherie ("secure") affects Odysseus as children are affected who see the life flood back into their father who has long lain stricken with a wasting disease. (This curious reversal of roles—for Odysseus is, after all, the father in this story—may among other things serve to remind us how important his survival is to Telemachos as well as to himself.) But because he can see and hear and reason, Odysseus soon realizes that, if he approaches this security directly, he will probably be smashed on the rocks. Even as he considers the nearly equally dangerous alternative of swimming along the shore, a great wave hurls him among the reefs, where "he would have been flayed alive, and his bones all crushed together/if Athena had not given him an idea" (5.426–27). This momentous idea is simply to seize a rock and hang on: obvious enough, to be sure, but absolutely crucial; and Athena's participation has the effect of putting it in a larger context. Paralleled here is Odysseus's own characteristic reaction of distrust: not to be swept to destruction at the sudden offer of what he craves and seems to need most at the moment—in this case, solid ground beneath his feet. In the words of the later Stoic motto, Hold on and hold off!

The grip needed for such holding is inimitably suggested in the simile of the cuttlefish dragged from his hole in the reef (5.432–35), to whose suckers the pebbles still stick, thick as the bits of skin from Odysseus's hands that were left sticking to the rock as the wave swept him out to sea again. The simile works by contrast more than by comparison: the cuttlefish wants to stay in its hole, but once caught, it is pulled forth into the light, dragging fragments of its security with it; Odysseus, to remain in the light uncaught, must hold himself away from the offered false security with such force that in the backwash he leaves fragments of himself behind. Athena's share in the matter inspires the thought that only the gods give that kind of strength.

Saved by this strength, Odysseus makes the indirect approach to his goal of a safe shelter; no sea monster interferes. Encountering nature's kinder aspect in the shape of a river mouth breaking the line of cliff, he prays to the river in recognition of his dependence on nature's pity and comes ashore at last, kissing the ground in his relief. One more decision between the hard and soft remains: shall he risk the chill of the dank and misty lowland, or brave exposure to hostile beasts on the wooded height? Choosing as we would expect, he crawls beneath the leaves of the half-wild, half-tame, olive thicket on the hill to sleep there

> like a firebrand a man buries in the black ashes
> at the far end of the cropland, where he lives without neighbors,
> keeping safe a seed of fire, so he can light his own.
>
> (5.488–90)

This, then, is what Zeus and Poseidon between them sometimes allow to the strong and careful: a chance alone, stripped, but unextinguished, eventually to blaze with whatever light they may be capable of.

This sounds like allegory, but it is not. Allegory implies a second reality parallel to the overt narrative, point for point. Here we have only what happens to Odysseus, embodying the logic of the world as it presents itself to Homer through his muse. The island Scherie (root *sekh*, "to have, hold"), which "looked like a shield in the midst of the hazy sea" (5.281), does not stand for the concept *security*; but its name and appearance are appropriate to its function in Odysseus's story: to face Odysseus with a situation of great generality, analogous to many others with which both he and the rest of humankind are faced. This same generic way of seeing things is what produces Homer's similes. To see that the pattern of Odysseus's escape from being smashed against the cliff and obliterated is the mirror image of a squid's being dragged from its hole suggests a very high degree of organization indeed in the reality we all face. Whatever else he does, Homer presents us with an intensely ordered world.

The Maiden Unmastered

Scherie, Land of Security, land of the Phaeacians, will "hold" Odysseus for the next seven books. Indirectly, with great narrative tact, Homer tells us at once what it is like.

> So he slept there, enduring, noble Odysseus,
> worn out with sleeplessness and toil. And Athena
> went to the people and city of the Phaeacians,
> who used to dwell in spacious Hypereia
> near the Kyklopes, men of violence,
> who plundered them, being the stronger fighters.
> From there godlike Nausithoos moved them,
> settling them in Scherie far from the haunts of men,
> ran a wall around his city and built houses,
> raised temples to the gods and distributed lands.
> But now that he was dead and gone to the House of Hades,
> Alkinoos ruled, whose wisdom was from the gods;
> to his house Athena went, goddess with the gray eyes,
> contriving homecoming for great-hearted Odysseus.
>
> (6.1–14)

Ithaca, Pylos, and Sparta have no walls, no temples that we have heard of. Odysseus will now be confronted with what looks like a full-scale polis, with a history, secure upon its island far from the haunts of men. Like many a tentative colony of Homer's day, it has changed its original site because of hostile neighbors. Yet it is not a contemporary polis. The Muse imports no such anachronism into Odysseus' world. Rather, she sees there what we might call an ideal essence, a possible implication of what the cities of Homer's time might become. In their civility the Phaeacians are more than human, "near to the gods" (5.35), just as their bad former neighbors, the Kyklopes, are "near to the gods" (7.201–6) in their savagery. The Phaeacians, having avoided conflict with them, live without war. Having escaped the simple security of Kalypso's natural paradise, Odysseus is about to take the logical next step: among the Phaeacians he will encounter the peaceful world of what we might call an ideal social complex.

Appropriately for this new context, Athena arranges for him not the frank passion of a Kalypso but the awakening love of a princess, with all the social consequences such a situation entails. Marriage, for instance, is much on this princess's mind. Homer evokes the civilized felicity of her world with the utmost economy and grace, filling our minds with suggestions not only of her coming wedding to whomever it may be but also of a happy family, clean clothes, dances, a picnic by the sea. How fortuitous this picnic is! The river where the clothes are washed is the river which permits Odysseus to come ashore; the pebbles where the clothes are dried is the beach on which he lands. Above all, Homer tells us of a wagon for Nausikaa to ride in, a wagon with a rack to hold the clothes; and no doubt there is a road to drive on as well. This is all very unlike Odysseus's recent stormy passage over the barren sea, and when Athena, having arranged for the picnic, departs for Olympos,

> where the gods, they say, have their seat, ever safe:
> no wind shakes it, no rain wets it,
> no snow drifts upon it,
> but all is fair weather and brilliant light, (6.42–45)

the life of pain again begins to seem almost irrelevant.

Odysseus emerges from his thicket naked, holding a leafy branch to cover his genitals and looking

> like a lion bred in the mountains, confident in his strength,
> who goes through rain and wind with blazing eyes,
> in search of cattle or sheep,
> or the deer of the wilderness; and his belly bids him
> try for the flock and enter even the close fold. (6.130–34)

When Odysseus comes upon Nausikaa and her maidens in this fashion, the incongruity is so striking as to be amusing. All this terrible lion wants of these ladies at the moment is a rag to put around him and directions to the city. Nevertheless, this confrontation is the beginning of the major conflict of the

Phaeacian episode. There is something basically incompatible between Odysseus's world and Nausikaa's, as we are forcibly reminded when she attempts to reassure her companions.

> Stop, my maids; where are you running to, seeing a man?
> You don't think, do you, that he could be an enemy [dysmeneōn]?
> He is no dangerous person, nor will there ever be one
> who will come to the land of the Phaeacian people
> bringing hostility, for they are the gods' special friends.
> We live far off in the surging sea,
> most remote; no other mortals associate with us.
> No; he is some poor [dystēnos] lost fellow who has wandered here
> and whom we now must help. From Zeus come all
> strangers and beggars, and a small gift brings much love.
>
> (6.199–208)

Nausikaa has mistaken her man: in accordance with his name, Odysseus will bring hostility to the Phaeacians in a sense she has yet to conceive of.

Conflict or no, we can feel at once how Odysseus's ferocious and battered appearance attracts Nausikaa even before she herself is aware of it. She reports that at this stage she thought him ugly (6.242); nevertheless, when all her maids fled, she remained. We are told that this is Athena's doing, but this is evidently one of those divine interventions in which we can recognize a familiar fact of life, in this case the fact that awakening sexuality has aroused similar courage in many a sixteen-year-old girl face to face with a dangerous-looking male like Odysseus. In such cases civility generally comes to the rescue of both parties, as it does here. Homer has already told us, unforgettably, that Nausikaa looks like the goddess Artemis, and he has called her a "maiden unmastered" (parthenos admēs, 6.102–9). "Artemis the arrow-shooter," who "goes upon the mountains . . . delighting in wild boars and the fleet deer," is a version of the Mistress of Animals worshiped throughout the eastern Mediterranean (Burkert, 149). Here we can see in her the reverence-inspiring beauty both of emerging womanhood and of the inviolate wild. Presiding also over the female mystery of reproduction, she, more than any other divinity, inspires modesty, shamefastness, respect, and those other feelings of delicacy and restraint on which civil life depends (see also Euripides Hippolytos).

At the sight of Nausikaa Odysseus is at once affected by these feelings; indeed, his plucking the tree branch has already shown that he is susceptible to them. Rather than letting them master him, he makes use of them to take his first steps toward winning acceptance in this new and different world. They suggest to him that, in this particular situation, he had better not touch the maiden's knees in the standard ritual of supplication but instead "beseech her with honeyed words just as he was, from a distance," and Homer describes his ensuing speech as an artful one (6.143–48). Since Nausikaa looks like Artemis, what could be a more obvious yet effective expedient than for him to pretend to mistake Nausikaa for Artemis herself? She can now be confident that his feelings toward her are as respectful as she could wish. For Odysseus to capture her favor totally, however, she must not be left thinking that the man before her is unaffected by her beauty, and so he continues: if by any chance she is a mortal, how proud her parents and her brothers must be when they see her going to the dance; and as for the man who will marry her, he will be the happiest of mankind! Odysseus has never met another human being like her: he can only compare her to a young palm tree he once saw growing beside Apollo's altar on Delos. In short, it is clear how much Odysseus's art here owes to the civilized feelings which Apollo's sister Artemis inspires. As a result we are not surprised to find that Nausikaa is eager to relieve his misery.

Homer's simile comparing Nausikaa to Artemis evokes the pride of Artemis's mother, Leto, as she sees her go conspicuous among her nymphs playing on the mountains, and Odysseus's speech, as we have seen, evokes the pride in Nausikaa's beauty that her parents and brothers must feel. From these familial joys it is an easy transition to the thought of her future husband's delight in her, so that Odysseus is able to approach the subject of Nausikaa's marriage by way of Artemis, as it were, rather than by way of Aphrodite. All these thoughts suggest civility and community as contrasted with the possibility of instant sexual gratification implicit in Odysseus's and Nausikaa's presence alone together by the pleasant beach and stream. Odysseus, of course, is trying to appear as civilized as possible, and in the process he brings up Nausikaa's marriage one more, climactic time. In return for directions to the city and a rag to put about him, he prays,

> May the gods give all your mind is set on,
> a husband and a house, and grant that your hearts agree.
> For that surpasses everything,
> when two keep house in harmony,
> a man and wife; it makes their haters suffer,
> their friends rejoice, but they feel it most themselves.
>
> (6.180–85)

By this repeated praise of marriage does Odysseus hope to make Nausikaa fall in love with him? I think not. That would tend to make his situation in a strange country more difficult rather than easier, and Homer's audience may well doubt that even Odysseus would consider himself likely, in his present state, to take a princess's eye so quickly. We should understand him, I think, to have guessed correctly that marriage was on Nausikaa's mind and so to have wished her a happy marriage simply as the happiness she would most like to receive in return for helping him. What Homer does seem to intend is to provide an insight into the nature of a certain kind of happiness and at the same time to make us ask whether Nausikaa will be capable of it. The verb in the phrase I have translated "but they feel it most themselves" is a form of *kluein*, "to hear"; and this verb, in turn, is connected with the noun *kleos*, "fame," which we have seen to be important in the *Odyssey*. A large part of the delight the happily married pair take in their harmony comes from their consciousness (what they "hear") of how others feel about them; that is, from their consciousness of their friends' joy in addition to their own, and of their enemies' chagrin. In Homer happiness is a matter not merely of how one feels about one's self but of how others, including posterity, feel about one, and for anyone to arouse joy without at the same time arousing jealousy would seem to him not only unusual but insipid. In order to arouse jealousy, however, one needs enemies, and the Phaeacians are ill supplied in this respect, as we have seen. Supposing Nausikaa were to become Odysseus's wife, could she, not expecting ever even to see an enemy, be like minded with him; or without enemies to discomfit, could either of them enjoy to the full such harmony as they would have? At this stage in the poem this is still an open question; nevertheless, we may well suspect that it will ultimately be answered in the negative. Meanwhile Odysseus's advance along the road of civility succeeds perhaps too well. He may not have seen himself as Nausikaa's bridegroom, but she does, as we immediately discover.

Feelings connected with Artemis continue to help greatly in arousing Nausikaa's favorable response. The princess bids her maids bathe Odysseus in the river, anoint him, and dress him. Instead they "stood still and urged one another to do it" (6.211). Not a bit at a loss, Odysseus pretends that it is he who is shy and asks to be allowed to wash himself, whereupon the grateful maids at once report his delicacy to their mistress. Bored with juvenile sensibility, a modern audience might feel no wonder that, when Nausikaa sees him at last washed and dressed, he looks like one transformed "shining with beauty and charm" (6.237); Homer with greater appreciation of the phenomenon attributes the transformation to Athena, working "as a man does who edges silver with gold" (6.232). Nausikaa, in consequence, loses her heart.

> Listen, my white-armed maids, to this that I tell you:
> not without the combined will of the gods who live on Olympos

does this man come to mingle with the godlike Phaeacians.
Before this how unseemly I thought him;
but now he looks like the gods who hold broad heaven.
O that, just as he is, he might be named my husband,
dwelling among us, and be content to remain here! (6.239–45)

The result of this confession is that we follow the rest of the Phaeacian episode half afraid that Nausikaa will have her wish, and half afraid that she will not.

If in this civilized world Odysseus has shown that he knows how to use his sense of delicacy to advantage, so does Nausikaa. Simply by expressing her fears of what people will say if she is seen bringing this "big and handsome stranger" (6.276–77) into town, she is able to suggest to him, if he wishes to take it that way, that he might become her husband (6.277), that he seems to her like a god and an answer to her prayers (6.280), that she far prefers him to the local, and distinguished, competition (6.283–84), that her family not only is royal but attracts the best society as well (6.256–57), and that she holds herself to the strictest premarital standards (6.285–88). If he knows how to manipulate, so does she, and it is good to see her giving as good as she gets. If she must eventually fail, it is no doubt because she was born in the wrong place at the wrong time.

In her attempt to manipulate Odysseus, Nausikaa also gives a more detailed picture of how civilized the Phaeacians actually are. No landsmen-hunters they: not bow and quiver, but masts and oars and ships are their delight (6.270–72). They inhabit a fortified isthmus with good harbors on each side. Their city is equipped with sophisticated dock installations and a stone-paved market-place surrounding a temple of Poseidon (6.262–67). Most suggestive of all, Nausikaa emphasizes that, if Odysseus wants to get home, he must first win the favor not of her father the king but of her mother (6.303–15). In this secure land without war, a woman has the final word.

The book closes as Odysseus, left alone outside the city gates, prays to Athena in her own grove that he may meet with "love and pity" among the Phaeacians (6.327). Well as he has done with Nausikaa in this regard, he must now begin all over again, and Nausikaa's mother may be harder to convince than her daughter. It is noteworthy also that Odysseus claims Athena's favor on the ground that she has withheld it during his struggles with the sea. Remembering not only her assistance with Nausikaa (6.2–47) but also her advocacy of his case on Olympos and her careful tendance as he came ashore on Scherie (5.5, 382–87, 426–27, 491–93), we know that he is, in part at least, mistaken. It is a somewhat gratifying thought that, although Nausikaa may have failed to recognize the hostility that surrounds Odysseus, he himself can err in overestimating it. Telemachos, too, we are reminded, is only partially aware of the assistance the goddess provides. But in Odysseus's case, there is a special reason for his ignorance.

> So he spoke in prayer, and Pallas Athena heard him.
> But she did not yet appear to him face to face, respecting
> her father's brother. He raged unremittingly
> against good-as-a-god Odysseus until his homecoming.
>
> (6.328–31)

Even in Odysseus's case, things are not necessarily as bad as they appear.

The Happy City

In book 7, Homer continues to confront the Man of Pain with pain's absence: Odysseus, as he prays in Athena's grove outside the Phaeacians' city, is about to exchange hardship for ease. In fact, he is about to be offered an honored position in the first Utopia in Western literature. Nevertheless, even when at the end of the book he is safely put to bed in Alkinoos's palace, he has yet to win the favor of the queen, Arete, which Nausikaa has named as the one thing needful if he is to get home. Winning this favor, we shall see, provides the principal motive for the next five books.

The security, ease, and elegance of Phaeacian life has already been suggested in book 6 by Nausikaa's description of their walls, shipyards, groves, temples, and gathering places and by her praise of her father's house and her evocation of the scene within: her mother spinning the sea-purple yarn as her father sits beside her and "drinks his wine like a god" (6.309). Now at the beginning of book 7, the impression of ease is reinforced: her brothers unhitch and unload for her, and her old nurse lays her a fire and brings supper to her in her own chamber.

To us in the audience this is a most pleasant scene, and yet in the course of it we are made aware that such comfort has its disadvantages. The nurse comes from Apeiraia, a place geographers are unable to locate. Unfamiliar though it may be, the name is repeated in successive lines, and its sounds and possible meanings make their impression. It sounds very much like that shelteredness, that absence of experience and trial (*peira*), which Nausikaa is at the moment enjoying and which she has in a sense chosen by not herself bringing Odysseus to the palace—though we must admit she did well to face him at all. Warmth and security, then, with an attendant lack of experience of life, is strongly implied by this whole opening scene, and in particular by the nurse from Apeiraia, the Land of No Experience.

As he returns to Odysseus, however, Homer modulates from warmth and security to feelings of apprehension in a strange land. Nausikaa may be safe, but Odysseus is not; at least, he has no reason to feel so. Homer, sensing as he so often does the presence of Athena where we would think only of her protégé's own mental processes, tells us of Athena's anxiety for Odysseus rather than of his own trepidation. Physical violence from the Phaeacians does not seem very likely, even at this early stage of Odysseus's acquaintance with them, but there are other sorts of danger. Athena is afraid "that some proud Phaeacian in a chance encounter/might accost him rudely and ask him who he was" (7.16–17).

Of course, such a meeting would probably not be instantly fatal. Odysseus is no Priam making his way through the enemy camp. Yet for Odysseus to be challenged now, before reaching Arete's knees and making his supplication there, would violate those feelings, already made explicit by Nestor and Menelaos (3.69–70 and 4.60–62), which urge that guests be welcomed and fed before being asked who they are. Such feelings are natural in areas like ancient Greece where, because the political units are small and independent, the traveler is at the mercy of whatever community he happens to be in at the moment. For any intercourse between communities to take place at all, the stranger must by custom be accorded a certain inviolability. He must even be reasonably sure of his entertainment. Homer indicates that the advantage is mutual, for the host may one day be a guest: we remember how in his indignation at the mere suggestion that he might turn away the strangers at his door, Menelaos exclaimed,

> Great was the hospitality we enjoyed
> at other men's houses on our way here. . . . (4.33–34)

But if one knows the stranger's name or connections, it may be hard to feed him. The guest may turn out to be an enemy, and the host's honor may require him to exercise the power which, for the good of all, he might better withhold. Once the meal is shared, of course, the convention in such societies is that the enemy ceases to be one, but until that happens any guest may well feel anxious. No doubt subtler considerations of a psychological nature are also involved; even the least superstitious of us probably feel that, when we give our name, we give ourselves away to a certain extent. In Homer's world, however, social conditions intensified the feeling.

It is thus natural in the present case that Athena should be anxious to preserve Odysseus's anonymity. With this in mind she shrouds him in a mist so that he may pass through the city and even Alkinoos's hall unseen (7.14–15,

40–42, 139–40). The mists in which gods convey characters hither and thither in both the *Iliad* and the *Odyssey* are familiar, and Homer has sometimes been smiled at because of them; nevertheless, they seem an excellent expression of what must have been a common experience. In this they are similar to Athena's transformations of people's looks, such as her transformation of Odysseus in book 6. Just as, under certain circumstances, people look unbelievably better or more impressive than they did before, so we often escape the notice of everyone, even when to our own apprehensive eye it seems inevitable that we should be observed. In Homer's world the traveler entering a strange community must often literally have prayed not to be noticed until he reached the door of someone he could be reasonably sure would protect him. Feeling that every eye was upon him, his relief, once he had obtained a hospitable welcome, would make him believe that the god he prayed to must have shrouded him in invisibility. Viewed in this way, the mist in which Athena hides Odysseus as he arrives among the Phaeacians is not such a bizarre conception after all.

Odysseus's apprehension is therefore real as, following Nausikaa's hint that "even a child could guide you" (6.300), he asks directions to Alkinoos's palace from a young girl. This girl must be more than a mere infant, since she carries a water jar and the advice she gives is sophisticated. When we consider how fortunate it is that, instead of betraying Odysseus's presence to the Phaeacians, she urges him to remain inconspicuous, we ought to be more than content to recognize in her, as Homer does, the goddess herself. Before she and Odysseus approach the city together, his young guide informs him of further reason for apprehension: the Phaeacians are cold toward strangers from abroad, depending rather on the great speed and safety of their own ships, granted by Poseidon, for such foreign contact as they require. These ships, in fact, are "fast as a wing-beat, or a thought" (7.36). We have already observed that the Phaeacians are near and dear to the gods, but this is the first of their blessings that seems quite beyond ordinary human capability. We shall soon meet with more such blessings. Meanwhile we may note that this one has the same negative effect as Nausikaa's security: it inhibits the Phaeacians' experience.

Phaeacian blessings and lack of experience, together with apprehensiveness on Odysseus's account, remain our dominant impression as the episode progresses. The Phaeacians' freedom from war is stressed in Athena's description of Arete's pedigree. Nausithoos, the king who brought the Phaeacians to this remote island in order to escape the hostility of the Kyklopes, was child of Poseidon and Periboia. Periboia's father was Eurymedon, king of the giants, who "brought his reckless people to ruin, and was ruined himself" (7.60). Homer's audience probably knew, as we do not, the story alluded to here, but even without such knowledge we shall not be far off the track if we assume that its function is to suggest the violence in the Phaeacians' heredity which they now eschew. Nausithoos, Athena continues, had two sons, Man Smasher (Rhexenor) and Mighty Mind (Alkinoos). In this context, the opposition between brawn and brain is inevitably suggested, and if to us this pedigree begins to seem too pat to be credible, we must remember that, to Homer's Muse, its patness would on the contrary guarantee its truth. By transferring his city to Scherie, Nausithoos, apparently wisely, chose prosperous peace in preference to conflict with the Kyklopes; analogously, Nausithoos's heir Man Smasher, by dying soon after his marriage, gave place to Mighty Mind, leaving behind only his daughter Prayed For (Arete; cf. 19.403–4), whose name suggests the longed-for peace and civility impossible as long as there was conflict with the Kyklopes. No wonder Alkinoos married her "and honored her as no other woman on earth is honored" (7.67); no wonder that the people "regard her as a goddess/and address her in greeting as she walks through the town" (7.71–72). No wonder, finally, that, "for those who have her favor, even men, she settles quarrels" (7.74). In a city without war, the queen may well be king.

Parting from Nausikaa in book 6, Athena went to an ever calm and sunny Olympos; leaving Odysseus, she now departs for Athens and "the many-chambered house of Erechtheus" (7.81). Her going by way of Marathon may indicate that Homer imagines the Phaeacians as living in the dim and distant reaches of the Black Sea; or it may suggest that Homer and his audience, located at Chios, say, or Smyrna on the Asia Minor coast, naturally think of Marathon as Athens's port; or both may be true. In any case, just as Olympos served to characterize Nausikaa's felicity, so this evocation of Athens is probably intended to provide a standard of technical and political sophistication against which the city of Alkinoos may be measured. Homer's audience, including ourselves, may reasonably suppose that Odysseus has seen Athens. Yet he

> wondered at the Phaeacians' harbors, and shapely ships,
> at the assembly places of their noble owners and their long walls,
> high ones, with palisades, marvelous to behold.
>
> (7.43–45)

From such description, we may properly conclude that this sight surpasses the other.

Comparability ceases, however, as Odysseus surveys Alkinoos's palace through its open door (7.81–102). Its threshold is of bronze, and its walls are bronze with a frieze of lapis lazuli. The doors are gold, with silver posts and lintel, and the doorknob is of gold; in addition, these doors are guarded by "immortal" watchdogs of gold and silver, made by Hephaistos. Gold too are the "youths" who, standing on their well-built bases, hold the torches for the nightly feasts. We learn also that Alkinoos has fifty maidservants who grind and weave for him and that Athena has made the Phaeacian women as skillful at the loom as the men are in their ships (7.103–31). The house itself is sur-rounded by a large orchard of pear, pomegranate, apple, fig, and olive trees which never cease to bear, winter or summer; as one fruit is plucked, another ripens. An extensive vineyard provides a similarly perpetual supply of ripe grapes, and the vegetable garden has the same virtue. Last and perhaps best, since Greece is not a well-watered country, Homer tells us that Alkinoos's estate is watered by not one but two springs, one for the plants and the other for the people. "Such were the splendid gifts of the gods enjoyed by Alkinoos," Homer concludes (7.132), evidently intending to portray the Phaeacians as supremely blessed by heaven. When, having gazed his fill on these wonders, Odysseus enters the palace and embraces Arete's knees, it certainly seems that he is encountering what we would pray for if we thought we could get it: freedom from war, ships which move with the speed of thought, houses of bronze and gold, immortal watchdogs and torchbearers, fruits and vegetables which are always in season, and all the water we want, whenever we want it.

That the Phaeacians are exempted from the inconveniences of ordinary human life is even more strongly suggested when Alkinoos describes what Odysseus's voyage home, assuming it is granted to him, will be like.

> Free of toil or annoyance our guest
> escorted by us will reach the land of his fathers
> happily and swiftly, far off though it may be;
> in the meantime he will suffer no harm or ill
> until he sets foot on his own country; thereupon
> he will suffer whatever fate and the grim Spinners
> spun in his life-thread when his mother bore him.
>
> (7.192–98)

Apparently the Phaeacians can supply, at least temporarily, exemption from all pain whatsoever.

As we have seen, this happiness inhibits the Phaeacians' experience in various ways. Odysseus's appeal to Arete meets with silence, and it is only after an embarrassing pause that their oldest and wisest councillor, Echeneos, finally instructs Alkinoos in his duties toward the suppliant (7.155–57). If we remember that both Nausikaa and Athena have implied that foreigners seldom or never come as far as Scherie, it may well seem that Alkinoos is simply not used to receiving strangers and that only Echeneos remembers, or has heard, how it is done. Remoteness, special privilege, and lack of experience of Greece are most wondrously combined, however, when Alkinoos boasts for a second time of Phaeacian nautical prowess. He says that his men can bring Odysseus to his home and return on the same day,

> even if it is far more distant than Euboia,
> which those who saw it say is farthest,
> those of our people, when they took blond Rhadamanthys
> to look upon Tityos, the son of Earth. (7.321–24)

There is humor here in that, for Homer's original audiences, dwelling as they did around the shores and on the islands of the Aegean, no place can have seemed more central than the island of Euboia. For Alkinoos to be able to say what he does, his homeland must be remote indeed. The visit of Rhadamanthys to Tityos is similarly exotic. It is consistent with the rest of the poem in that we hear of Rhadamanthys as presiding over the "Elysian plain at the ends of the earth" at 4.563–64, whereas at 11.576–81, the gigantic Tityos lies in torment in Hades for raping the goddess Leto "on her way to Delphi by pleasant Panopeus" in Phocis, comparatively close to Euboia. At the same time, the Phaeacian journey cited, since it must have occurred before Rhadamanthys and Tityos were fixed in their present locations, must be as remote in time as Scherie evidently is in space. Thus Alkinoos's information about Euboia is evidently based on experience that is not only extremely ancient but apparently unrepeated, for all the unerring swiftness of his vessels.

Such are the gifts of the gods to Alkinoos, particularly of his ancestor Poseidon, and we can see that, in their felicity, the Phaeacians, although they are mortal, are much closer to the gods than to humankind. Most remarkable in this closeness is the way Homer can suggest that it confers a certain disadvantage, first and foremost, in the matter of receiving a mortal wanderer like Odysseus. To Odysseus's appeal Arete makes no answer, so that Alkinoos, as we have seen, must take the responsibility upon himself. He graciously raises Odysseus from the ashes of the hearth and seats him in the chair occupied by his favorite son (7.168–71), but he seems not to feel free to preempt what Nausikaa and Athena have implied will be Arete's power to decide, namely, the question of Odysseus's escort home. He promises merely to discuss (7.192) the matter on the morrow, "before more councillors" (7.189). Thereupon he somewhat wistfully considers whether Odysseus may not after all be a god in disguise (7.199–206). That would obviously relieve Alkinoos's doubts about what to do, since, unlike mortals, gods visit the Phaeacians frequently and evidently pose no problems for their hosts. Unfortunately, their very familiarity tends to dash Alkinoos's hope: he remarks that, hitherto at least, the gods have never felt it necessary to disguise themselves. Thus, for purposes of receiving Odysseus, being "near to the gods/like the Kyklopes and the wild tribes of the Giants" (7.205–6) puts the Phaeacians at a disadvantage.

Quite simply, the Phaeacians lack experience of evil, and the rest of the book will show us how Odysseus, in working his way through what is potentially an extremely dangerous situation, is able to capitalize on that lack. He, of course, is as unlucky as the Phaeacians are fortunate. Observing his misfortune, Nausikaa at once exonerates him from responsibility for it, observing that Zeus metes out good and bad indiscriminately (6.187–90); but will Arete, older and less prejudiced, show an equal tolerance? May she not consider Odysseus's misfortune evidence of guilt in the eyes of the gods? Her silence in response to his appeal is ominous, and Alkinoos's hesitation may have been due to more than inexperience: evidently he was waiting for her to speak, just as the others, according to Echeneos, were waiting for him (7.161). We can infer that the pause that resulted was a bad moment indeed for the suppliant Odysseus as he crouched in the ashes of Alkinoos's hearth.

This is especially so, since his appeal, brief though it necessarily is, should have succeeded. As he did with Nausikaa, he bases it on what is evidently of most interest to the person or persons addressed—in the Phaeacians' case, their prosperity and political stability.

> Arete, daughter of good-as-a-god Rhexenor,
> in my trouble I approach your husband and your knees
> and these banqueters here, to whom may the gods grant prosperity
> while they live, and to hand on to their children
> their houses' wealth and the rank their city has bestowed.
> Grant me in return passage to my native land
> without delay; long have I suffered far from my own people.
>
> (7.146–52)

The Phaeacians, with their unsinkable ships, will never be stranded far from home like Odysseus, and their security from foreign attack would seem to guarantee perpetual possession of their astounding wealth. Since no external enemy will overturn their social order, each Phaeacian seems assured of passing on his goods and privilege to his children. Not so, of course, Odysseus, whose long absence makes almost inevitable the usurpation which we know threatens at home. Why does not this abundant happiness, invoked in Odysseus's prayer for its continuance, arouse Arete's and the other Phaeacians' pity for the wanderer, who so obviously lacks what they enjoy?

Eventually, of course, they are moved, but not before Odysseus has made his misfortune even more palpable. He does so, naturally enough, in response to Alkinoos's suggestion that he may be a god in disguise. Moved by the incongruity of Alkinoos's notion as well as by the clear hint that now would be a proper time to tell his hosts who he is, Odysseus does not reveal his name and country but rather identifies himself by his very distance from divine felicity, punning on his name twice in the process. In the first part of his answer he implies that he has received at least as many injuries at the hands of the gods as the Phaeacians have blessings, claiming that he equals or surpasses any persons "loaded down with pain" (*okheontas oïzdun*) they have ever heard of (7.208–14). Thus he equates his identity and his name (albeit disguised) with the distinctly un-Phaeacian troubles he could tell of if he would. In the next section of his speech, he nevertheless refuses to recount these troubles on the ground that his "miserable belly" makes him forget all he has suffered by demanding that he fill it (7.215–21). Presumably he is not as ravenous as he pretends and merely wishes to postpone his tale, but the essential point is clear: desperate necessity is itself a kind of anodyne, and in acting under its compulsion, Odysseus has experienced an intensity of life which the Phaeacians will never know. Rejection of the Phaeacians' world follows, as it were, inexorably.

> Send me home in the morning;
> Set me, Man of Misfortune [*ton dystēnon*], on the land of my fathers,
> whatever I suffer; I would die gladly
> once I have seen my estate, my slaves, and my big high-roofed house.
>
> (7.222–25)

Odysseus has only recently paused in awe before a far larger and richer house than the one he recalls here, a house with more numerous and more skillful servants than he has ever possessed, a house in which Phaeacians have pursued a most pleasant life year after year; nevertheless, if after all his suffering he can but see his own house again, he will have no need of any such pleasant life as theirs: seeing what is his will be enough.

We see what Odysseus has done. Whether or not he or the Phaeacians are aware of it, he has made clear the way in which his existence is more vivid than theirs. He has also, by withholding his actual name and by hinting at his unequaled tale of woe, excited the Phaeacians' curiosity still further. When he finally begins that tale in book 9, we ourselves will be more than ready for it. Here then is the issue of those mists which enshrouded him and of his successful preservation of his anonymity: he is waiting for the right moment to reveal both the name and the meaning of himself as Man of Pain.

Impressed, presumably, both by Odysseus's misery and his passion to return to it, the Phaeacian lords unanimously urge his escort home (7.226–27). Tomorrow's meeting to discuss the question seems hardly necessary, and we begin to doubt whether Arete's approval is essential after all. But again we are mistaken. No sooner have the guests departed than Arete breaks her silence.

> Now, stranger, I shall question you myself:
> Who are you, and from where? Who gave you those clothes?
> Did you not say you wandered here over the sea? (7.237–39)

In effect, Arete is asking, "How is it that you, who claim to be a foreigner, are wearing clothes I recognize as having stitched myself?" (7.234–35). Obviously this can be a very dangerous question. In many communities mere suspicion of what might have passed between Odysseus and Nausikaa would be enough to cause his death. Therefore, even though Arete has asked his name and country point-blank, this is not the moment for the stranger to reveal that he is Odysseus of Ithaca, famous for his guile and his sacking of Troy.

Since the truth is on his side, Odysseus more or less confines his reply to what actually happened, but there is more to it than that. As before, he offers the multitude of his tribulations sent by the gods (7.242) both as a substitute for his name and country and as an excuse for not telling his complete history. He then emphasizes that Nausikaa was not the first to give him clothes: Kalypso loved him and gave him immortal ones (7.259–60, 265), with the result that his tears kept them wet for seven years. Not even the promise of an eternity of such love as hers could persuade his mind (7.256–58). Finally she let him go, and his joy at sighting Scherie (7.269) is calculated to suggest how much better he hopes to find life there than in her cave, as well as his relief at the sight of land after seventeen days adrift. His subsequent battering by storm and surf and final bedding down in a pile of leaves, which he also recounts, serve not only to inspire pity but also to emphasize how gladly he would exchange unvarnished nature in the company of a single female, however beautiful, for a civilized existence. When after this introduction Odysseus praises so highly Nausikaa's precocious understanding of the treatment due a stranger and suppliant, it seems that Arete can hardly fail to accept him as a man of the most proper sentiments.

Tantalizingly, Alkinoos leaves no opportunity for such an acknowledgment. Having such slight acquaintance with evil, Alkinoos is instantly convinced by Odysseus's words and sees only that his daughter may have been to blame: how is it that she herself did not bring her suppliant to the palace? Here the Man of Guile tells his second lie of the poem. Appropriating Nausikaa's delicacy as he did her maids' in book 6, he says that Nausikaa herself bade him come with her but that he felt fear and shame that he might anger Alkinoos by appearing in her company. "We earthbound humans," he adds, "are a jealous lot" (7.307).

Initially we applaud Odysseus's tact in telling a lie to protect his young benefactress; but when we see the result, we can be certain that more selfish motives played a part. By pretending to fear an anger that Alkinoos is too innocent to feel, as Alkinoos himself avows (7.309–10), Odysseus both obscurely excites and compliments him and at the same time wins credit for a fear of giving offense which is far from his true nature. Completely taken in, Alkinoos hails him as exactly his kind of man.

> Father Zeus, Athena, and Apollo, if only,
> seeing that you are as you are and feel exactly as I do,
> you would marry my daughter, be my son-in-law,
> and stay here! (7.311–14)

Nausikaa mistook Odysseus's nature because she was convinced that the gods would allow no one "bearing hostility" to visit the Phaeacians; Alkinoos mistakes it because he is himself too little used to people's taking advantage of one another and too unfamiliar with the world's evil. Alkinoos's evocation, already discussed, of the virtuous Rhadamanthys's visit to the criminal Tityos follows almost immediately as he protests his willingness, in spite of his desire to make Odysseus his son-in-law, to send Odysseus home; and Rhadamanthys's far journey, in turn, only accentuates the distance between Alkinoos's blessed innocence and Odysseus's importunate pain. A marriage between Odysseus and Nausikaa would certainly have its incongruities. Odysseus opts for going home.

> Father Zeus, may he but perform all he says,
> Alkinoos! Then his fame over all the generous earth
> would never die, and I would reach my homeland.
>
> (7.331–33)

There seems little chance that the speaker of these words will stay willingly on Scherie. Also, it may strike us that Alkinoos's fame has in fact survived not at all because of his superior happiness but as a result of Odysseus's leaving the Phaeacians behind: had he stayed, neither he nor Alkinoos would be famed "over all the generous earth." But the decision, we know, still rests with Arete. She has not spoken, although she does now go as far as to allow Odysseus a civilized bed in the happy city. The book can therefore end with the following contrast:

> So slept there much-enduring noble Odysseus
> in his intricate bed in the echoing porch;
> but Alkinoos lay in the alcove of his high house,
> and beside him his wife the queen brought him love and comfort.
>
> (7.344–47)

Odysseus still lacks his wife.

The City Sacker

In book 8, Odysseus, already "loved and pitied" as he had prayed that he would be (6.327), is about to become "loved . . . and feared and respected" (8.21–22), as the lionlike, city-sacking side of him, suppressed in book 7, begins to be revealed to the Phaeacians. In the book's opening lines, as he sets out with Alkinoos for the Phaeacian assembly, he is called *ptoliporthos*, "city sacking," for the first time in the poem (8.3). Immediately thereafter Athena

> poured wondrous grace upon his head and shoulders
> and made him taller and stouter to look upon,
> so that he might be *loved* of all the Phaeacians
> and *feared* and *respected*, and complete the many contests
> with which the Phaeacians made trial [*epeirēsant'*] of Odysseus.
> (8.19–23)

Thus this opening also announces the games at which the Phaeacians are to experience Odysseus, little inclined toward experience in general though book 7 suggested they were.

Athena, taking the form of a herald, assembles a huge crowd, expressive of the interest such a stranger as Odysseus would arouse in such a place as Scherie; nevertheless, Odysseus still has far to go. In recommending that the Phaeacians assist his return home, Alkinoos emphasizes not his impressiveness but his anonymity.

> This stranger, I don't know who, has come to my house a wanderer,
> whether from eastern or western lands. (8.28–29)

Pity, too, is still very much in the forefront.

Let us forward the stranger's journey, as is our custom.
No one in future either, who comes to my house,
shall wait here long in sorrow for lack of escort.

(8.31–33)

The poet now recounts the launching of Odysseus's ship, with full formulaic circumstance. Its crew returns ashore for the feast of farewell, and for the next six books that ship remains ready and waiting to take Odysseus home. If it does not depart on the present day as Alkinoos promised (7.318) but rather on the next, that is not a discrepancy, as has been thought, but the result of Odysseus's increased stature, of the process of his becoming "loved and feared and respected." Suspense, too, has been increased.

At the banquet following the launching, the Muse inspires Alkinoos's blind bard, Demodokos, to sing, with fateful appropriateness, "the quarrel of Odysseus and Achilles,/how they once disputed at the gods' rich feast," a song in which Odysseus is both placed on a par with Achilles and surrounded with all the sorrow and glory of the Trojan War (8.72–82). The Phaeacians of course do not yet realize that their guest is Odysseus. Again suspense is increased as we watch for realization to occur. This will happen at the beginning of book 9.

Demodokos's song, even though Homer tells us that its "fame at that time reached the spreading heavens" (8.74), and although the whole matter has usually been viewed otherwise (Nagy, 22–25), probably was never part of the repertoire of songs we think of Homer as inheriting from his predecessors. In all the material that has come down to us, there simply is no independent reference to a quarrel of Odysseus and Achilles at a feast of the gods, or to Agamemnon's consulting the Delphic oracle before the Trojan War, or to a prophecy that Troy would fall when "the best of the Achaians" should quarrel. I suspect that, as the Muse presents Odysseus's sojourn among these impossibly remote Phaeacians, she also—irresistibly!—presents their bard as singing by mere coincidence a song that is then all the rage, about how Odysseus and Achilles quarreled at a feast of the gods and Agamemnon rejoiced. He rejoiced because Apollo had told him that, when "the best of the Achaians" (i.e., Odysseus and Achilles) quarreled, Troy's end would be near. Why should the Muse make Demodokos sing precisely of this quarrel at which Agamemnon rejoices? The answer is that Odysseus is about to have a very profitable quarrel with the Phaeacians. Why at a feast of the gods? Because in *Iliad* 19.154–356, Odysseus and Achilles *do* quarrel at what Odysseus hopes will be a feast of reconciliation given to Achilles by Agamemnon. The reconciliation, ensuring the death of Hektor and the downfall of Troy, does take place, but the feast is

95

prevented by Achilles' resolve not to eat until his revenge is consummated. Odysseus gains his limited point, that the Achaians cannot fight for long on empty stomachs (19.160–70), and also (ultimately) his general one that mourning for the dead must have some limit (19.225–37). Nevertheless, for the reason stated, the grand feast which Odysseus had in mind does not take place. Why, then, does the Muse impel Demodokos to sing that there was a "feast of the gods"? Perhaps to point, for those who know the *Iliad*, to the superiority of Homer's version as compared with Demodokos's. In any case, we have before us the *Odyssey*'s first hint that, by its end, it will ask us specifically to compare the glory of Odysseus with the glory of Achilles.

The paradoxically welcome quarrel of Odysseus and Achilles in the song is the prelude to a quarrel between Odysseus and the Phaeacians which wins him the love, fear, and respect which Athena desires for him. It all begins when Odysseus, instead of showing satisfaction at the opportune introduction of his name, begins to weep, apparently at the woe of Zeus's contriving for Greeks and Trojans alike mentioned in the song (8.81–82). Weeping at the song of Troy, its tragedy and its sack, begins to signal for the Phaeacians who and what Odysseus, the Man of Sorrow, is. This is the way he differs from others like the Phaeacians: they do not weep at the quarrel of Odysseus and Achilles; they delight in it (8.91).

First and foremost, Odysseus's weeping about the Trojan War occasions the games at which the Phaeacians are to experience him (8.23): Alkinoos tactfully suggests "making trial of contests" (8.100) as an alternative to the singing which distresses his guest, and so the Phaeacians duly "try one another in running" (8.120), "make trial of the painful wrestling" (8.126), and invite Odysseus to "try the contests" (8.145–149). All these words alluding to experience and trial are expressed in Greek by the verb *peiran*, derived from the noun *peira* we have noticed before.

What emerges from these trials? First, we discover that even the Phaeacians, though in their peace-loving way they regard the contests simply as entertainment, think that a man's physical prowess is a matter of the first importance. Alkinoos would dearly love his people to be known as great athletes, hoping

> that the stranger tell his friends,
> when he reaches his home, how much we surpass others
> in boxing and wrestling, in jumping and running.
>
> (8.101–3)

The courteous prince Laodamas, inviting Odysseus to show his skill, says, "There is no greater fame, so long as a man lives,/than what he can do with his hands and his own swift feet" (8.147–48). In taunting him after he has excused himself from competing, the uncouth Euryalos shows the utmost scorn for the mercantile as opposed to the athletic virtues.

> Stranger, you don't look to me like a man who even knows
> games, common as games are among men,
> but rather like someone who travels about in his ship,
> giving orders to a crew of traders like himself,
> careful of his cargo and thinking only of the greedy profits
> he can make by the way. No, you are no athlete.
>
> (8.159–64)

Odysseus of course shares Euryalos's values. To be thought a merchant rather than a man of his hands makes him marvelously angry, and he risks everything he has gained so far among the Phaeacians in order to refute the charge. Physical prowess is clearly an essential ingredient of manly virtue in this poem.

We may note in passing that what an appeal to his present happiness could not do—Laodamas bade him cast care aside and compete, since the ship which would take him home was now in the water (8.149–51)—the "stinging speech" of the scoffer Euryalos finally achieved; namely, to make him "make trial of the contests." Odysseus answers the taunt in these words:

> You have roused the heart in my breast,
> speaking so out of due order. I am no ninny at games,
> as you tell it, but I think I was among
> the first, as long as youth and strength of hand were by me.
> Now I am caught in evil and sorrows; for I have endured much,
> passing through [*peirōn*] the wars of men and the painful waves.
> Even so, much though I suffer, I will try [*peirēsom'*] the contests;
> for that was a stinging speech; your words have roused me.
>
> (8.178–85)

The pun on *peirōn*, by associating Odysseus's painful career with trial by games, suggests that that career too is a kind of contest and a way of showing his excellence. Instead of being a deterrent by tending to break his strength, as Odysseus says in trying to decline the contests, his suffering is actually a spur to his engaging in yet more danger and struggle; for the "trial of contests" is all of a piece with his career and is, in fact, his element. We may compare this with his words to Kalypso to the effect that he is willing to endure shipwreck because he has suffered so much already.

Pain rouses Odysseus, where pleasure will not, to drop some of his anonymity, "be tried," and brave the whole Phaeacian people in order to prove his prowess. How great the risk is, Homer indicates through Odysseus's relief at finding a friend in the crowd, (8.199–201) the "Phaeacian" who marks his discus throw and applauds it as unbeatable. (The Phaeacian is really Athena. Once more, as he did when she was a herald, Homer uses the goddess not to take the action beyond the human realm into the supernatural but to convey the momentousness we sense when ordinary human actions are also crucial.) The risk is great, but it is not unconsidered or imprudent like the risk which Euryalos took in taunting him. Euryalos did not know what he was talking about—neither what the stranger could do nor what was due to the stranger; he spoke "out of due order," without respect (aidōs, 8.172), and so Odysseus calls him atasthalos ("reckless," 8.166). Odysseus, on the other hand, angry though he is, knows what he is doing and behaves with prudence and restraint. He exempts Laodamas from his general challenge—"Let [whoever wishes] come and be tried [peirēthētō], for you have angered me much" (8.205)—remarking that it is foolish, vulgar, and inexpedient to compete with one's host in a foreign land (8.209–11). He is aware that he may be defeated in running (8.230) and that he is inferior in archery to Philoctetes, with whom he reveals that he competed at Troy, as well as to the heroes of earlier times (8.219–25). He shows that he is also aware of the penalties for competing with gods (8.226–28). In a word, anger does not make him ignore or forget the realities of the situation (except perhaps when he boasts that he can throw a spear farther than another can shoot an arrow [8.229]). He is not reckless. Yet he is angry, with the sort of anger which will risk all, even life itself, for respect. It is clear that, if he had not been provoked, Odysseus would have preferred to remain anonymous and pitied in exchange for his voyage home. Yet when his virtue is called in question, reputation comes even before the homecoming for which he has struggled.

Stung, therefore, by Euryalos's words, he leaps to his feet, cloak and all, and, seizing a discus far heavier than any the Phaeacians have used, hurls it well beyond all the rest. Then he challenges all but his host to match him at this or any other sport, adding:

> Of the rest of you I forbid or reject no one;
> I want to know and be tried [peirēthēmenai] against you.
> For there is no game of all men use in which I am deficient;
> the bow I handle well, with its beautiful finish;
> I would be first to hit a man with my arrow in the throng

of those ranged against us, thick though my comrades
stood by and shot at them. Only Philoctetes
surpassed me with the bow in the land of the Trojans
when we Achaians competed at archery. (8.212–20)

Odysseus hereupon proceeds to decline rivalry with the archers of former times
like Herakles and Eurytos, boasts about his spear throwing, and admits that his
seafaring may have impaired his speed of foot. We may notice in particular
about this speech that it enables the Phaeacians to recognize that this is the
anger not just of a slighted athlete but of a sacker of cities who not only will die
for reputation, if necessary, but manifestly will kill for it as the Achaians did at
Troy.

The amiable Phaeacians are less proud. At the sound of Odysseus's discus
hurled in anger,

they cowered down to the ground,
those long-oared Phaeacians, renowned for their ships,
beneath the rush of the stone. (8.190–92)

These are the people, we remember, who, when plundered by the Kyklopes,
turned their backs on conflict and removed to this safe island. They will never
sack any cities. Alkinoos, avoiding the unpleasant as usual, in the face of
Odysseus's challenge backs down. No one ventures to "make trial" of Odysseus's prowess further. Alkinoos withdraws the Phaeacians' claim to excellence
at the more aggressive sports, boxing and wrestling, reserving only running,
and changes his boast to excellence at hot baths, singing, and the dance. Thus,
when it comes to the point, Odysseus is willing to try and be tried at the
contests, and the Phaeacians are not. The nurse from the Land of No Experience does characterize them after all.

In the career of Odysseus, Homer is showing us what a life of peira is like.
Like a lion whose belly drives him to try even the sheepfold, Odysseus,
approaching Nausikaa in his need, sallied forth, though naked and battered, to
"try [*peirēsomai*] and see" what men he had come among now (6.126). Similarly when his self-respect is attacked, he insists, with no less lionlike courage
and willingness to meet peril, that the Phaeacians *experience* his strength. The
repeated pattern is pleasing and artistic in itself; it also suggests that the two
things have a real connection: the need to go and see in order to live, and the
need to come forth and be seen in order to live with honor. A Man of Trouble
will not preserve his anonymity forever.

The Phaeacians exemplify the opposite: they are neither driven to bold action by need for livelihood, nor do they get angry in defense of their honor. "We do not find what you have said disagreeable" (8.236), Alkinoos replies as the Phaeacians refuse Odysseus's challenge. It is evident which alternative the poem favors. Those who "make trial," like lions and heroes, are also tried. Driven to it they find out, and others find out, what they can do. Phaeacians, on the other hand, enjoying a "happy" life, avoid the test and so are condemned, like Odysseus with Kalypso, both to not knowing and to not being known.

The Phaeacian games end in an exhibition of dancing so that Alkinoos may demonstrate what his people really are good at. That this and the following postponements of Odysseus's departure are unpremeditated, entirely produced first by Odysseus's weeping and then by his self-assertion, is shown when Homer notes the necessity of sending back to the palace for Demodokos's lyre. Furthermore, the attention given the lyre and the bard both here and when Demodokos was first introduced tends to make us conscious of how much this book is concerned with song and its uses. For the exhibition of dancing is also an exhibition of song, and if Demodokos's first song was a song to make Odysseus weep, this one will be one to make everybody laugh.

The Song of Ares and Aphrodite occupies just one hundred lines (8.267–366). It is apparently presented at full length, unlike the sketches which Homer gives us of Demodokos's other songs. As we have said, it is a song for laughter, not tears, and as such is as different as possible from Demodokos's earlier song of the strife of Odysseus and Achilles. In it Homer seems quite consciously to be making the point made later by Bergson, Max Eastman, and others that, excepting the laughter of pure delight, we humans mostly laugh in order not to cry. Hephaistos, learning that Aphrodite is betraying him in his own bed with Ares, catches the culprits in his cunningly forged invisible wires and exhibits them for all the Olympians to see.

> Father Zeus, and all you other blessed gods who live forever,
> come and see a thing for laughter, a thing not to be endured. . . .
>
> (8.306–7)

Hephaistos is roaring with anger (8.305); but all the same, because he cannot bear what is happening, he has turned both his shame and his revenge to laughter. Things are no longer serious, and this is Homer's point. The contrast with the Achaians' attitude toward the adultery of Helen is obvious.

Laughter of this sort insists that what is before us is not serious; it does not matter; it does not count. When we laugh like this (Eastman, 20), we take the attitude of play. This suspension of reality is the fundamental attitude of the humor which laughs in order not to cry. Hermes suspends reality when he boasts that he would gladly change places with Ares, even if the bindings were tripled. He actually refuses to believe in Ares' plight, for if he gave it his full emotional participation, it would be too painful to bear with equanimity. Similarly the triumph of Hephaistos's justice as hailed by the other gods is a mock triumph which they do not take seriously. We cannot take Hephaistos himself seriously without emotionally sharing his shame; therefore we prefer to laugh. He is already a natural butt of joking because he is ugly and a cripple, two further deficiencies we would rather not take seriously. Hephaistos manages easily enough to subject Ares' and Aphrodite's passion to ironic contemplation, and so to destroy its reality at least for the moment. As he puts them on exhibition, he gloats,

> I don't think they will lie longer like this even for a moment,
> however great their love; they will soon lose their desire
> for bed. . . . (8.315–17)

But Hephaistos can score this success only at the price of exhibiting his own shame, a shame the gods laugh at rather than sympathize with. In effect they are saying that neither Hephaistos nor what he does nor what happens to him matters—and what a relief it is not to have to care! Homer, then, in the song of Hephaistos, Ares, and Aphrodite, even as he delights us with a comic piece, shows us what it is to let one's self be laughed at rather than to insist on being taken seriously, as Odysseus has just done in challenging the Phaeacians.

Hephaistos's buffoonery in the song dissipates the ugly atmosphere caused by the quarrel between Odysseus and Euryalos; both Odysseus and the Phaeacians delight in Demodokos's performance (8.367–69); but even for Alkinoos that is not enough; he too feels the need to be taken seriously, and so he bids Laodamas and Halios perform their acrobatic dance with the purple ball (8.370–71). Though this dance is only a game, a form of play, such is their skill that it awakens Odysseus's "awe" (*sebas*, 8.384), and Alkinoos is overjoyed. Evidently now that Odysseus has become angry and challenged the Phaeacians' self-respect, his approval means a great deal more than it did previously. Alkinoos suddenly discovers that his guest is a very wise man indeed and proposes to load him with guest gifts (8.388–89), unmentioned before, in this way reminding us of Zeus's promise at the beginning of book 5 that the Phaeacians would "honor Odysseus like a god" and give him more wealth than he would have got from Troy if he had brought his booty home safely. Such are the advantages of arousing "fear and respect" as well as pity; such are the rewards of the anger and pride of a sacker of cities.

Now that respect between both sides has been established, Euryalos, on orders from Alkinoos, makes Odysseus handsome amends, including the gift of a sword. When Odysseus hangs this weapon about his own shoulders (8.416), he seems quite on a level with his hosts at last, or indeed even a little superior. His prayer that Euryalos never miss the weapon may remind us how little likely the Phaeacians are ever to need such things. The still-anonymous Odysseus, on the other hand, has risen in the world. "The sun went down, and he had his famous gifts" (8.417). With these words this phase of the Phaeacian episode ends, as if to accentuate the stature Odysseus has achieved.

Because of the interruption caused by the games, another farewell feast becomes necessary. All return to the palace, and Odysseus is brought face to face once more with Arete, whose favor he has yet to win. Alkinoos, now completely convinced of his guest's importance and anxious to do whatever he can to mollify him, directs Arete to prepare a bath for Odysseus's comfort and a chest in which to store his gifts of gold and fine clothes. She obeys, but she still withholds her enthusiasm. As Samuel Butler noted (91), she is in a hurry to have her guest close the chest and lash it securely, ostensibly so that no one may rob him on the journey in his sleep (8.444–45). Her hurry, however, is not I think for the reason Butler suggested, namely, in order to avoid contributing one of the talents of gold levied on each king by Alkinoos (8.393), for he has named a drinking cup, presumably even more precious, as his own corresponding gift (8.430). Rather, she is saying as clearly as possible, "All this may be very fine, but now, enough: no more gifts." Odysseus is still far from having won his way to Arete's heart. Yet as he lashes the chest with a knot, "an intricate one, which Kirke once imparted to his mind" (8.448), we may be encouraged to feel that Odysseus has come off well in his dealings with wise women before, and may do so again.

In contrast to Arete's reserve, we are shown, for the last time, Nausikaa's love for Odysseus. Once more, herself "clothed in beauty by the gods" (8.457), she observes the stranger freshly bathed and looks on him with eyes of wonder. This time she bids him good-bye.

> Fair journey, stranger, so in the land of your fathers too
> you may remember it was I who rescued you.
>
> (8.461–62)

We should not be too disappointed, as some have been, that Odysseus does not now fling his arms about her, marry her, and live happily ever after. He has work to do in Ithaca, and Nausikaa has done very well as it is. It is no small thing to be remembered in the terms she has suggested; and Odysseus's reply suggests that she will get her wish in larger measure than her father, Alkinoos, who sets such store by being remembered in Ithaca whenever Odysseus shall use the cup he has given him (8.431–32). In the *Odyssey* it is more important to be remembered even than to be successful in love, and Odysseus promises to remember Nausikaa, in words that leave nothing to be desired on that score.

> Nausikaa, daughter of great-hearted Alkinoos,
> May Zeus only grant it, Hera's thundering lord,
> that I come home, that I should see that day!
> There too then I would pray to you as to a goddess
> all the days there are. To you, girl, I owe my life.
>
> (8.464–68)

Nausikaa has done very well, but only if Odysseus really does get home. We should note that he himself makes this reservation even as he fervently assents to Nausikaa's good wishes, and this in turn reminds us that his homecoming is not yet assured. Arete is still to be won. Thus, in addition to giving Nausikaa her due, the scene of Nausikaa's farewell points out to us both how far Odysseus has come since he landed naked and unknown on Scherie and how far he still has to go. Nausikaa gave him life, and for that he may some day be able to remember her like a goddess in his prayers; but that day has not yet come.

As the feasting resumes, Odysseus takes it upon himself to choose the song which the bard will sing. He has heard Demodokos sing of the Trojan War and his own anger in such a way that he weeps; he has also heard him sing of the gods' turning wrath to laughter in a way calculated to make him smile; which sort of subject will he choose? He deliberately chooses to weep, for he calls for nothing less than the climax of the Trojan War; namely, the ruse of the wooden horse, contrived by himself, and the sack of the city. It might be thought that he does this simply in order to call attention to himself; that, since he already intends to reveal who he is, he is making sure that the revelation will come with the greatest possible effect. But something else more direct and more fundamental is involved. Both uses of song, both the tragic and the comic, have already been displayed to him by Demodokos, and of the two he prefers to weep with the one rather than to laugh with the other. He prefers the mode which says, "What is about to pass before your minds is to be taken without irony." He prefers to live again a real revenge for a real adultery (Helen's) than to mock at Hephaistos's "punishment" of Ares and Aphrodite.

> And the bard sang how the sons of the Achaians sacked the city,
> pouring from the horse, issuing from the hollow hiding place.
> And he sang how one ravaged in one place, another in another,
> but Odysseus made for the house of Deïphobos
> along with godlike Menelaos. Like Ares he strode;
> and there, the poet said, daring the direst battle,
> he conquered, at the last, with the help of fierce Athena.
>
> (8.514–20)

Odysseus prefers to be and to remember the city sacker, in spite of all the pain that means.

Odysseus is not seeking simply to live again the exaltation of victory, however, for he weeps to hear the song of Troy's fall. Paradoxically, he is said to weep not like a victor but like the victim of a city's sack, a woman dragged from embracing the body of her dying husband, fallen in defense of his home and children.

> Beating her back and shoulders with their spears
> they take her off to slavery, to suffer toil and pain [oïzdun],
> her cheeks gaunt with a grief to break the heart.
>
> (8.528–30)

By means of this paradox Homer suggests that the essential meaning in the fall of a city is the same for victor and vanquished. Both experience the event completely; neither is able to withdraw from it by means of irony (comedy) or even aesthetic distance (tragedy) or in any other way. Odysseus and the woman in the simile, because they have actually experienced a city's fall, both know something that the Phaeacians with their essentially playful and aesthetic approach to life will never know, and though it is a knowledge to call forth tears, it is infinitely preferable to laughter. As Man of Pain, Odysseus deliberately chooses to weep at the song of the fall of Troy, in which he was personally involved, rather than to engage in ironic laughter at the foibles of the gods, or even to enjoy as literature the fall of Troy, as the Phaeacians do.

We may be the more confident of this way of looking at it when we remember that the question of "weeping after supper" has arisen at least once before. In Menelaos's hall all fell to weeping at the thought of the absent Odysseus (4.183–86) until Peisistratos, expressing distaste for such mourning, broke the spell. Thereupon Menelaos gave orders to renew the feast, and Helen made sure no further pain would be felt by infusing her drug, nepenthe, into the drink. Homer has evidently very much in mind the human tendency to soften the impact of life's pains by one means or another and the loss of value attendant on doing so. Therefore I think that, with the simile of the weeping captive, Homer is showing that, greatly though it matters who wins and who loses, even more important is the human capacity to feel sorrow completely, a capacity without which life becomes trivial.

Alkinoos is an example of someone who does not understand the satisfaction of sorrow. He is nearly frantic at the thought that his guest is not enjoying the singing like everybody else, and so he puts an end to it. But the very acuteness of his concern about Odysseus's sorrow makes him value him the more. The guest whom he once had to be prompted even to receive is now to be treated "like a brother" (8.546), as he clearly perceives. His name—he *must* have one—his homeland, and his travels and experiences are now of vital importance, and he will not allow him to remain silent. Why does he weep at the song of Troy when no one else does? Has he perhaps lost an in-law or a friend, who might be almost as close as a brother? "In-law" or "friend" is as close to sorrow and death as Alkinoos will let his mind reach, and he hopes to comfort his guest with the thought that such things are arranged by the gods so that there will be songs for future generations (8.579–80). We see that he and the other Phaeacians much prefer to take life as literature rather than straight. *They* do not weep at the song of Troy, for they have not participated. Hearing about things rather than living through them, their life is, as it were, theoretical, not actual, and so it is appropriate that their ships behave like thoughts or wishes, going whithersoever their masters direct them without the need of steersmen or steering oar, invisibly and absolutely safely (8.556–63).

But there is a penalty for this painless method of taking people from place to place. There is a prophecy that, because of this practice of theirs, Poseidon, the same god who plants so much evil in Odysseus's path, will wreck a boat of theirs on its return from escort and will cover their city with a great mountain (8.564–69). Even as we hear Alkinoos reminding the Phaeacians of this prophecy, we can perhaps infer what lies behind it in the poet's mind. Neither Homer nor the oldest member of his audience can have met in real life a race of people for whom reality was suspended to the degree that it is for the Phaeacians. Therefore, if they ever existed, they must have disappeared long ago. Only Poseidon's own children can have sailed the sea as safely and effortlessly as they did; yet if they lived so securely, their life must have been dim indeed. Poseidon's very favor condemned them to a kind of nonexistence at the same time that it encouraged them to show him insufficient respect (13.128–38). Should he not, then, be the one to blot them out finally, "for giving painless escort to all" (8.566)?

The Kyklops

Alkinoos is unable to hold back his questions any longer. The moment has come for Odysseus to give up the relative security of his anonymity and reveal himself to the Phaeacians in word, as he already has in deed. This revelation is the function of his famous tale of his wanderings, occupying the next four books.

It is a well-articulated tale. Three sets of three adventures each, two short followed by one long in each case, frame the great adventure of Odysseus's journey to the underworld, two sets preceding it and one following. Occupying the whole of book 11, the underworld adventure holds a climactic position, nearer the end of the four-book group than the beginning. At the same time, it is given a feeling of greater centrality because Odysseus tells the three adventures of book 12 twice: once in Kirke's admonitory forecast, and again as they actually happen. In this way it seems as though book 11 were followed, as well as preceded, by two sets of adventures. Book 11 itself is divided at its center when Odysseus offers, presumably not entirely sincerely, to cease his tale for the night; and it is here, at this so-emphasized central point, that he wins the respect and approval of Arete, which has been suggested as the one thing needful for his return. It will be obvious that such a structure is neither accidental nor without effect.

Alkinoos's questions are essentially four: what is your name? where do you come from? what have you seen of the world on your wanderings? why do you weep at the song of Troy? (8.548–78). The moment Odysseus answers the first of these, the Phaeacians will realize that the man standing before them is the man whose sacking of Troy Demodokos has just portrayed in grim detail. If that sack has called forth bitterest tears even from Odysseus, how will it affect Arete? How can Troy's sacker possibly win the approval of the queen who "settles men's quarrels as well as women's" and who is the living symbol of the Phaeacians' freedom from war? To win Arete's favor Odysseus must do no less than win acceptance for all the pain, given and received, which his name implies.

He begins, cleverly enough, by contrasting the sorrows of his own story with the pleasure (for others) of listening to the bard Demodokos at the feast.

> To my mind this is a happiness second to none.
> Yet your heart has moved you to inquire about
> my lamentable sorrows, that I may groan the more in pain.
>
> (9.11–13)

After such a preface his audience will have the pain he himself has suffered prominently in mind at the moment that they discover that he is the sacker of Troy, and for that reason they will be less likely to condemn him out of hand.

Alkinoos has asked him his name with what by this point in the story has become almost desperate impatience.

> Tell us what name your mother and father called you by yonder,
> and what your fellows, both townsmen and country folk.
> No one, surely, of human kind is completely nameless,
> good person or bad, once he comes to his birth.
> Parents give names to each of their children as they produce them.
>
> (8.550–54)

Odysseus responds, as he has before (7.222–25), as though his name were equivalent to his woes.

> So what shall I tell you first? What should come last?
> for the sorrows are many that the gods in the heavens gave me.
> Now first I shall tell you my name, so that you also
> may know, and I, if I can escape the day without pity,
> may be your guest-friend in foreign parts, far away though my home is.
>
> (9.14–18)

Odysseus explicitly chooses to begin the story of his sorrows with the announcement of his name. Obviously to become Alkinoos's guest-friend he must reveal it, as he says; but knowing what his name means, we can understand that it is the first of his sorrows as well. In babyhood he was named Man of Pain, and his life since has matched that description.

The name itself he brings forth with the utmost panache.

> I am Odysseus, Laertes' son; the whole world
> knows of my stratagems, and my fame reaches the heavens.
> (9.19–20)

Here before the Phaeacians, in the flesh, is the man whose stratagems brought the fall of Troy. That fact makes Odysseus weep where others enjoy; nevertheless, he is proud of it.

After the name, the country. Odysseus describes Ithaca as being as distant as possible from Scherie both in space and in character (9.21–27): it is an island far off toward the west and the dark; even its neighboring islands are all of them closer to the sun; and it is rough. There are redeeming features: a tall mountain renders it conspicuous, like Odysseus himself, and it produces strong youth. Nevertheless, as compared with Scherie, the island's characteristics definitely remind us of the contrast, sketched in Odysseus's opening words, between the Phaeacians' happiness and his own pain. To explain adequately why Kalypso and Kirke and, by implication, Nausikaa cannot make him forsake such a place, Odysseus points to the special attraction exerted by the land of one's forefathers and the place where one's parents live.

> Truly,
> I can find nothing sweeter than the land [*gaiēs*] a person is born in.
> Oh yes, she kept me with her, the lovely goddess Kalypso,
> in her vaulted cave desiring me to be her husband.
> In the very same way Kirke detained me in her palace,
> the Aiaian witch, desiring me to be her husband.
> But never did she persuade the spirit within my breast.
> So true is it that nothing sweeter than fatherland [*patridos*] or parents
> exists, no matter how sumptuous one's dwelling
> far off in a land of strangers, away from mother and father.
> (9.27–36)

In praising Ithaca, Odysseus indirectly invokes both *Gaia*, the mother principle, and, in the word *patridos*, fatherhood itself. His feeling for family and fatherhood shows also in his including Laertes' name in the announcement of his own. All this of course adds point to Homer's referring to him simply as "Laertes' son" when he is about to go forth to "be tried" by the Phaeacians in the games (8.18). The piety in the present passage has the ring of truth, even on the lips of the master of stratagems, and in his love of home and parents we can find something at last for Arete to admire; nevertheless, his tale promises to be a grim one. Can a queen named Prayed For approve of such a life? Above all, can she approve of Odysseus's sacking of Troy?

Odysseus proceeds to justify both leaving home in general and the Trojan War in particular. The ninth book is in fact a compendium testing possible attitudes toward those who are not one's countrymen. Odysseus the city sacker, who "sacked Troy's sacred citadel" in the poem's second line, now tells how, on leaving Troy, he and his men sacked Ismaros, the city of the Kikones. His account is brusque, brutal even. Here is city sacking as a simple act of predation, divorced from any question of honor or justice. To be sure, Odysseus and his men suffer for it, but only because, according to him, his men disregarded his advice to "flee with slippery foot" (9.43) and did not reembark soon enough. Instead, they linger to feast on their booty, with the result that Kikones from the hinterland come down upon them "thick as the flowers that bloom/in the spring" (9.51–52). Odysseus regards this as the beginning of their "bad luck from Zeus" (9.52–53), but at the same time, the lightness of his tone suggests that he has no moral feeling about it. For him the lesson, if there is one, is simply to show a slipperier foot next time. Even when a storm, apparently the same one that came too late to catch Nestor but blew Menelaos to Egypt (3.288–90), wrecked Aias on the Gyraian Rocks (4.500), and took Agamemnon out of his way off Cape Malea (4.514–18), thus becoming presumably the storm the tradition offered as the main feature of the "woeful return of the Achaians" which Zeus and Athena were said to have caused (1.327; 3.132)—even when this storm, which Odysseus specifically recognizes as coming from Zeus (9.67), blows out the sails of his fleet, he is not overly impressed. After all, his men manage to row ashore, wait out the worst of it, and then continue on their way. They are subsequently blown past Cythera to the land of the lotus-eaters instead of homeward, but this too Odysseus seems to regard simply as more bad luck. Nevertheless, we are led to ask ourselves whether Odysseus is not too little sensitive to the gods' equally possible disapproval of city sacking. Why does it not occur to him, as it did to Nestor, that the gods are punishing the Achaians for what they did at Troy? Having followed Telemachos's experiences at Pylos and Sparta, Homer's audience has learned that Athena was not so hostile as Nestor believed—but what about Odysseus's Phaeacian audience? What will be the effect of his bravado on Arete? Can she accept with equanimity the assumption that foreigners are simply fair game for pillage?

The lotus-eaters show what may happen if foreigners are treated as friends. Odysseus tells how he sent a delegation to inquire "what men these were who ate bread upon the earth" (9.89), only to discover that they ate not bread but lotus, a "flowery food" (9.84). Bread is obviously what Homer and his audience consider the normal diet of humans, including meat; lotus is the flowery diet of herbivores, as Odysseus's description of his men as "champing" it (*ereptomenoi*, 9.97) indicates. Converted to the lotus-eating (we might say, grass-eating) life, his men no longer wish to return to their fellows, let alone to Ithaca. They have ceased to be normal, predatory humans who kill a large part of what they eat. Hence the horror we sense in Odysseus as he drags his ambassadors back to the ships by force, ties them beneath the rowing benches, and bids all hands embark at once, "lest by chance anyone eat lotus and forget the voyage home" (9.102). Sacking cities may be painful, but the episode of the lotus-eaters suggests that to refrain from city sacking would be to deny one's humanity. Even the Phaeacians kill and eat meat (8.59–61), and when Odysseus and his men are divinely conducted to the isle of goats off the Kyklopes' shore and to the hunting and feasting which ensue (9.142), it seems to be for the express purpose of showing how humans are meant to behave. Thus as they approach the climactic episode of the Kyklops, the Phaeacians may be expected to be the more willing to accept city sacking as natural to the human condition. The Kyklops himself will then demonstrate by his cannibalistic excess the limits to be placed on normal human predation.

City sacking is not just a matter of filling one's belly, however. Odysseus's adventure with the Kyklops is one in which beginning as Nobody he is able to escape from the cave and proclaim himself Odysseus by virtue of ramming a white-hot, pointed, six-foot log of olive wood into the giant's single eye. The parallel between this act and becoming known to all the world by sacking Troy is obvious, and it poses the same question: does becoming known justify inflicting such pain? On at least four levels the adventure with the Kyklops suggests that it does.

On the first level, we can see that we have here an analogue to human birth: the stake in the eye suggest the sexual act; the cave, a womb; and receiving a name upon issuing from it, the birth of a child. The text itself alludes to the pain of childbirth when Odysseus speaks of Polyphemos as "travailing with pains [*ōdinōn odynēsi*]" as he himself is about to escape from the cave (9.415). The inference that, from the biological point of view, at least, we owe our existence to pain, is obvious, together with the secondary implication that not to inflict pain is not to be born and therefore to be nobody.

Second, the blinding of the Kyklops is a most satisfactory act of vengeance. Odysseus is forced to stand by helplessly while the giant kills and eats two of his men at each of three successive meals, and as a result even the modern reader may empathize with the intensity of his desire to get even (9.316–17). Realizing that, in Homer's world, revenge was not only accepted but admired, we can guess that the grisly details of the blinding (9.378–97) are intended to provoke only the most thoroughgoing emotional assent. Similarly we do not necessarily begrudge Odysseus his satisfaction when, at a later stage, his intellectual superiority prevents Polyphemos from getting help from his hitherto neglected countrymen.

> So they spoke in departing; and my dear heart laughed
> to think how my name had deceived him, my resourceful trick.
>
> (9.413–14)

Homer's Greek here for "resourceful trick" is simply the word mētis, "resource"; but mētis irresistibly recalls the two-word phrase mē tis, "not anyone," in which the other Kyklopes thrice voice the error which Odysseus's naming himself Nobody has induced (9.405, 406, 410). We remember too Odysseus's frequent epithet, polumētis, "resourceful." The adventure with Polyphemos, then, is portrayed as a most wittily satisfactory vengeance. If it now occurs to the Phaeacians that the sack of Troy too was an act of vengeance for an egregious violation of hospitality, Troy's pain will seem more acceptable.

Intentionally or not, Odysseus makes it more likely that the Phaeacians will associate Troy with the blinding of Polyphemus when, at the beginning of the episode, he allows the giant to seem to score a point against him in regard to Troy. There is in the poetic tradition a stock question which people at home ask of sailors from abroad. Nestor asks it of Telemachos and Athena at 3.71–74, and now the Kyklops repeats it.

> Strangers, who are you? Where do you sail from over the paths of the water?
> Have you some business, or do you rove on chance
> as raiders do on the sea, who rove
> risking their lives [psukhas], bringing trouble to people abroad?
>
> (9.252–55)

Thucydides (1.5) is doubtless correct in pointing out that the way in which the question is asked shows that there was no moral condemnation of piracy in more ancient times. Nevertheless, the terms in which the formulaic expression describes raiding make it seem, prima facie, less reasonable than "business," and when Odysseus, hiding his terror at the size of the giant as best he can (9.256–58), replies to Polyphemos that he is now thwarted on his homeward journey after helping Agamemnon sack Troy, his boast that that sack has made

Agamemnon the most famous man in the world sounds rather hollow. Once the giant is defeated and Odysseus regains his name, however, city sacking seems vindicated insofar as it can be compared with the adventure with Polyphemos.

Third, by taking vengeance on Polyphemos, Odysseus succeeds in bringing him to respect the gods. Early in the episode Polyphemos answers Odysseus's appeal to the protection of Zeus, god of strangers, by saying that the Kyklopes, being much stronger, pay no attention to Zeus and the other gods; Odysseus therefore, after he has blinded him, taunts the giant first with the fact that Zeus and the other gods have punished him. The only reply this receives, however, is a rock thrown by the Kyklops which washes him back to the Kyklops's shore. Only by Odysseus's second taunt, in which he names himself, is Polyphemos enabled to remember that a prophet predicted he would lose his sight "at the hands of Odysseus" (9.512). Let no one argue that for Odysseus to reveal his name to Polyphemos was a mistake, enabling the giant to curse his punisher: as a result of this proof of an order superior to his own will, Polyphemos turns to pretended friendliness and offers to urge his father Poseidon to give Odysseus a safe homecoming, tacitly admitting for the first time that the gods have more power than he does. It even occurs to him that Poseidon might restore his sight. A strong instinct, which I think the audience tends to share, informs Odysseus that Poseidon will do no such thing, and even Polyphemos abandons the idea, praying Poseidon instead that Odysseus not come home; or if it is fated that he shall, that he "come late and miserably, with the loss of all his comrades,/on a foreign ship, and find trouble in his house" (9.534–35). Here at last even the Kyklops completely accepts fate and the power of the gods. The divine pattern is made manifest to Kyklops, Odysseus, and audience alike. Odysseus's act was not only a satisfactory revenge but one planned by the gods, and for the Kyklops to realize this, it is absolutely required that Odysseus proclaim his name.

Fourth and finally, Odysseus justifies the blinding of the Kyklops in terms of human advancement. In the *Odyssey* the fear of the gods is the beginning of civilization—to judge, at least, from the traditional question, the counterpart of the one just cited, which the civilized sailor asks of the unknown shore.

> Are these people full of hubris, wild and without justice,
> or are they kind to strangers, and is their mind god-fearing?
> (9.175–76; cf. 6.120–21; 8.575–76; 13.201–2)

It was for no other reason than to "make trial" of the possibility of civilized human contact expressed in this question that Odysseus and his ship left the security and abundance of the island of goats to visit the Kyklopes across the way (9.174–76), and it was for no other reason that, against his men's advice, he chose to wait for Polyphemos to return to his cave (9.229). Of course, as he admits, it would have been "much more profitable" not to have done so in that particular case, but if the chance is not taken, what becomes of civilized enterprise and the growth of knowledge, useful in the first instance to those who may come that way in the future? Flight would have been "more profitable" because in fact Polyphemos turned out to embody precisely the description "full of hubris, wild and without justice"; but without remaining, no one could have been sure of this. Odysseus's spirit of enterprise gets him into trouble here; but without it, the episode suggests, humans would be condemned to live in brutish isolation.

"Brutish isolation" characterizes the Kyklopes from the moment we first hear of them.

> To the land of the Kyklopes, violent, innocent of laws,
> we came; leaving it all to the gods
> they put hand to no planting or plowing;
> their food grows unsown and uncultivated,
> wheat, barley, vines which produce
> grapes for their wine; Zeus's rain makes it grow for them.
> No meetings in council for them, no judgments or dooms;
> instead they dwell on the tops of the mountains
> in hollow caves, and each gives laws
> to his own wife and children, not heeding his fellows.
>
> (9.106–15)

Nature is good to the Kyklopes, but not because they are virtuous. Rather, the kindness of nature has deprived them of the stimulus to develop human institutions.

The island of goats provides a text for Odysseus to suggest what the Kyklopes might achieve with a little more sophistication. Odysseus tells how the island teems with game because no one ever goes there. It is crying out to be cultivated: there are no crops it could not bear. It has pasture, plowland, vineland, and a perfect harbor. Yet all is for naught.

> For the Kyklopes have no red-cheeked ships,
> no craftsmen among them, who could build
> ships with their rowing benches, all that is needful

> to reach the towns of the rest of the world, as is common—
> that men cross the sea in their ships to meet one another;
> craftsmen would have built them handsome buildings as well.
>
> (9.125–30)

If the Kyklopes had more contact with the rest of the world, it would be impossible for even Polyphemos to think the Kyklopes were stronger than the gods. Even he would know when to stop drinking the wine that brought his downfall. Even he would not have to learn the virtues of hospitality through the loss of his eye, nor need to hear Odysseus's words on the subject.

> Here, Kyklops, drink this wine to wash down that human flesh,
> so you may see how good was the vintage our ship held within it.
> I brought it to give you if you would take pity
> and send me home; but you are insane.
> Cruel host, how will anyone else come here again
> in all the world? What you did was not right. (9.347–52)

Ignorance of ships means ignorance of the world and ignorance of justice. Therefore it is fitting that knowledge of ships and shipbuilding should be associated with the means of Polyphemos's punishment. The pole from which the blazing billet is cut looks to Odysseus "as big as the mast of a twenty-oared black ship" (9.322). Odysseus and his four helpers twirl the billet in the Kyklops's eye in the same way that shipwrights drill a ship's timber with an auger (9.382–88). The Kyklops's eye sizzles with the same sound a smith produces when he dips an ax or adz in cold water to temper it (9.391–94). It was ax, adz, and auger that Kalypso lent Odysseus so that he might make the craft on which he left her (5.234–37, 246).

Here we have the final implication of Odysseus's blinding of the Kyklops. First and last, he got into trouble with Polyphemos because he showed nautical enterprise and the spirit of discovery. How valuable that attitude is, is shown throughout the episode by the Kyklops, who exemplifies the consequences of the lack of it. In Homer's world not to sail the sea is finally unthinkable. To sail inevitably exposes one to Poseidon's malice, but that is no reason to refrain. This, then, is the beginning of an explanation of Zeus's answer to Athena in book 1. Odysseus incurs divine hostility not from recklessness or impiety but from attempting to make contact with the rest of the world. This may lead to shipwreck and to the Trojan War, but it also leads to greater human development and greater fame.

Odysseus's adventure with the Kyklops has strong affinities with folktale: with one folktale and two unrelated folk motifs, to be exact, which all may be older than Homer (Glenn). In the first, a one-eyed giant shepherd holds the hero and his companions captive in a cave. He cooks and eats some of his prisoners and then goes to sleep. The hero then heats the spit on which his comrades were cooked and blinds the giant. In the morning, when the giant opens the door to let his sheep out of the cave, the hero escapes by crawling out on all fours covered with a sheepskin or underneath a living sheep. Once outside he taunts the giant, and the giant, pretending reconciliation, throws him a ring or other object of value. No sooner does the hero put it on or take it in his hand than it begins to cry out, "Here I am," and the hero must cut off his finger or fingers before he can get rid of it and escape. To this well-constructed story Homer has added the "nobody" trick and the motif of making the monster drunk, which are very ill attested as folktale. He has obviously made other changes also.

For these variations the explanations are not far to seek; in fact, the way in which Homer adapts traditional material to his own purposes is nowhere clearer than in this tale of Polyphemos. The giant's name, Much Fame, was very likely Homer's choice. It relates not to anything in the generic story itself but rather to Homer's use of the tale as a figure for winning identity. The addition of the nobody trick obviously contributes to the same end. In the supposedly parallel folk motif the trickster almost always, if not invariably, calls himself not Nobody but Myself. The demon who is the usual enemy in this case is foiled when the only accusation he can make is "Myself did it." Could there be a clearer indication than this that Odysseus's explicit achievement of identity in this adventure is the product of Homer's own mind rather than of the tradition?

The second folk motif imported into the basic story, making the shepherd drunk, also has nothing to do with the traditional giant shepherd but is due rather to Homer's conception of the Kyklops as the embodiment of the un-civilized. So too is the use of an olive log instead of a spit as the instrument of blinding. The absence of metal puts the Kyklops at a lower cultural level, as does Homer's modification of the story according to which he eats his victims raw. More important, the log, explicitly a section of a mastlike pole, conduces to the nautical theme; at the same time, the fact that it is of olive wood suggests Odysseus's undying fertility, as we shall see when we compare it to the olive thicket in which he awoke on Scherie and to the rooted olive stump which forms one corner of his and Penelope's bed.

It is obvious too why Homer discarded the sequel (if he knew it) involving the talking ring or other magical gift in favor of Odysseus's voluntary proclamation of his own role in exacting the gods' justice. He is not the man to fall for a pretty bauble like the ring; he is also not the man to skulk nameless for fear of Poseidon's hostility, any more than he can endure to remain hidden with Kalypso.

The conception of shepherd-as-ogre seems especially appropriate when one considers the lonely, primitive life of the Mediterranean summer sheepsteading. When a Greek audience hears of the solitary cannibal Polyphemos with his cave-cum-stockade and his sheep pens, cheeses, and milk pails, it must find the account both particularly familiar and particularly hair-raising. Above and beyond this, it is interesting to see how Homer makes his own use of the pastoral aspect. Odysseus and his companions do nothing so simple as to crawl forth draped in sheepskins. Instead, for his companions Odysseus ties sheep together in threes with willow withes, then himself twines his fingers and feet in the wool of the lead ram's back and hangs beneath his belly, waiting for dawn and release. All this is in the highest degree impractical. I hope nobody whom I hold in regard ever has the task of tying three sheep together with willow withes in a manner calculated to last more than five minutes, let alone to support a grown man beneath the middle sheep's stomach. Homer succeeds only moderately in gliding over this difficulty by not telling us that the men are tied underneath until somewhat later in the story. As for Odysseus, if his feet are hooked over the ram's back, as in the nature of things they must be, Polyphemos will inevitably discover him. Yet none of this is of the slightest consequence. We accept that Polyphemos may let his sheep out at any time; therefore Odysseus and his men must be constantly ready. We accept that Odysseus is incomparably more enduring than his men; therefore they need three sheep and a hammock apiece while he hangs beneath the leader of the flock by his own muscle; finally, we accept that everyone can hang on until dawn arrives. It all results in a marvelously suspenseful story, and I intend no witticism. Odysseus's preeminent ability to endure is probably not Homer's invention, but it took Homer to see, first, how that endurance suited the story of the Man of Pain who achieved the survival of his ghost and, second, how it could be shown to advantage in the story of the trickster and the one-eyed, man-eating shepherd.

The question arises, What is the relation of Homer's use of traditional folk motifs to what may be called his narrative thinking under the inspiration of the Muse? Certainty in such matters cannot be arrived at, but it is important to have as plausible a theory as possible. Ordinarily, folktale is marked off from serious reconstruction of the past by its unlimited tolerance for the fantastic. It would be hard, on the other hand, to draw a line between folktale and, say, sailors' yarns, of which there were surely a great number current in Homer's day, the Greek age of colonization. At the same time, much that sailors told was true, more was believed, and, particularly with increased knowledge of foreign parts, it all found its place in the fund of what was considered possible human experience. For Homer as he brooded on what happened to Odysseus during his ten years' absence after Troy's fall, the story of the one-eyed giant shepherd would float into his mind, tagged not "folktale" but simply "possible." One-eyed giant Kyklopes already existed in the epic tradition (cf. Hesiod *Theogony* 139–46), and Homer's sense of the appropriateness for Odysseus of an encounter with such a being surely overwhelmed the trivial difficulties of tying sheep together with withes or eluding Polyphemos's groping hands. The events of the folktale, or rather of Homer's revised version of it, were so appropriate that they must have happened to Odysseus, and therefore, guaranteed by the Muse, they did.

When Odysseus recounts the story to the Phaeacians, however, he has not yet achieved the survival of his ghost. On the one hand, his triumph was a great one: he successfully cast his name in the Kyklops's teeth, and he now knows that Poseidon will not kill him (5.341). When he rejoined the rest of his fleet, his men awarded him the ram in addition to his share of the booty, despite the loss of six men (9.550–51). The ram he promptly sacrificed to Zeus. Yet, as he relates it to the Phaeacians, the whole affair is clouded by hindsight.

> The ram on the beach
> to Zeus-of-the-Black-Clouds, son of Kronos, I sacrificed,
> and burned the thigh pieces; but he had no regard for my offering;
> he was pondering how all my ships with their beautiful benches
> would be lost, and my cherished companions.
>
> (9.551–55)

Therefore it may be with foreboding rather than elation, and a good deal less than convinced of the value of city sacking, in spite of Odysseus's conquest of the Kyklops, that both the Phaeacians and we ourselves approach the events of the tenth book.

Kirke

Kirke provides the climactic adventure of book 10, but the preceding shorter episodes involving Aiolos and the Laistrygonians are essential. With Aiolos Odysseus suffers a failure as great as his Kyklopean success, whereupon the Laistrygonians destroy all his ships except the one in which he himself is carried. In this state of deepest misfortune and discouragement, he confronts Kirke, overcomes her enchantments, and wins her love and tendance to such good effect that he and his men recover the courage and vigor with which they set out for Troy. Comparing this part of Odysseus's story with the events of book 9, Arete and the Phaeacians can learn what failure, as well as success, can mean to mortals less favored than they, and also what harm and what benefit the female dispenses as compared with the male. They can learn, too, by what right Odysseus is the leader of his men. Finally, the Kirke episode will introduce the Phaeacians, as well as Odysseus and his men, to the meaning of mortality.

In Homer's time following "the watery paths" of the sea gave great opportunity for daydreaming, whether one rowed or sailed before the wind, and many of Homer's images seem likely to have had their source in such fantasy as it came, via sailors' yarns, into poetry. It is easy to imagine, for example, how the sight of an island cave filled with seals suggested an image like that of the sea-god Proteus shepherding his seals (4.400–406, 411–13). Aiolos (Variable), King of the Winds, on his floating island is another such image of fantasy (10.1–4). For the winds to blow from different quarters, the island must be mobile (10.3), and its unbreakable bronze wall (10.4) is required to restrain the winds' force. At the same time, it would not be beyond the powers of a "friend of the gods" like Aiolos (10.2) to confine these same winds, all but the right one, in a leather bag and give it to Odysseus. How many sailors since the world began have dreamed of some such gift! Aiolos's incestuous sons and daughters (10.5–12) seem also to be creatures of fantasy, exhibiting as they do the structural simplicity Norman Austin (134) has noticed of twelve winds "married" to each other in the sense that each blows to its opposite quarter. In their perpetual round of feasting, song, sex, and sleep, they also serve in the poem as further comment on the sheltered life of the Phaeacians, to whom Odysseus is now telling his story in the same way he describes himself as having told it to Aiolos and his children (10.14–16). Phaeacian too in its suspension of the normal frustrations of seafaring is Aiolos's present to Odysseus of the bag confining the unfavorable winds.

Everyday reality and human weakness intervene at last in connection with this bag. Had Odysseus not fallen asleep and his men not opened it, he and his whole fleet of twelve ships would have come safe home to Ithaca without ever meeting the cannibal Laistrygonians; as things turned out, however, the bag of winds merely made it possible for Odysseus and his fellows to ruin themselves by a storm of their own rather than Poseidon's making, as Odysseus twice admits: "We were ruined by our own stupidity" and "Worn was my men's spirit by the woeful rowing/caused by our own fecklessness, since that was the end of our escort" (10.27, 78–79). The one thing that could make the disaster of losing Ithaca still harder for Odysseus to bear is his sense, here attested, that it was in part his own fault.

It is not completely obvious what Odysseus feels he should have done differently. He says that sleep overcame him because, throughout the voyage, he had minded his ship's sail himself, letting no one else touch the rope, in order to reach home as quickly as possible (10.28–33). Modern taste might suppose that he regrets not having put more trust in his men. On the other hand, their opening the bag of winds as soon as he goes to sleep suggests that trusting them would only have brought the disaster on earlier. It is more likely, and more in character, that he should blame himself for not holding out a few minutes longer.

> For nine days and nights we sailed without a break;
> on the tenth at last the land of our fathers came in sight;
> we could even see people lighting fires, so close we were.
> Then sweet sleep came over me in my weariness.
>
> (10.28–31)

It would not be surprising if, to the weary Odysseus, it should seem that nothing could go wrong now, or that this should be one of the very few times when he is mistaken. I am convinced that it is for this misjudgment that he includes himself in the stupidity and fecklessness just mentioned.

At all events, nothing else which Odysseus suffered, not even the loss of his fleet to the Laistrygonians, ever came so close to breaking his will to exist. As he tells it:

> They opened the bag, and all the winds rushed forth;
> the squall caught them at once and carried them out to sea,
> weeping, away from their fatherland. As for me,
> I woke, and debated within my perfect heart
> whether to leap from the ship and end it all in the sea,
> or silently to endure and remain among the living.
> I endured and I remained; muffling my head [*kalypsamenos*], I lay
> in the ship; and my fleet was borne by the wicked wind-squall
> back to Aiolos's isle, while my companions groaned.
>
> (10.47–55)

Subsequently, when Odysseus learned from Kirke that he had to visit Hades before he could steer for home, he tells us that his heart no longer desired to live and see the light of the sun (10.497–98); but that is not the same as contemplating actual suicide, as he does here. To wake, only to realize that he and his men had proved unequal to the homecoming that seemed assured, evidently convinced him that he had lost the favor of the gods after all. Lying in his ship with his head wrapped in his cloak, too discouraged even to groan, he does not look like a man who will "win his ghost." His men, perhaps, have some hope that Aiolos will repeat his assistance, but Odysseus seems to anticipate what Aiolos will in fact say when applied to a second time.

> Begone from this island at once, most reprehensible of all that live!
> Religion forbids that I favor and forward
> a man the happy gods hate.
> Begone, since you have come to be hated by the immortals.
>
> (10.72–75)

Evidently Odysseus does not need Aiolos to tell him that he is the unluckiest of men.

Odysseus's companions are not so perceptive. Actually, it is much more their fault than his that they lose Ithaca when it is within their grasp. Jealous of the rank and prestige which won their leader not only a much larger share of the Trojan booty but guest presents besides from foreign hosts like Aiolos, they open Aiolos's bag to see how much "gold and silver" it contains (10.38–45). As the squall sweeps them out to sea again, they are grief stricken, but they do not realize that they have effectively destroyed their leader's prestige, which a few minutes previously was bringing them all home. Even after Aiolos has named their captain an utter outcast, they do not get the point. Although their despair begins to match Odysseus's own at last, all he finds to say of them is the lines already quoted:

> Worn was my men's spirit by the woeful rowing
> caused by our own fecklessness, since that was the end of our escort.
>
> (10.78–79)

His men regret only that, by their own mistake, they must row their way home, whereas Odysseus has realized that he may in actual fact be the most god-hated man on earth.

In this way the Aiolos adventure makes the immediately ensuing defeat at the hands of the Laistrygonians as devastating as possible. We have seen how Odysseus's victory over the cannibal giant Polyphemos (Much Fame) is a paradigm for the winning of renown. When, on the contrary, Antiphates (Opposed to Fame) and his cannibal friends crush Odysseus's fleet under a barrage of boulders and spear his men like fish, all Odysseus can do is to cut his cable and run for it. Assuredly, he wins no glory this time. Nevertheless, he has already made the crucial decision for winning his ghost: even the terrible disappointment with the world and with himself which he sustains in the Aiolos affair cannot keep him from enduring and remaining. After that, for him the Laistrygonians are just more of the same. As though to emphasize this, the formula which concludes the episodes of Ismaros and the Kyklopes serves to end the tale of the Laistrygonians as well.

> From there we sailed on, grieved at heart,
> glad to escape death, missing precious companions.
> (9.62–63 = 9.565–66 = 10.133–34)

Daughter of Helios the Sun and the nymph Perse, whose name like Persephone's suggests death, sister of the wizard Aietes and inhabitant of Aiaia (Isle of Wails), Kirke (Hawk) is indeed a "dread goddess endowed with speech" (10.136). Yet as Odysseus and his men arrive at her island, they receive a sign of divine favor at last.

> At her shore we brought in our ship in silence,
> into a safe harbor, and a god was our guide. (10.140–41)

The silence is the silence of fear after what happened with the Laistrygonians, but the safe landing is propitious. Odysseus speaks of the same divine guidance into harbor at the beginning of the Kyklops adventure, with the addition that nobody saw or heard anything in the fog until the ships beached themselves (9.142–48). Indeed throughout his narrative Odysseus refers often to divine help. He tells how, on the island of the goats off the Kyklopes' coast, nymphs started the game for the hunters (9.154); how a god gave them good hunting (9.158); and, later, how he grimly imagined what revenge Athena might give him on the Kyklops (9.317). He remarks that the lot which selected the men who helped him blind Polyphemus fell fortunately (9.334) and that, although he himself did his best to encourage them (9.376–77), "divine agency" made his efforts succeed (9.381). Suspicion, or a god, made the Kyklops bring into the cave the sheep under which they later escaped (9.339). First and foremost, "Zeus and the other gods" punished the Kyklops (9.479), and in evident recognition of this fact, Odysseus sacrificed the Kyklops's ram to "Zeus, who is lord of all" (9.550–53). As we have seen, Odysseus complains that on this occasion his prayers were not heard and that instead Zeus was planning to destroy his ships and men (9.553–55), an event which we have just witnessed. Aiolos and the Laistrygonians certainly represent a run of bad luck. Nevertheless, on Kirke's island the bad luck is beginning to lift, however dread the goddess may turn out to be.

For two days Odysseus and his men lie in weariness and woe on Kirke's beach (10.142–43). On the third day Odysseus gets to his feet, takes spear and sword, and sets forth in search of human habitation and speech. He sees smoke, and we remember the smoke of the Kyklopes, observed across the water (9.167), and above all the smoke which led to contact with the Laistrygonians (10.99). Well may Odysseus pause to consider how, and whether, to make an approach (10.151–52). When he decides to return to the ship, give his men a meal, and send a delegation to discover what people they have come among (10.153–55), we are apt to be disappointed. The method of sending two men and a herald certainly did not work with the lotus-eaters or the Laistrygonians. Would it not be better for Odysseus to go himself? Is he perhaps afraid?

Only gradually does it become clear that Odysseus has made the right decision. "Giving his men a meal" turns out to imply re-creating from the beginning the capability of joint action which succeeded against Polyphemos. There is still food of a sort in the ship, but as though to bless Odysseus's decision, "some god" once more befriends him by sending in his way a magnificent stag (10.157–59). In his telling of it Odysseus presents the experience in full, even to the hot sun which caused the thirst which drove the stag to the river to drink. Aside from reinforcing the theme of surrender to impulse, which is so pronounced in this book, the reason for so detailed an account is that killing the stag is an instance of the predatory act, the opposite of lotus-eating, which signifies the Man of Pain. Odysseus even tells us how he made a rope of withes, tied the animal's feet together, put his arms through, and heaved the stag onto his back like a coat, "leaning on my spear, since there was no way on my shoulder/I could carry it with one hand, so huge was the creature" (10.170–71). Casting the stag down before his ship, he gently arouses his men one by one, whereupon "uncovering themselves" (*ek de kalyp-samenoi*, 10.179), they all gather around and admire his catch. The result is that we invest his inviting them to feast and return to life with all the feelings of a supremely successful hunt, recognizing as we do so how exactly suited such feelings are to overcome the despair caused by Aiolos and the Laistrygonians.

The feast of warriors reestablishes community, as it so often does in the *Iliad*; next day comes deliberation in formal assembly (10.183–88). Odysseus's speech is short.

> Hearken to my words, comrades, bad though our luck has been:
> friends, we know not where the dark is nor where the dawn,
> where the sun that shines for mortals goes beneath the earth
> nor where it comes up. We must decide at once
> whether any resource [*mētis*] remains. For my part, I think not:
> climbing a lookout among the crags I surveyed
> the island, wreathed about with endless sea.
> There it lay below me; in its midst
> I saw smoke through the thicket and the wood.
>
> (10.189–97)

What Odysseus means by "any resource" is clear to all: a way to get home without confronting those responsible for the smoke. There is no resource because Odysseus and his men are utterly lost and must inquire their way. To see where the sun rises, they have only to look, but where is that? Is Ithaca where the sun rises or, on the contrary, where it sets? They have seen their homeland only recently, but where did the winds they released from the bag take them from there? Where was Aiolos's floating island when they, and the winds, returned to it? The sleepless land of the Laistrygonians was at the world's end, where the sun never sets (10.82–86)—but which end? For all their renewed despair, his men must acknowledge that the peril must be confronted. Only Kirke can tell them where the sun rises or where it sets, or, in other words, how to get home.

How Odysseus's speech applies to the immediate problem of finding their way is clear enough, but his language sounds as though it meant something else as well. It sounds almost as though Odysseus and his men did not know what was bright and what was gloomy, what was hopeful and what was not; it even sounds as though their sense of good and evil might be reversed. Those who are tempted to read Homer's poem in something like the sense I have been reading it can realize how well this would fit a situation in which Odysseus has in effect undertaken to show the Phaeacians that the pain they have hitherto avoided has its advantages. As for the question "whether any resource remains," it is a nearly exact pun in Greek for "whether anybody will still be nobody," a pun we can scarcely miss, since Odysseus has so recently proved to Polyphemos that he was not Nobody after all. After the Laistrygonian disaster, proving that point may look less attractive than it ever did; nevertheless, we now see that it is absolutely necessary. If Odysseus and his men are to make their way home, they cannot remain anonymous: they must reveal themselves to the being or beings who cause the smoke to rise "through the thicket and the wood."

To make the approach, Odysseus devises an improvement on the familiar method we feared he would use: he divides his crew in two so that half of them may do the inquiring, while half are held in reserve. Far from shirking the danger, Odysseus himself takes as great a chance as anybody, since the active party is chosen by lot. In fact the division itself gives Odysseus's worthiness to rule, of which we spoke, explicit demonstration. Eurylochos, the leader of the group on whom the lot falls, provides the contrast which shows why Odysseus deserves to lead them all. Eurylochos is as wary as his captain, but he lacks Odysseus's ingrained sense that there are more important things than survival and so neither experiences life's higher joys himself nor leads others to them. We applaud when we discover that he has not followed the rest of his group into Kirke's house but withdraw our assent when he refuses to guide Odysseus to their rescue. He may well be right that Odysseus will only disappear with the others, and it makes a sort of sense to flee instead with those who remain, as Eurylochos urges; nevertheless, our instinct tells us that such concentration on survival at any price is too drab, that it would be infinitely better to die if necessary, trying to save the others. Life should mean more than survival, more than mere eating and drinking, and Odysseus taunts Eurylochos with this truth.

> Eurylochos, by all means stay right here on this spot,
> eating and drinking by the hollow black ship;
> as for me, I am going; I can't help it. (10.271–73)

We should remember that unreflective eating was the image chosen to characterize human failure in the poem's invocation. "Right here on this spot" (*autou tōid' eni khōrōi*) also has its barb. Eurylochos may as well stay here as anywhere, since with his attitude one place is as good as another. Without risk he will never get to Ithaca. Odysseus, on the contrary, feels driven to risk the rescue. What drives him he does not say, nor probably could we, but we feel it all the same. We can even feel that it is not too obscurely connected with the joy of bringing in a mighty stag to share with one's companions. The man who cheers his men by his predatory prowess is the kind of man who will risk pain to rescue them from peril, and he is also the kind most likely to succeed in doing so.

Odysseus's luck is now definitely in. For the first time in his narrative, he meets a major deity face to face. Hermes appears (not by chance, we may be sure) and gives Odysseus the magic herb, together with instructions, that makes him proof against Kirke's enchantments. Aside from indicating that heaven is by no means as unfriendly to him as Aiolos supposed, Hermes' intervention above and beyond all else serves notice that strength of mind like Odysseus's comes from the gods. To think otherwise is hubris, and Odysseus's account shows that he is far from making that error. Since Kirke is a goddess, her power is irresistible. No mortal, not even Odysseus, can withstand its full force. Only Hermes' herb, which "the gods call 'moly'" and is "hard for mortals to dig" (10.305–6), can render his mind "unseduceable" (*akēlētos*, 10.329) by her. Therefore when Odysseus's favorite kinsman Polites accepts without a second thought the invitation offered by a female whom they all have just heard singing at her weaving and leads Eurylochos's group into Kirke's hall, he is not to be regarded as imprudent but rather as simply human. We do not need to be told how attractive, as well as how innocent, such an invitation must sound to this band of battered sailors. The refreshment Kirke offers, a sort of thin porridge of cheese, barley, honey, and strong wine, would not sound so strange to Homer's contemporaries as it does to us. They would recognize it as the kind of restorative which Nestor's spear-bride provides for her master and the wounded Machaon in *Iliad* 11.638–41. It is therefore not at all surprising that Eurylochos's men, hungry as they are for both psychological and physical comfort, swallow down the mixture to the last drop, unaware of the drug Kirke has added to it. It is not their excessive greed that turns them to pigs but a power no one can resist without help from the gods, the craving for the kind of emotional and physical comfort and care which, consciously or subconsciously remembering our mothers, we tend to think of the female as uniquely providing.

Obviously this power can and does enslave. When it does, its victims become like those lions and wolves who once were men but now fawn about Kirke's door, "as dogs about their master home from the feast/fawn for the sake of his tidbit" (10.216–17). That Odysseus's men even so cannot help being frightened of these "lions and wolves" (10.219) only adds to our regret for the native ferocity the lions and wolves have lost. The condition of Odysseus's men as pigs is similar. Odysseus tells us that, behind the piggish head, voice, bristles, and form, human consciousness lingered (10.239–40). If, according to the well-known saying, inside every fat person there is a thin one trying to get out, so inside every female-dependent male there is a full human being trying to escape. The Kyklops ate Odysseus's men; Kirke fed them, but as surely, and perhaps even more horribly, robbed them of their proper selves. Once more we are reminded of unconsidered eating as the mark of human failure, with the added sense that not to fail is in the end a gift of the gods.

As Hermes showed Odysseus, there is not only an antidote to Kirke's drug but, when the gods grant it, a way to secure its benefits without succumbing to its harms. When Kirke strikes him with her wand, the previously instructed Odysseus draws his sword and leaps at her "as though burning to kill her" (10.322). With a great cry she slips under his weapon, seizes his knees in supplication, and begs to know who he could be, the first to withstand her enchantment, the first whose mind is unseduceable (10.329). He must be, now she realizes, Odysseus of the many shifts, who, Hermes has told her, would come here on his way back from Troy. Let him put up his sword and come to bed with her so that, mingling in love, they may become true friends. Flattering though this recognition and outward surrender may appear, Odysseus, warned by Hermes, keeps his head. Before they make love, he makes her swear that she intends him no harm. It seems right that the female who seduced Odysseus's crew by a bogus offer of love and care should really become interested in the man before her only when he shows himself both able to resist her gratifications and willing to kill her if necessary to preserve his men's identity and his own. The most interesting person is, after all, the one for whom some things are more important than survival, whether one's own survival or another's, or so Homer seems to say. The knowledge that Odysseus would kill her before surrendering his selfhood to her only further convinces Kirke of the value of that self. It does not matter that technically, being a goddess, Kirke need not fear for her life and that Odysseus has no hope of taking it; the point remains obvious and eloquent.

Although not one to quail in the presence of deity, as will become particularly plain in book 13, Odysseus has felt understandable trepidation (10.309,

313) at the prospect of obeying Hermes' instructions to swallow a goddess's drugs, threaten her with violence, and sleep with her after securing her oath not to "unman" him (10.341), a peril of which the changing into beasts seems but the outward sign. We may conclude, as noted before, that he is not hubristic, at the same time that we sense in him the courage needed to hold one's own in such a love. For that is what the two are entering upon. Feeling the value and the threat of Odysseus's fierce independence, Kirke suggests sleeping together, as we saw, so that they may "become true friends" (*pepoitho-men alleloisin*, 10.335). Odysseus implies that, even though she has transformed his men and attempted to unman him, he could feel kind toward her if she would swear she intends him no further evil (10.337–44). She swears, and while they make love, as a sign of further favor, Kirke's servant nymphs prepare for him a delicious meal. Then, when the lovemaking is over, they give him a warm bath and seat him at table. Lulled by the usual succession of formulas for serving a meal, we expect the normal outcome, that he now will eat, and it surprises us when Odysseus reports instead,

> [The stewardess] bade me eat, but my heart was not pleased;
> I sat with other thoughts, my heart brooding on evil.
>
> (10.373–74)

Here, again, is the Man of Pain. We are apt to have forgotten them, but Odysseus has remembered his men. It is like the end of book 23 of the *Iliad*, where the funeral games have served their announced purpose of making everyone forget Patroklos. The reader forgets also, until he is suddenly made aware that Achilles' grief has not been affected in the slightest. In the *Iliad* our minds behave like the generality of the characters in the poem and not like the hero, thus emphasizing the strength of his sorrow; similarly here in the *Odyssey* we tend to respond as Odysseus's men would respond and unreflectingly assent to the eating, emphasizing, by contrast, Odysseus's strength of mind. Odysseus's refusal to eat here is in fact the critical point in winning Kirke's love. After she restores his enchanted men and witnesses the happy tears shared by them and their captain, she feels pity (10.399), apparently for the first time in her existence. Before sleeping with him, she speaks of him as "Odysseus . . . of the many shifts" (*polutropos*, 10.330); but now that she has experienced the affection between him and his men, she gives him his full titles (10.401), "Zeus-sprung son of Laertes, ingenious Odysseus," and invites him to put up his ship and bring the rest of his men to her hall so that she may care for them as well, her heart evidently wholly set on entertaining them all.

When Odysseus returns to the ship to fetch the others, we see the degree to which their identity is bound to his. Their dependence on him is emphasized when in their happy weeping they are compared to calves, crowding about their mother cows and bawling when their mothers return from pasture (10.410–15). The image reminds us of the dependence of Kirke's victims on her, and if we compare the two dependencies, it may well occur to us that, whereas Odysseus is leading his men to where they have a chance of winning their ghosts, Kirke's effect has hitherto been the opposite. In fact Odysseus first states, and then quotes his men's own words to the same effect, that his return makes them feel as though they had already reached Ithaca (10.415–17, 419–20). He is their king there as he is their leader here, and to that extent wherever they are together they constitute Ithaca, or home. Ithaca, in turn, is the ground of the identity of each. It would seem to be something in the propriety of their relationship to him and of his to them, and of all to their home, that has already awakened love and pity in Kirke. We may well be reminded here of Odysseus's praise of home at the beginning of his tale.

To establish even more firmly Odysseus's right to the relationship just described, precisely here his leadership is again called into question. Eurylochos is still without faith. He thinks they yet may all be changed to pigs or wolves or lions and that returning to Kirke's dwelling would be

> like what the Kyklops did when our comrades entered
> his cave, and bold Odysseus followed them in.
> His recklessness destroyed them as it now does us.
>
> (10.435–37)

Is any reader of the poem surprised that, in response to this speech, Odysseus has it in mind to draw his sword and sweep Eurylochos's head from his shoulders, "even though he was a very close relative by marriage" (10.441)? The encounter with Kirke has indeed something in common with the encounter with the Kyklops—but both are victories, not defeats, as Eurylochos alone fails to understand. Odysseus's men save Eurylochos's life by suggesting that he be allowed to "guard the ship" (10.444) while Odysseus "leads" (10.445) the rest to the palace. Eurylochos finally follows along from fear and shame (10.448); but it would have been better if Odysseus had killed him. It is he who later persuades the others to eat the cattle of the Sun (12.339–52).

The need not to surrender thoughtlessly to impulse but rather, when necessary, to risk and endure exposure and pain has been prominent throughout the episode: Odysseus himself failed to stay awake long enough to profit from Aiolos's gift; he and his ship escaped when the others were lost because he alone preferred to anchor in an exposed position rather than to trust the trap of the Laistrygonians' bottlenecked, deceptively secure harbor (10.87–96); to learn their way home he and his men have "no resource" except to expose themselves to Kirke; when Ithacans disappear, they must be rescued if possible, and to rescue them Odysseus "in his nakedness" must risk emasculation in Kirke's embrace (10.301, 341). But as we have seen, Eurylochos does not understand any of this: unlike Odysseus, he does not know when to take a chance.

Contrary to Eurylochos's dire expectations, happiness follows the successfully assumed risk. A third joyous reunion of Odysseus and his men takes place when the two groups join at Kirke's palace, and this in turn inspires Kirke's warmest expression yet of favor and support.

> Zeus-sprung son of Laertes, ingenious Odysseus,
> rouse no more this swelling lamentation. I too know
> how much sorrow you suffered on the fishy sea,
> and how much hurt hostile strangers did you on the shore.
> Come, eat food, drink wine,
> until once more you gain that spirit in your breasts
> with which at the start you left the land of your fathers,
> rugged Ithaca. Now you are dried up, spiritless,
> no thought in your minds but hard voyaging. Never
> do you feel lighthearted, since indeed you have suffered much.
>
> (10.456–65)

It is not only ironic but significant that the joy of such an occasion expresses itself in tears and that, welcome as the tears are, Kirke seeks to replace them by a lightheartedness that forgets the sorrow of which the tearful joy is the function. This forgetting is necessary in order that her new friends may recover from ten years of war and two of wandering. Nevertheless, it is clear that these joyful tears hold more meaning than the gladness Kirke promises does and that the recovery of spirit has as its purpose the undergoing of further trials. As for Kirke herself, we see how Odysseus's way of dealing with her, inspired by Hermes, changes her from a goddess who unmans men to one who is happy to enhance them by her fostering care. I have no doubt that Homer is conveying here how important willingness to injure and suffer is for a proper relation between the sexes; how it is, in fact, the necessary complement of the restorative joys of home.

Kirke becomes, as it were, a lover of those who have an Ithaca, and this is fortunate for Odysseus and his friends, since getting there, as they discover, depends entirely on her directions. We must not expect these directions to add much to our knowledge of Homeric geography, however. Homer's Muse has more interesting things to tell than whether Aiaia physically lies east or west of Ithaca; things like, for example, that, truly to come home, one must have something on one's mind more important than eating. After a year of feasting by all hands, his men call Odysseus out of Kirke's apartments and say:

> What ails you? Think now of your fatherland
> if it is indeed your fate to come home alive
> to your strong-founded household and the land of your fathers.
> (10.472–74)

Has Odysseus forgotten Ithaca? Not if he is the man who won Kirke's respect. He never did think of his stomach first; it is his men who, only after a year, have gained enough spirit to think of home. We should notice, too, how aware they are that their fate depends on his. Odysseus has already received Kirke's promise to help them with their journey when the time comes (10.483–84), and no doubt he has been waiting for this moment as the sign that his men, too, are ready. He consents at once and, not without some tactful exaggeration both of his men's importunity and of their consideration for their hostess's feelings, breaks the news to Kirke.

Kirke is quite willing, but nevertheless her response reduces Odysseus to weeping and writhing on her couch: she informs him that, before going home, they must go to the underworld to consult the psukhē of the blind seer, Teiresias of Thebes. When we think about it, the appropriateness of this jolt to our expectations is not difficult to see. After a year of Kirke's lightheartedness, taking up the struggle again must seem very like going down to death. Again, if the encounter with her suggests that there are things more important than survival, that conception itself implies a look at life from beyond the grave. Odysseus would rather see himself dead after having tried to save his men than live forever not having done so. In similar fashion he and his men, however reluctantly, would now rather see themselves die trying to return to Ithaca than fail to make the attempt. Since she is the goddess who embodies for them the truth that survival is not the highest good (and here we may contrast Menelaos), Kirke is the one to introduce them to the way life looks from beyond the grave.

As if this were not enough, Homer suggests a second, and simpler, reason for the journey to the realm of Hades and Persephone. Teiresias, already famous in song and story long before Homer's time, in his very name seems to pose the riddle of Odysseus's suffering—the problem of evil. When Odysseus reported that his men's spirit was "worn . . . by the woeful rowing," he said in Greek,

> *teire*-to d'andrōn thumos hup' *eiresiēs* alegeinēs
> (*worn* was my men's spirit by *rowing* painful). (10.78)

Teiresias in the underworld ought most of all to be able to tell Odysseus and his friends the reason why their progress must yield so much pain.

I treat in the next chapter Kirke's instructions about how to reach the House of Hades and Persephone and what to do when they get there, remarking here only that a ram and a black ewe are needed for sacrifice. In the bustle of departing, Elpenor, the youngest and least capable of Odysseus's men, falls from Kirke's roof and breaks his neck, a victim of lack of reflection and surrender to impulse. We will see him again in the underworld. Odysseus understandably delays telling his men where they are actually going until the last moment, at which point, like him, they rise to the challenge despite their grief. At the moment of departure one further detail strikes Odysseus's attention.

> But as we were going to the swift ship and the beach of the sea,
> filled with woe and letting the warm tears fall,
> Kirke meantime set off and by the black ship
> tethered a ram and a black ewe,
> eluding us easily; who with his eyes could see a god
> passing here or there, unless the god willed? (10.569–74)

The Dead

It is hard to imagine a better introduction to Homer's book of the dead than the concluding image of the previous book: the miraculous appearance, safely tethered by his ship, of the ram and ewe Odysseus needs for sacrifice in the underworld. Realizing that this is Kirke's doing, Odysseus remarks on the inability of mortal eyes to perceive the comings and goings of a divinity who does not wish to be seen. Here we have perhaps first and foremost the poet's desire to prevent impertinent questions about where Odysseus got these animals when the time comes to offer them, but above and beyond that there is a titillating coalescence of the utterly practical and concrete with the finally inexplicable. The underworld is like that. Kirke informs Odysseus that Teiresias will tell him "the way, and the measures of the path,/and your return, how you shall go over the fishy sea" (10.539–40)—to Ithaca, we assume. Not so, or not only so; in the event Teiresias prophesies a further journey and the manner of Odysseus's own death. What Odysseus ultimately discovers in the underworld, we shall see, is not so much how to get to Ithaca as how to "win his ghost."

Kirke's further instructions combine the familiar with the finally mysterious in the same way. She answers Odysseus's question "Who will be my guide?/For Hades no one ever yet has reached by ship" (10.501–2) by replying, "Raise your mast, set your white sail,/and sit; the North Wind's breath will take you there" (10.506–7). Must not this be Virgil's (and Aristophanes') "Easy is the descent to Hell"? This is to be a real journey into the beyond, to be taken literally. Yet here already we find expressed the humorous or half-humorous tension between the sense in which it is easy to get to the underworld and the sense in which it is hard, the distinction between what we nowadays call the literal and the figurative modes of apprehension.

This double vision also suggests why we need not worry about the discrepancy which some feel between those passages which seem to speak of going "down" to the underworld (10.174, 560 [= 11.65]; 11.475, 625; 12.383) and the so-called normal Homeric view that Hades' house is beyond the stream of Ocean (10.508; 11.155–59). Surely Odysseus's question here to Kirke implies that going down to the underworld is normal and crossing Ocean to get there is not? He himself says that nobody has ever yet done it by ship. Homer and his characters think of the dead as being burned and then buried in a tomb heaped over with earth (1.239, 291; 3.258, 285; 4.584; 11.74–75; 24.32, 65–84; cf. *Iliad* 23.45, 126, 164–77, 245–48). Penelope therefore speaks of dying as going beneath the earth (20.81), and the dead are depicted as hidden in, or held by, the earth at least seven more times in the *Odyssey*. Even Antikleia in the underworld, who remarks that her son must have crossed many rivers, including Ocean, to get there (11.157–58), says, as Odysseus does to Elpenor, "How did you come *beneath* the dark air?" (11.57). The dead are in the dark, beneath the earth—but more, they are not even in this world, for were we to reopen their tombs and look for them, we would find only their bones. As Antikleia puts it, their ghosts (*psukhai*), all that is left of their real selves, have "flown away like a dream," (11.222; see Vermeule, chap. 1). To follow them out of this world, Odysseus must sail across its boundary, Ocean; furthermore, he must sail beyond the light of the sun, for it looks on the dead no longer, nor they on it. Hence he must reach the land of the Kimmerians, which "Helios never looks on with his rays" (11.15–16). When he has done so, he will find himself "down" in the House of Hades, as he himself regards it (11.164; 23.252).

Hades' house is "down" because the dead are buried "beneath the earth"; it is beyond Ocean and the sun's track because the psukhai of the dead have "flown away," out of this world which Ocean bounds and the sun looks on. For purposes of storytelling the two conceptions are harmonious, however inharmonious they may be from the point of view of practical action. If there is any difficulty about the geometry of this, we can infer that for Homer the world is spherical, but I do not think he or his audience bothered about it. For them, for purposes of description at least, the world of dreams and shades was contiguous with the waking one, but to ask whether horizontally or vertically contiguous would be as irrelevant as asking whether a thought comes to one from the east or the west. Again, as we did in the case of the "easy" way to the underworld, we come up against the difference between the Homeric attitude and our own toward the world of what for us are mental events. Our way of thinking perhaps distinguishes more clearly and consciously between that realm and the physical, but our appreciation tends to suffer in consequence as mental events become more and more a figment, something we willfully create rather than a part of our environment. We must never forget that for Homer a thought or a dream is just as real as smoke or a shadow, and they all exist in the same world.

If geometry really does not apply to Homer's world of the dead, why does Kirke specify a north wind as the one to take Odysseus there? Probably because, for an Aegean Homer, that was the wind to take you, as according to Nestor it did Menelaos, "into a sea so vast that not even the birds return/out of it in the same year, for it is great and terrible" (3.321–22). It will be remembered that Menelaos had been driven beyond Crete, and Nestor's description implies that some of Homer's audience at least did not realize that the Mediterranean was landlocked on the south. A traveled Greek's general feeling would be "land to the north and east and west, sea to the south." If he wanted to sail beyond the Ocean Stream, that would be the way to go. Second, though the land, too, might be unknown, it never seemed as indefinite, dangerous, and uncanny as the sea. Thus the southern sea is the place for the Hider, Kalypso, for the bulk of Odysseus's adventures (for he too was blown south), and above all for the way to the land of the dead.

Kirke's description of the scenery and topography of Hades' realm is equally appropriate. For Homer's audience and all who accept the world of the imagination, "the shelving shore and Persephone's groves,/the tall poplars, and willows which lose their fruit unripe" (10.509–10)—these as well as "Hades' dank dwelling" (10.512) are perfectly real and satisfactory. So too is the spot which Odysseus must seek out.

> There into Grief Flood flow Fireblast River
> and Wailing Stream, which comes from Loathing Water;
> a rock stands at the confluence of those two loud rivers;
> there, good hero, approach as close as you can. (10.513–16)

In Greek these waters are of course Acheron, Pyriphlegethon, Kokytos, and Styx, respectively, but we must not let too much familiarity with "mythology" dull our ears to what their names suggest and to their appropriateness in the land of the dead. Acheron must remind us of the *akhos* ("grief") we would feel when the *kōkutos* ("wailing") went up all around the corpse of a comrade as the "fire blazed" about it (*puri phlegethōn*; cf. *Iliad* 23.197 of the burning of Patroklos's pyre: *ophra tachista puri phlegethoiato nekroi*). Styx ("hate") will recall not so much the enmity we feel for our human enemies who killed the man whose corpse now lies on the pyre as it does the loathing and dread which disease, old age, and particularly corpses of the dead characteristically inspire, for such is the Homeric use of the related words *stugein* and *stugeros*. In short, the underworld landscape is marked by streams and lakes whose names and relationships reflect the feelings and actions of the living in the presence of death and the dead.

Pyriphlegethon and Kokytos we understand because of the meaning of their names, but "Erebos" and "the streams of the river" in the following passage are more difficult. Kirke tells Odysseus that he must turn the throat-cut sheep "toward Erebos, but turn away yourself/setting your heart on the streams of the river" (10.528–29). Kirke's instruction means, as similar ritual prescriptions to "turn away" probably also do, "Dissociate yourself from what is happening; do not let yourself flow away to the dead along with the sheep's blood. Keep your grip on life." Erebos then seems to be the "Dark Place," from which the dead will come, while "the river" is simply the one that separates the dead from the living, which Odysseus aims to recross, in this case the Ocean Stream (10.508).

In the *Iliad* Patroklos's ghost apparently speaks of the same stream when he tells Achilles that the other ghosts do not let him join them yet "beyond the river" (23.73). Patroklos's river, strictly speaking, separates not the living from the dead but dead Patroklos from the other dead. This is almost universally thought to be because he has not yet had his funeral. In that case the river would separate the buried from the unburied, but we shall see, when we come to discuss Elpenor's death, that Patroklos is excluded not so much because he is unburied as because Achilles treats him as though he were alive. This river in the *Iliad* is like the one in the *Odyssey* not only in what it separates but also in the vagueness of its location. Patroklos's ghost says,

> Bury me the quickest way you can; let me pass Hades' gates;
> the ghosts keep me afar, the images of those who have died,
> and do not let me join them yet beyond the river;
> instead I wander forlorn through Hades' wide-doored house.
> (*Iliad* 23.71–74)

Patroklos is across the river and outside the gates, and yet he is in "Hades' house." This should not trouble us. Part of the explanation is that "Hades' house" is the term for the whole underworld realm, but also the gates and the river stand in no particular spatial relation to each other; they merely keep Patroklos from the dead. This is no ordinary physical landscape. It obeys the rules of dreamland, not those of geometry, and in dreamland Patroklos's ghost, treated by Achilles as though it were the living man, cannot join the other dead beyond "the river" and inside Hades' gates, though all are together in Hades' house. I think, then, that we may conclude that this river of Patroklos's is the same one, separating the living and the dead, which Odysseus aims to recross. In both the *Iliad* and the *Odyssey*, the landscape of the underworld is real enough and makes sense even in its more puzzling features; but from our point of view it is a mental, not a physical, landscape, and consequently its geometry may from time to time grow fluid. Odysseus must "set his heart on the streams of the river" between the living and the dead, but we need not precisely locate or even name that river.

Kirke's picture of what Odysseus is to do in the underworld is as consistent and reasonable as her picture of its landscape. First, the idea that an occasional great hero or prophet might be singled out as able to impart his wisdom to the living after his death we may assume to have been a common one through the ages and around the globe. Doubtless it reflects actual visionary experiences which in themselves are real enough, even though we would regard them as psychological disturbances. Therefore we can easily imagine Homer's contemporaries assenting to the idea that a particular dead man might still be able to communicate with the living as Kirke says Teiresias is.

> To him even in death Persephone has given intelligence
> so that he alone has wisdom; the rest only flit as shadows.
>
> (10.494–95)

Given this situation, how are the living to communicate with such a prophet? First, by going as near as possible to where he is: this Odysseus will manage to do better than anyone ever has before; he will reach the confluence of the River of Fire and the River of Wailing. Second, he must attract the prophet's attention and win his favor. For this the prayers and the promised sacrifices (or holocausts), both to Teiresias on the spot and to the other dead after Odysseus goes home, the digging a pit, pouring the three libations about it and sprinkling barley over all, and finally the cutting the sheep's throats so that they bleed into the pit—all these seem reasonable. It is unlikely that Homer was the first to invent these ways of waking the dead, and certainly necromancy must have been practiced in early Greece, but as usual it makes no real difference to the poem whether Homer is inventing or reporting. Wherever the rites come from, they so obviously ought to work. That is why Homer put them in. Burnt offerings such as Odysseus promises may be thought of on occasion as going up to "heaven," but they also go wherever burnt bodies go, and that is evidently (in Homer) beneath the earth. Again, the dead so obviously ought to like liquid refreshment of the nature of Odysseus's libations, and such libations soak so nicely down to where the dead must be. (Let no geometrician object that, when he pours them, Odysseus is already "down" in the underworld.) Finally, if Teiresias is to come close enough for conversation face to face, an even choicer offering must be near at hand under Odysseus's eyes. This of course is the blood in the pit, "a cubit long and a cubit wide" (10.517); for Teiresias, even though he still has his intelligence and does not need the blood in order to speak, is after all dead and is attracted by the same things as the other shades. The pit, in the *Odyssey* at least, is quite simply the best means to contain the blood and attract the dead. A pot or similar vessel would lack the advantage of allowing some of the blood to soak down to the shades below and give them a foretaste of what awaited them in Odysseus's presence.

The blood is there to attract Teiresias, but fortunately for the poem and ultimately for Odysseus, whatever attracts Teiresias is going to attract the other shades too. Furthermore, the resulting disturbance will certainly come to the attention of the rulers of the underworld. Accordingly, Odysseus's men must propitiate Hades and Persephone by burning the bodies of the sheep in their honor (10.533–34), whereas Odysseus, in order to make sure of speaking with Teiresias, must sit holding his sword outstretched over the pit in order to keep the other ghosts back (10.535–37). Thus everything Kirke tells Odysseus to do makes perfect sense, given the problem of communicating with a ghost who has retained his faculties. Doubtless similar actions were performed more usually at certain famous tombs, like that of Amphiaraos between Athens and Thebes, and perhaps Homer had heard of them, but how much better if one were able, like Odysseus, to perform these rites in the underworld itself!

Odysseus's account of the actual adventure differs in detail from his account of Kirke's forecast of it. Furthermore, it differs in such a way that the one seems complementary to the other—evidence, I should say, that both belong together in the same *Odyssey*. First, note that, unlike Kirke, Odysseus says nothing of willows or poplars, of the low coast of Persephone's grove, or of Pyriphlegethon, Kokytos, and "the rock"; he simply says, "We went along the shore of Ocean until we came to the spot which Kirke indicated" (11.21–22). With characteristic sangfroid Odysseus, far from dwelling on the weird and picturesque aspects of the place, makes it seem comparatively ordinary.

> Our ships reached deep-flowing Ocean's outer boundary.
> There men called Kimmerians have their land and city,
> wrapped in perpetual cloud. Never does shining Helios
> look down upon them with his rays, neither
> when he goes forth into the starry heaven, nor

> when he turns back again out of the heavens to earth;
> hateful night overspreads the sad inhabitants. (11.13–19)

What takes Odysseus's eye is not the rivers of the dead but the fact that living humans have colonized even beyond the sun's track. Those who like to assail the reasonableness of this adventure from the point of view of the everyday world will note that Odysseus is about to perform many complicated actions, and to "see" and be "seen" many times—all in pitch-blackness. Yet this is not stupidity, of course, but the way the world of the dead must be. If the beginning of Odysseus's account is relatively matter-of-fact, that suits his by now familiar intrepidity. Besides, it is as well to dispel the atmosphere of dread for a little; it will be all the more effective when it returns.

The story continues with no less consequence. Odysseus goes about summoning the dead in nearly the same words that Kirke used in her directions. Presumably his heart is sufficiently set on the streams of the river, for though he is frightened at the coming of the dead, he does not lose his presence of mind and carries out the rest of Kirke's instructions. Still, there is no doubt that he, and we, have been through an awesome experience.

> To them, the tribes of the dead, with prayers and promises
> I made supplication. I slit the throats of the sheep
> into the pit; the blood flowed blue-black; and they came,
> the ghosts, out of Erebos, dead people who had left this life:
> young blooming women, stout lads, and old men who had suffered much,
> skittish girls whose hearts were new to sorrow,
> and many, many pierced by bronze-shod spears,
> men slain in battle, their bloody armor still on them.
> All these were moving back and forth about the pit
> with a tremendous din; pale fear seized me.
> Then I bade and spurred on my comrades
> to take the sheep which now lay slaughtered by the pitiless bronze
> and skin and burn them. (11.34–46)

Though we have for long been meditating this journey to the underworld, here for the first time both we and Odysseus are brought face to face with the full meaning of death. Merely to have the list begin "young blooming women, stout lads" is to make us feel in half a line the enormity of death's deprivation, while by the end of the list we have no doubt about what it is about death that we all unconsciously flee. Odysseus, we know, will eventually choose to die like any other mortal rather than to exist forever in Kalypso's embrace. We begin to see something of what it means so to choose.

Homer has confronted Odysseus with the fact of death. He has next to show us what happens when people die and what kind of memory they wish to leave behind them. As I noted in the previous chapter, one of Odysseus's men, Elpenor, in the hurry of departure and his own witlessness, has fallen off Kirke's roof and broken his neck. This gives Homer the opportunity to compare Odysseus's extremely abnormal descent to the shades with Elpenor's normal one. Expecting as we are the arrival of Teiresias, we probably have not remembered any better than Odysseus and his companions the comrade whom they were too preoccupied to bury (11.53–54). Odysseus weeps when he sees the young man's ghost and asks in pity,

> Elpenor, how did you come beneath the dark air?
> You got here more quickly on foot than I did in my black ship.
>
> (11.57–58)

Odysseus can speak to Elpenor without violating Kirke's instructions to let no ghost approach the blood before "learning from Teiresias" (10.536–37) because Elpenor shows no interest in the blood at all. Odysseus's asking how he came there suggests the poignancy of the difference between living and dying. It is like Kirke's implication that to get to Hades is not difficult but easy. Elpenor's speed of movement is both natural and touching: first of all, an "Elpenor" apart from the body exists, a psukhē which at death must have departed elsewhere with uncanny speed, since the living presence that was Elpenor ceased within moments to be visible in the dead body. It is nearly impossible not to feel that it still exists somewhere, and does it not, for example, reappear in dreams? When he broke his neck, then, "Elpenor" must have arrived almost instantaneously in the land of the dead—and yet he must have gone on foot, since the living Elpenor had no other means of transportation. Indeed, his passage through space is as mysterious as Kirke's was when she brought the sheep to the ship just before they sailed. Things are very different, Odysseus's question makes evident, once we die; with a strong feeling of that difference, we watch the scene between him and his dead companion.

> So the two of us, holding grisly converse
> sat, I on the one side holding my sword above the blood,
> while on the other side the likeness of my comrade spoke of many things.
>
> (11.81–83)

Elpenor wishes only to be buried. With considerable emphasis on what we have called the world of mental events, he begs Odysseus by the dear ones he has left behind, who "are not present" (11.66) except in memory, that, when Odysseus returns to Kirke's island, Odysseus will "remember" him (11.71). He continues,

When you go from there do not leave me unwept, unburied,
as you depart, lest I become for you a cause of the gods' wrath,
but burn me with such armor and weapons as I have;
heap me up a tomb on the beach of the gray sea,
the monument of an unhappy man, that even those to come may learn about me;
perform this for me, and fix on the tomb my oar
with which when still alive I rowed with my comrades.

(11.72–78)

Next to Thersites, Elpenor is the most unheroic person in Homeric epic. As indeed his fate suggests, he is "very young, not very bold in battle, and giddy minded" (10.552–53). Yet the evocation of his tomb "on the beach of the gray sea" with his oar fixed on top suddenly gives him significance. His rowing, performed with no little pain, becomes his epitaph. "I rowed with my comrades," his oar-topped tomb seems to say, and one does not doubt that "those to come" will find the statement eloquent. It would be a shame and a "cause of the gods' wrath" for his career not to receive this crown. It seems worth all the toil it cost—far preferable, for example, to an eternity of bliss with Kalypso, of which men to come certainly would not hear, or be much moved if they did. Elpenor asks that he receive a "monument for an unhappy man" (*sēma . . . andros dustēnoio*, 11.75–76), and Odysseus replies, "All this, O unhappy one, I shall do and perform" (11.80). In the address *ō dustēne*, elsewhere applied so often to Odysseus, we hear Elpenor's accolade, earned with the oar which will rise above his tomb. Elpenor has showed us both what it is like to die and that only in death is the meaning of our life made clear, a thought which will be familiar to Herodotos and Sophokles. As signs of this meaning, a funeral and especially a tomb are important, as for example Hektor too makes clear at *Iliad* 7.85–91).

Elpenor wants to be properly cremated and laid in a conspicuous tomb primarily so that he may be remembered, not so that he may "cross the river" and join the other dead. Though he is apt to lie unburied for some little time, we hear from him not a word of how he wanders and will wander disconsolate far from the other ghosts because of this. In fact he obviously is doing nothing of the sort. What then are we to make of Patroklos's complaint to Achilles in the *Iliad* that the other dead exclude him, and of the usual view that this is because he has not yet been cremated? We must look at that complaint again.

> You sleep, Achilles, and have ceased to regard me.
> You neglect me not as living, but as dead.
> Bury me the quickest way; let me pass Hades' gates.
> The ghosts keep me afar, the images of those who have died,
> and do not let me join them yet beyond the river;
> instead I wander forlorn through Hades' wide-doored house.
> Give me your hand, I beg; for not a second time
> shall I come out of Hades' house, once you grant me my due of fire.
> Not in life shall we sit by ourselves apart from our comrades
> and plan our plans, but the loathed death
> has swallowed me up, which was my lot from birth;
> you too, godlike Achilles, have it as your fate
> to die before the wall of the rich Trojans.
>
> (*Iliad* 23.69–81)

Patroklos goes on to ask that Achilles' bones be buried together with his when Achilles too comes to die, so that, even as they were brought up together, so they may be together in death.

Patroklos's ghost asks essentially two things: he asks to be buried, so that he may pass Hades' gates and cross the river. This is clear. But he also asks Achilles to give him the hand of farewell, on the grounds that he is dead and will not return to their living companionship ever again; on the contrary, Achilles is soon to join him in the companionship of death. So far, he says, Achilles has refused to recognize this fact: "You neglect me not as living, but as dead [*ou men meu zōontos akēdeis, alla thanontos*]" (*Iliad* 23.70).

Achilles seems to substantiate that complaint when, instead of giving the hand of farewell, he tries to embrace Patroklos and hold him, "even if only for a little" (*Iliad* 23.97). This of course is impossible, and the ghost flits gibbering beneath the earth (*Iliad* 23.101). Achilles concludes from this, with no little astonishment, that "even in Hades' house there is/a ghost and an image, but no consciousness [*phrenes*] in it at all" (*Iliad* 23.103–4). By "consciousness" Achilles means "living consciousness." Patroklos's ghost shows no interest in the slaughtering of captives and giving Hektor's body to the dogs, which Achilles has promised him and just reminded him of (*Iliad* 23.19–23), but Achilles carries out these promises even so, as though the dead Patroklos demanded it as the living might. This is what it is to treat Patroklos as though he were alive, not dead, and this is why an unburned Patroklos cannot cross the river and join the other dead, while an unburned Elpenor can.

The purpose of the funeral and the fire is to help the living get over their shock and grief and to enable them to treat the dead, however loved and glorious, as dead. Achilles himself knows this, for just before Patroklos's appearance he has said to Agamemnon,

> Let wood be brought, and all the things provided
> which a corpse should have as it goes beneath the murky gloom,
> so the weariless fire may burn this one
> the more quickly from our sight, and the people turn to their work.
>
> *(Iliad* 23.50–53)

The purpose of the funeral is to let people "turn to their work," but in Achilles' case, from what we have seen, there is every reason to fear that it will not be effective. Therefore Patroklos's ghost appears. For it to beg to be buried, as it does, at the very moment when Achilles is concerned with nothing else, is to make us wonder what is wrong with Achilles' conduct of the funeral, and once we have asked the question, the answer is not difficult to see. The ghost pleads with Achilles to say good-bye, but Achilles cannot do so. His attitude, his grief, and his rage remain unchanged.

We see the result at the beginning of *Iliad* 24; the pyre has finally burned to the ground, and in the games everyone else's mind has returned to normal. The book begins:

> The ceremony was over; the people scattered and went
> each to his own swift ship. They took thought for supper
> and the enjoyment of sweet sleep. But Achilles
> wept for his dear companion, remembering, nor did sleep
> take him, which subdues all, but he tossed this way and that,
> longing for Patroklos's manliness and his strong might,
> and all they had been through together, the hardships
> amid the wars of men and the passage of stormy seas.

I think we may say that the funeral has not burned Patroklos from Achilles' sight and that therefore Patroklos does not cross the river until Achilles restores Hektor's body to Priam. This view of the dead is after all completely consistent. Though their ghosts flit to "Hades' house" the moment they die, still, as long as

those above are unable to get over the sense of their living presence, they are
not yet among the dead, where it would seem they would desire to be. Even
Achilles, who we may well feel has suffered the ultimate bereavement, must
learn to say good-bye. His greatness, and the greatness of the *Iliad*, are revealed
in the scene where he eventually shows that he has done so.

Patroklos's wishes, then, are in no way inconsistent with Elpenor's. In
Patroklos's case the function of burial as a way of saying good-bye comes to the
fore, whereas with Elpenor that is not the problem. There is no question of
anyone's grief keeping his ghost among the living; on the contrary, his words to
Odysseus show how burial and a tomb, if they set the seal on a life of toil and
danger, can lend dignity to the memory of even the most insignificant of men.
"The weariness of rowing," execrated in life, beyond the tomb becomes full of
meaning. If this is true for Elpenor, how much more must it not be true for
Odysseus? Sub specie aeternitatis—that is, on a tombstone—the life of effort
looks better than a life of pleasure.

With Elpenor and his oar, Homer has prepared us for what should be the
climax of the adventure in the underworld, the words of Teiresias. In effect,
Teiresias predicts what we knew already, that Odysseus's woes will be many and
his chances of success will seem small. He underscores the problem that has
been with us ever since Athena posed it at the beginning of the poem: why do
even good men suffer?

Teiresias begins his prophecy,

> You seek homecoming sweet as honey, stout Odysseus;
> heaven [*theos*] will make it hard for you. (11.100–101)

He continues: if Odysseus can keep his men's and his own hands off the cattle
of the Sun, all may yet be well—but we in the audience have known ever since
the first nine lines of the poem that that is not to be. Instead, we ourselves have
been witnesses to Odysseus's attempt to get home "late, in evil case, with all his
comrades lost," just as the Kyklops threatened and Teiresias now reiterates
(11.114). If he gets there, we know he will find "trouble in his house"
(Teiresias's words), and we know what that trouble will be; but neither we nor
Teiresias know whether Odysseus will be able to take his revenge on the suitors.
If he can, Teiresias gives him this injunction:

> Go then, taking your well-shaped oar,
> until you come to those who do not know the sea,
> men who do not even put salt on their food,

who have never heard of ships, with their red-painted prows,
nor of shapely oars, which are what ships use for wings.
I will tell you the manifest sign of this; you cannot mistake it:
at whatever time another wayfarer falls in with you and says
it's a winnowing fan you are carrying upon your heroic shoulder,
there and then plant in the ground your well-shaped oar;
perform a splendid sacrifice to Poseidon the Lord,
a ram, a bull, and a boar, mounter of sows;
then go back home and make sacred hecatombs
to the immortal gods who hold broad heaven,
all of them in their proper turn. For you, your death will come
out of the sea, in the gentlest way, and slay you
stricken in a sleek old age. Your people about you
will be prosperous. This is the truth I tell you.

(11.121–37)

All this is the prophecy of "the way, and the measures of the path" which Odysseus has come to the underworld to hear. Appropriately enough, it concerns not only his course through the Mediterranean to Ithaca but his course through life up to and including his death. After all, a trip to the beyond should produce more than merely navigational information. None of Teiresias's predictions are certain; there are many if's. At the best, it is a hard fate; yet if Odysseus wins through it, the end will be good. After witnessing the example of Elpenor, we should not be too surprised that an oar will be associated with that good end, for in Elpenor's case we saw how, as the mark of a hard and adventurous, painful and paingiving career, an oar might proclaim the meaning of his life. Teiresias furthermore, if we may detect the weariness of rowing in the syllables of his name, may be expected to be especially aware of the significance of an oar. Odysseus, however, is to set his up not on his tomb but among those who do not even know what an oar is. We must inquire a little further into what this direction may intend to suggest.

Sailors notoriously hate the sea. They are forever proclaiming what a miserable life it is and assuring one and all that they would follow any other in preference if they had the chance. Indeed a type of joke has arisen among them in many places to the effect that they will travel inland with an oar on their shoulder, or with some other nautical implement, and will not settle down until they meet a person who mistakes it for something which has nothing to do with the sea. The human mind works in very much the same way at different times and in different places, and the story I have sketched is simple and obvious enough to have occurred over and over again independently. A version of it must have been current in Homer's time, for we can recognize it clearly enough, even though he has reversed its meaning for his own purposes. He has in fact raised it to a higher power. He has made the oar suggest not merely toiling on the sea but also that toil's reward; and he has made the inland journey not an escape from, but a celebration of, the struggle with Poseidon, named by Teiresias as well as Zeus as the source of Odysseus's pain (11.102–3). The emphasis on what the inlanders do not know and the salt which their food lacks shows us which way we are to understand all this; the inlanders, not the bearer of the oar, are the underprivileged ones. To begin with, their life lacks savor, and they do not know the meaning that Elpenor has shown us. Odysseus, by planting his oar and making that male-fertile sacrifice to Poseidon, will rebuke their stay-at-home comforts and refute the one-sided sailor's joke in the name of the paradox that pain can be more worth having than any pleasure. Then he can go home and sacrifice to "all the gods" in peace.

We should consider as well the likeness between what Teiresias tells Odysseus to do in the future and the effect he is presumably having in the present on the Phaeacians. His story told in their peaceful and painless midst is like an oar planted among those who "do not even put salt on their food." Furthermore, our own listening to Homer's *Odyssey* can be seen in the same light—if, that is, it establishes among us the paradox which Elpenor's and Odysseus's oars embody.

Teiresias charts not just the way home to Ithaca but Odysseus's whole career, including his death. Seen from beyond the grave in this way, it can be seen truly for the first time, like the career of Elpenor. In the underworld Odysseus contemplates what the possibilities of his life actually are by seeing what it can look like after he is dead. This "learning from Teiresias" is a matter of fundamental importance for a man who hopes to leave behind a significant image of himself, and it should come first, before any other contemplation whatsoever. Kirke's instructions "not to let the strengthless shapes of the dead approach the blood before learning from Teiresias" seem only reasonable, given the notion of a pit full of blood to which the dead in their multitudes are attracted. Now, as it turns out, her words are appropriate also to the singleness of purpose and concentration of mind, the strength not to be distracted by conflicting images, however powerful, which Odysseus must exhibit if he is to achieve his goal. He must "learn from Teiresias" not just the way to Ithaca but the way to winning his ghost.

With Teiresias's help Odysseus sees his life clearly and sees it whole, but this by itself is in no way sufficient to establish its value: that life, Odysseus learns next, has killed his mother. When he left Ithaca she was still alive, but in the underworld, even before Teiresias appears, he sees her ghost. Shaken though he is by pity, he is strong enough not to let her approach the blood before Teiresias does. Once he has heard the possibilities of his fate from Teiresias, however, the thought of his mother takes over.

> Teiresias, no doubt the gods themselves have ordained this.
> But tell me this other thing and explain it truly:
> here before my eyes is the ghost of my dead mother;
> she sits in silence near the blood and has not favored
> her own son with a glance or any spoken word.
> Tell me, lord, how she may recognize that I am he?
>
> $$(11.139-44)$$

Odysseus has chosen to hear his fate from Teiresias before giving his mother his full attention; nevertheless, once heard, that fate recedes into the background at the thought of his mother. As we shall see, she means a great deal to him indeed.

Teiresias replies that any ghost Odysseus admits to the blood will speak truth to him; those he does not admit will retire. As a result of Teiresias's words, we now have the impression of three kinds of ghost, or three levels of ghostly communication. Ghosts like Elpenor, with strong claims on the living, will, and obviously can, speak without drinking blood. Then there is Teiresias, who by special dispensation is still an independently functioning personality but has to be summoned and propitiated. Finally, the great mass which "flit as shadows," of which Odysseus's mother is one, are almost completely passive, analogous to the mental images we can call up and examine or not, as we choose. Odysseus can refuse to contemplate his mother's spirit, in which case it will not recognize him, will not speak to him, will have nothing to do with him, but will just remain one more possibility in a world of ghosts. What it does on its own, how it feels, and whether it converses with the other ghosts are matters not even considered at this point, for we are looking at the situation from Odysseus's point of view only. If, however, Odysseus decides to give the ghost his attention, then it will recognize him and may even tell him things he did not expect to hear. The whole emphasis is on Odysseus's control of the situation, not on the ghost's weakness. It is simply right and in accord with normal experience that in general the spirits of the departed should be able to communicate with the living only to the degree that the living choose to contemplate them.

For Odysseus the mechanism of choosing whether to contemplate individual dead people or not is the sword and the pit. By means of these he not only talks with his mother but explicitly sees to it that the heroines of old, whom he sees next, approach one at a time and not all together, just as we must do with mental images when we try to think straight. Once this mechanism is established, however, our consciousness of it withdraws further and further into the background, especially in the second section, when Odysseus has resumed his tale after the interruption, or intermezzo. The mechanism has fulfilled its purpose, which was to suggest the tension between the crowding of these ghostly impressions and the necessity of dealing with them one by one—which of course is much more often a mental necessity and a necessity of narrative, than it is a physical one. I have several times called attention to the fact that the underworld adventure in particular obeys the laws of mental more than of physical experience.

When we keep this distinction in mind, the varieties of behavior among the ghosts all seem appropriate. The heroines, selected and marshaled by the sword and blood, appear to come faster and faster until toward the end we experience them at the rate of three per line. Finally Odysseus says that he cannot tell or name all the ladies he saw; the night would be gone before that (11.328–30), and so he makes a pause.

The second half of Odysseus's account of his vision of the dead achieves an even greater crescendo, with a suggestion that even a mind as strong as his may be about to lose control. At first, matters proceed at a leisurely pace, and the pit and the sword come to the fore again: Agamemnon drinks the blood (11.390); Achilles, if we stop to ask, probably does so also (11.471). The other heroes who appeared accompanying the first two all converse with Odysseus (11.541–42) and, if we insist, must have partaken of the blood before they did so. Even Aias may have drunk, listened to Odysseus's words, and then departed in silence. But the tables are now turned; we now see Odysseus as attracted to the dead, instead of them as attracted to him. Odysseus pleads with Aias, but Aias stalks off, still angry over losing to Odysseus in the contest for the armor of Achilles. Aias thus becomes the first ghost who does not need to speak, whose actions alone proclaim his meaning, and at the same time we feel Odysseus's mind as it follows Aias back into Erebos, reaching out toward the dead instead of waiting for them to come to him. The sense of this impulse continues in Odysseus's next words.

Then, still, even though angry, he would have spoken with me, or I with him,
but in my breast the heart within me desired
to see the ghosts of the others who had died. (11.565–67)

Some may think that this makes an anticlimax of Aias's proud exit; but I think we ought to sense here the contrast between stiff-necked Aias, who through all eternity will not forget or put aside that one unfortunate incident, the award of the arms, and Odysseus, who can now wish that he had never won them (11.548). Odysseus's suggestion that, in spite of everything, Aias might eventually speak suggests that all things must change and grow dim, even Aias's wrath. For that very reason, however, Aias's wrath does not matter so very much now; better, thinks Odysseus, to see the other ghosts. This way of presenting things seems to me very Homeric indeed, and I would go as far as to think that it is out of the contrast suggested by this passage that Sophokles developed his tragedy. However that may be, Odysseus's mind, and ours, is now fixed on Erebos behind the pit, and in Erebos various shapes appear—Minos, Orion, and the rest, whose actions, like Aias's, convey their meaning without the use of words.

By now it should be unnecessary to point out that the new spatial problems involved are as little hindrance to our acceptance of what is going on as the fact that the pitch-darkness continues. Similarly when Heracles, the last ghost to appear and the climactic one, hails Odysseus with a fairly long speech, we ought not to worry about whether he has had his blood to drink, even though he speaks. Odysseus is having something very like a visionary experience: after hearing Heracles, he says that he "remained steadfast," willing to see even further apparitions (11.628–31); but the throng of ghosts closes in again, again with "a tremendous din" as it did at the first. Again fear seizes Odysseus, and he thinks how Persephone might send up the Gorgon's head to turn him to stone. Odysseus, at last, has had enough, and we can sympathize. What he has seen would strain any mind, and as the ghosts close in again and he thinks of the Gorgon's head, we can feel him losing control—the control that he exercised at first by means of the sword and the blood. The sword and the blood by now have served their turn, and it is best that only the general impression remain as he and his men return to their vessel. Taking the events in the underworld in this way, as they occur, we experience not a hodgepodge of inconsistent eschatology but a most persuasive externalization of a visionary experience. We shall find that not just part but all of it is relevant to Odysseus's winning of his own soul.

From his mother Odysseus learns first not how she died but how things are at home at this stage of his journey. His wife remains with his son and keeps his house; she weeps, but that is only natural. His son is still treated with respect. So far, things are better than he hoped, for the way he asks his question shows that he knows it is only a question of time before he is given up for lost and his privilege passes into the hands of some other family (11.175–76). He seems to expect also that his wife will marry again (11.179). On these points, now, he is reassured, but as regards his father and mother it is different: Laertes in his longing for his son has withdrawn almost completely into himself, caring neither to go to the city nor to keep up even the show of aristocratic life; he sleeps in the ashes in winter and in piles of leaves in summer. As for Antikleia herself, she died of pure tenderness for her absent son.

Odysseus's reaction to this shattering news is to try to embrace his mother so that he may at least share her grief (11.211–12), but even this is denied him. There is nothing there for him to touch. Is her ghost, then, some cruel deception? His mother tells him that she is real enough, but has no body to embrace.

> Alas, my child, unluckiest of all men,
> this ghost of mine is no deception from Persephone, daughter of Zeus;
> rather this is the way of mortals when they die.
> The tendons no longer hold the bones and flesh together;
> them the strong might of blazing fire
> subdues once the life leaves the white bones,
> while the ghost, like a dream, flies off and is gone.
>
> (11.216–22)

The body is burned (or rots) once the life leaves it, while the ghost speeds off to the underworld. That ghost is what Odysseus sees before him. Understanding this, Odysseus knows that his mother is forever beyond his grosser reach. If his absence from home has killed her, he can do nothing to change that now. She is dead, and that is that. When he has reached his own life's close, with luck he may be able to say, "I took Troy, I came home and punished the usurpers, I rewon my position, I leave my people prosperous"; but what is all this if he killed his own mother in doing so? He must now reconsider the meaning of his life in the light of this new fact.

We should note in passing that Odysseus's experience in the underworld parallels Menelaos's experience on the island of Pharos, especially in this matter of receiving crushing news. Menelaos, like Odysseus, needs instruction concerning "the way and the measures of the path,/and the homeward journey, how [he] shall go over the fishy sea" (4.389–90 = 10.539–40). He too is directed by a nymph to consult an unerring prophet. He too discovers not only how he may come home but the nature of his own passing from life. Above all, he hears news that makes his heart "no longer desire to live and see the light of the sun" (4.540); namely, that Aigisthos, with twenty men, slew Agamemnon

in ambush while Menelaos, as a result of going off on his own with Nestor
(4.488), was away in Egypt (4.90–92). Therefore he takes no joy in all the
wealth he has amassed (4.93). As it can be said of Odysseus that he is
responsible for his mother's death, so it can be said of Menelaos, that he is
responsible for Agamemnon's. He takes what comfort he can, and it seems to
be relatively little, from the fact that he will spend eternity in the Elysian fields.
Odysseus's consolation will be of another sort.

Antikleia is now a ghost, a psukhē. She is beyond Odysseus's reach as
Patroklos was beyond Achilles', but all is not necessarily in vain. Odysseus's
mother does not complain or recriminate; instead, hailing him as unfortunate
beyond all other men (11.216), she bids him seek the light of the upper world
as quickly as possible, having noted well "all this" in order that he may tell it to
his wife (11.223–24). As we consider what in particular Antikleia wishes
Odysseus to tell Penelope, we begin to see the possibility of good. What
remains for a woman after death? Odysseus can say to Penelope that, even
though the body decomposes, there is a ghost in the underworld. That ghost,
furthermore, is no longer subject to hazardous change, but rather, like Elpenor
and his mother, now definitely *is* what its story, now finished, proclaims it to
be. For example, it can be said of Antikleia that she died of longing for her
absent son. But is that all that can be said, and are we to regard it as glorious, or
the reverse? These questions lead naturally to the consideration of what is the
best and the worst that can be said of a woman after she is dead, and "all this" is
something which Penelope should find of vital interest. Once we know which
women look best beyond the grave, it may turn out that Antikleia's death was a
good one after all.

The list of heroines whom Odysseus contemplates next (11.225–332) seems
arranged to tell us at once what is the best and worst that can happen to a
woman. Though the list as such, "all who were wives and daughters of the
noblest" (11.227), reflects the masculine notion that a woman's chief glory is to
be descended from and married to and to produce great men, the centers of
interest seem to be particularly feminine ones: pride of birth, conception of
children, and the growth of children. Could a highborn lady dream of anything greater or more glorious than sleeping with a god? The list begins at once
with Tyro, "of noble lineage," descended from Salmoneus, whom Poseidon
"lay with in the estuary of the eddying river" (11.242) and who from this union
conceived twins, each of whom became a mighty king. She is followed by
Antiope, daughter of a river-god, who in Zeus had an even mightier lover than
Tyro did and whose resulting twins built the walls of Thebes. Alkmene, next,
was another whom Zeus loved, and she produced Heracles, the most worthy

son of all. Heracles' wife, Megara, on the other hand, introduces a more somber note if Homer is referring to her husband's madness and her death together with their children's at his hands. In any case we turn definitely from the most blessed of mothers to the most accursed with Epikaste (later Iokaste), who slept with her own son Oidipus. She hanged herself and left him to suffer "all that a mother's Furies bring to pass" (11.280). Such are the heights and depths that a woman's fate may attain.

Odysseus's attention is next directed to those whose beauty made them much sought after by mortal suitors. Surely this is a fate to be envied? Chloris's beauty won myriad bride gifts from Neleus, and she bore him Nestor, among others. Her daughter Pero, "that marvel among women,/whom all the dwellers-round courted" (11.287–88), was apparently even more beautiful. Her father, Neleus, made the price of her hand the lifting of Iphiklos's perilous cattle; failing in the attempt, a great prophet spent a year in close confinement for her sake. He was released at last, "and the will of Zeus was fulfilled" (11.297). There is a sinister ring to this story of fatal beauty, with its cryptic conclusion reminiscent of the first lines of the *Iliad*. We learn further on in the *Odyssey* (15.225–40) that the prophet avenged himself on Neleus once he had won the girl for his brother. In the context of such a story, it is quite possible that we should think of Helen, whom we already know from book 4 as the cause of ill to many men. Helen's mother, Leda, "the wife of Tyndareos" (11.298), appears next in the train of heroines and makes the association inevitable. We may well think of Klytaimnestra, Leda's other notorious daughter, too, since Odysseus has described the heroines as proclaiming their offspring to him each in turn (11.233–34). Therefore it is in the highest degree surprising that Leda says nothing of her famous daughter, begotten of Zeus. This silence is eloquent. At this point in the list, female beauty seems an ambiguous blessing at best, and so, on second thoughts, it seems appropriate that Leda bases her claim to consideration by posterity not on her daughters, one of them by Zeus, but on her mighty sons, Kastor and Polydeukes. They, though in this account explicitly begotten by a mortal (11.299), share one immortal life between them beneath the earth and in this are "honored like the gods" (11.304). Homer has achieved a climax here: those of lofty birth like Tyro and Antiope have slept with gods and produced mighty sons, and then there is Epikaste, who fell into incest unspeakable and left only shame to her son. There have been great and much-wooed beauties, but their beauty has led to sorrow more often than honor. The result is that Leda, who could boast both of sleeping in the arms of Zeus and of having produced the beauty of the age in her daughter Helen, prides herself instead on the semi-immortality of her sons sprung of a mortal father.

The emphasis has passed from sleeping with a god or the splendor of a woman's beauty to the quality of her offspring.

But maternal pride too must have its limits. Iphimedeia, who next appears, bore to Poseidon the twins Otos and Ephialtes, next to the handsomest, and certainly the biggest, children earth had ever seen; at nine years old they were nine fathoms tall (11.305–12). But the world cannot afford such exaggeration of a mother's hopes: the twins threatened to pile Ossa on Olympos and Pelion on Ossa in order to climb to heaven itself and war with the gods. This they would actually have done if they had reached their full growth, but Apollo killed them before the down grew thick on their cheeks (11.313–20). Here is bereavement indeed. If Leda, in spite of Helen and Klytaimnestra, is an example of successful motherhood through Kastor and Polydeukes and the limited immortality they won, Iphimedeia is an example of motherhood impossibly exaggerated and gone wrong.

The series concludes with the rapid thronging of spirits mentioned above. "Phaidra, Procris, and fair Ariadne" together give an impression of blighted love; they may also be women who never had children at all. Of the group "Maira, Clymene, and abhorred Eriphyle," though two are more or less obscure, the third at least leaves us with a sense of the wickedness of which a woman may be capable, and of the sort of psukhē such a woman achieves: Eriphyle, "who for precious gold betrayed her husband" (11.327), provides for the second part of the list the negative contrast which Epikaste did for the first. The general result is that the so-called Catalogue of Women takes its place in the *Odyssey* as a kind of survey of the possible fates of womankind, a survey motivated by the revelation that Odysseus was responsible for his mother's death. We gather from the survey that, whether Antikleia's fate is happy or the opposite, all rests with him. She will not be able to say as her final statement, "I slept with a god," but she can say, "I bore Odysseus." If, like Kastor and Polydeukes, he achieves a measure of immortality, it will not matter; it will instead be to his mother's credit, that in achieving it he indirectly caused her death. Antikleia died because of her son's absence (11.202–3). Her first question, after her initial surprise at seeing him here in the world of the dead, is to wonder that he has not even yet come home from Troy or seen his wife (11.160–62). In reply, Odysseus names Troy as the beginning of his own woe.

> I have not yet come near Achaia, nor yet on my own
> land set foot; instead I wander in constant grief
> since that day when first I followed splendid Agamemnon
> to Troy of the fair horses, that I might fight with the Trojans.
> (11.166–69)

Troy was the cause of all his woe. It brought his mother's death. Yet it also began to make his name immortal, the name whose echo we hear when he characterizes himself as "wandering in constant grief": *aien ekhōn alalēmai oïzdun.* "Odysseus" may yet win immortality—not in spite of, but rather because of, all the pain he has caused and suffered.

Final judgment of Antikleia's fate depends, then, on the answer to the question "What kind of a man is Odysseus?" When after telling of the ghosts of the heroines he offers to break off his story, his most distinguished listener, Arete, is prompted to ask that very question. Her own opinion of him, she implies, is extremely high. Odysseus in fact has won Arete's approval at last. We should remember that both Nausikaa and the disguised Athena have said that Odysseus's return depends on Arete's favor (6.313–15 = 7.75–77). Odysseus clasped her knees at his first appearance in the Phaeacians' midst, but she said nothing (7.154). Later she asked him who he was (7.238) but did not respond to his evasive answer. So far her only other words to him have been those in which she bade him lash his box full of gifts securely (8.443–45), evidently meaning that, in her opinion, he had had enough presents. Now, however, she has changed her mind.

> Phaeacians, *how does this man here seem to you*
> *in looks and stature and the mind and heart within him?*
> *He is my guest,* though we all share the honor of it.
> Therefore do not hasten to send him off, and do not stint
> your gifts to one so needy; you are rich,
> and by the gods' grace have much stored up at home. (11.336–41)

Arete at last has accepted Odysseus as her own particular guest, and she approves of him so much that she wishes to reopen the gift chest which she herself caused to be tight shut.

Concerning this approval two questions may arise. First, was it after all so necessary? The boat which is to take Odysseus home has already been launched and manned (8.48–56), and his chest of presents is already packed (8.438–48). Can Arete really stop him now, however she feels? Second, what is there in Odysseus's story to arouse this belated enthusiasm on Arete's part? As to the first question, Homer has encouraged us to feel that Arete's approval is still necessary. Odysseus has made supplication directly to her, and until this moment that supplication has not been answered. In spite of the ease with which he has won, first, the "love and pity" (6.327; cf. 7.226–27) and, then, after his wrath, the "affection, fear, and respect" of the other Phaeacians (8.21–

22; cf. 387–432), Arete has shown how little she shares these feelings both by her silence and by her grudging words about tying up the chest. Can the poet have made her utter these words for any other purpose than to show her lack of enthusiasm? We are made aware of this attitude in her just before Odysseus begins his tale, and if we remember also how influential Athena has said that she is among her own people (7.67–77), we may well feel that everything will depend on Odysseus's account of himself. If it is not to her liking, may not her grudging acquiescence in his escort turn to outright refusal? (In Odysseus's tale we have seen him incur such a refusal at the hands of Aiolos.) Arete, who "settles even men's quarrels" (7.74), might well disapprove of a man who sacks cities, as I suggested in my account of book 9. Therefore we ought not to feel, when Odysseus begins his tale, too confident that his safe return to Ithaca is assured.

The intermezzo relieves us of our fear that Arete may prevent Odysseus's return. His painful and violent career, far from antagonizing her, has won her to his side. She may well have felt that the sack of Ismaros was brutal, but having considered the alternative of the lotus-eaters and seen true brutality in the Kyklops, may she not have begun to change her mind? Having lived through, as we have, Odysseus's failures with Aiolos and the Laistrygonians and his success and joyous reunions on Kirke's island, must she not have come to admire and value him and his painful life as we do? If a woman can know no higher destiny than to be the mother of a child of immortal renown, as the vision of women in the underworld suggests, must not Arete feel that it was right after all for Odysseus to go to Troy, even though it killed Antikleia? Her response to what he has told of himself so far shows that she does.

As a result she preempts her husband's role in the matter of gift giving, as we have seen. Alkinoos therefore has to struggle for his self-respect. Arete may preempt his role in the matter of guest presents, but he at least will see to Odysseus's journey. In the words of the *Odyssey*'s usual formula for reestablishing male authority, he says,

> His departure shall be the men's affair,
> all of ours, and mine especially, since I rule this house.
> (11.352–53; cf. 1.358–59; 21.352–53)

It looks very much as though Odysseus's tale, with its emphasis on male dominance, particularly in the Kirke episode, has given Alkinoos the strength to assert himself against his powerful wife during the very time that she was being inspired with the admiration for Odysseus that ensured his return. In the reactions of Arete and Alkinoos in the intermezzo, at the structural center of Odysseus's tale, we see what a powerful effect his identity, as that tale presents it, can have. We may well recall how strongly Odysseus's image affects Telemachos and Penelope in the first book of the poem. Both these observations suggest how greatly one's psukhē, the image one leaves behind one in death, can matter.

To the suggestion that he postpone his departure by one day for the sake of further presents, Odysseus replies that, if his return were assured, he would be glad to stay a year for the sake of arriving "with fuller hand" (11.359). That way he would be "more respected and loved" by everybody when they saw him return to Ithaca (11.360–61). To us this may sound crass, but it should not. Gifts mattered in the *Iliad*, too. The *Odyssey* recognizes as well as we do that some gains may be ignoble (8.161–64), but the gifts in question here are exactly what Odysseus says they are: marks of affection and esteem. Waiting for them will not involve "forgetting Ithaca" and abandoning his goal, even temporarily, but instead will enhance his return, as he says. Homer is not being unaccountably careless in the characterization of his hero here or introducing a note discordant to his theme of homecoming but rather showing us that Odysseus's return means more than simply getting to Ithaca as quickly as possible. We have already seen in the case of Nestor what that sort of return amounts to. Here, then, are two purposes served by the intermezzo: we see Arete convinced at last of Odysseus's worth, and we see in what light the gifts he is in the process of winning—"more than those he won at Troy," Zeus has promised (5.36–40)—are to be regarded. Alkinoos answers Arete's question about Odysseus's looks, stature, mind, and heart as follows:

> Odysseus, as we look upon you, you seem in no way
> to be a deceiver and dishonest, like so many
> the black earth lavishly breeds and feeds,
> stringing lies together, no one can tell from where;
> your speech is clothed in seemliness; your mind within is sound;
> you told your tale as wisely as a bard,
> the woes of all the Argives and your own. (11.363–69)

It is like Alkinoos and the Phaeacians generally to be more impressed by the telling of Odysseus's deeds than by the doing of them, but we may suppose that Arete responds more deeply.

Continuing his tale, Odysseus relates how he admitted Agamemnon's ghost to the blood (11.390). Here begins, in response to Alkinoos's desire to learn about the heroes of Troy, a kind of review of the fates of men, parallel to the comparison of women's fates afforded by the parade of heroines just before the intermezzo. As Homer portrays it, Agamemnon's fate is the "most piteous" that could happen to anyone (11.412)—not tragedy, but pure pathos. From the moment his ghost appears stretching feeble arms to Odysseus (11.390–94), like Odysseus we probably feel intense pity, but no terror and not even very much respect. (For all that, in the tradition Agamemnon's is evidently the reversal of fortune par excellence until Sophokles portrayed Oidipus's even greater one; there is much of Aeschylus's *Agamemnon* here in embryo.) Homer's Agamemnon is purely an example of simple trust betrayed: he and his men were slaughtered about the full tables and the mixing bowl (11.419), he like an ox at the manger (11.411), they like boars at a wedding (11.413–15); all this happened where he had thought to be welcomed with joy (11.430–32), and to feast. He paints himself tossing in his death throes on the sword, stretching out vain hands (as he has but now to Odysseus) to Klytaimnestra, who turns away and will not even close his eyes or tie up his mouth, now going slack in death (11.423–26). Almost naively he shows his love for Kassandra in that, even as he died, her death cry was most piteous to him (11.421). Odysseus politely blames Zeus for the woe that comes to the sons of Atreus through the treachery of women (11.436–39), but Agamemnon himself draws the moral: do not trust even your wife too much (11.441–43). Agamemnon is frankly envious of the homecoming he foresees for Odysseus, the opposite of his own (11.444, 450–53). As a result we cannot help feeling not only that Odysseus, for all his woe, will be happier than Agamemnon—Athena has made this point already at 3.232–35—but that he is the better man. Everything we know about him so far suggests that he is not the sort to be caught so unsuspectingly. In this way, Agamemnon's ghost explicitly illumines Odysseus's eventual fate by showing us its opposite.

A positive measure of that fate is provided by the next ghost to appear, Achilles, attended by Patroklos, Antilochos, and Aias. Odysseus compares Achilles' fate with his own and says that it must have been the happiest that ever was or will be (11.483), for he was honored like the gods while living and in death is a great one among the dead. Not so, Achilles says, for Odysseus is still alive, and life in the lowest station of all is preferable to being dead. This carries conviction and puts Odysseus's sorrows in yet another light; in this respect the meanest man can carry off the palm from the greatest of the heroes, and Odysseus is certainly happier than he. Furthermore, Odysseus wins Achilles' respect and amazement for his hardihood in coming down among the dead alive (11.473–76), and it adds to our sense of Odysseus's superiority that he is able to make Achilles happy by telling him of the prowess of his son Neoptolemos (11.538–40).

In another way too, in their concern for those they have left behind, Agamemnon and Achilles add to our sense of Odysseus's achievement. We have seen how Achilles was affected by a good report of Neoptolemos; Agamemnon too yearned for news of Orestes, and Achilles would give anything to be able to protect his father, Peleus, in his old age (11.494–503). We may hope both from Teiresias's prophecy and from the general course of the story that Odysseus will be able to fulfill during his lifetime the dreams of happiness of both these dead men: the indications are that he will get home to free his father from oppression and to see his son not only behaving as a hero should, like Neoptolemos, but engaged in the vindication of his father's honor, like Orestes. Odysseus is beginning to look, in prospect at least, like the happiest of men.

We can see Agamemnon and Achilles, then, not only as obvious old friends for Odysseus to visit but as types of the worst and best that a man may expect in death. The poem shows Odysseus conversing with Patroklos and Antilochos also (11.468, 541–42) but does not tell us what was said, since the main point—Odysseus's superiority to these perished heroes—has been made. This conversation serves rather to contrast with Aias's silence, caused by his anger that Odysseus and not he won the prize of valor at Troy. But what purpose does this famous episode serve? As must be evident from what has been said above, I do not think that Aias comes off best here. Certainly we are reminded that, after all, Odysseus won, and surely the judgment is meant to be a fair one, since Athena and the Trojans made it (11.547). Odysseus regrets his victory not because of a bad conscience but because it was not worth Aias's suicide (11.548–51). On the other hand, we are told twice in a short space that Aias was fairest and best after Achilles (11.469–70, 550–51). We have no doubt that he could beat Odysseus in a duel, that he was better looking, and that, by the simpler standards of heroic virtue, he would have been considered the better man. In short, the scene makes us compare the obvious hero with that much more complex and, after all, valuable being which is Odysseus. Greatness is something more than physical prowess. Aias was the greater warrior, but Odysseus took Troy. Aias died for an honor which Odysseus would give up to have Aias still alive. Aias can never forget that he was defeated, whereas Odysseus rises above defeat and victory alike. Certainly the *Odyssey* contemplates that Odysseus's fate will be the happier one of the two and his stature greater—despite his notorious life of pain.

In book 11, in the middle of the hero's own tale, Homer continues to define

Odysseus by contrasting him with Agamemnon, Achilles, and Aias. He ends the book by comparing him to Heracles. In between he broadens the field of comparison by a more schematic, more mythical series of images than he has yet given us. Agamemnon, Achilles, and Aias come from the tradition. So evidently do Minos, Orion, Tityos, Tantalos, and Sisyphos (all of whom Odysseus now "sees"), for it would be hard indeed to believe that the Greeks did not people their underworld, as soon as they had one, with something more than the "strengthless heads" of the ordinary dead. If we allow Hades, Persephone, and the special vitality of Teiresias, then there is no reason why we may not have these more "mythical" figures as well. As usual, Homer has chosen them because they seemed right. Minos sits in judgment, the hunter Orion with his club pursues his quarry as in life, and Tityos suffers vastly, two vultures tearing at his liver, for an act of irresponsible and senseless violence, the rape of Leto.

If Homer could see in the juxtaposition of Agamemnon and Achilles the contrast of the worst and best of deaths, we may be allowed to find in these three figures the moral range of divine and human activity as it has been suggested by the poem so far. Minos applies the rules of right and wrong (11.569), the same ones we have come to know in the story of the Kyklops; Orion embodies the predatory life that we have come to associate with Odysseus and to find justified in his adventures; whereas Tityos is immensely punished for the *Odyssey*'s typical crime—the reckless violence exhibited by figures as various as Aigisthos, who killed Agamemnon, though he knew it would be fatal to himself; the Phaeacian Euryalos, who could not resist taunting the sacrosanct stranger Odysseus; and the Kyklops, who thought he was mightier than Zeus. We have seen indeed that a main concern of the poem is to distinguish between the violence that is inevitable and even desirable among men and the violence that is senseless and violates *themis*, "the rules." Tityos's crime is recounted that we may know what to think of his punishment and his pain, but the crimes of the other two sufferers whom Odysseus beholds, Tantalos and Sisyphos, are not told. Their pains bear a different relationship to our theme, embodying as they do in the one case the frustration of appetite and in the other the frustration of effort. From Tityos's pain, which we both see as punishment and feel as an analogue of desire, we pass to these pains of frustration, deprivation, and toil, so typical of our human lot and so marked a feature of Odysseus's career. This indeed is the sort of evil which Athena has called upon Zeus to explain in the case of Odysseus.

In the ghost of Herakles, who last appears, a sort of answer to Athena's question in book 1 is forthcoming. His salutation of Odysseus is even more honorific than the similar ones made by Agamemnon (11.405) and Achilles (11.473) and surely makes up for Aias's silence; yet it is framed in terms of pain.

> Zeus-sprung son of Laertes, ingenious Odysseus,
> alas! for surely you pursue the same evil lot
> as I had to bear above in the sunlight.
> Zeus son of Kronos was my own father, but pain [oïzdun]
> I had in abundance; to a far inferior man
> I was bound, and he set me hard tasks.
> Once he sent me down here to steal hell's watchdog,
> thinking there could be no task harder than that one.
> I brought that dog out of Hades and made him my prize;
> Hermes was my protector and gray-eyed Athena. (11.617–26)

Odysseus is like Herakles in his sufferings, even in their seeming injustice, as Herakles says. He is like Herakles also in that he has braved the underworld. Again, if he confronts the world with the aspect of hostility, so does Heracles.

> About him the dead clamored like screaming birds,
> scattering in all directions; and he like black night,
> with bow unsheathed and arrow on string,
> glaring terribly seemed ever about to shoot.
> The baldric encircling his breast was horrible,
> a golden shield-strap, in which were wrought marvelous figures,
> bears and wild boars and lions with shining eyes,
> battles and fights and violent deaths and killings of men.
> No such artwork as that, or any other,
> may the man who made that shield-strap ever again create!
> (11.605–14)

But this is only Herakles' seeming (eidōlon); his reality (autos) dwells in bliss with the immortals (11.602–4). Does not this sound like the double aspect of Odysseus's own pain and hostility? We have seen his hostility flower with balm and solace once before, with Kirke, and now book 11 seems to have been telling us throughout that Odysseus's lot, so ill seeming on the surface, looks from beyond the grave like the most enviable fate of all. Herakles' toils, with all their pain given and received, will never be forgotten, and neither, it seems, will Odysseus's if he succeeds. If Herakles descended into the abyss and brought away a prize from the very gates of Hades' house, may it not be that Odysseus will match Herakles in that too? The fifth line of the *Odyssey* speaks of him as "winning his ghost." If his toils end, as Teiresias suggests, in homecoming, revenge, reunion, and the reassertion of all he holds valuable, if time succeeds neither then nor later in blotting his image out, may we not say that he has planted his oar and "won his ghost" in a survival far outshining any merely physical immortality which Kalypso could offer?

Helios

After the dark of the underworld, Odysseus's tale brings us to the dawn of a new day—chronologically, emotionally, and even geographically.

> Now when our ship had left the streams of the Ocean River,
> and come back to the billows of the far-traveled sea
> and the Aiaian island, where early-born dawn
> has her house and dancing grounds, and the sun rises,
> arriving, we beached our ship on the sand
> and ourselves disembarked at the water's edge.
> There we lay down to sleep until splendid dawn should come.
> Now when early-born dawn with her rosy fingers appeared . . .
>
> (12.1–8)

The new day is marked by new knowledge, and the new knowledge is that Kirke's island is literally the island of the dawn. Odysseus and his men had gone to see Kirke, it will be remembered, because they did not know

> where the dark is, nor where the dawn,
> nor where the sun which shines for mortals goes beneath the earth,
> nor where he rises. (10.190–92)

Now they do.

It contributes to the atmosphere of wakened hope and fresh beginnings that Aiaia (whose name echoes a Greek cry of woe) is where the sun rises and not in the west, as up to now we have probably more or less subconsciously assumed it to be. Aiaia has seemed to be west of Ithaca because it is the second landfall after Aiolia, from where the west wind brought Odysseus to Ithaca in nine days (10.25–29). But as befits the home of the winds, Aiolia is a floating island

(10.3), and when "all the winds" (10.47) loosed from the bag blow Odysseus's fleet back there, it may be anywhere. After the discouragement of that catastrophe and the Laistrygonian terror which follows it, Odysseus has no idea whether he is east or west, just as he says. Therefore when, after the underworld adventure, we are told that Aiaia is in the farthest east, we are free to realize that there is no reason why it should not be there as well as anywhere. This geographical fancywork shows us once more how physical and mental events coincide in Homer's poetry. The sunrise is the awakening which his characters feel and is, at the same time, firmly located in the physical world.

When Odysseus was first lost on Kirke's island, his whole aim was to find out where he was. Now that he knows where he is, this knowledge turns out to be just a pointer to something much more important. In the underworld he and his men have already experienced mortality. On their return Kirke hails them as "twice-dying, when other men die only once" (12.22). They now know what dying means and so should know how to live better than other men. When on their return even before meeting Kirke they bury Elpenor and heap his mound, raising his oar on its top (12.8–15), Odysseus and his men should know, if anyone does, how to win their ghosts, the goal of the poem. They are in truth awakening in the dawn of a new possibility.

All three of the perils which Kirke now points out to them, the last dangers of their journey together, involve the knowledge of life and death which the underworld affords. The encounter with the Sirens demonstrates that, if life is not to be lost, it must be lived, not merely heard about; the adventure of the Planktai and Skylla and Charybdis shows that life, precious though it is, must even so be ruthlessly risked; finally, the cattle of the Sun, the adventure which Homer's invocation seems to nominate as the most crucial of all, shows how much, in order to win one's ghost, life must be valued.

The Sirens at first glance seem to show the extreme case of the resisted impulse to pleasure. We know by now that Odysseus is not one to snatch unreflectingly at a proffered tidbit. It was not he who wanted to stay too long eating and drinking at Ismaros or who ate the lotus and forgot his goal; it was the Kyklops, not he, who drank the fatal wine of Maron; and, in perhaps the clearest instance of all, where his hungry, weary men fell unsuspecting into Kirke's trap, he avoided it by foreknowledge and conscious resistance. Therefore when we see him face to face with Agamemnon in the underworld we feel that Odysseus would never be caught as Agamemnon was, however much he longed for his homecoming feast. But the Sirens provide a seduction less physical than any yet and, for those who can hear it, more powerful. They can sing irresistibly of all that happened at Troy—indeed, of all that ever happens anywhere. Anyone as sensitive to heroic poetry as we have seen Odysseus to be might spend his whole life listening to them and never do anything else, and this in fact is what happens to those who come within range of the Sirens' voices. Their meadow is heaped with bones and rotting flesh and withered skin (12.45–46), all that is left of those who come ashore to listen (12.184–85). Even Odysseus, it is suggested, steadfast though he is, would have succumbed to this fatal pleasure if he had not, forewarned, plugged his men's ears with wax and made them lash him to the mast. As it is, they row him safely by, and the harder he signals to them to untie him, the more rope they apply. In this figure of Odysseus lashed to the mast, we find, on the one hand, complete assent to the delight offered; on the other, complete resistance to it. Could a more powerful example of the resisted impulse be imagined? The adventure of the Sirens therefore suits Odysseus as one who is supremely able to resist his own impulses, and it is already clear that this sort of strength will be needed to survive the ordeal of the cattle of the Sun.

By having himself lashed to the mast so that he may hear the Sirens, Odysseus has chosen to feel the temptation and be thwarted rather than not to feel it at all. This too is characteristic of him. Kirke described the purpose of her advice as follows:

> so that from pitiable looseness of intellect
> you shall not meet with any grief, or suffer either on land or sea.
> (12.26–27)

The simple and straightforward implication is that Odysseus and his men are to use forethought and willpower in order to avoid pain, but the sounds of Kirke's words themselves hint that there is more to it than that. "Meet with any grief, or suffer either on land or sea" is in the Greek *ē halos ē epi gēs algēsete pēma pathontes*. In sound *halos* and *gēs*, "sea" and "land," nearly make up *algēsete*, "meet with grief," as though grief were indeed inextricably implicated in the sea Odysseus sails and the land he walks on. The point would then be not so much to avoid pain as to turn it to one's advantage, not to suffer from the suffering. It seems in accord with this that Odysseus, though he can if he wishes plug his own ears with wax and pass the Sirens quite painlessly, chooses instead to endure having the pleasure of the Sirens' song snatched from him for the sake of experiencing it.

This choice in turn illumines less clear-cut ones of the same nature. When Odysseus, against his men's advice, chooses to wait and see whether the Kyklops will give him gifts, he is choosing to have the experience, though he is at least partially aware of the pain it may entail. Leaving Kalypso and leaving Kirke both involve accepting greater pain for the sake of the fuller experience of life which going home will bring. Another case in which we see Odysseus deliberately choose to suffer is his request that Demodokos sing of the fall of Troy, a song which he must know will bring him pain, for earlier he weeps to hear Demodokos sing a similar composition, the quarrel of Odysseus and Achilles. Odysseus prefers to relive his sorrows here, rather than not to have the experience at all. And finally, even though he has seen the underworld and heard Achilles' dispraise of it, he turns his back on immortality when Kalypso offers it; for the sake of going home he consents to go beneath the earth at the end of his days like anyone else. Just as he chooses to hear, and lose, the Sirens' song, so in leaving Kalypso he chooses to live, and then lose, his life in preference to not really living at all.

The adventure of the Sirens is especially appropriate both to Odysseus's positive and to his negative impulses, both to his thirst for experience and to his wariness. It points also to what is wrong with the Phaeacians and gives us perhaps our clearest indication of the reasons why Odysseus will not settle down and remain with Alkinoos, Arete, and Nausikaa. Though the Phaeacians seem to lead an ideal existence, in reality they do not live life; instead, they merely hear about it like the Sirens' victims. The Sirens tempt Odysseus with the claim that they know all that the Achaians and Trojans *suffered* at Troy (12.190), putting us in the presence of the familiar paradox that what is most painful to experience is most satisfying to hear about. Alkinoos makes of this paradox, as we have seen, an explanation for the sorrows of our mortal lot, suggesting that the gods are "weaving catastrophe into the pattern of events to make a song for future generations" (8.579–80, trans. Rieu). This is his answer to the problem of evil with which he endeavors to comfort Odysseus, who has just wept so bitterly to hear the song he himself requested, the song of Troy's fall (8.492–95, 521–31).

But Odysseus is evidently doing more than enjoying a tragic song; his reaction is different from the Phaeacians' (8.538, 542–43) precisely because he has lived through these events and they have not. This is what the simile of the weeping captive and Alkinoos's remark that Odysseus must have been close to one of the participants (8.581–85) imply. Thus the line between participant and nonparticipant is clearly drawn. Odysseus by asking for the song as a participant has chosen to live its events over again.

The same confrontation of participant and nonparticipant is continued as Odysseus tells his own tale to the Phaeacian audience. Again their reaction is pleasure (11.334), while his is pain (9.13); yet, as we watch him with his painful story complete the process which he began by his appeal to Nausikaa's pity, the process of building himself up from a naked castaway to one whom the Phaeacians "honor as a god" (Zeus's phrase at 5.36), we can feel sure that his painful participation in the ills of life is a thing of more value than Alkinoos's literary appreciation of them. Leading an ideal existence themselves, the Phaeacians have lost touch with life. We know that, to avoid conflict with the Kyklopes, they moved away "far from mankind" (6.8), and as they listen to Odysseus's tale, it is evident that they prefer to hear about life rather than to live it. Even their ships move like thoughts (7.36; 8.556–63) and the voyage home which they bestow upon Odysseus, "lapped in sleep," will be more like dream than waking (7.317–28).

"Near to the gods" (5.35), the Phaeacians are also insubstantial, and the penalty for this insubstantiality is that they will one day vanish and leave not a wrack behind. We know that Alkinoos has heard that, for such "painless escorting of strangers" as theirs (8.566), Poseidon will "smite their ship . . . and hide [*amphikalupsein*] their city under a mountain" (8.567–69). It seems that, without experience of pain, they may indeed be doomed to oblivion. Like the Phaeacians, those who succumb to the Sirens give up reality for a shadow; but Odysseus prefers to continue on his painful way, and so to live. The adventure of the Sirens communicates, above all else, the fact that life is more than any song; it is something to be lived, as well as heard about.

To leave the Sirens behind means to choose to participate rather than to be an onlooker; in short, to act. To act, however, means to incur risk. In the episode of the Planktai and Skylla and Charybdis, Odysseus is faced with two contrasting sorts of risk. Skylla and Charybdis present the antithesis between, on the one hand, accepting loss of the part for the sake of gaining the whole and, on the other, risking the whole on the chance of saving the part. The choice between Skylla and Charybdis is usually thought of as simply a choice between two evils.

> enthen gar Skullē, heterōthi de dia Kharubdis,
> On this side Skylla, and on that great Charybdis. (12.235)

But the situation which faces Odysseus in the poem is actually a good deal more complicated. After the Sirens, Kirke says, there are two routes he can take, and she will not tell him by which he will in fact go; he himself must take a hand in the decision (12.55–58). The choice to be made, however, is not between Skylla and Charybdis, as one might expect, but between the route by the Planktai, on the one hand (12.59–72), and by Skylla and Charybdis, on the other (12.73–110). Why this added alternative? Why were not Skylla and Charybdis sufficient?

One reason is that Jason and the Argo took the route by the Planktai. Kirke tells Odysseus explicitly that not even birds, not even the doves which bring ambrosia to Zeus, pass the Planktai unscathed; no ship has ever passed them except the Argo, *pasi melousa*, "about which everybody has heard," and even the Argo would speedily have been wrecked on the great rocks if Hera had not loved Jason (12.72). This is the way Homer presents the hero of what was evidently a contemporary poem which rivaled his own, intending to show his own hero to be the greater man.

Kirke sets up a choice, and the choice is between Jason's exploit and something peculiarly Odysseus's own. To do it Jason's way and succeed is to be the world's luckiest, or, in Homeric terms, most god-favored man. This is certainly a type of heroism, but most of us would probably admire more the man who is willing to accept suffering for the sake of a statistically better chance of success. This is what Skylla and Charybdis represent. Homer, however, makes us see more clearly than we usually do what a ruthless thing a calculated risk really is. If in dangerous situations any sizable number of men is involved in taking calculated risks over any length of time, some are going to get killed. Odysseus, for example, apparently considered the Trojan War worth the risking, yet he knew that some would not come back (18.259–60). Similarly, he knows that, unless he expects to be as fortunate as Jason, he must pass through Skylla and Charybdis and that the only way to pass through them without risking losing everything is to lose six men to Skylla (12.99–100, 109–10). Skylla's aspect itself suggests the inexorability of this prospect: the unscalable peak, ever shrouded in cloud; the cave "turned to the dark, and Erebos"; the small, terrible voice; the unforeseeable, unpreventable attack. Furthermore, this inevitability is knowledge he cannot share, for then his men, less strong minded than he, will drop their oars and ruin everything (12.223–25; cf. 203). He must deliberately, on his own responsibility, lead six men unforewarned to their deaths. Their deaths are inevitable, and yet Odysseus tries to prevent them. He tries to fight this "immortal evil . . . not to be fought with" (12.118–19). Here is one case where it seems eminently human and right not to "submit to the will of the gods" (12.117); it is also, as Kirke implies, particularly characteristic of Odysseus (12.116–17). We may observe that Odysseus's unrealistic behavior, if that is what it is, does not suffer the consequences which Kirke fears of losing six further men (12.121–23; cf. 245–61).

Yet what happens is bad enough. Odysseus hears the six as they are swung aloft in Skylla's jaws "call out [his] name for the last time" (12.248–50), but he cannot help them. Instead he must watch them being eaten alive at the door of Skylla's cave, shrieking, and stretching out their hands to him in agony (12.256–57). Odysseus calls this the most piteous sight of all his wanderings (12.258–59), and no wonder, for he, and we, are made to feel every detail of the suffering he himself has had to cause. The meaning of the name his men have called upon becomes nearly unbearable. It looks, then, as though, in contrasting Skylla and Charybdis with the Planktai, Homer were showing us the difference between a lucky stroke like Jason's and that really much more difficult and painful thing, the well-considered acceptance of a calculated risk.

There are indications that, in thus revising the traditional estimate of Jason, Homer has changed the shape of the adventure as well. He has probably even changed the name of the peril invoked. Kirke describes it thus:

> One way there are overarching rocks, and against them
> surges a great surf from blue-faced [kuanōpidos] Amphitrite;
> "Planktai" the blessed gods call them. (12.59–61)

What men call them, she does not say, but in later times it was well known, to Pindar (*Pythians* 4.208–10) and Euripides (*Medea* 2), for example, that Jason had rowed between two rocks, called alternatively *Kuaneai* (Blue) or *Symplēgades* (Clashing), which trundled together "faster," Pindar says, "than the ranks of the roaring winds" to catch whatever passed between. The association of "blue-faced" Amphitrite with the Planktai, on the one hand (12.60), and of a "blue" cloud with Skylla (12.74–75; see Stanford ad loc.), on the other, suggests that Homer has made his whole episode out of Jason's two clashing, blue rocks. Two rocks suggested to him a choice, and to carry out that idea the rocks had to be differentiated, one becoming the Planktai, the other Skylla's lair and the rock above Charybdis. Homer's rocks, unlike Jason's, clearly do not move. One sails past the Planktai rather than between (12.62, 69). Thus, instead of the fantastic "Clashers," Homer has given us in the Planktai something much more like the terror of an actual lee shore, heightened by "smoke" (12.202) and "blasts of fire" (12.68), perhaps suggested by the spume which one sees in heavy surf. He has changed the traditional picture of Jason's rocks, it would seem, and then tells us what the gods call the first of them the better to convince us that he knows more about them than the composer of the poem on the Argo. Their name Planktai is clearly intended to suggest that objects are "dashed" against them rather than that they themselves "wander."

We may still ask, however, why the contrast between Odysseus's heroism and Jason's would not be adequately expressed by a simple choice between the Planktai and Skylla? Why Charybdis? The answer is that, even though both the

Planktai and Charybdis are perils which involve the loss of everybody, they are not equivalent. To pass the Planktai requires a miracle, while at first sight, Charybdis is not a bad gamble. She only sucks the water down three times a day (12.105–6). Nevertheless, Kirke strongly advises Odysseus to choose Skylla, evidently believing that it is not worth taking even a relatively small chance of losing all hands. Thus what Kirke's advice amounts to in the end is, "Go ahead and do it Jason's way if you think the gods love you enough; but if you are like most people, it will be better to sacrifice some lives, hard as that is, than to risk all, even when the chances are fairly good. If all hands go down, *no* one wins his ghost."

The active, predatory life which he who would win his ghost must espouse inevitably presents choices like the one between Skylla and Charybdis, and to choose rightly (to choose Skylla) is a painful thing indeed, as we have seen. Yet accepting the certain loss of some lives in a dangerous enterprise is mitigated by not knowing which lives will be sacrificed and by the reasonably good chance any particular individual has of coming through unharmed. For Odysseus deliberately to take his ship past Skylla when there is a fair chance of surviving Charybdis unscathed is thus less cruel than it seems. Nor is it unfair. Odysseus is taking the same, or a greater, chance of dying than any of his men.

In spite of Kirke's advice to the contrary, Odysseus puts on his armor and, snatching up two spears, mounts the foredeck, hoping to fight Skylla when she appears. He says he forgot Kirke's warning not to oppose her (12.226–33). Indeed Kirke implied that to try it, though characteristic of Odysseus, would be mad, would be fighting the immortal gods (12.116–17). Nevertheless, this is one of Odysseus's greatest moments. Not only is he taking a greater chance than any of his men in the forlorn hope of warding off the danger, but in forgetting Kirke's words, he is showing a very humane inability to take a calculated risk in a calculating manner. All humane leaders share this double vision of Odysseus's. Though they know Skylla is "not to be fought with," that some lives will inevitably be lost, including very possibly their own, they put this knowledge behind them and behave as if it were not so. They make every effort to save every life. When Odysseus proposes the idea of fighting Skylla, Kirke answers that, by trying it, he is likely to lose twelve men instead of six and suggests that he resort to prayer instead. The sequel, however, indicates that Skylla conforms to the original calculation. Odysseus's defiance does neither good nor harm. Doubtless prayer would have been equally ineffective. Under the circumstances, is defiance not a nobler and more human response than either submission or prayer? At all events, it is characteristically Odyssean, as Kirke remarks.

More encouragingly still, book 12 shows us how such a loss as the loss to

Skylla may be turned to account in retrospect. In the affair of the Kyklops also, Odysseus lost six men. There too he had brought his men into danger through choosing to act rather than to avoid an encounter. He regrets the adventure himself (9.228), and he has had it very inappropriately cast in his teeth by Eurylochos (10.435–37), as we have seen. In book 12, however, when his men drop their oars at the sight of the Planktai, the memory of this very loss serves to put heart in them. Odysseus says to them:

> Friends, never yet have we been found unacquainted with trouble;
> this pass is no way worse than when the Kyklops
> cribbed us in his cave with all that force.
> No, even then, by my courage, will, and strategy
> we survived; this too I think we shall live to remember.
>
> (12.208–12)

The more desperate the peril was then, the more encouragement it affords now; if six men were lost, others were saved. That is the sort of reflection which gives men heart to face the greatest dangers. Homer's showing the affair of the Kyklops in such a light at such a time shows that he meant it to be not Odysseus's reproach but his glory. Death turns out to be not only something which men have to risk if they are to live fully but something which, risked and remembered, encourages. Kirke's advice to choose Skylla substantiates this conclusion.

The Sirens are an indication of the peril of taking life as a story, however full of death and derring-do; Skylla and Charybdis are an exercise in consciously risking death, both one's own and one's friends', to win a satisfactory home-coming. As such, both episodes appropriately follow Odysseus's and his men's experience of the underworld. Compared to hearing about life, living it is a painful, dangerous thing, but as seen from beyond the grave, infinitely to be preferred. Life with Kalypso or the Phaeacians or on the Sirens' meadow leaves little for the rest of the world to remember.

Even more than the underworld adventure, the adventures of the Sirens, Skylla and Charybdis, and the cattle of the Sun gain from Kirke's projecting them before they occur. Odysseus, she says, may hear the Sirens "if he wishes" (12.49); we are glad in the event to discover that he does. In the case of the Planktai and Skylla and Charybdis, she gives him a choice, and we are anxious to see how he will choose: can he really deliberately sacrifice six men, and what will it be like if he does? The most prepared-for adventure of all, however, is the cattle of the Sun: it is the only one mentioned in Homer's invocation of the

Muse; in the underworld Teiresias singles it out as the major peril of Odysseus's wanderings; and Kirke repeats Teiresias's warning with greater detail as the climax of her instructions for Odysseus's last three adventures. Those instructions, furthermore, begin with the words "now hearken/to what I say, and heaven itself will remind you" (12.37–38).

No reminding from on high takes place in the adventure of the Sirens; in the presence of Skylla and Charybdis there is even a forgetting of Kirke's advice, as we have seen; but when Odysseus and his men approach the island of the Sun's cows, the reminding at last takes place. Odysseus says:

> Then I, still at sea in my black ship,
> heard the lowing of the cows as they settled for the night,
> and the bleating of the sheep. And there fell into my mind the word
> of the blind prophet Teiresias
> and of Aiaian Kirke, who both prompted me strongly
> to avoid the island of Helios who gladdens men.
>
> (12.264–69)

Not very surprising, surely, that Odysseus, hearing the lowing of the cattle, should be reminded of what he had twice been told with the greatest emphasis. But Homer, through Kirke, has alerted us to look for divine prompting, and this is manifestly a case of it. As when Odysseus was inspired by Athena to hang on to the rock in the surf at Scherie, it is not the difficulty but the importance of the mental act that is stressed. The idea "fell into" Odysseus's mind. How disastrous if it had not! It is therefore god-sent: not that Odysseus is going to succeed in avoiding the island, but if he had not been aware of the peril and tried to combat it, Zeus might well have drowned him along with his men.

Homer's invocation of the Muse singles out the eating of the Sun's cows as the typical human failure against which Odysseus's success is to be gauged. Now we are to see what that failure consists in. It consists in preferring death to life. The failure begins, significantly enough, with the attempt to avoid pain and danger. Eurylochos—would that Odysseus had killed him, as he was tempted to on Kirke's island (10.438–42)—for the sake of greater comfort and safety persuades the crew to land, in spite of Odysseus's warning. They swear, of course, that they will not touch the flocks and herds; but when, stormbound, they feel the pressure of starvation, they change, and Homer makes us see this change as literally a choice of death over life. As Odysseus tells it, "As long as they had bread and good red wine/so long they spared the cows, wishing to stay alive" (12.327–28). However, "when all the food in the ship was spent" (12.329), Eurylochos began to talk of death.

> Hear my words, comrades, in pain though you be.
> All deaths are hateful to us poor mortals,
> but the saddest thing of all is to meet one's end from hunger.
>
> (12.340–42)

He urges them to kill some of the cows, ending his argument as follows: "I prefer to die at one gulp in the sea/than to waste away by inches in this desolate island" (12.350–51). "So spoke Eurylochos," Odysseus concludes, "and my comrades agreed" (12.352).

Because they are hungry, Odysseus's comrades are no longer minded to stay alive as long as possible, hoping to come home at all costs. Instead they are selecting one form of death as preferable to another. In spite of having seen the underworld and having heard Achilles praise the meanest life on earth above the highest rank in Hades' house, they have not the passionate will to live which is necessary if one is to win one's ghost; or if they have, they cannot keep it constant under the stress of pain or desire. This is why they fail where Odysseus succeeds, and why he cannot save them.

The crucial adventure of the cattle of the Sun shows us in the crew the weakness that keeps men from winning their ghosts. It also shows us in Odysseus the corresponding strength. Not only does he keep firm his will not to eat the forbidden cattle, but in the sequel, in one of the most powerful images of the poem, he clings "like a bat" for hours to the fig tree above Charybdis, refusing to drop and be comfortably engulfed (12.430–38). Unlike his men, Odysseus can hang on.

For a Greek, to live is to look on the light of the sun. After the book of the dead and the perennial darkness of the underworld, it is appropriate that this should be the book of Helios and the living, starting at the island of the Dawn. In this book, as we have seen, the central issue is life and death. When the crew in effect choose death over life by eating the Sun's cattle, the natural order is reversed, as Helios's threat to shine among the dead if the crew are not punished implies (12.382–83). If death is to be preferred to life, the sun may better shine below the earth than above. As for the crew, they are turning their backs on the light and scorning the days and nights of life above ground. Indeed it is difficult not to think of days and nights in connection with the cows and sheep of the sun. The fact that there are 350 of each is suggestive, and even more so the fact that their number remains constant.

> [Helios has] seven herds of cows, and seven fair flocks of sheep,
> each fifty; of them there is no increase,
> nor do they diminish ever. (12.129–31)

When we get to Helios's own words about them, the suggestion of days passing is irresistible:

> my cows, in which I
> delighted when I climbed the starry heaven,
> and again when back to earth from heaven I turned my way.
> (12.379–81)

At the very least, there is a strong suggestion of the periodicity of the sun and the succession of days and nights, which gives special flavor to the crew's mistake, the crucial mistake of the poem. What can be seen here is a sin against the light of the days of our lives, and a willful disrespect for the time that is given us. When we come to the half-line which recounts the end of the crew, "and the god took away their return" (12.419), it seems right to be reminded of the last lines of the invocation.

> For of their own witlessness they perished,
> fools! who killed and ate the cattle of the Sun
> Hyperion, and he took away the day of their return.
> (1.7–9)

Days are Helios's delight, and his province. Odysseus knows "where the sun that shines for mortals rises, and where it sets." The men of the crew, still incompletely aware of the preciousness of life, even after experiencing the underworld, finally do not.

It is Zeus, of course, with his thunderbolt, not Helios, who actually destroys them, but that is as it should be. In the *Odyssey*, unlike the *Iliad*, there is no resistance to Zeus's control. When gods wish to do anything important, they ask his permission, as Poseidon does, for example, in the next book when he wishes to blot out the Phaeacians. Zeus invariably lets them do as they wish, exhibiting surprise each time that they had not realized that this was what he intended all along (1.64–65; 5.22–24; 13.140–45). But Helios's complaint is different. As we have seen, he demands vengeance on the crew, threatening that otherwise he will shine among the dead. This time there is no amazement, none of the air of "how could you ask?" in Zeus's answer. Instead he grimly tells

Helios to go on shining for gods and living men and then, for the only time in the poem except at the very end, bestirs himself. That Zeus deals with the crew's offence in person indicates its seriousness. This offence, we should note once more, is not stealing, for both Odysseus and his grandfather steal cattle with impunity; it is not greed, in the ordinary sense, for these are starving men; it is not even precisely disobedience to the gods, for Odysseus in a manner disobeys them, as we saw in the case of Skylla. It is preferring death to discomfort, it is lack of steadfastness in the conviction of the preciousness of life, it is losing the passion to round out one's life and come home to Ithaca. Like Aigisthos, Zeus's example of human folly at the beginning of the poem, Odysseus's comrades indulge themselves even when they know it will prove fatal, *eidōs aipun olethron*, "in the consciousness of sheer ruin" (1.37).

One more small problem concerns us before we leave book 12. How is it that Hermes knows all about the wrath of Helios here (12.389–90), whereas he did not appear to in book 5? Here, I think, at last is a real inconsistency. Aiming at the utmost verisimilitude, and this in itself is interesting, Homer looked for a way in which Helios's words to Zeus could have been passed on to Odysseus. He found it in Hermes' conversation with Kalypso, of which he had already told us in book 5. It does not matter that, as that visit is actually related, there was no time for such an exchange, or that Hermes there seems to mention Athena rather than Helios as responsible for the loss of Odysseus's companions. Details like these Homer simply forgot once their usefulness was past.

Athena and Odysseus

So speeding lightly onward the ship clove the billows of the sea
carrying a man full of wisdom like the wisdom of the gods, a man
who had suffered much in his heart in the time before,
undergoing the wars of men and the painful sea waves—
but now at last he slept, forgetting all he had suffered.

$$(13.88–92)$$

With these words Homer sets Odysseus on his way from the Phaeacians' land to
Ithaca and pauses, as it were, to let us view him whole. Here, in words that
echo the poem's invocation, he is named knower, doer, and sufferer, with his
knowledge, action, and suffering in a sense complete. His return to Ithaca is
now certain, and he has proved to the full those qualities by which he won it.
Now he rests, and we see him almost sub specie aeternitatis as we did the dead
Elpenor, buried beneath his oar. Indeed, this sleep in which Odysseus is
lapped is described as "most like death" (13.80). Though we cannot let the
story end here, remembering as we do Telemachos's need, and Penelope's, and
the suitors' outrages, we can see that Odysseus has in a manner already won his
ghost.

He has certainly "won his ghost" with the Phaeacians, as Homer has just
pointed out. The process whereby, from being a miserable castaway, he grew to
be honored by them "like a god" has just reached its culmination in Alkinoos's
magnificent levy of thirteen bronze tripods and caldrons which completes the
Phaeacian gift giving (13.13–15). Zeus predicted that Odysseus would win
"bronze and gold and clothing in abundance" among the Phaeacians (5.38),
and now Alkinoos, after mentioning (13.10–12) the gold and clothing Odysseus has already obtained (8.443), duly provides the bronze (13.19) as prompted
by Arete (11.339–40). Arete even adds an extra cloak and tunic as a farewell
present (13.67). Here is the culmination of the process of winning his identity

with the Phaeacians which began when, naked and unknown, he sallied forth
from his thicket like a hungry lion to confront Nausikaa in the sixth book.

Best of all in this success story is the realization that, through the operation
of his powerful personality, Odysseus is now as good as safe at home. Alkinoos
responds to his tale as follows:

> Odysseus, since you have come to my house (bronze is its threshold,
> lofty its roof), I judge that you will come home
> without any further check, much though you have suffered.
>
> (13.4–6)

This bears out Poseidon's admission that Scherie was the fated end of Odysseus's trials (5.288–89), and it is natural to feel, by the time Odysseus has come
so far, that there is nothing more Poseidon can do to him; in fact we have seen
Poseidon's departure and heard his farewell:

> So now go on and suffer, straying over the waters,
> until you join a race of men cherished by Zeus.
> Not even so, I think, will you make light of your troubles.
>
> (5.377–79)

Whatever Odysseus has to suffer after Scherie will be at home, at the hands of
the suitors. He has survived the enmity of Poseidon.

To arrange for the Phaeacians' second donation, the one involving the
bronze tripods, Alkinoos asked for and got permission to postpone his guest's
departure for one day (11.350–61). On this day little happens, but this too has
its purpose. Odysseus's impatience to depart can now have time to gather
strength and provide the tension which will be released in the image with
which we began this chapter, of the ship speeding along as it carries him home.
In contrast to the day before, songs and tales are as nothing in contrast to the
reality of homecoming. Though Demodokos performs again, Odysseus's head
keeps turning away toward the westering sun, "in his urgency that it should set;
for truly he was passionate to depart" (13.30). Now follows the simile of the
plowman, who, faint with hunger and fatigue, also yearns for the sun to set so
that he may leave his work and go to his supper. The plowman's physical
weariness is compared to Odysseus's mental anguish, just as earlier Odysseus
implicitly compares his physical anguish as he clings to the fig tree above
Charybdis to the mental anguish of a judge weary of hearing cases all day long
in the marketplace (12.437–41). In both these cases physical and mental

weariness are sensed together to the great enhancement of both. But the greater the pain, the more welcome the relief. In the passage before us, the sun finally sets, the farewells are finally said, Odysseus goes aboard to sleep, and the ship speeds on her way. Such is the sensation of longing fulfilled, of rest after toil, with which the *Odyssey's* first half finds its end.

That "the star which most especially heralds the dawn" (13.93) should be shining as Odysseus approaches Ithaca in the Phaeacian ship is quite in Homer's manner. It lends to the start of the second half of the poem that air of hope and new beginnings which we have met before, for example, at the beginning of book 12, but with the difference that this time the start is earlier—before dawn, in fact—and hope is only a glimmer.

So much for the time of day. The landing place is introduced as follows:

> There is a certain harbor belonging to Phorkys, that old man of the sea,
> in the confines of Ithaca. In it two headlands,
> steep ones, fall abrupt to the water. (13.96–98)

For the appropriateness of this spot we may note first the security of the harbor itself, where boats can lie without even tying up (13.100). This fits the atmosphere of "safe home at last" which has been building ever since Alkinoos concluded that Odysseus's return was assured (13.4–6). At the same time, remembering not only what awaits Odysseus in Ithaca but also another similarly "safe" harbor on his travels, that of the Laistrygonians (10.93), we are invited yet again to regard security with a suspicious eye. The next feature mentioned, the olive tree at the head of the cove (13.102), not only serves eventually as a mark of recognition and a place to put Odysseus's wealth, but the tough, vital olive is also becoming a sort of banner or motto of Odysseus himself. We remember the olive in the thicket which sheltered him after his struggle in the sea off Scherie (5.477), and the olive trunk which blinded the Kyklops so that Odysseus might have a name.

Most remarkable of the features of Odysseus's landing place, however, is the cave of the nymphs. As local spirits embodying the beauty and mystery of certain particular spots on the earth's surface, nymphs are ideally suited to objectify love for one's native land. The Ithacan nymphs who live in this cave serve this function for Odysseus, and as the episode unfolds we see him greet them most touchingly. Their function, however, and that of the cave itself, goes beyond even this. They are expressly Naiads (13.104), the "dripping, flowing ones" who are associated with springs and other cool, shady, wet spots which delight the beholder and at the same time affect him with a sense of mystery. Odysseus's nymphs inhabit what is evidently a pretty (13.103) limestone cave, with its stalactites and stalagmites and ever-dropping water (13.105–9). From one point of view, that is all there is to be seen, but to Homer's imaginative eye it is evident that the stalagmites are the nymphs' bowls and jars, "in which the bees make honey" (13.106), and that the stalactites are their looms, "on which they weave their sea-purple garments, marvelous to behold" (13.108). No sensitive Greek of Homer's time could fail to recognize that nymphs lived here, though of course he could not see them, at least not usually. Odysseus is no exception. The instant Athena shows him the cave, he remembers and greets the maidens of his youth, "Naiad nymphs, daughters of Zeus, never did I think/to see you again" (13.356–57)—and with the eye of the imagination he does see them, though they are physically invisible, even in the story. The cave of the nymphs, then, is a place where the presence of divinity is especially evident.

As though to make the point unmistakable, Homer continues his account of the cave as follows:

> There are two entrances to it:
> the one to the north humans may pass; but
> the one to the south is for the gods. That way
> men do not enter, but only the immortals. (13.109–12)

From these words particularly we may conclude that, as he begins the second half of the poem, Homer wishes to emphasize both the separateness of the divine and the human and the idea that there are places where they intersect. This not only prepares well for Athena's entrance, soon to follow the description of the cave, but accentuates the numinous aspect of Odysseus's return. This last has been further indicated both by the more-than-natural impetus of the Phaeacians' ship, driven "half her length" on land (13.114), and by the statement that the Phaeacians came ashore "knowing the place before" (13.113), which seems in the context to refer to their ships' uncanny ability to make any landfall one names to them (8.560). With the Phaeacians Odysseus has been "near to the gods" (5.35; 7.199–206), and with Kalypso and Kirke he has actually associated with them. The underworld adventure too took him beyond the human realm. Now he is returning to the world of men. Thus it is all of a piece that, here at the beginning of the second half of the poem, Homer should call attention to the cave of the nymphs as a place where human and divine may merge. For example, even Odysseus's newfound wealth has its double aspect. With our own eyes we saw him win it from the Phaeacians.

Now we are told, somewhat unexpectedly, that he gained it "through great-hearted Athena" (13.121), as she herself will later remark (13.304–5), and we realize that this also is true. Accordingly, with the image of Phorkys's harbor and the cave of the nymphs before us, it is perhaps not too much to say that the interaction of the divine and human, or more simply, the ways in which a goddess may help a hero, have been announced as the topic of the thirteenth book.

Before going on with Odysseus's adventures, however, Homer gives us a last look at the Phaeacians. They came into the poem, at least in part, as the embodiment of an impossible dream: that navigation should be absolutely safe and without effort. Alkinoos, however, has heard a prophecy that, for this very "painless escorting of strangers," Poseidon will one day smite their ship and "bury" (*amphikalupsein*) their city beneath a mountain (8.569). By the time we have reached book 13, we can understand the appropriateness of this fate: the penalty for a painless existence seems indeed to be oblivion. Now that Odysseus has been safely deposited in Ithaca and the unreality of the Phaeacians in comparison with his reality has been fully demonstrated, it is time for the prophecy to be fulfilled. Painless sailing is only a dream. Odysseus's safe, dreamlike voyage during the last stage of his homecoming was an exception, a violation of the laws of nature, and such dreams do not accord with reality. Accordingly, Zeus gives Poseidon permission to bury the Phaeacians forever, later sentimental emendation of the passage to the contrary notwithstanding.

That a suitably shaped offshore rock was once a ship, now in some miraculous manner turned to stone, is an idea exceedingly likely to occur to any seagoing community, and there must have been in Homer's time hundreds of such stories current in the Mediterranean world. Homer took this motif and used it to mark the end of the Phaeacian dream. Poseidon goes to Scherie, awaits the returning ship, strikes it with his hand, and turns it to stone before the very eyes of the Phaeacian onlookers (13.159–69). The punishment fits the crime: the offending ship which once sped so proudly is motionless forever, and the finality of its petrification is a sufficient commentary on the hope of things ever becoming so easy again. Poseidon will not allow it. As for the rest of the prophecy, Homer breaks off the account before the Phaeacians are actually buried, but that they should be buried fits the situation. It suits Poseidon as god of earthquakes, and it is a peculiarly effective way of removing a fantasy from the everyday world to which Odysseus is now returning. All these appropriatenesses we can see in what may be called Poseidon's revenge, but certain problems remain.

First, why must the Phaeacians, his own children (13.130), suffer for

Poseidon's wrath against Odysseus (13.126)? All they have done is to pay the stranger his due of hospitality, and conventionally such action should bring reward, not punishment. Not to mention Nausikaa, must Alkinoos and Arete, from whom Odysseus has just parted with such good wishes for the future, all be buried under Poseidon's mountain? The answer is to be found in the words of Poseidon's complaint to Zeus. He complains of lack of respect, and we must realize that it is the Phaeacians, not Odysseus, who do not respect him. "I said he would come home having suffered much," Poseidon says in effect, "and now they have taken him home while he slept, and given him more wealth than he ever could have brought from Troy" (13.131–38). We recognize at once that both statements are true. Odysseus has suffered much; yet he has come home successfully and in comfort. Even if Poseidon understandably feels that the second statement rather tends to cancel the first, its validity is attested by Zeus's reply. Poseidon's honor, he says, is secure among the gods, for he is "preeminent in majesty and worth" (13.142). This is no exaggeration on Zeus's part. Poseidon's functions are fundamental to the universe, for there is certainly no fear that we will see the end of storms at sea or earthquakes, or that trouble in general will disappear. As for Poseidon's honor among men, Zeus continues, he can do whatever he pleases to those who dishonor him "out of the violence of their natures." This also makes sense, for of course storms and earthquakes are much more powerful than any mortal. All this is Poseidon's half of the truth and is an accurate description of the world as far as it goes.

On the other hand, as in Odysseus's case, people do succeed. This is the other side of the truth: Poseidon is not the only god there is, and for this reason Homer sees Poseidon both as deferring to Zeus's and fate's decree that Odysseus should reach home alive (13.132–33) and as asking permission before he acts against the Phaeacians. Success happens, in spite of hardship and pain. But will it go to men's heads? Actually, we realize that Poseidon need not worry about Odysseus. As he once hinted, Odysseus will never be able to make light of his troubles (5.379; cf. 5.290), nor is there any danger that he will take life as a song or appreciate insufficiently the reality of pain. It is the Phaeacians, privileged as Poseidon's children to pass the sea painlessly, who by that very fact are prevented from truly knowing or respecting him. For this they will receive their appropriate punishment by the will of Zeus. They do not belong in a world where Poseidon is "preeminent in majesty and worth," and so they will be blotted out.

A second problem: why is this episode left incomplete? As Homer tells it, we last see the Phaeacians sacrificing twelve bulls to Poseidon, hoping to avert the prophesied obliteration. As Stanford says in his note on 13.187, "Here we leave the good Phaeacians standing round their altar, their fate uncertain forever." Is this carelessness, or intended? Does Homer really mean us never to know what happened?

In one sense we probably do know what happened; literary prophecies of this nature generally do come true. Nevertheless it is just as well that we are not shown the actual burying of our friends Alkinoos, Arete, and Nausikaa. It would violate our sensibilities not so much by its seeming injustice as by making too sharp something that should be vague. Ever since Telemachos in the first book demonstrated his need to know definitely whether his father, Odysseus, was alive or dead, the poem has been impressing upon us the importance of having a definite, known fate up to and including death. That was in large part the point of the underworld adventure. We saw what dignity a known end lent to Elpenor, and Teiresias offered the same to Odysseus in telling him what his death could be. We saw that this mortality, which Odysseus deliberately chose, was preferable to Kalypso's immortality, consisting in an endless survival about which there was nothing to say. So here, not witnessing directly what happens to the Phaeacians, we feel less able to say anything about them. They can make no very strong impression on us because we can form no final judgment about them until we see how their story comes out. Actually, since they have resolved never again to carry strangers (13.180), they have in a manner buried themselves from the rest of the world, whether Poseidon lends a hand or not. In these ways Homer both leaves us unsure of what will become of the Phaeacians and makes us reasonably certain that we have seen the last of them. The result is to remove them from our regard as effectively as Poseidon's mountain could do, without the dignity of a definite end. And this is fitting: they were always too "happy" to be true.

Book 13 closes the first half of the *Odyssey* by bringing Odysseus safely home and disposing of the Phaeacians. It begins the second half by starting Odysseus out again at the bottom. Though he is home, he does not even know where he is.

> Thus making prayer to Poseidon their lord,
> the chiefs and councillors of the Phaeacian people
> stood about the altar. But noble Odysseus awoke
> from sleep in the land of his fathers and did not recognize it,
> being so long away. (13.185–89)

This is a marvelously dramatic conception, full of pathos and irony. It makes us feel as keenly as possible what Odysseus's homecoming means, by letting us experience both the fact and its negation at the same instant. It allows Odysseus himself, when he realizes the truth, to experience his homecoming not as the familiar achievement of the long expected but with the sudden impact of "the lost is found." It allows us too to compare Odysseus in the dark with Odysseus enlightened: there are few more gratifying reversals in the *Odyssey* than when the plaintive Odysseus who wrongly suspects the Phaeacians of treachery changes to the Odysseus who, having satisfied himself that he is home and that Athena is really on his side, feels a match for three hundred men.

The only disadvantage in this procedure is that it seems improbable that Odysseus would fail to recognize his own island, even after the vicissitudes of his twenty years abroad. Of this improbability, however, Homer has deftly made capital. We can imagine him, as he thought over what must have happened to the real Odysseus, concluding that he must have gone un-discovered until his revenge was in his grasp. As we saw in book 7, however, going undiscovered was for Homer peculiarly the gods' affair: "divine agency" must have concealed him in a cloud. This cloud, in turn, this once at least, can be made to serve a double function. If it is hard to see into, it must be hard to see out of, and thus can account for Odysseus's not knowing his own island. Accordingly Homer follows his statement that Odysseus did not know his native land with the words:

> For the goddess poured a mist about him,
> Pallas Athena, daughter of Zeus, both to conceal
> the man himself, and that she might tell him all,
> lest his wife and townsmen and friends should know him too soon,
> before the suitors paid for their crime in full.
> Therefore all seemed strange to Ithaca's king,
> the wandering footpaths, the sheltering harbors,
> the high-rising cliffs and the luxuriant trees. (13.189–96)

As he did with the Phaeacians, Odysseus must evidently start all over again from the bottom, with Ithaca as strange and unknown to him as he is to it. So Homer sets the stage for Athena to bring about the first great recognition scene of the *Odyssey*—Odysseus's recognition of his own land.

Furthermore, this will be the first occasion in the poem in which Athena appears to Odysseus openly, for until now she has feared the wrath of her brother Poseidon (6.328–31). Thus the scene also involves the mutual recognition of Odysseus and Athena. It transpires that, although Odysseus is utterly dependent on Athena for success and welcomes her aid as essential, he is at the same time absolutely independent of her as far as his own character and sense of himself are concerned.

The demonstration of this point begins with this very business of not recognizing Ithaca. There is no doubt that the gods can blind the keenest eye, when they will. Compared with the gods, men are helpless, and so, as we have said, Odysseus, counting his tripods and cursing the Phaeacians, is a sorry sight as he

> mourned for the land of his fathers,
> creeping along the beach of the loud-roaring sea,
> making lament. (13.219–21)

Once Athena appears, however, Odysseus immediately begins to look better, not because of her help, but in opposition to her. His independence is beginning to be established.

That Athena appears disguised as a handsome young princeling may serve to remind us of an important aspect of Homer's conception of the gods. This conception begins with the conviction that no man is master of his fate. For any human to succeed, or even to survive, the presence of good luck or the absence of bad luck is obviously necessary. In Homer the gods are felt as being responsible for this good and bad luck. Here in the thirteenth book, at the beginning of the recognition scene between Odysseus and Athena, it would be extremely lucky if Odysseus's first encounter in Ithaca should be with someone young enough not to have kown him and well bred enough to respond to a suppliant stranger with grace and decorum rather than panic and outcry. Therefore that is the way Athena appears. It does not matter that she later drops the disguise and these particular advantages are not made use of: she brings Odysseus good luck, and so her disguise is a lucky one.

We shall see, however, that there is more than luck to Odysseus's success and that he has something of his own to contribute. The mutual recognition between Odysseus and Athena takes place in two stages, the first ending as both drop their outward false identities, and the second after a more inward revelation. At the climax of the first stage, Athena in rueful admiration hails Odysseus with the epithets "Wretch, rogue, stuffed with guile" (13.293); in the second stage she is impelled to say that she can never abandon him in his trials because he is so "understanding, perceptive, and steady minded" (13.332). In the first stage Odysseus shows that, gods or no gods, good luck or bad luck, it is difficult even for a goddess to make him give himself away; in the second, we see him trust his own judgment even in preference to Athena's word, and therefore she gives him her second, and nobler-sounding accolade. In brief, the scene is a recognition of Odysseus by Athena even more than of Athena and Ithaca by Odysseus.

In her prince's guise Athena tells Odysseus that they are indeed in Ithaca, rough but very fertile, whose name is known to the ends of the earth, even to Troy (13.242–49). She implies that the island achieved this fame by its fertility alone; but we in the audience tend to think rather of Odysseus's description of his island as "rough, but a good nurse of men" (9.27). If Ithaca is known in Troy, we would prefer it to be for the man or men it has bred. Odysseus rejoiced to hear this, Homer says, but did not tell the truth (13.254): "He seized back the word that was on his lips" and instead told a lie. The word which Odysseus kept back was evidently, "I am that Odysseus through whom Ithaca's name is known in Troy, and not from its fertility, as you suggest." The temptation to reveal himself to the charming young man seems irresistible, but Odysseus resists it and invents for himself instead a character as a dangerous man of Crete. This is enough to win the admiration of Athena. What she is among gods for cleverness, he is among men, she says. She throws off her disguise and from now on treats him as in some sort her equal. Yet his ability to withhold himself at all times and places is at bottom only a kind of deceit. It is, we saw, as a rogue that she recognizes him, and though Homer doubtless paid roguery more respect than we do, the shape of the passage shows that he knew of a higher form of intelligence still.

This level too is reached by way of distrust. Athena has already revealed both the island as Odysseus's home and herself as his protectress. What mortal could ask more? and yet Odysseus is not satisfied. He is not satisfied because, as Homer means to show us, though gods may be blessed with divine certainty, a human never can be. With the characteristic insouciance of Homer's gods, Athena says, in effect, "I love your tricks, but this time they are inappropriate. How is it you did not recognize your old friend?" (13.287–310). Odysseus can only respond with mistrust (13.311–28); he patiently explains that it is not so easy for a mortal to recognize a goddess who takes so many shapes. As a matter of fact, did she not abandon him from the time when Troy fell and heaven scattered the Achaeans to the time when she helped him among the Phaea-cians (13.302)? May she not even now be deceiving him? Is this really Ithaca?

First, let us remark what marvelous use, even in rejecting it, Homer has made of "the Wrath of Athena," the tradition that, after the fall of Troy, Athena's anger caused the scattering of the Achaians and the disasters of the return. By the time Odysseus reaches Ithaca, we have been shown that not Athena's wrath but Poseidon's was the chief cause of his troubles; still, during the period in question there has been a notable lack of Athena's help, which might well be taken as anger. Odysseus seems to be considering that possibility in asking his question, and as members of Homer's audience we can easily understand how the erroneous impression of Athena's hostility arose. Athena's answer that she only held aloof out of respect for Poseidon both rejects the traditional view and accounts for it; more than that it frees Odysseus once and for all from the imputation that she was ever displeased with him; and best of all, it shows that he can go it alone. Athena may have saved his life by inspiring him to hang on to the rock off Scherie, but in an equally crucial situation before she appeared on the scene, Homer remarks that "he did not forget his raft" (5.324), and this is apparently his own idea. In the Kyklops's cave Odysseus looked forward to how Athena might give him the glory of victory over the monster (9.317), but he achieved it without her explicit help. The intellectual feats of that triumph seem to be his own. This does not mean that he could have done it against her will or that he could do without luck: indeed he is aware, as we have seen, that divine agency gave his men the necessary courage when they needed it (9.381) and probably also brought into the cave the rams by means of which they escaped (9.339). Nevertheless, our sense of his independence may reasonably be enhanced by his achieving so much in Athena's "absence."

Athena's admission that, to some extent, she abandoned even her beloved Odysseus proves that no mortal can be sure of a god's help. Therefore Odysseus's distrust of the gods, strangely enough, is the beginning of wisdom, as Athena's admiring answer shows. He is right: she did leave his side out of respect for Poseidon. To be sure, she knew he would get home in the end and so felt confident (13.339–40), but we cannot help realizing that such confidence based on such knowledge is only for gods. Odysseus has correctly read the situation: no human can be certain of divine help.

From this distrust Athena draws her second, more complimentary conclusion, a rather involved one. I paraphrase 13.330–38: "You always think like that," she says. "That is why I cannot desert you in your trouble; it is because you are understanding and perceptive and steady minded. Another man in your situation would feel impelled to go home and see his wife and children. You do not even want to ask about them until you make trial of your wife, who sits at home all this time and does nothing but weep." First, how can Athena tell from Odysseus's lack of confidence in herself that he means to "make trial of" Penelope? And what is so understanding and steady minded about that? The answer, I think, is that she goes by what he does not say as much as by what he does. Another man, told as he has been by a now-undisguised Athena that she has come to help him, would accept such apparent fortune without another thought, and in the assurance of success would rush straight home or at least would ask his patron-goddess eager questions about his family. Odysseus, however, has done no such thing. So steady minded is he, in spite of the proffered seductive hope, that he remembers that, of his own knowledge, he is not even sure of where he is. In the uncertainty of all things human, it will take more than the words "This is Ithaca" to make him believe. Similarly, rushing home and falling into Penelope's arms, even if it were safe to do it, will not tell him what he wants to know of her, nor will any hearsay, even from a goddess, help him in the slightest. He must test her for himself. For this is the unforeseen happy corollary of universal uncertainty and the need for universal distrust: one must find out for oneself. But in that case, what one comes to know one will know through and through, by and for oneself and not as the pawn or dupe of any god or man. Realizing that this is what is in Odysseus's mind, Athena at last declares, "Here is Phorkys's harbor, here the olive tree, here the nymphs' cave, here Neriton" and takes away the cloud (13.345–52). Odysseus rejoices, for he himself now recognizes harbor, tree, cave, mountain, and therefore Ithaca.

The statement of Odysseus's independence of Athena is now complete: she may smooth his path, and she may put before him what ideas and information she will, but what he knows and what he believes and what he trusts still depends on himself alone. Still, we must not slight Odysseus's dependence on Athena either, and sure enough, the statement of it follows at once as Odysseus greets his old friends, the nymphs of the cave.

> Naiad nymphs, Zeus's daughters, I never thought
> to see you. Now with my warmest prayers be pleased;
> afterward we shall give gifts as of old,
> if the daughter of Zeus, driver of the spoil, graciously lets me
> live myself, and lets my son grow tall. (13.356–60)

His mind is his own; but his life and success depend on the gods, and he knows it. And so he makes his prayer.

Because success depends on Athena, Odysseus puts himself completely in her hands for the rest of the scene. It is she who finds hiding places in the cave for the treasure, makes plans against the suitors, and disguises Odysseus, not because he cannot do these things himself, but because she can do it better. This is not meant to diminish Odysseus in our eyes but to magnify him. Athena helps him, as she says, because he is wise, not because he is unable to help himself, and this would agree with Homer's experience of life, which showed him, as it does us, that the gods help those best able to help themselves. In the present situation the only thing she promises to do which he cannot do is to fetch Telemachos, and though it is indeed lucky, perhaps essential, that Telemachos should arrive in time ready to play a part in the campaign against the suitors, we do not begrudge Odysseus this luck. We have seen that Telemachos is prepared for such a role on his own account. All the rest is well within Odysseus's powers: we know, for example, how he was able to disguise himself for his secret entry into Troy (4.240–50). Even the detailed information about Eumaios and the suitors which Athena now gives Odysseus is such as he could have got for himself. The essential point is that, in the *Odyssey*, the gods help those who are capable of helping themselves, and in just those ways in which they are most capable.

With this principle firmly in mind, we can understand an otherwise curious feature which occurs at the end of the scene. Odysseus seems, but only seems, to imply that this is the first time he has heard about the suitors and that he could not have found out about them by himself—implications both of which are palpably false. In the underworld, Teiresias told him about the suitors, and Agamemnon warned him not to trust even his wife. Nevertheless, after Athena has invited him to plot his revenge on the suitors, he says,

> Ah me! the death of Agamemnon, son of Atreus,
> would surely have been mine in my own halls
> if you had not told me everything, Goddess, just as it is. (13.383–85)

I am sure this is meant to be taken literally: Odysseus would have met his end if, at this point in the story, it had not come into his mind that there were suitors in his halls. As Homer sees it, on this occasion the idea reached him by way of the spoken words of Athena. This does not mean, however, that, if she had not been there, he would not have remembered it for himself. As Athena said to Telemachos at 3.26–27, some things men think of themselves, others the gods put into their minds. Still other things, on very special occasions like this one, the gods tell one face to face. When they do, it is up to men to be grateful in proportion to the importance of the information; whether they might otherwise have thought of it by themselves is profitless speculation. In other words, Athena's telling Odysseus face to face about the suitors is simply an extreme case of what her help to him usually is anyway, a heightened version of what he would naturally have done himself.

Homer manages the intrigue against the suitors on the same principles: Athena invites Odysseus to make his own plan for the campaign against them (13.376), but even though he is the best strategist on earth, he knows better than to rely on himself when a god is at hand. Wisely, he asks her to do it for him (13.386), and she graciously complies. By himself he could perhaps do much, but with her help he feels confident against three hundred (13.390); he could manage to disguise himself, no doubt, as he did when he entered Troy in secret (4.240–50), but Athena can actually transform him (13.397–403), and that is how Homer sees the situation as having occurred.

To those who can believe happily in Homer's gods, all this may be reasonable. For most of the rest of us, though, why is Athena's interfering not merely annoying? The answer is, I think, that Homer converts us temporarily to his theology. His gods do glorify, they do not violate, the reality we actually know. Athena helps Odysseus do a little better only what we already think of him as supremely able to do: to remember, to plan, to disguise himself. This accords both with our sense of the aesthetic fitness of things and with our sense of how the world works. There may be exaggeration, but there is no falsification. Nor are things made too easy. We are still permitted to regard Odysseus as one of the most sorely tried individuals the world has ever seen. In fact in this very episode, where Athena's aid to Odysseus for the first time looms large, Homer shows how far she is from making the world a softer place than we know it to be, even for her favorites. Concerning Telemachos, Odysseus asks her,

> Why did you not tell him, when you knew it all in your heart?
> Was it that he too might wander and suffer woes
> on the sterile sea, while others ate up his livelihood?
>
> (13.417–19)

Athena answers:

> Trouble your heart about him no more than you must.
> I was his escort, that he might win good fame
> by his journey. Not toiling, but at ease,
> he sits in Menelaos's house in the midst of plenty.
> To be sure the young men in their black ship lie in wait
> meaning to kill him before he returns to the land of his fathers;
> but I do not think that will happen; sooner the earth will cover
> one or two of those suitors who now devour his livelihood.
>
> (13.421–28)

Athena's words are confident, but with exactly that confidence with which a brave man faces the chances of life. Danger, toil, and uncertainty are not remitted but accepted and even welcomed as an opportunity to win fame.

Eumaios, the Faithful Slave

Odysseus is safely home, Athena has promised to stand by him, and she has given him an impenetrable disguise. Why does Homer's Muse not see him as proceeding at once to the rescue of his wife and son and to his own revenge? Why does Athena send him to "the swineherd, who, of all the slaves Odysseus possessed,/took best care of his livelihood" (14.3–4)?

In the story this visit serves to fill the time until Athena can fetch Tele-machos from Sparta, as she has promised to do (13.412–13), but if that were all the poet was concerned about, he could have disposed of his problem in a pair of sentences. Instead he treats the visit at length. I think he does this chiefly to show how Odysseus would have instructed himself about the situation in Ithaca if Athena had not "told him everything" (13.385). Another reason he does so, minor but still important, is suggested by the already-quoted words "took best care of his livelihood," for Homer takes this opportunity to show us Odysseus's economic resources in detail. The poem constantly stresses the importance of having the means to fill one's stomach, and we shall soon see what it is like to be without such means, as Odysseus begins to play his role of beggar. Pigsties therefore are important (14.5–28), and it is neither by accident nor through naïveté nor for the sake of parody that we are given at the beginning of the episode a most satisfactory account of Eumaios's arrange-ments for his 600 sows. In addition, the fact that the boars have dwindled to a mere 360 is our first and best index of the damage the suitors have done to Odysseus's estate. Later on in this book Eumaios will catalogue Odysseus's remaining flocks and herds, both in Ithaca and on the mainland, demonstrat-ing that he is indeed "richer than any other twenty men" in that part of the world (14.96–104). This is the livelihood which he has come to dispute with the suitors, and the visit to Eumaios enables us to appreciate how extensive and important it is.

Better still, the new character Eumaios serves to define Odysseus in two important ways: first, Eumaios is a slave, and it is of the essence of Odysseus that he is a free man; second, the fact that Odysseus can command such loyalty as Eumaios's increases his stature in our eyes. For not only is Eumaios a slave, he is an absolutely admirable one. He is so faithful that, even after twenty years, he still yearns for his master, than whom, he says, he will never find a kinder. He would rather have him back than see his home and parents again, much as he longs for them (14.139–44). Furthermore, this love is very profitable to Odysseus: Eumaios is a prodigious builder and worker; he directs the efforts of four underherdsmen; the flocks prosper under his care (14.61–66). As we hear of all he has accomplished, even of the sandals he is cutting (14.23), or watch him tighten his belt as he strides off to get his guest's dinner from the sties (14.72), we are invited to applaud the good he is doing and the energy with which he does it. With regard to the rest of the world, his heart is in exactly the right place: he cannot bear that even so humble a stranger as Odysseus seems to be should come to grief under the teeth of his dogs or go without food and shelter; his reverence for the gods and his pity for his fellow man alike forbid it. In short, Eumaios could scarcely be a nicer man.

Yet in the presence of all this goodness, we have one overriding impression, and that is of Eumaios's powerlessness. Without Odysseus none of his wishes— a house, a wife, a little land—will come true (14.64). He exists now entirely on the suitors' sufferance, in fear and trembling (14.59–60). Apparently he has just saved the life of a man, Odysseus, who is absolutely dependent on his bounty and protection, but actually it is the dependent guest who holds the keys to his host's happiness. Eumaios's fate depends not on himself but on whether Odysseus succeeds or fails. This is what it is to be a slave.

That Homer has slavery prominently in mind in this episode is evident also from the story Odysseus tells of himself, pretending to be a Cretan chieftain down on his luck. By his own account his life has been one long struggle against falling into servitude. He was born of a slave mother, he says (14.202), and though he overcame this handicap, rising to be a leading man in Crete (14.237), slavery threatened him again after the Trojan War as a result of a disastrous raid he made in Egypt. A treacherous Phoenician befriended him and entertained him in his house but then took him abroad, ostensibly on a trading venture, but actually intending to sell him in Libya. Odysseus suspected the plot, he says, but had to go anyway, "perforce" (14.298), a vivid indication of how far his fictive self has sunk on the power scale since his return from Troy. Although the Phoenician's designs are prevented when Zeus sinks his ship and saves Odysseus alone of all on board, it is not long before a ship's company of Thesprotians tries to play the same trick on him, and this time it nearly comes off (14.340). Odysseus is already dressed in rags and lashed beneath the thwarts: who now would believe him if he tried to claim his freedom? He manages to escape, but only barely, and it is in these same rags, he says, that he comes to Eumaios's hut. This is what has become of the once-proud Cretan chief. His desperate struggles both show how easy it is to slip into slavery and make us feel what a desperate thing it would be to do so. In all these ways Odysseus's tale makes us fully aware of the disadvantages of Eumaios's position, good man though he is.

As a free man, then, Odysseus enjoys a certain superiority over Eumaios, even in his role of beggar. But this is not all: his fundamental mastery over his servant is shown in the way in which he deceives him. Man of many devices that he is, he can and does make Eumaios do what he wants without Eumaios's realizing it. This is doubly appropriate: in the first place, maintaining his disguise in Ithaca obviously demands that Odysseus deceive most of his friends as well as his enemies; and second, the role of beggar itself, disguise or no disguise, consists almost entirely of manipulation. From Odysseus we get a virtuoso performance, as we might expect. Set upon by his swineherd's dogs, "he sat down with guileful intent, and let fall his staff./Then he would have come to unseemly grief in his own steading" (14.31–32) if Eumaios had not dashed to the rescue.

Why did Odysseus act in this curious way, instead of defending himself with his staff? Scholars in antiquity thought that such behavior would allay the dogs' ferocity, and recent research in animal behavior suggests that they may have been right, but Homer can hardly have had any such idea in mind. As Stanford remarks in his note on the passage, Homer explicitly states that, without Eumaios's intervention, Odysseus would have come to grief. The truth must be, as Stanford says, that Odysseus is playing his role of beggar well and feigning fear. Not only that, I would add, but feigning helplessness as well. The irony, in any case, could not be more marked. To all appearances the rightful king of Ithaca is at the mercy of his own slave's dogs, but actually he is so confident of Eumaios's response that he takes what would seem to anyone else a serious risk of wounds or death in order to arouse his sympathy, such sympathy as only comes with the consciousness of having saved someone else's life. Thus, good as he is, Eumaios becomes and continues to be Odysseus's dupe. By the end of the book we see Odysseus in disguise extract from Eumaios the loan of a warm cloak by telling him how at Troy "Odysseus" got him the loan of a warm cloak by deceiving a fellow chieftain. At this stage Odysseus has so much the upper hand that, pace Stanford, I cannot suppose that Eumaios is meant to see the story for the fabrication we all know it is. Pretty clearly

Eumaios believes every word of it, for he has believed the whole Cretan story except the part about Odysseus's return (14.361–62). His respect for his guest has grown to the point where he actually dares to sacrifice for him one of the hogs destined for the suitors (14.414–17; cf. 80–82). He honors him with the chine, or best cut (14.437), and this manifest regard of Eumaios for him, even in disguise, inspires Odysseus to try for the cloak.

> Odysseus spoke among them, making trial of the swineherd,
> if he might perhaps take off his cloak and give it him
> or bid another to, for he showed him immense concern.
>
> (14.459–61)

To be sure, Odysseus apologizes for the presumption he is about to exhibit in his story, blaming it all on the wine (14.463), but surely that is to excuse the boldness of his request (14.504–6), not to imply that he is about to tell a lie. Odysseus gets his cloak, and we are led to see at the end of the book, as we were at the beginning, that Eumaios is only ostensibly host and protector. Actually he is Odysseus's man, and the irony of the situation is reinforced by his master's ability, even playing the role of suppliant and beggar, to get him to do his will. At the very end of the book, though the night is dark and stormy (14.457), we see Odysseus lying warm in Eumaios's cloak (14.523), while Eumaios himself, to his master's great delight, "set forth to lie down where the swine with their gleaming tusks/slept beneath a hollow in the rock, out of the north wind's gusts" (14.532–33).

Whatever Odysseus's apparent circumstances, and whether he is acting in his true role or in disguise, Eumaios works for him and not the other way round. It seems fitting that this should be so, not because Eumaios is in any contemptuous sense a gull or a patsy, but rather because in Homer's world the goodness of a Eumaios, to be rewarded, depends on the ability of men like Odysseus to gain and keep power.

In book 14, Homer has shown us Odysseus's livelihood; he has shown us his faithful slave and why he is his faithful slave; but the most interesting thing of all in this episode is Odysseus's unsuccessful attempt to make Eumaios believe that his supposedly absent master is alive and coming home "between the waning of this moon and the waxing of the next" (14.162). From a practical point of view it may seem dangerous for Odysseus to call attention in this way to the identity he is trying to hide, but the pattern of the story demands it. We cannot forego the ironic titillation of hearing the Returned One in Disguise talk of his own return. As usual Homer not only accepts the literary challenge involved but transcends it. He includes in the irony first a rejection, and finally an affirmation, of Odysseus's name and nature.

For here we reach the point at which Eumaios boggles. He refuses to believe in Odysseus's return not only for the same reason that everyone else does (namely, that he has been gone so long), but also because he thinks Odysseus has incurred the displeasure of the gods—this immediately after we have seen Athena promise Odysseus her aid. Much as he loves his master, he cannot approve of his having joined in the war against Troy and having sacked the city, for this action, he thinks, won him the hostility of heaven. Surprisingly enough, it is the wickedness of the suitors which convinces him of this. Before the episode is many minutes old, he addresses his guest as follows:

> Eat now, my friend, such food as slaves are allowed to eat,
> young pigs; the full-grown hogs are reserved for the suitors' dinners.
> They fear no wrath to come, nor do they think of pity.
> Wicked deeds, be sure, find little favor with the gods;
> they honor what is just, and the equable deeds of men.
> Men at war, natural enemies, even they, when they make a landing
> in foreign parts, and Zeus grants them taking of booty,
> and they, loading their ships, set out on the homeward voyage—
> even on them the strong fear falls of retribution.
> But the suitors must know something, have heard some word from the gods
> of my master's bitter death, that they will not fairly court
> my mistress, nor go home either; instead in utter comfort
> they take our goods by force, devour all, and spare nothing.
>
> (14.80–92)

It cannot escape our notice, as it did not escape Eumaios's, that the Odysseus who went to Troy was a "man at war," a "natural enemy," who landed on an alien shore, and Zeus granted him booty. If such men have reason to fear the wrath of the gods, and if the gods have given the suitors word of Odysseus's "bitter death," it seems only too likely that the gods themselves have punished him. In fact Eumaios later says that he is quite sure that the gods hate Odysseus because they have not granted him a known death at Troy or on the way home (14.365–68). It is interesting that this is consonant with what I have argued was the traditional view of the aftermath of the Trojan War, "the bitter return Athena gave when they left Troy" (1.327). Eumaios shares this view. He regards city sacking as a perilous proposition and a mistake, even if he thinks that what the suitors are doing is worse.

No wonder then that, having such trouble accepting the warlike aspect of Odysseus's career, he cannot accept the meaning of his name, "man of pain." When Odysseus asks him who his "so wealthy and so mighty" master is, Eumaios replies at length, emphasizing both the certainty of Odysseus's death and Odysseus's kindness while alive, greater even than a father's or a mother's (14.122–43). Then at last he utters his master's name for the first time, evidently well aware of its significance.

> It's for *Odysseus* that yearning takes me, so long gone.
> Even absent, I feel shame to say his name,
> for beyond measure he loved and cherished me.
> No; "dear friend" I call him, even though far away.
>
> (14.144–47)

It has been clear all along that Odysseus will have to make Ithaca accept his identity. Now, Eumaios's rejection of the meaning of his name makes it apparent that he will have to win approval for that meaning, even in the heart of this most faithful slave. As long as Eumaios is convinced that gods have punished his master for sacking Troy, it will be impossible to persuade him that this disguised Odysseus is the real one. Therefore Eumaios must be brought to see that city sacking is not such a doomed occupation as he thinks. Odysseus wastes no time in setting about the task. When Eumaios in his turn asks him who he is, instead of indulging Eumaios's prejudices and playing the role of a man of peace, he gives himself out to be nothing less than a darling of the war-god. Born of a slave mother and of slender inheritance, even so, he says:

> I won for myself to wife a woman of family and fortune,
> by my courage and prowess, for I was not one of your weaklings,
> I never ran from the fighting. All that is gone by this time;
> still, I think you can tell from the straw what the crop was;
> you can believe there's been plenty of grief since then to change me.
> Make no mistake, I had valor—Athena and Ares gave it—
> and the smashing of men, those times I led on an ambush
> warriors, men of rank, sowing seeds of doom for the enemy.
> Never did my proud heart see death in its expectations:
> dashing forward in front of them all I caught with my spear thrust
> any enemy man who was slow in escaping.
> Such I was in war; I never delighted in labor
> nor good husbandry, though it makes children grow big and fine looking.

Instead, the ships with their oars always took my fancy,
battles, and finely polished throwing spears, and arrows—
grim things, which in others inspire fear and trembling.
But I—I suppose I liked what the gods put it in me to like:
one man likes one sort of thing; another, another.

(14.211–28)

This is the sort of man Eumaios is being asked to accept as his guest. We see that he has connections with the Odysseus we know. He pictures himself as "sowing seeds of doom for the enemy" (*kaka dusmeneessi phuteuōn*), and it is not much more than one hundred lines since we have seen him in his own character "sowing seeds of doom for the suitors" (*kaka de mnēstērsi phuteuen*, 14.110). In fact "sowing seeds of doom" is a translation of Odysseus's name, as we have known since the fifth book. The same phrase is used of him twice more in this part of the poem (15.178; 17.159), as it already has been used of him by Halitherses in a prophecy (2.165) and will be used twice of Telemachos (17.27, 82). It describes the mind of the city sacker and of the avenger of insult and exactor of justice alike. The problem is, can Eumaios be brought to accept it?

On the face of it, it would seem unlikely. However prosperous the warlike stranger may claim to have been once, he is clearly a beggar now, and he seems rather a proof of Eumaios's thesis that heaven punishes city sackers than a refutation of it. But Odysseus can manage even that. He pretends to accept Eumaios's theory and, with it, the traditional doctrine of "the Achaians' grim return" (1.327; 3.132). He speaks of the Trojan War as the turning point in his fortune, the cause of all his misery.

Before the sons of the Achaians boarded their ships for Troy,
nine times as captain I led my men in their fast-faring warcraft
to foreign shores, on venture; and great the success it brought me.
I had privileged pick of the booty, and my regular share besides,
a large one. At once my household increased, and not long after,
I became a figure of dread and respect.
But when Zeus, who sees far and wide, contrived that foray
hated of all, which loosed the knees of so many men,
then they chose me and famous Idomeneus
to be their leaders in the ships to Ilion; there was no
way to refuse them. The voice of the people compelled us.
There for nine years we fought the war, we sons of the Achaians;

then in the tenth, having sacked Priam's city, we departed
for home with the ships; and the god scattered the Achaian fleet.
And for me too, poor man, Zeus-contriver planned evils.

(14.229–43)

The speaker here evidently blames Troy for his troubles, but he goes on to
tell his story in such a way that we must doubt his interpretation, just as we
doubted Nestor's in the third book. In the first place, he gets back from Troy in
perfect safety. The beginning of the evils which Zeus allegedly planned turns
out to be this Cretan's decision, only a month after his homecoming, to go on
a raid to Egypt (14.244–47). This hardly seems Zeus's fault. When he and his
men arrive there, the natives meet them in force and put them to flight. Zeus
is blamed for the flight (14.268), but the speaker himself admits that the battle
never should have occurred, that it was brought about by his men's recklessness (14.262). When in addition we find him regretting that Zeus saved his life
by putting it into his head to throw himself on the Egyptian king's mercy
(14.273)—far better to have died, he says—it is difficult to agree or to regard
this life saving as punishment at the hands of Zeus; it is much more like the
normal ups and downs of life.

Even supposing that Zeus can be blamed for the Egyptian disaster, the
speaker himself makes it explicit that, ever since that event, the gods have been
helpful. Reverence for Zeus, he says, led the king to spare his life and treat him
as his guest (14.283). Zeus's thunderbolt saved him from the Phoenician and
from slavery (14.300, 305). In the ensuing wreck Zeus put the ship's mast
between his hands and saved him (14.310). Finally, "the gods themselves"
untied the knots the Thesprotians had bound him with (14.348), hid him from
their search (14.357), and brought him to the steading of the god-fearing
Eumaios (14.358–59). Such a tale ought to shake Eumaios or anyone from the
conviction that the gods punish city sackers out of hand. It is possible, of
course, that they are merely preserving this Cretan for still further misery; that
is what he seems to think himself (14.273–75, 338). We know better; rather,
the climax and denouement of the poem will teach us better. Then, clearly, by
his success Odysseus will vindicate himself, his sufferings, his city sacking, and
his hostile name; it will also vindicate this Cretan, insofar as he and Odysseus
are the same. In short, the Muse has so arranged the Eumaios episode that
what is at stake in the coming conflict is not only Odysseus's livelihood but the
justification of his life and his hostile name.

We have said that Odysseus's attempt to convince Eumaios of his own
imminent return remains unsuccessful. This is strictly true, but it does not

mean that he does not succeed in changing Eumaios's attitude considerably. In the beginning, even though Eumaios has some hope that his master may be wandering in foreign parts (14.42–44), the more he thinks about it, the more he is sure he is dead. The gods have prevented his return, he says (14.61). He is dead and gone—would that instead, the whole race of Helen were (14.68)! The suitors must have had from the gods some assurance of his death to dare to do what they do (14.89–90). His body has long since been torn by dogs or eaten by fish, his bones are lapped in the sand of the seashore (14.133–36). This is the frame of mind which Odysseus sets out to change.

In his role of stranger he begins the attempt with an elaborate oath that Odysseus will return (14.151–64). Eumaios replies that this will never be (14.167), but he finds being strongly reminded of Odysseus so painful (14.169–70) that he tries to dilute the effect of the stranger's oath by substituting for it a pious wish.

> So, friend, let us speak no more of oaths; Odysseus,
> may he come home as I, for one, wish, and Penelope also;
> as old Laertes does, and handsome Telemachos.
>
> (14.171–73)

This wish has not much reality, but at least it is an improvement over the picture of Odysseus's bones lapped in sand. The very pain of the thought that Odysseus is gone leads ironically to an expression of the possibility that he may still return. Slight as it is, this affords encouragement.

Odysseus makes further progress toward convincing Eumaios that his master is alive by telling his fire-eating Cretan tale, in which we have seen that Zeus *does not* destroy the city sacker. When Eumaios doubts that his guest really crossed Odysseus's track in Thesprotia, Odysseus counters by offering to let himself be thrown off a cliff if Odysseus does not return (14.393). Though Eumaios reacts to this proposal with horror and evidently refuses the bet, this time he does not explicitly refuse to believe. Instead, as he turns to preparing dinner, his actions seem to show an increased sense of his absent master's reality. For one thing, he shows his guest, the bearer of the ostensibly rejected news, increased respect by offering him the best cut of meat. He is bolder against the suitors as well, and as he sacrifices the hog he once named as reserved for them, he prays the gods formally and emphatically for Odysseus's return (14.423). Then, as he hands the wine to "Odysseus, sacker of cities" (14.447), he no longer seems so sure that the gods punish city sackers; he has concluded, indeed, that the gods are unpredictable. When Odysseus, delighted at having been given the best cut of meat, prays that Eumaios may be as dear to Zeus as he is to him, Eumaios replies in a kind of exasperation,

> Eat, my god-touched guest, and enjoy what is set before you,
> the way it is; the god will grant, and the god will fail
> to give, just as he pleases; for he can do anything.

(14.443–45)

At this stage Eumaios is not betting on his master's return, but he is not betting against it either.

The Return of Telemachos

Odysseus's encounters, first with Athena and then with Eumaios, have fixed our eyes firmly on the revenge to come. It is time to summon Telemachos from Sparta so that he may take his part, as he so well has earned the right to do. Homer therefore shows us Athena starting him on his way home and then tells us of his departure. In the process he brings our sympathy with Telemachos back to where it was when we left him in the fourth book; he reinforces our feeling of peril from the suitors; and he puts us in mind of the temptations women are subject to, a factor of obvious importance in the circumstances.

Athena's summons takes place in the most natural way in the world. Peisistratos is comfortably sleeping, but Telemachos lies awake thinking about his father, his troubled state one more instance of the pain which Odysseus characteristically causes. As Telemachos continues to ponder his problem, the thought occurs (I paraphrase 15.10–42):

I can't leave my house like this, with those men in it. I must go home. Besides, Mother may marry one of the suitors, and then her interest and affection will turn to her new husband. She may even take some of the household goods with her when she leaves. I must get a housekeeper to take care of things until I get married. And I must be careful how I go home; I have a strong feeling that the suitors, who so clearly would like me out of the way, have laid a trap.

Remembering Nestor's observation that some things we think of for ourselves while others the gods put into our heads (3.26–27), we can see that an impulse of this importance may very well come from Athena. Homer's Muse tells him that Telemachos's thoughts did so in this case, and so our text reads, "As Telemachos lay awake, Athena came near him and said . . . " Though they come from a goddess, however, these are mortal thoughts. For this reason

Athena says here, rather curiously from our point of view, "You will get a fair wind/from whichever god it is who keeps you safe and defends you" (15.34–35). This is not a dream. Telemachos is awake (15.7–8), and so far is he from having a vision of Athena, that he does not presume even to identify his protectress. The thought comes from Athena, but only the Muse and Homer and his audience can be sure of this, certainly not Telemachos. It is thus in a very real sense Telemachos's own thought as well, and only when we understand this can we properly appreciate his realism about women and his willingness to trust heaven when necessary.

Telemachos is not yet a complete Odysseus, however. There is a headlong quality in his urgency which betrays his youth. He at once wakes Peisistratos and has to be persuaded not to go to Menelaos then and there, in the middle of the night. Nevertheless, when the conversation with Menelaos does occur, we are glad to see Telemachos refuse Menelaos's offer of a gift-gathering tour of Greece. We remember that it was a similar tour in Egypt and Phoenicia that prevented Menelaos not only from saving Agamemnon's life but even from avenging his death (3.311–12, 4.90–93). Telemachos, by contrast, is not to be distracted from the thought of Odysseus and the problem Odysseus's absence causes, and so when Menelaos asks to be remembered to Nestor, he bursts out,

> Would that I might so surely
> come home to Ithaca, and finding Odysseus there,
> tell *him* how, having received all courtesy at your hands,
> I am back, bringing much good treasure! (15.156–59)

In response to this wish the omen of the eagle and the goose occurs immediately, and Helen interprets it as meaning the return and revenge of Odysseus, something which interests us now as much for Telemachos's sake as for Odysseus's own. It is interesting that Helen interprets the omen in terms we have come to associate with Odysseus's name and the problem of evil.

> Just as this eagle seized this goose, a fatling of the house,
> coming from the mountain, where he was born and bred,
> so Odysseus, coming from hardship, coming from far,
> shall come home and take his revenge; or else he's
> already at home and sowing seeds of doom for the suitors.
>
> (15.174–78)

Better to be a weather-beaten eagle than a comfortable goose. The pain of Telemachos's sleepless nights too will turn out to have been worth it.

After the éclat of his departure from Sparta, Telemachos's journey to Pylos settles into the quiet of familiar travel formulas, the stopover at Pherai being duly noted for the return, just as it was on the way out in book 3 (3.486–94 = 15.184–92). Even this I do not suppose was included just because it "happened." More likely part of the reason is that this is the rhythm Homer wanted. The twelve lines of everyday between two scenes of strain and stress seem appropriate. Above all, the poem's structure is underlined. The repetition in reverse of Telemachos's route in book 3 shows us Telemachos's journey as framing Odysseus's. We become increasingly aware of the shape of the poem as its end comes nearer.

The second scene of strain and stress, the taking on board of Theoklymenos, is prefaced by the unforgettable touch of Telemachos's avoiding Nestor in order to save time. There is no doubt that this is, if nothing worse, at least a breach of etiquette: Telemachos has promised Menelaos to give Nestor his regards, and there is no doubt that the old man himself will be "furiously angry" if Telemachos does not stop to be entertained (15.214); but Telemachos has the strength of character to break the rules and endure the hostility, and in the circumstances we feel that he is entirely right. Furthermore, it certainly does not diminish the credit which will accrue to Odysseus and his son for their triumph if Menelaos and Nestor both, who might have sent aid, instead turn out to be little more than potential impediments to their success.

We sense, I think, the relevance of the episode in which Telemachos picks up Theoklymenos, yet we find it hard to spell out. It seems to me to contribute in several ways. In the first place, it increases the atmosphere of peril. Telemachos is already trying to avoid an ambush, the laying of which we have witnessed, and now he takes aboard an obviously desperate fugitive who says, "I think I am pursued" (15.278).

Incidentally, the episode expresses well the difference between our preconceptions and Homer's. We feel that, before helping somebody who says he has killed a man, we ought to make sure somehow that he is in the right. This is of course difficult, and is even more difficult in a heroic context. In any case, nothing could be further from the spirit of the institution of supplication as we see it in early Greek literature. There, a person throws himself on another's mercy, by implication asking among other things not to be judged; and the gods, especially Zeus, recognize and even enforce the suppliant's right to a favorable reception.

In the case before us we share Telemachos's sympathy with this fugitive, feeling, as Telemachos himself may be expected to feel, that they are brothers in their peril, if in nothing else. The generosity of his response wins our further approval (we would not expect Eurymachos to act in this way), and more particularly, we sense an increase in Telemachos's stature. We have already seen him, and Helen, looking forward to the time when he will be married and master of a household (15.26, 125–27). He is in fact playing that role already in his care for his possessions in the supposed absence and loss of Odysseus. Theoklymenos's supplication heightens this impression of responsibility by putting Telemachos in the position of protector and man of power. He will sail back to Ithaca in the stern sheets of his vessel the superior figure of the two, just as, on the outward voyage, he was inferior to Athena disguised as Mentor.

There is in fact much to make us associate the two pairs. Theoklymenos may be in an inferior position, and a mortal, but he possesses the divine power of prophecy. More specifically, the language and, as it were, the gestures of Telemachos's reception of him remind us of his reception of Athena in book 1. In both places (1.123 and 15.281), we find the word *philēseai*, "you will meet with love [among us]," associated closely with the ceremonious taking of the stranger's spear. In the first book Telemachos "took the stranger's right hand and relieved him of his bronze-pointed spear" (1.121) and then

> took it and stood it against the tall pillar
> in the polished spear-stand where many other
> spears of Odysseus the enduring hearted were set.
>
> (1.127–29)

Here "he relieved [Theoklymenos] of his bronze-pointed spear/and laid it on the deck of the ship with its shapely end-posts" (15.282–83). Hearing this, we can feel that divine power has accrued to Telemachos's side, just as we did when Athena's spear was set beside those of Odysseus in book 1, especially since Helen has recently interpreted the omen of the eagle and goose in Telemachos's favor.

The Theoklymenos episode also completes the story of Theoklymenos's ancestor Melampus, already sketched for us at 11.287–97. There Neleus of Pylos, Nestor's father, offers the hand of his daughter Pero to whoever shall "lift from Phylake/the broad-browed cows of mighty Iphiklos,/a difficult task—" and Melampus undertakes it (11.289–92). He is caught and imprisoned, but later released on account of his prophecies, "and the will of Zeus was fulfilled" (11.293–97). Neleus meanwhile, we now learn (15.229–40), under the influence of *ate* (delusion) and a "dread Fury," sequesters Melampus's considerable wealth, a "foul crime." As a consequence Melampus on his escape not only delivers the cattle and wins the maiden for his brother but takes such drastic revenge on Neleus that he himself must flee the country and settle in Argos, "for there he was destined/to dwell and be king of many Argives." All this last part of Melampus's story we learn as part of the Theoklymenos episode, and it suits the occasion admirably, for in it we see a just revenge taken by one who, like Odysseus and to some extent Telemachos, returns unexpectedly from abroad to punish those who have violently appropriated his possessions. Even dividing the story between two different contexts has its effect. In book 11, it seemed simply a case of a man's mental and verbal prowess winning his homecoming after long imprisonment abroad, as Odysseus wins his by telling his story to the Phaeacians; to this, book 15 adds not only the revenge but the exile it is apt to cause, a problem Odysseus too faces at the end of the poem.

With Theoklymenos safely aboard, Telemachos sets sail for Ithaca, "pondering whether he would escape death, or yet be caught" (15.300). Profiting a second time from the suspense afforded by the ambush, the poet changes scenes, returning us to Odysseus and Eumaios. When we last saw them, they had just settled down for the night; now they are at supper, synchronous with the sunset which Telemachos and his crew have just experienced. What has happened in Eumaios's hut in the interim, or even how many days have elapsed, should not concern us. The illusion of continuity is all that is necessary.

Ever since Telemachos's night thoughts, managed by Athena as we have seen, suggested that, on arriving in Ithaca, he should go first to Eumaios's cabin (15.36–39), the poem has clearly been headed toward the meeting of father and son. Having reawakened our interest in and feeling for Telemachos, Homer might have proceeded at once to the recognition scene, but it seems better that he does not. The excitement is greater because Telemachos is still in doubt and ignorance as we turn to find a further matter of interest in the encounter between Odysseus and Eumaios. For how long can Odysseus count on Eumaios's hospitality? Odysseus offers to go to the palace and find work as a serving man for the suitors, only to meet with Eumaios's violent opposition, as he had hoped. Not only is our impression of Eumaios's real delight in and love for this stranger confirmed, but there is the irony of Eumaios's doubtless accurate prediction (15.326–34) that Odysseus will not be thought good enough even to carve the suitors' meat. Odysseus's emphatic thanks to his host for being spared the insult and injury attendant upon his wandering life and his invective against the hungry belly which drives him to it (15.341–45) produce a curious double feeling; relief and pleasure at the kindness of Eumaios and the avoidance of this pain are opposed by the realization that the suitors are not to be avoided, and that the wandering, suffering, and hunger which are the essence of Odysseus are going to contribute vastly more to the eventual triumph than this temporary ease will do. All this not only heightens our impression of the arrogance of the suitors but, more subtly, keeps us in touch with the poem's main concern with pain and its meaning.

This concern develops further as Odysseus proceeds, without Eumaios's being in the least aware, to subject himself to a much greater pain than any the suitors can inflict: what about your master's parents, he asks; are they still alive (15.347–50)? Eumaios describes the life of Laertes and the death of Antikleia alike in the most pitiable terms, pointing out that their suffering is due entirely to Odysseus's absence. We have seen Odysseus face his responsibility for his parents' sorrow in the underworld and see it in its true light. That he can bear to evoke the same sorrow now shows how much better he is at facing reality than those around him, even Eumaios; and it also suggests the depth of feeling and meaning that will be involved as he and his son reassume their rightful place in Ithaca. The suitors' hopes and fears are trivial by comparison.

Eumaios is led by these memories to recall, with the pathos of a happiness gone forever, his own upbringing at Antikleia's hands along with Odysseus's sister Ktimene (15.361–71). This sorrow too heightens our sense of Odysseus's greater hardships (alluded to later by Odysseus himself, 15.486–92) and thus increases Odysseus's stature. Odysseus now asks Eumaios to tell how it was that he became a slave so young. The tale is interesting, but almost more interesting is the gusto with which Eumaios tells it. He directs Odysseus to sit right there, drink his wine, and listen (15.391–97). It is not late. People sleep too much anyway, and these nights are terribly long. Whoever wants to can go outside and sleep; of himself and Odysseus Eumaios says:

> We two, eating and drinking in the cabin,
> will regale one another with our piteous histories
> as we recall them. Afterward, a man enjoys his troubles,
> one who suffers much and wanders far. (15.398–401)

Here is a real brotherhood of the woebegone, and the demonstration of the point Eumaios is making. We too enjoy these sorrows as they are recalled, and this of course is relevant to the poem's concern with the meaning and value of pain.

Eumaios's tale is no exception to his statement. Without the foreseen sadness of its denouement, his enslavement, much of its effect would be lost. As it is, we learn that a certain Phoenician seduced a slave girl in the palace of Eumaios's father, king of Syrie. The slave girl was the nurse of a small child whom she offered to the Phoenicians as the price of rescuing her from slavery.

That the small child was Eumaios himself—this is not revealed until we come to Eumaios's words "she took me by the hand" at the story's climax (15.465)— generates great excitement. Nothing in ordinary life seizes our attention so readily as an impending catastrophe, for we hope to avoid it. When recalled, the catastrophe impends again. If it is in fact avoided, that affords a climax of a certain power in the retelling. If not, that affords an even stronger climax, since we relive the catastrophe in the realization that it has been in some sense survived. Small wonder, then, that Eumaios, and we, enjoy so much the account of the unluckiest moment of his life.

Eumaios's tale is interesting as an example of the pleasures of remembered pain. It also characterizes Eumaios as one who has lost, and misses, the love he would naturally receive from the women close to him. Betrayed by his nurse, he gained a foster sister and a foster mother in Ktimene and Antikleia, only to lose the first when she married and the second when she died. At the end of the story he explains that he gets no good of his mistress Penelope because of the suitors. Thus we are given a sense of the importance of women and also of their openness to temptation at a point in the poem where it is most appropriate, just as we are about to meet Penelope for the first time since Telemachos left for Pylos.

There is, then, nothing irrelevant to arouse our impatience in the poem's return to Odysseus and Eumaios after we have encountered Telemachos. To be sure, both the meeting of father and son and the final revenge are delayed by this scene, but in such a way that our interest is increased, not diminished.

Eumaios's tale incidentally affords a good example of one of the further satisfactions of the *Odyssey*, the quiet way in which expectations are fulfilled even in minor matters. Eumaios implies that the storytelling may take much of the night. Actually the story requires only eighty-two lines, but the illusion of its length is kept up. When it is finished, Homer tells us that "they lay down to sleep for no long time; indeed it was short;/for at once came the resplendent Dawn" (15.494–95). Similar is the line Homer adds to a common day's-end formula in his account of Telemachos's return to Ithaca.

> The sun set, and all the ways were hid in shadow,
> as the ship made for Pheai, sped by a wind from Zeus.
>
> (15.296–97)

No putting ashore this night, as Athena and Telemachos have determined (15.33–34).

Book 15 ends with another of those uniquely Homeric touches, like Telemachos in his urgency waking Peisistratos in the middle of the night, or his avoiding a second interview with Nestor. The morning that dawns after the storytelling in Eumaios's cabin shows us not Eumaios and Odysseus but Telemachos landing in Ithaca, and he is immediately faced with an embarrassment. Because of the danger, he must leave the ship before it reaches the town. What is he to do with his guest and suppliant, Theoklymenos? He finds that the most disinterested advice he can give him is that he apply to Eurymachos, one of the leading suitors and his own mortal enemy. So great is the shift in power occasioned by Odysseus's absence, making equally great the danger in which Telemachos himself stands. Telemachos is spared this necessity of sending his friend over to the enemy by the immediately ensuing omen of the hawk and dove and Theoklymenos's interpretation of it, but the point is made all the same, and very vividly (15.525–34).

We leave book 15, then, with our interest in Telemachos reawakened, our respect for him increased, and our sense of his danger heightened. Meanwhile, with Eumaios and Odysseus, we have contemplated sorrow itself and sorrow recalled. Mostly indirectly, through Eumaios, we have had an impression of Odysseus's softer side, his tenderness toward his mother and father and sister. If Eumaios's feelings for these people are so strong, what must Odysseus's not be, especially when he must hide them? This contrasts with the previous book, where Odysseus the city sacker is so much the center of our attention. In book 15, not only Odysseus's tenderness but the female element comes strongly to the fore, pointing toward coming encounters with Penelope. All in all, though this is not the book one thinks of first when one thinks of the *Odyssey*, there is probably not a line in it we can do without.

Father and Son

Book 15 has prepared us for the imminent meeting and mutual recognition of Odysseus and Telemachos. As book 16 begins, we hear immediately that, inside the cabin where Odysseus and Eumaios are preparing breakfast,

> the noisy dogs writhed in delight at Telemachos's coming
> and did not bark. Odysseus noticed the fawning dogs,
> and the sound of footsteps came to his ears. (16.4–6)

This is the sudden yet inevitable way in which the recognition begins: the dogs are the first to know who is coming, Odysseus realizes that it must be someone close to Eumaios (16.8–9), and then Telemachos stands in the door. Not a word about what Odysseus feels at this point. We realize that he must not give the slightest sign. Instead, it is Eumaios who leaps to his feet, dropping the bowls he is holding, and covers Telemachos with kisses. The result is that, before we witness Odysseus's emotion directly, we feel its counterpart first in the dogs and then in Eumaios, realizing that, whatever they are experiencing, Odysseus is experiencing to an even greater degree. This is one of the great literary advantages of Odysseus's disguise in the poem's second half: the necessity of inferring his feelings from the reactions of others and the heightening which results as we make the inevitable comparison. When Odysseus is able to act freely, as he soon is in this case, the effect is all the greater.

As though to make sure that we see through Eumaios to Odysseus, Homer compares Eumaios's joy to a father's.

> As a father lovingly greets his son
> returned in the tenth year from distant lands,
> an only son, much cherished, for whom he has suffered much,
> so then to Telemachos-the-godlike the noble swineherd
> clung, covering him with kisses, for he knew the death he had escaped.
>
> (16.17–21)

The irony is heightened in that, in the simile as well as in fact, the son, not the father, is being welcomed home, even though for us Odysseus is the principal home-comer in the scene. We notice too that Homer does not let us overlook the contribution to this joy made by grief and danger.

Though he must give no sign, Odysseus is aware from the first that this is his son; Telemachos, on the contrary, does not know that the beggar is his father, and the ironies afforded are numerous. One of the most poignant occurs when Odysseus, as an inferior, offers his son his seat. It is indescribably satisfying when Telemachos generously declines. Again, Telemachos and Eumaios give information about Penelope, the effect of which on the stranger they cannot imagine: although Eumaios reports that she "remains staunchly" in what he now refers to as Telemachos's house, grieving for her lost lord (16.37–39), Telemachos reveals what is equally true, that she cannot decide whether to remain with him or to marry one of the suitors (16.73–77). Another irony is Telemachos's embarrassment when the question of the stranger's entertainment in the palace comes up; as in the case of Theoklymenos, he does not feel he can expose his guest and suppliant to the suitors, the guest who in reality is the rightful owner of the hall. Telemachos's embarrassment in turn gives Odysseus a chance to express his indignation against the suitors as he tells what he would do if he were Odysseus's son or Odysseus himself. He says that he would rather face the suitors alone and die in the struggle, if it came to that, than go on witnessing their outrageous behavior. That a stranger, even a bogus one, should respond in this way is calculated to fortify both Telemachos's resolve and our own sense that the coming revenge will be utterly justified. The main point, however, is the irony of Odysseus, on his way to his revenge, wishing that he were Odysseus on his way to his revenge. If he were Odysseus, he says,

> On the spot let him who wishes cut off my head,
> if to all those fellows I would not be a bane
> going into the house of Laertes' son, the Man of Pain.
>
> (16.102–4)

Nor is the irony dropped when the scene goes on to show us that Telemachos is like his father in his ability to control, when necessary, even the softer emotions (16.130–53). Eumaios, under instructions to go to the palace to tell Penelope that Telemachos is back, asks whether he shall not also tell Laertes, who, if possible, is even more grief stricken. Telemachos, though it pains him, says no, remarking that mortals cannot have everything they wish for. If they could, he says that he would choose Odysseus's return. As it is, Eumaios must come back at once, having told Penelope to send her house-keeper to the old man. Telemachos is no more to be betrayed by his impulses than his father is, however strong their appeal to his gentler nature. As a result, Telemachos too is a Man of Pain to others as well as to himself.

Moreover, it is worth asking, why it would be so bad if Eumaios should, as Telemachos puts it, "wander about the fields looking for Laertes" (16.150–51). The tone and content of the phrase itself is all Homer needs to suggest the answer. Conscious as he is that the suitors intend to kill him, Telemachos wants to keep his arrival a secret as long as he can. Eumaios's straggling about the fields might make a stir. Besides, absolutely alone as he thinks himself to be, Telemachos wants Eumaios at his side. It says much for his consideration for his mother that he lets Eumaios go at all.

When the recognition of Odysseus by his son finally comes, it comes with due impressiveness. Athena not only presides over it but passes a barefaced miracle. With a touch of her golden wand, she changes the bald-headed down-at-heel wanderer she has made of Odysseus in book 13 back into a handsome, tanned, black-bearded hero in a freshly washed cloak and tunic. Of course the battered stranger will look different to Telemachos once he sees him as his father, but the present case obviously goes far beyond this, so far that modern taste is apt to wish that Homer had not been on this occasion so "unrealistic." But I think Homer was right. The key to the situation lies in Odysseus's final comment on it.

> It is easy for the gods, who possess the spacious heavens,
> either to glorify us mortals or to bring us to disgrace.
>
> (16.211–12)

This is one of the two or three truths most central to the poem, and to use Aristotle's terms, Homer has chosen the philosophically likely, though histor-ically impossible, illustration for it over the merely possible, which would be less instructive. Homer's own mind, of course, was not troubled by this. He lived at a time when history was still poetry, and for him Athena's transforma-tion of Odysseus was as true as any other statement about the past.

Homer implies that, for Telemachos's benefit, Athena restored Odysseus to his original shape (16.175–76), but there is at least one difficulty in believing this. When she disguised him in book 13, Athena "took from his head the yellow locks" he had at the time (13.399, 431); here she presents him with a fine blue-black beard (16.176). Editors fuss about this, but I imagine that

Homer simply forgot. In any case the real point seems to be that, in the last analysis, Odysseus's looks do not matter. What makes his real identity is not a given set of physical characteristics but a style of action. In the present circumstances he is the only person capable of filling the role of Telemachos's father, husband of Penelope, and lord both of Ithaca and more particularly of "the house of Laertes' son Odysseus" (16.104). This is what he is in Telemachos's mind at any rate, since Telemachos has no memory of his father's appearance, having been only a baby when Odysseus went to Troy. Odysseus makes this point, that he is something more than a physical image, when Telemachos, naturally impressed by his miraculous transformation, insists on taking him for a god. He says,

> Telemachos, when your father is home
> you must not marvel too much or stand amazed:
> be sure no other Odysseus will come here ever;
> only I, as I stand here, suffering much and wandering far,
> have returned in the twentieth year to the land of my fathers.
>
> (16.202–6)

Here is someone who fills the role which precisely answers Telemachos's need, the role of an Odysseus willing and able to be his father, to suffer, and to "sow evils" for the suitors. Telemachos would do well to accept this Odysseus. There is no other. In short, the main thing about Odysseus is that he does what he does, whether he looks old or young, blond-headed or black-bearded. Therefore we must not think, as some have, that Telemachos is persuaded of his father's identity on insufficient evidence; on the contrary, he accepts him on the very best.

The scene makes a further point about this Odysseus whom Telemachos accepts: how like he is, and yet how unlike, a god. We start with Telemachos's taking him for one, and we may further reflect that Odysseus's return is in fact close to miraculous and heaven sent. For Telemachos he is in some sense truly divine as well as mistakenly so. It is similar to Telemachos's promising to pray to Helen as to a god if her prophecy should come true (15.181) or to Odysseus's making the same promise to Nausikaa in return for her help and good wishes (8.467). We may remember as well Odysseus's wish that Eumaios might be as dear to Zeus as to him (14.440–41). From some points of view it comes to the same thing: Odysseus is in fact in a position to play Zeus for Eumaios, as we have seen. And yet all of this can only happen if the gods will it so. They are the ones who finally "glorify us mortals, or bring us to disgrace," and only they are always happy. Odysseus makes us particularly aware of how like, and at the same time how unlike, man is to god when he disabuses Telemachos of his error.

I am no god, be sure [*ou tis toi theos eimi*]; why make me like the immortals?
I am that father of yours [*alla patēr teos eimi*], on whose account, deeply groaning,
you suffer a life full of evils, bearing the outrage of men.

(16.187–89)

The pun on *theos eimi* and *teos eimi*, where the only difference in the Homeric pronunciation is that the *t* of *theos*, "god," is aspirated, while that of *teos*, "your," is not, makes the point vividly and neatly. In the Greek, "god" and "your father" are made to sound alike, yet the ambience of Odysseus is pain, of which, as he says, he brings Telemachos so much. If there is anything about Odysseus more important than his ability to endure pain appropriately, both that which he suffers and that which he causes, it is his ineradicable knowledge that he is not a god. All this seems implicit in the passage before us; but as my reader has doubtless long since wished to object, the final impression the passage makes is something still other. Odysseus's very emphasis on the unhappiness he causes his son adds to our sense of the happiness he brings now, and will bring when the suitors are overthrown. Odysseus is like a god after all.

In another way too this recognition scene makes us feel what a god is. Eumaios departs, and Athena shows herself outside the cabin doorway. Telemachos cannot see her, "for it is not in nature that the gods should appear to everyone" (16.161); but Odysseus can. The dogs for their part slink away whining, not daring to bark. Odysseus accepts Athena's epiphany calmly, having experienced it before; but how it might affect another man, even an exceptionally courageous one, is soon made evident: Telemachos, on the mere suspicion that his transformed father is a god, prays that he be propitious and spare him, promising sacrifices and gifts of goldwork (16.181–85). As a result, our respect for both Athena and Odysseus is increased. On the one hand, man is not a god: he cannot control even the way he looks. On the other hand, if the gods befriend him, he may suffer, but he will not lose in the end.

We must not leave the recognition scene without commenting on the simile—at first sight, curious—in which the joy of father and son is depicted.

Loudly they wept, with shriller sound than any birds make,
vultures or eagles with curving talons, whose tender young

rustics have stolen before they grew full fledged;
so piteous were the tears they poured from beneath their brows.

(16.216–19)

It has been said that this is a rather extreme example of the supposed rule that the Homeric simile applies only to the precise point of comparison—in this case, the shrillness of sound—otherwise being free to roam as it will. I do not believe this rule applies, either here or elsewhere. It seems to me rather that the simile as a whole always makes an impression that is poetically essential to its context. In the present case, the poem by this time has suggested enough about the relation between pain and pleasure, sorrow and joy, for us to realize that Odysseus's and Telemachos's rejoicing is to a large extent a function of the grief they have experienced in their enforced separation. The nest has indeed been robbed, and no feature of the situation contributes more than that robbery does to the happiness that ensues when what has been lost is restored: namely, when Odysseus and his son are reunited. The simile affords us the pain of the loss in order to enhance the joy of the recognition, while the act itself of weeping for joy communicates the close connection between happiness and pain, as it does so often elsewhere in the *Odyssey*. Above all, the image of the great birds of prey in their bereavement suggests the pain which drives the two humans to their revenge against the suitors. We may well compare the similar image at the beginning of Aeschylus's *Agamemnon*.

The intrigue which follows the recognition has the interest of all such scenes, and in particular, we must not be surprised if every detail of Odysseus's plan for the coming battle is not carried out—the leaving behind two sets of arms when the others are removed from the hall, for example. Rather, as elsewhere in the poem and as in life, some things work out, and others do not. Here in book 16, we are left with the impression that Odysseus and Telemachos plan to take on all 108 suitors by themselves. In that case, two sets of armor are appropriate. As things turn out, four are needed, for Odysseus and Telemachos are joined by Eumaios and Philoitios the cowherd. Anticipating this, Homer refuses to make Telemachos look silly in the event by leaving him two sets of armor short. Instead, when the time comes, Odysseus and Telemachos remove *all* the weapons, and Telemachos brings back four sets as the fight begins. At this early stage, however, the false impression is useful. It increases our sense of the fearful odds, and it adds to the stature of Telemachos.

At first he naturally feels that, against such numbers, help will be needed, and even when Odysseus asks him if Athena and Zeus are not helpers enough (16.260–61), he doubts that they would be interested, "sitting off there high in the clouds with so many others/to rule over, both men and the gods that never die" (16.264–65). For Telemachos to change his mind about what interests the gods, however, Odysseus has only to sketch for him in a few quick phrases the intensity of the coming fight (16.267–69). So effectively is he converted that, to Odysseus's later suggestion (16.305–7) that they might look for other slaves who might still be loyal, he replies that he would rather not waste time going around the farms testing men if Odysseus has "really some knowledge of Zeus's marvelous intent" (16.320). Odysseus concurs. Telemachos thus shows at one and the same time courage, intelligence, piety, and independence of his father. When in the sequel they are able to find two loyal servants to help them without wasting time, nothing is lost: on the contrary, we only feel that Odysseus is flexible and realistic, and we are glad to see the faithful slaves share in the revenge. So it is better that everything should not work out just as Odysseus, and we, expect. The surprises add to the interest, while for the present we are quite satisfied with Odysseus's plan, impressively elaborate and obviously well conceived as it is.

We may turn now to the second climax of the book: the scene of the suitors' chagrin (16.342–408). We are glad to see them fail in their attempt to murder Telemachos and glad to hear them admit that they have failed. Best of all is to experience their well-founded fear of Telemachos. The tables are certainly being turned. Remembering Telemachos's bold action in calling the assembly in the second book, Antinoos realizes that Telemachos is quite capable of accusing the suitors of attempted murder before the people. The good impression he previously made suggests that that will be too much for the people of Ithaca to stomach and that therefore the suitors must either get rid of Telemachos before he calls another assembly or else do what he wants and carry on their wooing from their own houses at their own expense.

In any case, the attempted ambush has made it clear to all that the suitors are completely in the wrong. Therefore they must fear Telemachos, even though they are 108 to his 1, as they see it. For Homer is showing us that justice has, after all, a certain strength of its own. The suitors have undertaken to act outside the boundaries of what men consider fair conduct, relying on force. If they were completely savage like the Kyklops and recognized no restraint on their own wills whatsoever, they might well succeed except for the fact that they then could not keep their hands off each other. As it is, they are too decent. In any group of 108 outlaws there are apt to be some who are too civilized to maintain the necessary ruthlessness, and the suitors are no exception. When one of them, Amphinomos, sees their murder ship returning, he laughs happily (16.354). Is it at his companions' discomfiture? Homer does not say, but it seems clear that one suitor at least is glad that Telemachos is still alive. Even his name, Amphinomos (Both Ways), suggests the ambivalence of his mind, and it is he who gives the answer, fatal for the suitors, to Antinoos's question about whether Telemachos is to be killed.

> Friends, I for my part would not wish to kill
> Telemachos. King's blood is a perilous thing
> to shed. (16.400–402)

He goes on to suggest that they find out the will of the gods, which presumably means to seek some divine sign of what will happen if they do kill Telemachos; if the sign is favorable, he says, he will be the first to urge the murder. To be sure, this sounds sufficiently bloody minded, but actually his words have just saved Telemachos's life and secured the doom of his own party. Released from the necessity of deciding to spill the blood of kings immediately, the suitors break up their meeting. They do not realize that they have missed their opportunity forever.

Their squeamishness saves Telemachos, Eumaios, and Odysseus all three, but that does not mean that the suitors deserve sympathy, for Homer proceeds at once to show how bad they really are. At the same time, he makes us realize, with something of a shock, how little time has elapsed since Medon told Penelope of the plot against her son. Odysseus's tale has created the feeling that years have gone by, but actually Telemachos has been abroad what seems to be less than a week. Of course, if anyone takes the trouble to figure up how long it took Odysseus to build his boat and drift from Kalypso's island to Scherie, events which technically at least occurred after Telemachos left Ithaca, the time will be nearer a month; but the poet does not mean us to regard his tale so narrowly. Ordinary hearers will almost certainly review only Telemachos's stay in Pylos and Sparta. When, therefore, in the process of recounting Penelope's resolve to face her tormentors, Homer reminds us of Medon's warning (16.411–12) and we are suddenly carried back to the scene of her distress at the end of book 4, we are encouraged to reflect that, although trust in Athena had to suffice her while her son and the more aggressive suitors were absent, the sudden return of both has made some action on her part imperative. A similar manipulation of our sense of time occurs in the *Iliad* when, at the opening of book 14, we find Nestor drinking the same cup of wine we left him with in the middle of book 11 (lines 638–41). It is a shock to realize that all the fighting of books 12 and 13 has occupied an hour at most.

Gallantly facing her wooers in person, Penelope reminds Antinoos that

Odysseus saved his father's life (16.418–33). As we might expect, this does no good, and it only increases our sense of Penelope's helplessness when Eurymachos, pointing out his own obligations to Odysseus, pretends to guarantee Telemachos's safety. Eurymachos's final remark, to the effect that of course death which comes from the gods is not to be avoided, is more than nauseous hypocrisy: it shows us with utter clarity what the suitors really mean to do. If they kill Telemachos in his own house, people will find out about it, and the suitors' position will be at least difficult, even if they do not incur banishment (16.381); but if they do as Antinoos suggests and kill Telemachos in the country or on his way to town (16.383–84), they can get rid of the body just as they would have if their ambush had succeeded, and report that the gods must have done away with the son as they have with his father. We should have no feeling after this that any case can be made for the suitors at all.

The return of Telemachos closes fittingly. The sight of the suitors' ship entering the harbor made Amphinomos laugh, and the same image of the ambush's failure conveyed to Telemachos by the words of Eumaios makes him smile at his father, "avoiding the eyes of the swineherd" (16.477). To be sure, the secret of Telemachos's return is out, but the return of the ambushers is a victory for father and son nonetheless, and there is much to make them, now reunited, confident of success even against these odds. There will be few moments in the lives of either Telemachos or Odysseus as satisfactory as this one, which could not have occurred without the "evils" so plentifully at hand for both.

Beggar on the Threshold

Matters now seem nearly ripe for Odysseus and Telemachos to take their revenge, but this will not be so quickly accomplished as we might at first expect; in fact, eight books will lapse before things are entirely settled. Is Homer dawdling here, as some have thought? No. To make the best literary use of the situation before us will require, as I think we shall see, virtually every line of the text we have.

Making literary use is, of course, not quite the same as solving the "real-life" problem. In real life quicker ways of getting rid of the suitors might be found—for example, the one the poem itself suggests, that Telemachos might call a second assembly of the people. But it is not difficult to see that Athena's method, disguising Odysseus as a beggar, is a much better way for purposes of delighting an audience. We have already seen how Athena's method provides effective ironies, and we may now note three further advantages: first, it allows Odysseus and Telemachos to win their revenge by themselves, except for some slight help from two of their own servants and a great deal of unconscious help from Penelope; second, it allows the suitors to reenact their crime against Odysseus even as his revenge takes shape, thus making the justice more "poetic" when it comes; and third, it allows Odysseus to win his identity starting from nothing, as we have seen him do twice before, with the Kyklops and the Phaeacians. From an artistic point of view this final winning of identity should be the most elaborate, to provide climax. At its end Odysseus will both know himself and know and be known by others, to an extent not otherwise possible.

Presumably to allay suspicion, Odysseus has decided as part of his plan that he and Telemachos shall go separately to the palace—Telemachos first, he to follow with Eumaios. Though it takes longer to describe, much is gained dramatically by this scheme because the two arrivals each have their individual effects, with the climax occurring as the master himself makes his way into the hall. Even before Telemachos sets out, the necessity of getting Odysseus to the palace without letting Eumaios in on the secret yields a foretaste of what is to come. In his disguise the only excuse for Odysseus's going there is to beg, but this means that Telemachos must appear to reject him as guest and suppliant and cast him out of Eumaios's cabin, exposing him to the insult and injury against which both he and Eumaios have hitherto undertaken to protect him. Telemachos is of course up to this, to Eumaios's sorrow, but even we who understand the true intent of the action feel some twinges of indignation. This is all to the good, for not only do we see another case where seeming evil is actual good, but it becomes even clearer, when we see Telemachos apparently mistreating an unfortunate, how contemptible it is of the suitors to take advantage of those who are weaker than they.

Once arrived at the palace, Telemachos, alone as it were in the enemy's camp, is brought face to face with his mother. In this encounter he shows the same apparent hardness he did in rejecting the beggar, for at first he refuses to tell her his news of Odysseus. Of course he cannot admit the truth, but why does he not tell her in the beginning what he heard from Menelaos instead of waiting until later? In the middle of their joyful reunion, as Telemachos is embraced in turn by Eurykleia, by the maids, and then by his mother, "looking like Artemis or golden Aphrodite" (17.37), it does seem hard that he should refuse such a lady anything, and editors, themselves yielding to these charms, speak of Telemachos's coldness. But not yielding to charms is just the point. With every temptation to blurt, Telemachos must not blurt. We are eager to see how he will parry his mother's question, and he does it in a way to show both how truly desperate the situation is and how able he is to face it: to speak of Odysseus now, he says, will only arouse his own grief and anger, since he has barely escaped being murdered by the suitors (17.46–47). We see that the thought of Odysseus is the highly charged thing it has always been: Telemachos is telling his mother the truth, even as he misleads her. She will take his words as meaning that he has had bad news or none at all, but actually the thought of Odysseus, whether with Kalypso or even as present, also arouses grief and anger, considering what the suitors have done and mean to do, and Telemachos must not indulge his emotions in indiscreet talk now. Instead he has the hard task of fetching Theoklymenos from the marketplace, braving the suitors as he does so, though he is quite aware that they may kill him at any time (17.79–80). I think, therefore, that the brusque way he treats Penelope is intended to show us how worthy of his charm-resisting father he is proving to be.

As a matter of fact, a third suggestion of this same beneficial cruelty occurs earlier in the episode as Telemachos sets out from the cabin. His openly admitted reason for going is to relieve Penelope's mind, but Homer colors his departure with the phrase which translates Odysseus's name, "and for the suitors he was planting evils" (17.27). In a good man the hard must coexist with the soft. In the present case what looks like a mission of comfort turns out to be an attack on the suitors as well, and we are glad that this is so. Even before Odysseus goes into action, we see his son successfully preparing the way by living up to implications of his father's name, implications which both create and are the identity to be established for the third and climactic time.

In the present situation Odysseus's name means vengeance, and it is hinted all through the scene that there is retribution in store for the suitors, of which both they and Penelope are as yet unaware. To his mother Telemachos suggests that, rather than chat about Odysseus, she

> wash herself, put on clean clothes,
> and upstairs in her room, calling her maids together
> vow hecatombs to all the gods
> in sacrifice if Zeus will grant revenge. (17.48–51)

These words echo the advice Eurykleia gave to Penelope in her distraction when she first heard of the suitors' plot against her son (4.750–53). On that occasion Penelope prayed Athena to protect her son from the suitors' ambush, so that we now recognize that the first prayer was answered, even as we look forward to the fulfillment of the second. Therefore we are glad to see Penelope obey Telemachos now, brusque though his words may sound and far though she is from understanding their full import.

The conflict to come is again implied when Telemachos takes his spear, first from Eumaios's cabin to the palace, where he "leaned it against a tall pillar" (17.29), and then from the palace to the marketplace (17.62). We remember how at the beginning of the poem also Telemachos took his spear to the agora, after Athena had put hers in Odysseus's spear rack. The connection is especially obvious because the whole image is repeated from the earlier scene: spear, two "swift" dogs, good looks bestowed by Athena, and admiration of the people. In fact, as the final conflict begins, there is much to remind us of the beginning of the poem.

Earlier we have had reason to associate the pair Theoklymenos and Telemachos in this part of the poem with Athena's aid to Telemachos in the first three books, and now we have more. Not only is there the companionship on the voyage and the matter of the spears, but Telemachos and Theoklymenos eat a private meal apart, in the course of which the suitors assemble for their dinner in the same hall, just as Athena and Telemachos did at the beginning of the poem. There the talk concerned the coming destruction of the suitors, and so it does here, the reprise suggesting the beginning of a new phase of the struggle against them. But a departure from the earlier scene is made, emphasizing the new factor in the situation, the return of Odysseus. Penelope joins her son and his guest, and Telemachos now feels free to tell what he has heard from Menelaos. We remember that Menelaos, after giving a rousing picture of what Odysseus would do to the suitors upon his return—they are like fawns left by a careless doe in a lion's lair—seemed to reverse himself by telling the story of Proteus, which implied that Odysseus was far away and unable to return. Telemachos repeats Menelaos's words to his mother, but this time Theoklymenos is present to amplify them. He points out that Menelaos did not know the whole story, and he swears a great oath that Odysseus,

> already in the land of his fathers,
> sitting or creeping, absorbing these wicked deeds,
> lives, and for the suitors, all of them, he sows evils.
> (17.157–59)

The kind of action to which Odysseus's name and presence are alike a prelude could not be more forcefully suggested. Thus Telemachos's separate arrival at the palace begins the account of the revenge against the suitors in a way which, among other things, recalls the opening of the poem, suggesting a new start, but, as is appropriate to this more advanced stage, brings the idea of the revenge itself more strongly to the fore.

Already in the marketplace Telemachos has said quite openly to a fellow townsman that he intends to "sow death and doom for the suitors" (17.82). As in the first book, there is no need to keep this secret, and it is a sign of the suitors' guilt that Telemachos fears no criticism of his project from the townspeople. This and the other references to the revenge which we have seen will prove to be only the beginning: by the end of book 20, the very walls of the palace will seem to be clamoring for the punishment of the suitors; but we should note that, even before Odysseus reaches his town and palace, Telemachos independently brings the idea of the coming revenge vividly to mind.

Particularly Telemachos brings it to Penelope's mind. Her hostility to the suitors becomes more and more evident as we see her first obeying Telemachos's instructions to pray for revenge, then excited by Menelaos's quoted words (17.150), and finally enthusiastic at Theoklymenos's clairvoyance. We have seen what good reason she has for her hostility, and also how powerless she is to rid herself of the men who threaten her son's life.

All this—Telemachos's emulating his father's identity as he creates his own, the growing sense of the revenge to come, and Penelope's favorable reaction to it—has emerged from Homer's account of Telemachos's arrival at the palace in the course of the first 165 lines of book 17. This is scarcely dawdling.

The suitors, against whom tension has been building, now enter the hall for their midday meal, and we are ready for Odysseus's approach. Coming after Telemachos's, it is intended to be climactic, as we have said, and from the very beginning the contrast between the two scenes is implicit. Telemachos carries a spear, but Odysseus asks Eumaios for a staff, adding, "For you say the way is very slippery" (17.196). Comparing Odysseus's staff to Telemachos's spear, we realize that it too represents a weapon and that the road ahead for Odysseus is indeed a slippery one. Furthermore, we have not only the double entendre of Odysseus's remark but the fact that, to the degree that Odysseus's weapon is outwardly less impressive, the sense of its hidden potency is increased. Again, Telemachos is shown reaching his house and going in without further ado as befits both his youthful speed of foot (17.27) and the comparative insignificance of the event for him. Odysseus's advance, on the other hand, is more deliberate (17.254); in addition, it is interrupted by an adventure on the way, and it ends with a suitable pause before his own gates, unseen for twenty years.

The adventure, Odysseus's confrontation with the disloyal goatherd Melanthios, is useful in several ways. In the first place, Melanthios provides a foil for Eumaios. Second, from now on we shall not expect all the servants to be faithful, and we see that the poem distinguishes the good and the evil at all levels of society. Third, as Melanthios abuses Odysseus and kicks him "in the groin" (17.234), we get a foretaste of what is likely to happen in the palace and a preliminary example of the restraint Odysseus must exercise. We are quite convinced that Odysseus can, as Homer says, either kill this wretch with his staff or pick him up and smash him to the ground headfirst; and we appreciate the feeling of suppressed power as Odysseus prudently refrains from doing so. Finally, Homer makes us feel the ugliness of this encounter more strongly by locating it in a beautiful and hallowed spot, by the public fountain and altar to the nymphs which the old kings of Ithaca built in a poplar grove. Odysseus must keep silence, but Eumaios vents his indignation in prayer to these nymphs, just as Odysseus expressed his homecoming joy to the nymphs at his landing place. With Eumaios's prayer the series of wishes for Odysseus's return and the suitors' destruction which marks this book receives a further addition, and we sympathize with it particularly strongly as the goatherd leaves the scene openly wishing for the death of Telemachos, even making his name a kind of talisman for the ruin of both father and son.

> May *Tele*-machos fall dead struck by Apollo's silver bow
> this very day in the palace, or else may the suitors slay him,
> so surely as far from here [*telou*] Odysseus's return was lost.
>
> (17.251–53)

There are various ways to interpret a name, and it depends on the individual and Zeus and the event which one is correct, as we saw in the discussion of book 2. Telemachos's name was meant to suggest that the scenes of his courage would, like his father's, extend to distant lands, but it might all have been as Melanthios wishes instead. We are glad to realize that it is not.

We have foreseen that Odysseus's entering the palace will follow climactically upon Telemachos's. Actually Homer gives us not just two but four entrances to compare. Instead of leaving Melanthios at this point, the poet shows us how the goatherd goes into the palace and, with the ease of long habituation, finds welcome at Eurymachos's table. Eumaios, when he arrives, has more difficulty. He needs to hunt for a chair and finally takes one ordinarily used by one of the carvers in order to take up a similar position near Telemachos. Obviously there is less room here for Odysseus's friends than for his enemies, and so when Odysseus himself appears and takes his seat on the threshold, he seems excluded from a nearer place not only as beggar but as himself, Odysseus. So economically does Homer use his materials: the encounter with Melanthios, the wicked herdsman, may seem after the fact more or less predictable, but the use made of his entrance into the palace was conceived by no ordinary mind.

Escorted by Eumaios, Odysseus at last reaches the house which is the physical goal of his return. In his role of guest he pauses to admire it, and here again we have a climax to a series of comparable scenes. Early in the poem (5.75), Hermes paused to admire Kalypso's pretty cave, for seven years Odysseus's dwelling; subsequently Odysseus stopped and marveled at the palace and gardens of Alkinoos (7.83, 133), which might also have become his home. What he sees before him now, viewed dispassionately as he must pretend to view it, is outwardly less impressive than the house of Alkinoos and promises infinitely less immediate satisfaction than either of the other two. As Odysseus describes it, it seems chiefly characterized by the sturdiness of its defenses.

> Eumaios, surely these are the noble halls of Odysseus,
> easy indeed to distinguish, even among a large number.

Building gives on building, and his courtyard
is walled and coped; the gates are strong
and double doored. No man could fashion better.

(17.264–68)

Yet all the same, we cannot miss the feeling that it is a climax in terms of a scale
of values which we are coming more and more to understand. In spite of its
comparative modesty and the difficulties and dangers which beset it, Odysseus's house is the place where we would most wish him to be.

Eumaios thinks it better that they go in separately. We could speculate about
the practical reasons for this, but there is no need for Homer or for us to
mention them as long as verisimilitude is not noticeably violated. The dramatic reasons are enough: Odysseus must go in alone and unsupported so that
his rise may start from as low a point as possible, and he must go in last, as we
have said, for climax. Thus when Eumaios asks whether he prefers going first
or following, we know what he must choose. Perhaps we get a certain satisfaction from seeing him choose as we would wish, but the chief advantage of
Eumaios's politeness is that it gives Odysseus, on the verge of his greatest
adventure, a chance to express the essence of himself, as he has several times
done before. He answers that he will go last and risk the abuse that may follow
if he remains alone and unsupported outside the door, justifying his choice as
follows:

For I know all about hitting and pelting.
My heart can stand much, for I have had many evils
on the waves and in war. Let this be added to that.
There is no way to hide a man's hungry belly,
that mighty curse, which brings on men such wealth of evils,
at whose bidding men fit out ships with their shapely rowing benches
to sail the barren sea, bearing evils to those not friends.

(17.283–89)

Odysseus's world is a world in which men inevitably prey on each other.
Odysseus himself, as we see, does not blink the grimness of that fact. Yet it has a
certain positive quality in that it inures men to hard knocks. In the passage
before us we can see that it is as true for Odysseus the king as it is for Odysseus
the beggar that his experience of the world's evils supremely qualifies him for
the present situation, and we cannot help but feel to some degree that his
success in the struggle to come would be worth many gentler satisfactions. We

are particularly convinced of this because we heard him make the same boast about his ability to withstand evils as he determined to leave Kalypso (5.221–24). There he deliberately chose a life of exposure to pain over an eternity of peace and pleasure, and for literary purposes at least we were forced to agree with him. Here, as there, we have nothing less than the wry solution which the *Odyssey* offers to the problem of evil: pain creates value. Odysseus is the living embodiment of that solution, and as he prepares to enter his house and deal death and doom to the suitors, we are reminded by this speech of the broadest implications of what is to follow.

But there is a further interruption, and to this one few readers have ever objected: Odysseus's dog Argos, full of fleas and lying on a dungheap, too old even to get to his feet, recognizes his old master and wags his tail. The reader will forgive me for yet again pointing out how much the pain involved in the situation adds to its poignancy and therefore to our sense of its value. Presumably not even dogs grow old on Kalypso's island. In this scene Homer has presented us with a softer emotion to contrast with the grimness of what we may call Odysseus's eve-of-battle speech, and both scenes have the same philosophical implication of the uses of pain and hardship. We are not surprised when Odysseus compares hunting dogs favorably to "table dogs" (17.306–10) with relevance to the same theme, or when Eumaios remarks on the carelessness of masterless slaves. Less obvious is the brilliantly laconic way in which Argos's death is described. We have almost forgotten about him, and then Homer tells us:

> Eumaios spoke and entered the well-sited dwelling;
> straight through the hall he strode, in among the lordly suitors.
> But Argos was struck by fate and the hand of death and its darkness,
> suddenly having had sight, in the twentieth year, of Odysseus.
>
> (17.324–27)

That is all. Odysseus's dog dies, as Odysseus's mother did, as a result of his absence, and the surprise doubles the effect. It is only too easy to tell a sad story about a dog's love for his master, but we begin to see why this one is one of the best.

The Argos episode is of course a recognition scene like the scene with Telemachos in the previous book. In fact perhaps the greatest dramatic advantage of Odysseus's disguise is the opportunity it gives for such recognitions. I shall not pretend to be able to add much to anyone's understanding of why such scenes are in general so effective: perhaps they speak to everyone because we all have had the sudden illumination of realizing what something hitherto unknown *is*, whether it is the solution of a puzzle or the identity of a face. Something which until the moment of recognition had no context suddenly receives one, and the richer and more meaningful the context, the more powerful the experience. There can even be the sense of complete revolution in one's own world, as there must have been for Argos. Nor is Odysseus unaffected: he allows himself a tear here, though he did not at Telemachos's first appearance; and though Homer with the phrase "easily escaping Eumaios's notice" (17.305) keeps us from feeling that Odysseus has lost control, we are aware of the power of his emotion.

We have seen that Odysseus's homecoming was to be essentially a matter of escaping Kalypso and getting to where he could know and be known in the fullest sense: thus the poem lends itself to recognition scenes to a peculiar degree. By the time we reach the Argos episode, recognitions both delayed and consummated are having their effect all around us. We have seen what the full awareness of each other means for Odysseus and Telemachos, and we can guess what recognition of Odysseus will mean for Eumaios when it comes. The effect which the same discovery will have on Penelope and the suitors is now being explored. Yet to discover what Odysseus means to the dog Argos and what Argos means to Odysseus is by no means inessential. Odysseus's right to his family and possessions is nowhere more clearly proclaimed than in the regard Odysseus and his dog have for each other, a regard in which the suitors have not even attempted to share. It remains perhaps to show how Odysseus's neglect of his dog and his family in going to Troy differs from the suitors' lack of regard for both, but that they do differ all must see. Thus the encounter with Argos, though it postpones Odysseus's entrance into his palace, is something we cannot do without.

Homer marks the significance of Odysseus's actual entrance first by repeating the lines which described him as he set out with the swineherd.

> Like a wretched beggar he seemed, an aged man,
> leaning on a staff; the sorry rags covered his body.
>
> (17.337–38 = 202–3)

Then he gives us the exact feeling of the doorway by telling us how it was made, as though we were viewing it close up.

> He took his seat on the ashwood threshold within the doorway,
> leaning against the doorpost of cypress which once the carpenter
> planed till it was smooth, and trued it to the line.
>
> (17.339–41)

At crucial moments such details of our surroundings do seem infused with meaning, and even more to the point, Odysseus's precarious position not even quite inside his own doorway is stressed. Of course the language which describes the doorway here is more or less formulaic, but that does not mean that the poet does not choose it. Homer knows that the right place to use such heightening of detail is at this particular emotional climax of the poem and not, for instance, at Telemachos's entrance or Melanthios's.

From now on, the book will concern itself first with Odysseus's impact on the suitors, especially Antinoos, and afterward with the effect of his presence on Penelope. As we have seen, Antinoos is the most forthright of the suitors in accepting the logic of their position, and that is one reason for his leadership. One of the possible meanings of his name, "hostile minded," is a near synonym for the meaning of Odysseus's own, and as we have suggested that this might indicate, he is personally aiming at taking Odysseus's place. As his advocacy of the murder of Telemachos shows, he will use whatever force is necessary and realizes that there is no possibility of compromise. Therefore it is fitting that he should be the first to come in open conflict with Odysseus, even in his beggar's disguise. Odysseus and Telemachos force the issue and succeed in putting him in an impossible position. Telemachos begins the confrontation by assuming command in his own house and encouraging the beggar to beg from the suitors, each in turn. All acquiesce in this and even pity the beggar until Antinoos, under the mistaken impression that Eumaios has invited him, objects. He says that there are enough "wanderers and beggars" (17.376–77) battening on the household already. Beggars are a nuisance and a drain, as even Eumaios agrees, and Antinoos has something of a point that the generosity of the other suitors is cheap in that they are giving away another man's substance (17.450–52). He implies that they would not do the same at home. To the extent that he is merely calling for a stop to the waste, he is acting like a reasonable man.

But he is wrong on two counts: first, though posing as a guest, he is treating Odysseus's property as his own; and second, whatever the other suitors would do at home, even they believe that beggars are under the gods' protection (17.483–87). Both Antinoos's errors come from what is, at bottom, the suitors' prime delusion: the idea that whatever they can get away with is permissible. Without this conviction Antinoos would not have joined in taking over Telemachos's house against his will and then presumed to oppose him about the beggar, nor would he have felt free to refuse the beggar and risk the anger of the gods. As it is, his pretending to be a guest exposes him both to Telemachos's charge that his real reason for refusing the beggar is to have more to eat himself, and to Odysseus's even more scathing accusation of stinginess.

So! after all you had not the mind I judged from your looks.
You would not give your own steward a pinch of salt from your own house,
you, who sitting at another's table had not the charity
to give me a piece of bread from all that plenty before you.

(17.454–57)

Of course Antinoos is not really so stingy, but his pose as a guest makes him look so. At the same time he cannot drop the pose, since even he is not so shameless as to give what is his true reason, namely, "I regard this as in fact our food, and I don't think we want to see it going to any more beggars."

So the weakness of the suitors' moral position exposes them to this attack, and Odysseus and Telemachos press it strongly. Telemachos even dares Antinoos to take his father's place, as it were, pointing out his incompetence for the role as he does so.

Antinoos, really your care for me is most fatherly!
See how you bid me chase from my hall the stranger,
the word of compulsion upon him—heaven forbid such a thing!

(17.397–99)

He leaves no doubt about who gives the orders in the hall as he continues:

Give him some food, I don't begrudge it. I myself bid you to.
Pay no heed to my mother, nor obey anyone else
of those who serve in this house, the house of godlike Odysseus.

(17.400–402)

Telemachos then goes on to accuse Antinoos of greed as mentioned above.

When all this is capped by Odysseus's description of Antinoos's stinginess, no wonder Antinoos hurls his stool at Odysseus. But his discomfiture would not have been possible if he had not in fact, in a deeper sense than the one he criticizes, been making free of another's goods, taking advantage of Telemachos and Penelope with the same disregard for the weak and unfortunate which he shows toward the beggar. Struck by Antinoos's missile, Odysseus makes the point:

Hear me now, you suitors of the far-famed queen,
as I say to you what the heart within me bids me speak:
It is no grief, for sure, to the feelings, nor any pain,

when, defending his goods, a man
gets hit, fighting for his cattle, or else his snowy sheep;
but me Antinoos hit for my wretched belly's sake,
that mighty curse, which brings on men such wealth of evils.
No: if gods and furies care for beggars at all,
let death find Antinoos before his wedding day. (17.468–76)

Recalling Odysseus's earlier remarks on how the belly causes men to prey on one another in war, these lines show us how different the present situation is. If you do violence to a man who is trying to run off your cattle, you do it to save your cows; if he kills you, it is in order to succeed in his venture. There is nothing personal about it, hence no one feels any great "grief" or "pain." But when Antinoos flings a stool at Odysseus it is as much as to say, "I reject your right to exist as a human being." In the world of the *Odyssey* every stranger has the right to hospitality because it is recognized that, essentially, he cannot exist without it. No doubt the right was abused, as Odysseus seemed to the suitors to be abusing it, but that was not for the host to decide—and besides, Antinoos was not even host. It is this being treated as though he does not count that conveys the deadly hurt to the beggar Odysseus's spirit and makes him pray for his enemy's death. Evidently we are meant to share his indignation; we are shown even the gentle Penelope calling for Antinoos's death because of this act (17.492–504); and from these reactions we can begin to imagine what it means in the *Odyssey*'s world to be denied one's status. Obviously the sense of wrong was so strong in such a case that people felt the gods *must* share it and therefore act out the hostility which the injured party was unable to implement.

Homer, through Odysseus, here defines (or redefines, since the Kyklops episode makes a similar point) the nature of crime. In the *Odyssey* a crime is an act in return for which you would kill the other person if you could, and so would any other right-minded person in your place; if you are unable to do so yourself, you would pray the gods to do it for you with every feeling of justification. Crime is thus that to which vengeance is the passionately desired and utterly appropriate response. It follows that, in this poem, forgiveness can hardly come into question. It did, in a way, in the *Iliad*: at its end, having finally identified the human condition as the ultimate source of injustice, Achilles no longer hates Priam (bk. 24). Odysseus, however, can demonstrate that the suitors ignored him at their peril and in a manner to arouse the vengeance of outraged human nature. In Homeric terms there is no room for forgiveness in such a case.

No one ought to argue that Odysseus is not really a beggar and therefore there is no crime. For the *Odyssey* it is enough that the suitors should demonstrate that they deserve what they get. They are simply reenacting their original crime, which is treating Odysseus and Telemachos as though they did not count. That crime deserves the same deadly indignation as this one, as Athena's words to Telemachos in the first book show and as we ourselves should be able to feel. What the suitors do here in book 17 to Odysseus the beggar is at bottom the same and springs from the same fundamental disrespect as what they are doing to him as absent king.

We may even take this back a step further. Refusing to honor Odysseus's right, even absent or dead, to control the disposition of his property, wife, and son (a right which they themselves admit exists, 1.386–87, 400–404), the suitors are almost literally eating Telemachos up.

> Bit by bit they devour
> my house; soon they will break me to bits as well.
> (1.250–51 = 16.127–28)

Refusing to honor Odysseus's status as stranger, guest, and human being, the Kyklops proceeds to eat Odysseus and his men at the rate of four a day. To deny another man his status not only consumes him but is like cannibalism in this also: it ignores the fact that he is a fellow human being, and this is the kind of callousness that we sense in the suitors as well as the Kyklops. From the *Odyssey*'s point of view, then, we ought to feel that Odysseus's hostility against Antinoos is justified—all of it.

Antinoos evidently counted on the suitors' joining him in violently expelling the beggar from the hall (17.407, 479); instead they are shocked (17.483–87). They suggest that Odysseus may be a god in disguise (we have seen him associated with divinity before); but they act on this idea only insofar as it prevents them from accepting the logic of their own position. For this they deserve no credit. Once they have undertaken to rely on power rather than decency, decent behavior becomes a luxury they cannot afford. Here we see again, as we did in the matter of Telemachos's murder, how feelings of decency work against the suitors and for Odysseus once the suitors have set themselves above the norms of their society.

Odysseus's disguise puts him in the position of having to reestablish his identity with those who knew him before, most intriguingly of all with Penelope. In real life he might be able to do this merely by telling her at the proper moment who he is, but in the poem Homer shows him doing something even more interesting. Not only does the beggar provide irony by exhibiting various similarities to Odysseus, but these similarities are themselves effective in creating the identity to be established. It is the beggar's own Odyssean qualities that arouse in Penelope vivid thoughts of her husband's presence before she ever hears the beggar's news, and indeed that impel her to ask for his news at all. The beggar makes his first impression on her when, as Man of Pain, he is struck by Antinoos. She responds with an Odyssean surge of hostility, calling on Apollo to strike Antinoos as he struck (17.494). Indeed it is not long before she is calling for the death of all the suitors, as she did in book 4. This develops in the following way: the stranger's "ill luck" (*dustēnos*, 17.501) and his quality of being "much battered abroad" (*poluplanktōi*, 17.511), descriptions which we know apply peculiarly to Odysseus, suggest to Penelope by their meaning alone that the stranger may have news of Odysseus. Therefore she asks Eumaios to bring him to her. Eumaios not only reports the stranger's claim to knowledge of Odysseus but also emphasizes the fascination exerted by his tale of misfortunes (17.517). Penelope, eager for the interview and in a mood to defy the suitors to get it, is impelled both to enumerate their crimes and to remark how easily Odysseus and Telemachos could dispose of them if only Odysseus should come home again (17.529–40). When the last statement is crowned by the omen of Telemachos's sneeze, Penelope's hostility at last finds itself hailing the death of all.

> Penelope laughed aloud,
> and straightway to Eumaios she spoke these winged words:
> "Go on my errand, and call the stranger to come here before me.
> Do you not see how my son's sneeze proved all that I said?
> That way the suitors' death would not come short of fulfillment,
> death for them all; not one would escape the spirits of darkness."
>
> (17.542–47)

The Odyssean characteristics of the stranger and the buffet he has withstood have combined with the idea of Odysseus's return to make Penelope contemplate the suitors' doom not only with delight but with hope.

Telemachos, as we saw, with the help of Theoklymenos, has almost brought Penelope to the same point, but there it is Theoklymenos who speaks the doom of the suitors, with Penelope assenting. Here she speaks the words and reads the omen herself. Thus Telemachos's sneeze marks a culmination of that series of wishes for Odysseus's return and the suitors' destruction which we have been noticing. It also marks Penelope's complete emotional assent to much of what the return of her husband will mean, even before she has seen him, even in disguise.

She has not seen him because, in typical Odyssean fashion, the beggar shows an apparently cruel, if prudent, restraint toward the woman who is his own wife. He postpones the interview until the suitors shall have left for the night, even while stressing his unique competence to speak about Odysseus: "Well do I know about him; the same suffering [oïzdun] has been ours" (17.563). Here of course he hints at his true name, as he does again a few lines later speaking of Antinoos: "Though I did him no wrong, he delivered me over to pain [odunēsin]" (17.567). He postpones the interview, pleading the suitors' violence and his own need to come "nearer the fire" (17.572), a thing he manifestly cannot do while they are present.

We may suspect that there are good literary reasons for the postponement: it seems too soon to bring Odysseus, even in disguise, face to face with his wife before he has had more to do with the suitors. Sensing this, we are especially glad of this further display of the Odyssean character: we know we will get the scene eventually and know it will be a good one. Besides, the touch about "nearer the fire" accords with the other progressions which mark this part of the poem. One of Odysseus's pretended reasons for delaying his departure from Eumaios's hut was that his old bones needed warming, especially considering his poor clothes (17.23–24). Odysseus has apparently been cold ever since he borrowed Eumaios's heavy cloak at the end of book 14. We are not allowed to forget this. As Odysseus and Eumaios are finally about to set out in the morning, Eumaios warns his companion that he must start while the sun is still high, for the evening will be cold (17.191). Later, conveying to him Penelope's invitation to an interview, Eumaios remarks that she has offered to give him better clothes, a thing he "especially needs" (17.557–58). With this preparation, Odysseus's mention of coming nearer the fire is very telling. We have seen how difficult the palace is to get into, and so far Odysseus has maintained himself only with difficulty on the threshold; but there are those, Penelope for one, who are eager to bring him farther in.

Before the book ends Eumaios has a last word with Telemachos, bidding him be careful first of all for himself, "for many Achaians harbor evil thoughts against you" (17.596). Telemachos replies, stressing the time of day:

> Let it be so, old man; eat your afternoon meal, and go;
> in the morning, come and bring the animals to be slaughtered.
> As for matters here, they are my care—and the immortals'.
>
> (17.599–601)

In strong contrast to this, but similarly stressing the time of day, we immediately hear of the carefree suitors. Eumaios

strode on his way to his hogs, leaving the hall and enclosure
full of the banqueting suitors. They with dancing and singing
pleasured themselves, for already the day's afternoon had come.

(17.604–6)

It is indeed the afternoon of the suitors' day, for we feel that their end is
approaching. In fact, we may even be reminded of a like effect toward the end
of the first book of the poem. There Telemachos in the same grim mood he
exhibits here has just concealed from the suitors the fact that a god has
appeared to help him.

So Telemachos spoke, though his heart knew the immortal goddess.
The suitors for their part turned to dancing and lovely song;
pleasuring themselves with these they waited for evening to come,
and as they pleasured themselves, black the evening came.

(1.420–23)

BOOK 18

Afternoon to Evening

Afternoon is at hand, and we look forward to the night, when the suitors will leave the hall and Odysseus will talk to Penelope alone. Before that happens, however, there is much to be accomplished. So far, since his return, Odysseus has been essentially the sufferer, the man hit by Antinoos. As he did with the Phaeacians, he has been winning pity before he wins respect. Now, however, changing to the active, he shows his prowess. Opportunely but not unprepared for, another beggar, a real one, appears to dispute with him his right to the threshold. We remember that Antinoos had said that there were such beggars. This one's nickname, Iros, with its casual, quasi-literary reference to Iris, the messenger-maiden of the gods, should help to remind us that this is not a primitive poem in any sense: we are told merely that the young men called him Iros because he used to go to and fro with messages whenever anyone required it; the suitors' sophistication is thus put on a level with our own. In any case, thanks to this Iros we are about to have the pleasure of seeing Odysseus stand up for his rights at last.

Both justice and identity are involved in the scene. We watch how the suitors' delight at the prospect of a fight leads, under Odysseus's and Telemachos's skillful management, to their willingness to see fair play (18.51–65), then even to their reading the moral situation correctly as they take note of Odysseus's muscles.

> Iros will be de-Irosed by the annihilation he asked for,
> to judge by the thigh the old man shows underneath his rags.
>
> (18.73–74)

The suggestion of Iros's loss of identity is perfectly relevant. Quite specifically the outcome of the fight proves that he is neither what he looked nor what he claimed to be. Furthermore, the suitors are unconsciously pronouncing on their own case. Like Iros, they too, in trying to take Odysseus's place, are pretending to a role they are unable to fill and are bringing on themselves annihilation in consequence—as is just, since they intend a like annihilation for Odysseus and Telemachos. Meanwhile the way in which, in spite of their basic rejection of justice, they find themselves upholding it is almost Platonic in its demonstration of the effectiveness of the Good. Willy-nilly as they observe his conduct with Iros, they respect Odysseus the beggar for the right reasons, not only for his courage, strength, and ability, but for his fair-minded-ness in being willing to share the threshold as Iros will not. Iros in turn loses their respect and in effect his identity as well, as Antinoos threatened before the fight.

> You'll wish you had never been born or existed, you mud-cow,
> if this fellow frightens you and fills you with terror,
> an old man, worn out with the pain he has suffered.
> Let me tell you what will happen and no mistake
> if by chance this man should win and come off the victor.
> I'll throw you aboard my black ship: then off to the mainland
> to King Echetos, spoiler of all mankind,
> who will cut off your nose and your ears with his cruel sword blade,
> then tear your genitals out and give them raw to his dogs.
> (18.79–87)

This threat, as used here, repeated by the suitors after the fight (18.115–16), and then used again by Antinoos against Odysseus himself at 21.308, is conventional scare talk, but, nevertheless, something much like what Antinoos suggests here is actually done by Telemachos and Eumaios to Melanthios at the end of the poem. To lose one's identity is no joke in any society, and here the physical effects are in keeping with the seriousness of the disaster, even as they suggest its nature.

The prudently "gentle" blow with which Odysseus strikes Iros beneath the ear

> crushed the bones
> within: and at once from his mouth red blood came;
> he fell in the dust bleating, and drove his teeth together
> as he drummed his heels on the ground. (18.96–99)

Some have thought that Iros's rage is being expressed here, but it seems more likely and more in keeping with the rest of the scene that he is responding to intense pain. A friend informs me that she has seen on TV a victim pulled from the rubble of the Mexico City earthquake behave as Iros does here. On the lowest level, Odysseus is to be respected for his physical strength, and we may agree that this scene conveys it powerfully.

In spite of themselves, the suitors are beginning to respect Odysseus. Antinoos, once so recalcitrant, is now happy to award him a choice portion of the food, and they all agree to give him a secure place in the hall as their favored beggar. This is as close as they will come to being on the right side either morally or strategically, and it will be now, if ever, that they can be made to change their fatal course. It is fitting, therefore, that in the next scene Odysseus should attempt to warn them. Amphinomos has been especially agreeable after the victory—we have already seen that he is only half a villain—and Odysseus tries to save him by pointing out a fundamental truth.

> The earth feeds nothing more helpless than man
> of all the things that breathe and move upon it.
> He never thinks that he will suffer evil later,
> so long as the gods give him success, and his knees are strong;
> but when at last the happy gods bring defeat upon him,
> that too he must bear as well as he can, unwilling.
> *For the mind of man that walks the earth is even such*
> *as the day which the father of gods and men brings on him.*
> (18.130–37; emphasis mine)

This is not a difficult idea, merely an important one. It may be the prime truth derivable from Odysseus's travels, for Homer asked the Muse to tell of the man who "saw the towns of many men and knew their mind" (1.3). It implies that men's notions depend on their circumstances and are, to that extent, deluded. Men in general cannot control what tomorrow will bring, and yet in success they cannot help feeling and acting as though they could. In prosperity they cannot imagine defeat.

Politely, Odysseus applies the idea first to his fictitious self, saying that, in his youth "giving way to force and violence,/relying on [his] father and brothers," he committed many "arrogant and insolent acts [*atasthala*]" (18.138–40). Now he wishes that instead he had taken what the gods gave in quiet gratitude (18.142). Some take this as a reference to his real career, particularly to the Trojan War, but I do not see how this can be. We never see him commit an arrogant or insolent act either in the *Odyssey* or in the *Iliad*. Both Athena and Zeus at the beginning of the *Odyssey* pronounce him exactly the opposite sort of man. He is not and never has been an Aigisthos, as that context makes clear.

Certainly, furthermore, he never "relied on his father and brothers." Instead, that detail applies rather to Amphinomos. It suggests that the whole purpose of Odysseus's present remarks, which are not a true confession in any sense, is to point out that there is no safety even in the suitors' numbers and that Amphinomos's fortune may change even as Odysseus is pretending that his has changed. The irony of the scene depends on the pretense: Odysseus's fortune is really in the ascendant; he is not an example of the loss of heaven's blessing at all. Meanwhile, what he is saying does apply to Amphinomos, though not to himself. Like most men, Amphinomos cannot sufficiently imagine in the midst of prosperity the evil that may come. His mind is such as the soon-to-end day which Zeus has brought him.

Odysseus gives Amphinomos absolutely fair warning. He tells him that what the suitors are doing is arrogant and insolent (18.143) and that Odysseus is near. He even prays for him: "May heaven/take you home out of this" (18.146–47). Amphinomos is much impressed, but he returns to his seat in the hall instead, "shaking his head as he went; his heart saw the evil to come" (18.154). As a piece of human behavior, this is only too familiar and likely: we can see ourselves acting in the same way, even though by this act Amphinomos makes his own death sure. Furthermore, if Amphinomos cannot tear himself out of this false and fatal position, no suitor can. From now on we must acquiesce in the justice of their destruction, though we are aware that they are not completely bad, either individually or as a group.

Amphinomos's fate reflects a truth about the way our world works, and so for Homer the gods are obviously involved. By naming Athena as responsible, Homer conveys the pathos of the human situation without detracting from the credit we accord to those who, like Odysseus, manage to keep their feet out of the toils by strength of will and intellect. Or do they possess this strength simply by the grace of heaven? We need not admire them any the less for that. Some such reflection I think is needed to understand passages like the following:

> The suitors raised a clamor along the hall; but Athena
> came, and standing close to Odysseus, son of Laertes,
> urged him on to collect alms among the suitors,
> to know who among them were decent, and who were lawless.
> Yet not even so would she save one from destruction.
>
> (17.360–64)

Similarly in the present passage, Athena is at work as Amphinomos returns to his fatal seat in doubt.

Not even so did he escape death, for Athena bound him
also, to fall to Telemachos's hands and the strength of his spear.
Back he went and sat in the seat from which he had risen.

(18.155–57)

We must admit, I think, that in real life Athena is like that.

The next scene, in which Penelope comes downstairs and asks gifts of the suitors, well depicts what it is that keeps Amphinomos from saving himself, but many have thought it an interpolation as being uncharacteristic of Penelope. It is indeed a scene which confounds our expectations in various ways, but even so I am sure it is a vital part of Homer's own conception, adding, as it can, so materially to our sense of the complexity of what is going on.

At the end of book 4, when Penelope was desperately worried that the suitors would kill Telemachos, she was compared to a lioness surrounded by hunters. Though there was little that she could do except pray to Athena, we felt her power as well as her helplessness. Now again in book 18, she faces the knowledge that the suitors mean to kill her son, and this time Athena sees to it that she does not remain passive. Athena bestows on her the impulse to show herself to the suitors

that she might flutter
their hearts and be more treasured
by her husband and son than she was before.

(18.160–62)

Athena is responding, as it were, to any sense we might have that Penelope has not yet in this poem received the respect she deserves. She really does play a large part in the revenge, as the bait which catches the suitors. The problem is to get her to play that role more prominently even when, as she says, she hates them. Athena can force her against her nature, but it will be more like Homer if in the end it all seems natural. People do do things against their own natures (obvious interference by the gods!), especially in situations as tense as the present one, and it finally seems utterly right that Penelope should do what she does here. Frustrated when she tried to recall Antinoos to a sense of decency, she has since then spent a day full of intimations of her husband's return and the destruction of the suitors, intimations she cannot completely believe but which nevertheless excite her. Theoklymenos has corrected Telemachos's repetition of Menelaos's story with all the authority of prophecy: he has asserted that Odysseus is even now in Ithaca. Later, her own words to the effect that, if

Odysseus should return, he and his son would requite the suitors' insolence have been answered by the omen of Telemachos's sneeze (17.541). At the same time, Antinoos's cruelty has called her attention to the mysterious beggar, but the beggar has postponed the interview she has requested. The only way she can break the passivity to which she finds herself condemned is to exercise her attractions on the suitors, even though to what end is not clear even to her.

Homer's account shows admirably both her uncertainty and the sources of her excitement. We hear of her irrational (*akhreion*) laugh as she speaks the following words to her housekeeper:

> Eurynome, my heart desires, as it has not before,
> to visit my suitors, much though I hate them.
> I could advise my son, and it would be better,
> to avoid the company of the suitors.
> They speak him well to do him ill hereafter.
>
> (18.164–68)

Here Penelope's natural concern for her son is partly responsible for her act, but both she and Eurynome know that it is not the whole reason. On Penelope's side there is the irrational laugh, showing that her impulse precedes her rationalization of it. Nor is Eurynome deceived: she knows that now is the time for Penelope to shake off her sadness and to summon all her powers and weapons. By all means go, she says, and do not forget your makeup (18.170–74). She even adds, cryptically,

> For now your son is of the age which most of all
> you prayed the gods for: to see the beard upon his chin.
>
> (18.175–76)

Within the next hundred lines we discover the particular relevance of this: the appearance of Telemachos's beard not only gladdens his mother with the evidence that he is raised but marks the time at which Odysseus told Penelope to give up hope and to marry again (18.259–70). Penelope herself violently rejects the idea of making herself attractive—Athena has to apply the makeup while she is asleep—but still, there it is. Marriage is one of Penelope's options, and her attractiveness is one of the most important things about her. To be herself she must use her charm; her woman's nature, triumphing over her more conscious thoughts, impels her along her proper course, even against her will.

Arrived in the hall, she seems to be thinking less of Telemachos, whom she meant to warn, than of the stranger, indicating a second source of her unease. She does the opposite of what she intended, rebuking her son for not getting more involved with the suitors rather than less: she blames him for not protecting the beggar better. Suppose, she says,

> something should happen to him,
> in all this pushing and hauling;
> what a disgrace that would be! (18.223–25)

In short, under the influence of her husband's disguised presence and in the spirit of his name, she finds herself urging on the conflict rather than trying to avoid it.

What she learns from her son can only tend to confirm her in this course. Telemachos's reply (18.227–42), although it deludes Penelope by suggesting that he is frightened of the suitors and without support, when the reverse is the case, puts before his mother his father's recent success against Iros. Odysseus has taken the offensive. Far from being the helpless victim of the suitors' violence this time, the stranger entered the fight of his own choice and came off the victor. We appreciate the irony of Telemachos's next remark: would that the suitors at this moment were as badly off as the beggar Iros, who is unable even to get himself home! For our delectation, if not Penelope's, the allusion to the beggar who did make it home is very clear. Furthermore, the beggar whom Telemachos knows to be Odysseus has just done to Iros what Telemachos would like to see him do to the suitors.

Next, we are shown Penelope's scorn for her admirers. Eurymachos makes the queen a compliment to the effect that, if all the Achaians could see her now, tomorrow there would be more suitors in the hall, so much does she surpass other women in beauty and intelligence. Eurymachos does not use the word *kleos*, "fame," but he pictures its essence: we visualize the "fame" of Penelope's beauty compelling large numbers, and we may remember Antinoos's remarking at the beginning of the poem that, by keeping the suitors dangling, Penelope is winning "for herself great fame [*kleos*]," but for Telemachos "loss of much livelihood" (2.125–26). Penelope's response to Eurymachos's compliment is most interesting; her real attractions and fame, she says, depend on the presence of Odysseus.

> Eurymachos, the truth is, my value, my looks, and my stature
> the gods destroyed that day when the men set sail for Ilion,
> the Argives, and with them went my husband, Odysseus.

> If *he* now should come and cultivate my life,
> then my glory [*kleos*] would be greater, and fairer that way.
>
> (18.251–55)

It would be a mistake to read these words too casually, assuming that Penelope was showing a more or less conventional grief. Actually this is one of the most important speeches in the poem, and Penelope is making a point of some subtlety. How can she say she is not beautiful, with the living evidence of 108 suitors there before her? She must mean, must she not, that, no matter how many suitors' "knees go slack" (18.212) as they behold her, she does not feel valuable or beautiful except when Odysseus is there. She rejects Eurymachos's assertion of her fame in the same way as his assertion of her beauty: if Odysseus should return and "busy himself about her life," she says, her fame would be "greater" and "fairer" than that which any number of suitors could provide. Is she thinking of still another public than the suitors and saying that she would be known to more people, and better spoken of, living a happy married life with Odysseus than as besieged by 108 admirers? We can see that such fame might be "fairer," but could it really be "greater"? I think rather that she is internalizing the idea of her fame just as she has the idea of her beauty. Whatever the external situation, she seems to say, her beauty is not beauty unless she feels beautiful to herself; similarly, no matter how much other people admire her, or how many, her fame is not really "great" or "fair" unless she feels it to be so, and she feels it so most as Odysseus's wife.

Homer provides another passage in which he actually sets a married couple's public and private image side by side and says that to them it is the private image that matters most. This would not be so remarkable or useful for our purpose if he did not at the same time imply, by using the verb *kluein*, that *kleos* (the related word we have been translating "fame") can refer to the private image as well as the public—which is what we have suspected that Penelope has been making it do. The passage is the famous one in which Odysseus praises marriage for Nausikaa's benefit.

> For that surpasses everything
> when two keep house in harmony,
> a man and wife; it makes their haters suffer,
> their friends rejoice, but they feel it [*ekluon*] most themselves
>
> (6.182–85)

Here is public and private image set side by side, and the statement that the latter counts most of all. The use of the verb *kluein* suggests that one can have *kleos*, or be famous, to one's self as well as to others, "hearing" (*kluōn*) internally one's own aural image (*kleos*) of oneself. Even more important, Odysseus is suggesting through these words that the best thing about a good marriage is the way the people concerned feel about themselves. This should make it the more likely that Homer is making the same point through Penelope's words here in book 18.

We have come this long way round to discover what precisely Penelope is saying as she rejects Eurymachos's compliment. It should be evident now, if it was not before, that she is saying that Odysseus can make her feel valued and glorious and that the suitors cannot. She also suggests how he does so, and this throws a sudden new light on Odysseus himself. Her fame would be greater, she says, if that man should come and "cultivate my life," *ton emon bion amphipoleuoi*. The verb *amphipoleuein* means "to busy one's self about; to tend to"; it is what Odysseus's father, Laertes, does to his orchard (24.244, 257), and an *amphipolos* is a servant. Obviously Odysseus is no woman's cavalier servente—the Kirke episode showed us that—but we can understand how the respect and concern of such a man, were he there to exhibit it, would make Penelope feel more valued and valuable than anything else in the world could; his presence would indeed make her life seem to blossom as if under the hands of a gardener. In fact it would not be inappropriate to be reminded here of the hero of Joyce's *Ulysses*, Leopold Bloom. Thus Penelope's phrase makes us see Odysseus's "heroic" qualities temporarily in a very different light. For the moment, the city sacker off at Troy may even seem antithetic to the husband Penelope would like to see safe at home. Yet would a stay-at-home really make Penelope feel beautiful and glorious? As we see, these stay-at-home suitors cannot.

Here we must point to an incidental implication of the use of such a phrase as *ton emon bion amphipoleuoi*, "should cultivate my life," in such a context: it makes it impossible to see Homer, oral technique or no oral technique, as the comparatively unconscious mouthpiece of the tradition some would have him. No doubt other bards had used the phrase to mean something like "take care of my livelihood"; but that is very different from the effect Homer achieves here, where it implies composition of the most conscious and subtle sort.

Penelope rejects Eurymachos's compliment, and we see how little she values the suitors in comparison with Odysseus. Yet she says she will soon go through with the marriage which Odysseus has advised, though she loathes the prospect. Meanwhile the suitors are to woo her properly, contributing their own cattle for the feasting and giving her presents. They balk at providing the cattle, for they mean to keep the pressure on her to marry, but they do bring the presents. Odysseus is delighted, observing how "she solicited their gifts, and

charmed them/with sweet-sounding words, with a different object in mind"
(18.282–83). How are we to interpret Penelope's actions? We have already
suggested that she showed herself to the suitors not so much to warn Telemachos as to have some effect on the crisis that is building. Though she is not
sure at first what she means to do, Eurymachos's compliment prompts her to
attempt to use "for the first time" (18.164) her beauty and the promise of her
wedding to make the suitors woo her properly. Although she fails of her object,
she affects the suitors strongly, and we are gratified to see her exercise her power
at the same stage of the action as her husband does. We are assured of her
reluctance to marry one of the suitors by the phrase "charmed them/with
sweet-sounding words, with a different object in mind," and she has even
prayed that death may relieve her of the longing she feels for her husband
(18.201–5).

We must not, however, take the words "with a different object in mind" as
meaning she has no thoughts of marriage whatever. We have known from the
beginning, when Telemachos said that she does not refuse the marriage
(1.249), that she must have some thoughts of it, and recently he has said the
same thing to his father (16.126). When Antinoos says in the assembly that she
encourages the suitors "with a different object in mind" (2.92), he means that
she intends to keep them dangling for her own glory rather than to marry one of
them; but when Athena uses the same words to Odysseus at 13.381, she means
what we have assumed all along and what Odysseus too would reasonably
suppose, that she is keeping her options open but will hold out as long as
possible. That is what Odysseus is admiring here. The scene being enjoyed by
him and Telemachos is not that of a wife and mother merely pretending to be
available in a bargain she knows she will not have to go through with but a
much more piquant one in which, however reluctant, her offer as far as she
knows is only too likely to be genuine. Hence her "irrational" laugh at the
beginning of the episode.

And so it seems to me, far from being an interpolation, this scene is
necessary for our understanding of Penelope and her role. Furthermore, there
now reigns in the hall a strong atmosphere of sex, on which the next scene
depends. We see how the suitors are affected by Penelope's presence.

> Their knees went slack on the spot, hearts spellbound with desire,
> and one and all they prayed to lie with her in bed.
>
> (18.212–13)

It accords with this heightened desire of theirs that they should, as they do, now
set up lamps in the hall and prepare to make a night of it instead of going home;

but first, as though not only to mark the passage of time but to show how much Penelope too contributes to their downfall, Homer repeats the passage from book 1 which the last book recalled so ominously. As Penelope goes upstairs with her presents,

> the suitors for their part turned to dancing and lovely song;
> pleasuring themselves with these they waited for evening to come,
> and as they pleasured themselves, black the evening came.
>
> $(18.304-6 = 1.421-23)$

As evening comes, we want the suitors out of the hall so that Odysseus and Penelope may meet in private, but the suitors have decided to spend the night, or a good part of it. What is Odysseus to do? It is another masterstroke of Homer's that Odysseus not only manages to get them out but threatens to disappoint them of their sexual satisfaction in the process. For the suitors not only have pretended to the future favors of his wife but have been enjoying the less loyal of his girl slaves in the meantime, and we do not need to assume that he is in love with these last to see how this violates some very strong human feelings. For this night at least, he manages to spoil part of the suitors' fun, and it is gratifying to see him, even before the revenge, begin to take away from them as it were not only Penelope but the maids.

As the process of getting rid of the interlopers develops, we see power growing on the side of Odysseus and Telemachos. The maids troop in to tend the lamps. Odysseus firmly suggests that their proper place is with Penelope and undertakes to keep the light going himself.

> I will furnish light for all the suitors here.
> Even if they wish to stay until bright morning,
> they will not wear me out; I am exceedingly patient.
>
> $(18.317-19)$

We not only appreciate the hint who this exceedingly patient person really is who is speaking and what kind of light he will give the suitors, but we also realize that he is coming "nearer the fire," as he wished to do in book 17. The maids, less well informed than we, look significantly at each other and laugh. They think the beggar misunderstands, and Melantho, Melanthios's sister, undertakes to point out to him how much in the way he is. She accuses him of being drunk, or crazy, that he should behave so above himself. But with a single word Odysseus scatters the maids in terror back to Penelope. Telemachos, he says, will cut them limb from limb for such talk. "They thought that he spoke the truth," Homer adds (18.342), and that they did so shows the respect which Telemachos has gained. Power, we see, is increasing on the side of Odysseus.

The suitors' mood is good, however, all unaware as they are, and at first they are quite willing to amuse themselves with the beggar instead of the maids. Eurymachos conceives the unhappy notion of twitting Odysseus on his bald head.

> Not without divine sanction this man comes to the house of Odysseus;
> anyway a shine of torches seems to come from him too,
> out of his head, which has no strand of hair upon it.
>
> (18.353–55)

The image is a good deal more ominous than Eurymachos knows. As a matter of fact, the suitors have a history of associating Odysseus with the gods, without realizing what they are saying. They were closest to realizing the truth when, as we have already seen, they rebuked Antinoos on the ground that the stranger might himself be a god, but Antinoos himself has imputed Telemachos's preservation to the gods (16.364). He has also blamed heaven for bringing "this killjoy to the feast" (17.446) and praised it for providing the fight between Odysseus and Iros (18.37). Now Eurymachos has made the same association of heaven and Odysseus in jest, but the light that seems to shine from Odysseus's head will prove to be no joke. Precisely as Eurymachos ironically pretended, Odysseus is, for him and the other suitors, a sending of the gods.

Eurymachos continues by making the immemorial jibe at beggars: I would be glad to give you work, but of course you are too lazy. For us who know the secret, however, this is an even less successful sally than the previous one. As Odysseus pictures himself competing with Eurymachos at mowing, "on an empty stomach until dark" (18.370), or plowing, or in battle, Eurymachos seems crushed by the comparison, and we are prepared for the culminating threat.

> You seem to think you are a great man and wielder of power
> because your fellows are few, and not of much account.
> If Odysseus should ever come safe to shore in the land of his fathers,
> suddenly those two doors, great though the span of them is,
> would be a tight fit as you fled for the porch and the outside air.
>
> (18.382–86)

Except for his warning to Amphinomos, this is the first time the beggar has mentioned the return of Odysseus to the suitors. Eurymachos is of course beyond warning. Instead, he is stung by Odysseus's implication that even he, a beggar, can outmow, outplow, outfight him—let alone what Odysseus could do. The rebuke stings him, but does not remove his deluded sense of security, accurately though it states his error. In fact, as he deliberately prepares to throw his stool, he repeats Melantho's rebuke: you must be drunk or crazy to act so much above yourself. We suddenly realize both that these are two of a kind and that Odysseus has come between them. We have already been told that Melantho is Eurymachos's light-o'-love (18.325); Eurymachos, apparently deprived by Odysseus of his evening's sport, has the more reason for his grievance.

His missile, however, is less effective than Antinoos's was: Odysseus avoids it altogether by crouching at Amphinomos's knees (18.395), and it knocks over the slave who pours the wine. We have another progression here. More missiles, when they occur, will be even less effective as power grows on the side of the rightful owners of the hall. As part of the same progression, the suitors' reaction is more drastic. Previously they blamed Antinoos; now they blame the beggar, in keeping with his changeover from passive to active. In a way, this is more respectful, and they come closer to realizing the nature of the man before them.

> Would that the stranger had died somewhere else in his wandering
> before coming here; he would not have made such trouble among us.
> Now we fight over beggars. (18.401–3)

The suitors, without knowing it, name the situation exactly. They may well indeed wish that the stranger had died abroad, as they assume Odysseus has, for the man before them is Odysseus himself, living up to his name by introducing trouble among those he meets.

The suitors' wish for the beggar's death may be dangerous, but Telemachos is equal to the situation. Gently and politely, as his father told him to (16.278–79), he restrains them, suggesting that it is they who are drunk and crazy, that they are not themselves, that some god is at work, and that they had better go home to bed. At this the suitors bite their lips. It has been said that this is to check their angry words, but that seems not to be the meaning of the gesture. When Telemachos rebuked them much more vehemently in book 1, they "bit their lips and wondered at him" as here (1.381–82 = 18.410–11), and when he repeated that rebuke in the assembly in book 2, the suitors all "were silent," and no one "had the hardihood to reply" except Antinoos (2.82–83). I think that, here as well as there, the suitors are abashed and have nothing to say. It is not like them to check their anger, but as we have seen they do have a sense of shame. So in the present situation, though they are growing increasingly hostile to the beggar, there is still room for Amphinomos's milder counsel to take effect: Telemachos is right, he says, and no one should be angry. Enough of throwing things at beggars and servants. They should pour one more drink, to the gods, and then home to bed. Thus Odysseus, Telemachos, and the suitors' own conscience expressed in the words of Amphinomos combine to clear the hall, impossible as that seemed at first. Ironically, the suitors even accord Telemachos his rights in the house: Amphinomos ends by saying,

> As for the stranger, let him stay in the house of Odysseus
> to be Telemachos's care: it was his house that he came to.
>
> (18.420–21)

Such is the strength of justice. As the book ends we realize that Odysseus's side has now taken the offensive and that the suitors, incapable of being warned, will pursue their fatal course, enthralled as they are by another man's wife, largely against her will. Though they still feel secure, the house already seems half cleared of their power as we await the interview, so long promised, between Penelope and her unrecognized husband. As we wait we notice that the tension has increased: because of it both Penelope and the suitors find themselves behaving in ways they had not expected.

The Man of Pain

But noble Odysseus remained, left behind in the hall
pondering, with Athena, how he should kill the suitors.
(19.1–2 = 19.51–52)

These two lines both begin and end the next episode, in which Odysseus and
Telemachos remove the weapons from the hall. In so pondering, Odysseus is
engaged in his most characteristic activity according to the meaning of his
name, and Athena is with him, though not necessarily in visible form. This is
how we should see him for the next three books.

So far Odysseus has been able to defeat his rival beggar, Iros, and to control
the wayward maids. Now with Telemachos's help he strikes a blow against the
suitors themselves by removing the arms from the walls, while Athena's presence is signaled by the brilliant light "as of blazing fire" which she casts over the
scene. That we may not miss the point, Telemachos guesses that some god is
present, and Odysseus, counseling silent reverence, confirms the fact. In this
way we have a visual picture of Odysseus preparing doom for the suitors with
Athena's help, which gives perspective to the meeting between Odysseus and
Penelope now about to take place. Yet even though the removal of the arms was
carefully prepared for in book 16 and will be referred to at least three more
times before the poem ends (22.23–25, 140–41; 24.164–66), overrationalistic
critics have cast doubt on it. Why, they ask, should Athena, "holding a golden
lamp," be needed to illuminate this rather trivial action of father and son?
Could not Odysseus carry the light and Telemachos the arms, as Telemachos
suggested (19.27)? To argue this way is to fail to see how well Athena's light
casting expresses the rightness and the fatality of what the humans are doing; in
fact, it expresses it so well that to Homer it seemed the actual way it must have
been. Do human actions on occasion have a luminosity about them, or do
they not? The luminosity before us has been in preparation ever since Odys-

seus expressed a wish to come "nearer the fire," and even before, when Eumaios warned him of the evening's chill. By now he has won the job of fire tender and illuminator in the hall (18.340–45); Eurymachos has remarked the light streaming from his bald head and laughingly imputed it to divine agency (18.353–55); and Telemachos has just nominated him torchbearer (19.27–28). In the event, Athena bears the light, but in a way it is as much Odysseus's as hers, for they both are determined to destroy the suitors. They are joining together to produce the deliverance of the House of Odysseus and the vindication of the justice of the gods.

Nor is this all: there is the irony that the menial task of torchbearer, with which Telemachos pretends he will afflict his beggar-guest, is actually of divine importance, and there is the deprecatory quality of Odysseus's excuse, intended for the suitors, for removing the arms: "Ah, the arms of Odysseus are not what they were once; the smoke has dulled them; and perchance, in your cups, you might quarrel and hurt yourselves with them" (19.7–13, in summary)—this contrasted with the bracing effect of the same excuse when used by Telemachos to Eurykleia: "I shall put away my father's beautiful weapons, till now uncared for while I was still too young" (19.16–20, in summary). Eurykleia shows us the tendency of these words by her reply,

> Would indeed, child, that you would finally take thought
> to care for the house, and protect its possessions.
>
> > (19.22–23)

This scene gives Telemachos something to do before he must leave the stage to his father and mother, and it shows the extent to which he has cast off his emotional dependence on his nurse, Eurykleia. Even as she utters her rebuke we know that he is taking care of the house in a manner she could not have dreamed of, and when he names Odysseus torchbearer in response to her objection that he needs the maids, he silences her as he did his mother when she inappropriately asked his news. Both ladies "had no winged words to reply" (17.57 = 19.29, trans. Lattimore), and they subside and do what he wants. This assertion of masculine capability fits the poem's picture of the proper relation between the sexes, and it seems especially useful just before Penelope's entrance. Splendid woman though she is, we have come to accept her assertion that, however it may seem to others, in her own mind her excellence and glory need Odysseus's regard to complete them.

As he dismisses Telemachos, Odysseus himself suggests the nature of his coming encounter with Penelope.

Now you go to bed while I remain behind,
still more to provoke the maids and your mother as well.
She, in her pity for me, will ask about every particular.

(19.44–46)

The way in which "in her pity for me" (*m' oduromenē*) combines Odysseus's
real and fictitious identities is arresting, but there is even more afoot. Athena
has suggested that Odysseus will use his disguise to test his wife for himself
rather than ask about her from others—this with the hint, ironic no doubt, but
still a hint, that such testing might be needless and cruel. Athena comments
that another would hurry straight home,

whereas you have no wish to know or find out from others,
but first must make trial of your wife, who unconsoled
sits in the palace halls, while endless and full of pain
the nights drag on and the days, filled with her falling tears.

(13.335–38)

Now, Odysseus says that he will "provoke" her, lumping her with the erring
maids as object of this treatment. The tendency of both these passages is to
make us ask, is not Odysseus about to give his wife a needless amount of pain?
We can guess at once where this is tending: if Homer can show us that this
seeming cruelty is in fact beneficial, he will have made further progress on the
way to justifying Odysseus's name and nature and to solving the problem of
evil.

Penelope's entrance, made more splendid by the full-line formula "like
Artemis or golden Aphrodite" (19.54), suggests among other things how far she
is above such a beggar as Odysseus appears to be and how far, for all her
favorable feelings toward him, he will have to go to win her. An elaborate chair
is set for her "near the fire" (19.55), that fire to which Odysseus has so evidently
been getting closer. No word is said about an interview; instead the maids come
in and clear away the remains of the recent feasting. For Odysseus to "provoke
the maids" it is enough that he merely be there. Melantho scolds him for the
second time (19.66–69); he replies; Penelope takes his part and is reminded of
her purpose toward him. Thus once again it is as the victim of hostility and the
inspirer of justly hostile feelings in response to that hostility that he arouses
Penelope's interest; once again we see how suffering and hostility can lead to a
good result.

Furthermore, the scene is so composed that we sympathize intensely with

Odysseus's own anger. Melantho's attack on him is, at bottom, a sexual one. Here he is, the rightful husband of Penelope, being scolded as unfit to look even at her maids. It is complete sexual rejection. Admittedly Odysseus's disguise invites it, but his reply to Melantho shows why it is cruelly unjust, even so. "Do you scorn me for my miserable filth and poverty?" he says in effect; "well, I was once as handsome and prosperous as anyone. If I am as I am now, no doubt Zeus wished it that way" (19.71–80 in summary). The implication here, that the consideration we are entitled to ought not to depend on our circumstances, must meet with any audience's sympathy, and we detect once again the essence of what is wrong with Melantho, her brother Melanthios, Antinoos, Eurymachos, and the suitors in general, even Amphinomos: they, in their fortunate position, act on the erroneous supposition that circumstances are what matter. They are living proof of Odysseus's great indictment of human folly: "the mind of man that walks the earth is even such/as the day which the father of gods and men brings on him" (18.136–37). That is indeed the state of mind of the generality of mankind, but it is a deluded state, as both Odysseus's words and his disguise attest. The temporary condition of things or people is never a sufficient basis for judgment.

Odysseus goes on to warn Melantho that her circumstances too may change. She may lose all that glorious attractiveness (*aglaïē*, 19.82) of which she is so proud. Suppose her mistress were to take offense, or Odysseus to return? And even without Odysseus, the beggar says, Telemachos is already man enough to punish her behavior. Penelope takes the hint. Even before she has had a word with him directly, let alone recognized him as her husband, she follows his lead in taking a justly hostile attitude. Odysseus has, in fact, exactly as he said, "provoked" her, if that means stirring her to hostility. At the same time, her hostility suggests their affinity by taking the same direction as his. Melantho may indeed "lose her splendor": Penelope tells her grimly that what she has done she will one day have to "wipe away with her own head" (19.92), and we rightly suspect that this prediction will be fulfilled. Thus Odysseus and Penelope are alike here in "planting evils" for the usurpers, even though Penelope has no faith as yet in the idea that her husband will return.

Odysseus and Penelope at last begin their conversation, and one of the most curious things about it is Odysseus's first words to his wife (19.107–14), the famous passage in which he compares her "glory" (*kleos*) to that of a god-fearing king in whose land the crops are abundant and fish plentiful because he successfully maintains justice among his numerous and powerful subjects. Not only does this seem a strange compliment to pay a lady, but some are troubled because Homeric kings are supposed neither to have had judicial functions nor to have eaten fish except when stormbound and starving (cf. 4.363–69; 12.329–32). We can perhaps dispose of the last two objections rather easily on the ground that we do not know whether either of them is a fact, the evidence being so scanty; furthermore, even though Odysseus and Agamemnon as Homer shows them may not "have judicial functions" in the sense of the objection, both kings are certainly in a position to "maintain the right" (*eudikias anekhēsi*), as the passage has it, or not, as the case may be. One need think only of what Agamemnon does to Achilles in the *Iliad*, or of what Odysseus is about to do to the suitors in the *Odyssey*. Nor should it give us trouble that Homer implies here a causal connection between royal righteousness and the fertility of nature. There is one, even if today we tend to regard it more as the benefit of good administration and less as the favor of heaven. There remains, however, the problem of why Odysseus should address the following words to his queen:

> Lady, no mortal in the whole world could find
> fault with you. Your glory reaches heaven
> like that of some blameless king who, respecting the gods,
> and ruling over a numerous and powerful people,
> maintains what is right and just, and the black earth brings forth
> harvests of wheat and barley, the trees are laden with fruit,
> the flocks increase without fail, the sea produces its fishes,
> because of his good guidance, and his people prosper under him.
> Therefore, ask me now in your halls about all the rest,
> but do not seek to know my race or the land of my fathers,
> for fear that you may fill my heart with greater pain
> as I recall them; I have much to groan for; and I must not
> sit in another's house sobbing and crying aloud;
> for it is the worst part to be always lamenting;
> I fear that one of the maids may blame me, or you yourself,
> and say that I swim with tears, being sodden with wine.
>
> (19.107–22)

On first reading this speech, one is surprised that Odysseus compares Penelope to a virtuous king, a man, whose virtues would ordinarily be of a considerably different sort; but when we realize that the point is not the nature of the virtue but its scope, all is in order. Kings whose good government ensures the prosperity of a whole community deserve the greatest glory of all, since they provide the broadest possible context of human happiness. In this way Odysseus outdoes Eurymachos in praising Penelope's glory. Eurymachos's picture of more suitors on the morrow suggests what a fine thing it would be to possess Penelope and the large number of men she can attract—both, to be sure, ideas conducive to glory. Odysseus, on the other hand, sketches a whole happy society, implying that her glory lies rather in her power to contribute to a situation of that sort. Unfortunately, as Penelope herself is only too well aware, it can be like that only if her husband returns, not only to "busy himself about her life" but to "maintain the right." In spite of what Odysseus says, there is a notable absence of *eudikia* ("right") in her present situation, and her kleos will indeed be greater and fairer if Odysseus can punish the suitors.

Under the circumstances, Odysseus's picture of Penelope's presumed happiness only forces her to recall her pain. She may be the more willing to do so, denying Odysseus's imputation of her happiness as she denied Eurymachos's, because that way he seems more likely to be willing to tell her who he is. She recounts to him, alone at last, the presence of the suitors, her longing for her absent husband, which "melts her heart" (19.136), and the pressure on her to marry. She repeats nearly verbatim Antinoos's account (2.93–110) of her attempt to put off marriage by her trick of weaving by day and unweaving by night Laertes' shroud, so expressive of one who "neither refuses the marriage she loathes, nor/can she go through with it" (16.126–27); and even as we respond once again to the suggestion, provided by the shroud, that to complete the marriage will mean the extinction of Laertes and his line, we are told how near at hand that marriage is: Penelope's parents and Telemachos's need are alike pressing it, and she has no more devices (19.157–61). "Now tell me," she says, "where you are from."

Odysseus can no longer pretend that his pain is unsuitable in Penelope's presence, so he consents to tell it, stressing that it is the pain of a wanderer far from home. In Ithaca he has told his story, or parts of it, three times before, changing the details to suit the situation. To Athena in her young-man disguise he had to account for his pile of treasure; therefore he claimed to be a Cretan who had killed a son of Idomeneus rather than relinquish the booty he won at Troy, thus indicating how determined he was to keep it. Next, for Eumaios's benefit, he retained Crete as his home and made himself the incorrigible city sacker who came to grief in a raid to Egypt, his purpose being to convince him eventually that city sacking was not necessarily a bad idea. For Antinoos he confined himself to his piratical expedition to Egypt, wishing in this case to emphasize his change of fortune. With Penelope, his purpose is different: he wishes to put before her as strongly as possible the image of her husband.

Crete has served him before (together with Egypt, Cyprus, and Phoenicia) as a place comfortably remote for the free spinning of his fictions. Now he stresses that Crete is the great world and that Odysseus counts for as much there as he does in tiny Ithaca.

> There is a land called Crete in the midst of the wine-dark sea,
> lovely and rich, surrounded by water; and in it are people,
> multitudes without number, and ninety complete cities.
>
> (19.172–74)

To prove his knowledge and the intimacy of his connection with Penelope's husband, he makes himself Odysseus's host. Odysseus in Crete deserves, and indeed asks, to be entertained by no less than its most prominent inhabitant, Idomeneus, grandson of Minos. Since Idomeneus's age and looks are doubtless well known to Penelope, even if only by hearsay, the real Odysseus pretends to be his younger brother, to whom the honor of playing host has fallen since Idomeneus has already left for Troy. A violent storm, with a north wind so strong one could not stand upright on land, ensures that Odysseus's stay will be long enough for the young Cretan to learn to know him well. It also suggests Odysseus's hardships abroad and his determination to go to Troy, both being matters calculated to give a sense of the true Odysseus and to increase Penelope's pain.

The story works. We remember that Penelope, in describing her pain, has said that her heart melts (*katatēkomai*, 19.136) with yearning for Odysseus. Now that his image is put so strongly before her, we are shown an intensification of that idea.

> Speaking, he fashioned many lies in the shape of truth;
> as she heard, her tears flowed, and her skin felt softer [*tēketo*].
> Just as the snow melts [*katatēket'*] on the topmost peaks of the mountains,
> snow the east wind has melted [*katetēxen*] which the west wind laid down;
> and as it melts [*tēkomenēs*] the rivers fill and flow away;
> so did her beautiful cheeks grow soft [*tēketo*] as she shed her tears,
> crying for her husband there beside her. (19.203–9)

If Odysseus set out to give his wife pain, he has done so now—the pain that melts the heart. I must remark again that this suits the meaning of his true name, if only because, in the image before us, it so well suits the meaning of his adopted name as well. Though this is the fourth time Odysseus has told his story, it is the first time he gives himself a name, and the name he gives is

Aithon. *Aithōn* means "red," or "ruddy," in the *Odyssey*, the color of oxen or iron; but a connection with fire is suggested by the fact that *aithomenos* is a regular epithet for fire and torches, apparently meaning "burning," and that the verb *aithein*, the participle of which is *aithōn*, means "kindle; set alight." We have watched, perhaps too attentively, Odysseus come closer to the fire, tend the "burning lamps" (*lamptērsi . . . aithomenoisin*, 18.343), and even seem to emit fire from his head (18.354–55); we have seen him attended by Athena's illumination, "like burning fire" (*hōs ei puros aithomenoio*, 19.39); now the effect of his burning, painful words has melted Penelope, as Homer has undeniably emphasized in the passage quoted above.

This is of course not sadism. Odysseus too "inwardly wept with pity for his wife" (19.210), though outwardly he was forced "with guile to hide his tears" (19.212). Why is this, we may well ask. Why does he not tell her the truth and spare her this pain? There is probably something to the answer that, from the point of view of the struggle against the suitors, it would be too dangerous. Penelope's knowing can add little to the strength of Odysseus's party and may do great harm. She may let something slip, and we have seen that her behavior can be unpredictable in her recent scene with the suitors. But the essential answer is the one we have already considered in our discussion of the recognition between Odysseus and Athena: if after twenty years Odysseus is really to know his wife again, he must subject her to this test.

Painful as it is for her, Penelope is vitally concerned to establish the truth of the stranger's story, and here again we see one of those cases where we all would prefer the pain to the absence of it. She tests him by asking for particulars of Odysseus's looks, his clothing, and his entourage. The stranger gives them, with the result that she is even more impelled to weep (19.249), as we can well understand. The tokens by which Odysseus is identified are most interesting, chief among them being a brooch and a tunic. The brooch is decorated with the figure of a dog throttling a fawn who struggles to escape, and it seems that Homer's choice of this device cannot be arbitrary. Here is a scene which, from one point of view, inspires pity; but from another, enthusiasm. We sympathize with the fawn but recognize that the dog is behaving as a good hunting dog should and that this is the moment of climax and victory for the hunter. To judge from the many similar scenes in art, such predatory images have been full of meaning for people of many times and places, and it seems to me the *Odyssey* is in the process of telling us why. Odysseus the Sacker of Cities, Odysseus the Plotter of Pain, is well expressed in this image of the dog and fawn, which conveys both his power and his ruthlessness when the situation demands it. But there is another side. The only part of his dress which is described in like detail is the tunic, and it earns the admiration of "many women" for its softness and sheen. This tunic serves to remind us that there is a gentle side to Odysseus's hardness and that the pain is there in the service of something else.

Odysseus has described the tokens correctly, with the result that Penelope is even more disposed to weep, and the pain has its expected result: the intensified image of her "absent" husband advances the kleos of the present beggar, as Penelope's response shows.

> Now indeed, my guest, pitied as you were before,
> you shall be loved and respected in my house.
> It was I who gave him those clothes. . . . (19.252–55)

This beggar has indeed won his way closer to the fire.

Now that the stranger has established his credentials, will he not be able to relieve Penelope's mind by telling her at least of Odysseus's return, as Eumaios has suggested that he will (17.525–28)? Circumstantial though his assurances are (19.262–307), he cannot persuade her. Her conclusion remains that it was a black day that her husband sailed to Troy (19.259–60), that he is gone and that there will never be his like again (19.312–16), and nothing Odysseus can do can convince her of the contrary. In the role of a third party, he tells the truth about the loss of Odysseus's men after eating the cattle of the Sun, backing it up with a confirmatory pun on his name, "for Zeus and the sun-god/had it in for [*ōdusanto*] him" (19.275–76). (Odysseus himself at this stage still misreads the paradoxical favor of Zeus.) He tells of the treasure Odysseus is bringing and broadly hints that he will return in secret; he swears by Zeus and the hearth of Odysseus that Odysseus will return before the next full moon— all to no avail. "She must believe now," we find ourselves saying to ourselves, but she does not. In other words, we have a frustrated recognition scene. Our desire that Penelope should discover at least that Odysseus is near grows and grows, and nothing happens. This of course adds to the pressure which is building for the final climax.

Some relief is obviously necessary, however, and Homer succeeds in letting us have our recognition while still keeping Penelope in the dark. This is most skillfully managed. Instead of believing in Odysseus's imminent return, Penelope, almost as though she enjoyed it, decides to play host herself in her husband's absence for the first time (19.134–35), and we begin to see that she has ideas of her own. She makes clear that she intends to make her guest comfortable, making sure that he has a rubdown and a warm bed for the night, and a proper bath to follow in the morning so that he may sit and have dinner at his ease with Telemachos. Any suitor who annoys him, she says, will lose his chance of marrying her. Thus she will win kleos, the only consolation for the shortness of life, for guests celebrate the kindness of their hosts throughout the world, while the hard-hearted win only curses from posterity (19.317–33).

Penelope, we see, is still laudably concerned with her fame, but in the absence of her husband is unlikely to get as much of it as she should. Courageous though she is, being a woman without a man she has no scope for the kind of activity that alone keeps a name alive in the world of the *Odyssey*. She believes that kindness will do it. Hard-heartedness is for her the greatest of all evils, and we must recognize that as yet she understands her husband's name as little as she understood his going to Troy. Furthermore, although there is no real fault to find with her intentions, we do have a sense that fame might reward something greater than dispensing baths and warm beds. So Odysseus gently demurs, and we agree. Such comfort does not suit his hard life, he says, nor do the attentions of young and pretty slave girls. If there were an old woman now, whose experience would be more like his own . . . To Penelope's credit, she at once sees the greater suitability of this and nominates Odysseus's old nurse, Eurykleia. We too agree that there is a point of view from which beds, baths, pretty girls, and clean clothes, pleasant as they are, are insufficient.

Eurykleia has a real sense of her absent master and so of the injustice of the world. Her opening speech shows a depth of mind and feeling which Melantho, for example, will never attain to. Apostrophizing the absent Odysseus, she cries:

> Alas for you, my child, and my helplessness. Surely Zeus
> hated you more than any, though your heart was god-fearing.
> Never did any man burn for the Lightning Hurler
> so many fat thigh-pieces, and hecatombs of the finest,
> as you offered to him, praying that you might reach
> a green and sound old age, and rear your stalwart son;
> now from you only he took your homecoming day.
> —So I suppose him too women treat with derision
> in a foreign land among strangers, when he comes to the house of any,
> just as these bitches here all revile and afflict you, . . . (19.363–72)

Eurykleia has seen enough of life for her sympathy to be worth something. Note further the double irony here of her seeming to address the stranger as

Odysseus, and note, too, that she repeats Athena's and Eumaios's assumption that Zeus hates Odysseus. Dwelling more and more on the likeness between the stranger and her absent master, she at the same time makes here the most eloquent accusation of heaven's injustice to be found in the poem. The result is that, when the almost unbearably postponed recognition finally takes place, Eurykleia discovers that heaven is just, not unjust, in the same instant that she discovers that Odysseus is present, not absent.

Instead of letting us enjoy the effect of her discovery, however, Homer instantly embarks on a seventy-line account of how Odysseus got the scar by which Eurykleia has recognized him. This is said to make for suspense, and it does, but we must remember that the seventy lines must be able to compete in interest with the recognition scene of which we are being cheated, or the audience will only yawn and beg Homer to get on with the story. Some critics seem indeed to be afflicted by this hypothetical yawn, to the point of thinking the lines not genuine; and according to received opinion, one of these critics is Aristotle himself. We have already seen that that is an error. What we must do, then, is to look at the passage as dispassionately as we can to see, first of all, whether it can compete in interest with the completion of the recognition which it postpones.

The first thing we discover is that Odysseus had what we would regard as a scamp for a grandfather: Autolykos (Himself a Wolf) surpassed mankind in "stealing and oath taking," and the god Hermes aided and abetted him in this. Odysseus's praise of Penelope's glory could be taken to imply that heaven rewards the virtuous. Here now we have the opposite case, of its rewarding roguery. And why not? Homer would be misrepresenting life if he pretended that rogues never prosper.

No one knows certainly what Homer means by Autolykos's "stealing and oath taking," but it is necessary to have a hypothesis in order to read the poem, and here is mine. From the Homeric poems one gathers that the great object of theft was cattle, about the lifting of which we hear on numerous occasions. The "Homeric" Hymn to Hermes concerns such an episode and may be instructive in this whole connection, especially in that Hermes, who did the stealing in the hymn, is mentioned here as Autolykos's patron. Autolykos, let us say, drives off someone's cows. In due course the someone appears to claim the "debt," this likewise being a familiar situation in Homer (e.g., *Odyssey* 21.16–23, where Odysseus and Iphitos have each gone to Messenia to retrieve stolen property: Odysseus, three hundred sheep together with their shepherds; Iphitos, twelve mares and their mule foals). Now is the moment for the "oath taking." How is the victim of the stealing to establish his right to a certain portion of the culprit's herd? We hear nothing of branding or ear marking in Homer. I assume that the victim would challenge the thief to "swear a dread oath" that all the cows present were his, or else give him back his own, in the manner of the Furies in Aeschylus's *Eumenides*, challenging Orestes to swear he was not guilty of his mother's murder or else pay with his life for his crime. The passage in Aeschylus suggests that few guilty parties would dare to take such an oath, even if not taking it meant death, and in Homer people seem usually to have been able to get back their stock. But Autolykos, Homer would have us imagine, was different. He took the oath cheerfully and often, kept the stolen cattle, and got away with it, perhaps by skillful use of equivocation. In any event, he was clearly helped by Hermes.

We now hear at last, in this digression in the course of Eurykleia's recognition, that it was this rogue of a grandfather who gave Odysseus his apparently ill-omened name; worse, he gave it in preference to the popular one, Aretos, "prayed for," which Eurykleia suggested (19.404). Autolykos implies that he prefers his own suggestion because he himself has "odysseused many men and women in [his] time [*polloisin gar egō ge odussamenos tod' hikanō,/andrasin ēde gunaixin*]" (19.407–8), and at this stage of the poem we know what he means. Zeus (1.62), Poseidon (5.339, 423), and, together with Zeus, Helios the sun-god (19.275) have all been spoken of as odysseusing Odysseus, and Ino-Leukothea has as much as said that "to odysseus" is to "plant evils for" Odysseus; Autolykos has obviously "planted evils for" those he has swindled. The metaphor "planting evils" itself suggests an early stage in the process of inflicting loss, pain, or damage, before the evils have grown, and this suggestion is confirmed by the number of times we hear of Odysseus and Telemachos "planting evils" for the suitors, before the evil has actually occurred. "Meditate pain for" will then not be a bad meaning for *odussasthai*, at least in this poem, the "pain" part of the meaning being recommended by the phonetic similarity between *odussasthai* and the noun *odunē*, "pain." Of the action itself we have seen an important example at the beginning of this book, "Odysseus . . . left behind in the hall/pondering, with Athena, how he should kill the suitors."

"Meditate pain for" is appropriate to Autolykos's swindling of his fellow men and women; he has found it extremely profitable and evidently thinks it a more successful attitude to carry through life than one which the name Aretos might imply. This is of course a paradox and no doubt flies in the face of even Homeric popular morality. Autolykos, however, sets great store by it. He promises that, if his grandchild will come to see him when he comes of age, he will enrich him and send him home rejoicing (19.409–12).

So Odysseus was given the name we all know. Furthermore, we understand now where he got his craftiness, enabling him to introduce himself to Alkinoos with the words "I am Odysseus, Laertes' son. My craft/is on every lip. My fame reaches the sky" (9.19–20).

Odysseus is thus the *polytropos* hero of the poem's first line, the man "of many shifts," and his "thievery" (*kleptosunē*), inherited from and encouraged by Autolykos, comes out clearly in Athena's compliment to him when he meets her in Ithaca.

> Sharp would one need to be, and a clever stealer to pass you
> in all your cunning tricks, even if it was a god.
>
> (13.291–92)

So we are not surprised to hear, as the digression continues, that the youthful Odysseus indeed paid his visit to his grandfather "to get the splendid presents" (19.413).

Once there, however, he raised the name his grandfather gave him to a higher power, as it were. The sons of Autolykos organize a boar hunt, and Odysseus joins in enthusiastically. Whether or not his grandfather had it in mind, this too is a case of "odysseusing." All, and particularly Odysseus, whom we see close up to the dogs brandishing his spear, in fact if not explicitly, "meditate pain for" the boar. And Homer makes us see it that way. For a moment we take the boar's part as we hear described first his snug thicket, exactly like the one Odysseus slept in on Scherie, and then feel his power and courage as he rises against the men and dogs, "bristling well his back-hair and looking fire from his eyes" (19.446). Odysseus gets to him first, the boar gashes his leg deeply, and Odysseus stabs him through, carrying out the meaning of his name.

This is not a new idea. A marginal note of uncertain but ancient date found in our manuscripts suggests not only that Odysseus enacts the meaning of his name here but that this is the act with which he becomes his mature self. Autolykos said that he was to come visit him "when he grew up" (*hēbēsas*, 19.410). Our perceptive annotator wrote in the margin, *hēbēsas—odussamanos*, "when he grew up—when he odysseused."

This then is the origin of the scar, to account for which was the ostensible purpose of the whole passage, but we now understand much else. As a form of odysseusing, stealing cows for profit is all very well; it reminds us of the dog catching the fawn on Odysseus's brooch, the simple predatory act. But killing a noble, dangerous beast is something different. The boar is magnificent, not pathetic like the fawn, and can and does fight back. Perhaps our armchair sympathies are not much engaged by the abstract idea of big-game hunting. We moderns, in our reaction against the predatory, hunting side of life, are in danger of forgetting that the meat we eat ever had to be killed. But it does not take much imagination to see what pleasurable human sensations are stirred in Homer's characters on this occasion. Autolykos had said he would send Odysseus home "rejoicing" (19.412); now, at Odysseus's feat, everybody rejoices.

> Him then Autolykos, and Autolykos's sons,
> healing well his wound, and giving him splendid presents,
> rejoicing, straightway dispatched him rejoicing to his beloved
> Ithaca. There his father and his queenly mother
> rejoiced at his homecoming, and questioned him of everything
> concerning the scar he got; and he told them well the story,
> how, when he was hunting, a boar with his white tusk struck him,
> the time he went on Parnassos along with the sons of Autolykos.
> (19.459–66; I read *khairontes*, with some MSS, for *es patrid'* in line 461)

This is not yet the satisfaction of taking Troy by the stratagem of the wooden horse or of defeating the Kyklops by the trick of "No-man." It is not contriving the richly deserved end of 108 suitors. But it will do. It is raising the clever, profitable predation of Autolykos into a realm where danger is risked for the sake of adventure, of trying one's self out against the hostility of the world. One may get hurt, and Odysseus does. His scar is the mark not only of what he has done but of what he has suffered, and his satisfaction is the greater for it. Now we understand why he went to Troy and why he faced the Kyklops, although in both cases he knew what danger he incurred.

This passage, then, is no digression, except in a chronological sense. It contains information absolutely vital for our understanding of why Odysseus does what he does, and it clarifies much of what we only vaguely knew about him before. I think most readers would feel that it competes successfully in interest even with the recognition which it interrupts and therefore constitutes real suspense. Suppose it were in its proper place chronologically speaking, at the beginning of the poem: that would be to put the answer before the question, to show the satisfactions of the hard life before stating the problem of its pain. Nor can we make the tale of the scar and Odysseus's name fit well as part of his recognition by Telemachos or by Penelope. There it would detract from the importance of the recognition itself. It is perfect here. As Eurykleia in her consternation lets Odysseus's foot drop and the washing water spills, we feel that, like her, we know now who this man is who has at last come home.

We can see now why Aristotle found in the boar hunt the essence of the *Odyssey*. It tells us how Odysseus got his name, what his grandfather wanted him to be, and what the rest of the poem shows that he is. It portrays in a single image the style of action by which he won his kleos and by which he is about to make it immortal, so winning his psukhē as well. It is the answer to the problem of evil, raised, with a like reference to Odysseus's name, by Athena at the beginning of the poem. By exposing Odysseus to Poseidon's pain, Zeus "odysseuses" Odysseus; that is, makes it possible for him to earn his incomparable identity. It seems right, therefore, that Homer has made the boar hunt part of the scene of Eurykleia's recognition, shortly before the main climax.

At last we are ready for Eurykleia's reaction to her discovery.

> Joy and pain together seized her consciousness, and her eyes
> were filled with tears; her voice choked in her aching throat.
> Touching his bearded chin, she spoke to Odysseus:
> "Surely you are Odysseus, dear child; and I did not
> know you before, till I felt my master all over."
>
> (19.471–75)

This is a pregnant piece of composition. First, as one of the most vivid, it may stand as the type of all those passages where pain and joy combine to produce moments of greatest meaning. It is enough to refer here in general to the many occasions in the *Odyssey* where people weep for joy, or "enjoy" (*terpesthai*) their weeping. We have just witnessed a striking illustration of the same point, as we saw how much Odysseus's getting hurt added to the joy of his exploit on Parnassos. This is relevant of course to the *Odyssey*'s concern with the problem of evil.

We may observe also that Eurykleia's speech has the air of meaning more than it seems to. For one thing, she has *not* felt her master "all over" (*panta*), or even thoroughly; she has only handled his leg. For another, the phrase "my master" seems brought in almost by force, as a balancing element for "dear child." And what did Eurykleia know of the stranger before? He was an object of pity, an example of human helplessness against the injustice of fate. And now? She has felt the scar which betokens the boar slayer, the Sacker of Cities. She has discovered that her "child" is also her master. The creature she loved as helpless, she now loves also in his power over her. This is the complete Odysseus. Some such reflections as these, at least, are needed to account for the strangeness of the passage.

Eurykleia tries to signal the good news to Penelope, but Athena prevents

Penelope's noticing. Earlier in this chapter I suggested why Penelope must be kept in the dark. As for Odysseus, he seizes Eurykleia by the throat and threatens to kill her if she breathes a word. Thus instead of a sentimental reunion with his old nurse, we have something much better, bearing out what Eurykleia has just recognized. This is her master, and much as he loves her, there are circumstances under which, unafraid of pain as he is, he would not hesitate to kill her. We may remember how he threatened Kirke also with death when his selfhood was at stake, building thereby a sound basis for the trust which grew between them.

Eurykleia's enthusiasm at any rate is not at all dimmed by such threats. She protests her staunchness, and we believe her; furthermore, far from quailing at killing, she offers to point out, when the time comes, which of the maids have proved to be disloyal. Odysseus rejects her proposal, sure that he can discover the guilty by himself, and thus leaves us wondering whether he may not need her help after all. He does, as it turns out, but in any case it will not be a mistake to see this as a poem which decries squeamishness. There is one note of moderation in the passage, however, and it is sufficient to hold Odysseus well within the bounds of the humility proper to a mortal: his last words to Eurykleia are "Keep my secret in silence, and leave the rest to the gods" (19.502). He knows that heaven, not he, determines the outcome of events, and as we shall see, he will commit no violence it does not sanction.

Homer rounds off this part of the scene by putting the everyday beside the violent and desperate, with fullest effect.

> He spoke, and the old woman went her way through the hall,
> to fetch water for his feet; what she had brought had all been spilled.
>
> (19.503–4)

The most important result of this scene between Penelope and Odysseus, however, remains to be discussed. Not only does Penelope refuse to believe either the stranger's news that a boat lies ready in nearby Thesprotia to bring Odysseus home or his oath that he will be in Ithaca "between the waning of this moon and the waxing of the next" (19.307)—this is understandable in view of the numerous times she has been disappointed by false information before—but she now tells Odysseus that she has had a dream in which Odysseus himself in the shape of an eagle has announced his presence in Ithaca and the coming destruction of the suitors. This too she refuses to believe, and again we need not be greatly surprised: as she says, not all dreams come true. What is startling is that, at this very moment, with all these signs of Odysseus's return multiplying around her, she resolves to marry a suitor. However skeptical she may be, we feel that she could surely hold out for another week or two to test The-oklymenos's prophecy, Telemachos's sneeze, the stranger's news, and her own dream.

The problem here is of course entirely one of Penelope's motivation. From the point of view of literary structure, nothing could be more effective than for the wife, in her beloved husband's disguised presence and under his influence, finally to decide to marry someone else at the very moment her husband is restored to her. This effect is of course lost if we solve the motivational problem, as some do, by assuming that Penelope knows, consciously or unconsciously, that she is talking to her husband; if that were the case, furthermore, it would be more in Homer's manner to give us some hint, as in the formula "but his/her mind intended otherwise." The real question is, can Homer convince us that an unknowing Penelope would decide to marry in the course of the present scene? I think he can, and indeed does, if we listen to him closely enough.

In book 18, we saw how the pressure of events led Penelope irrationally and almost involuntarily to encourage the suitors by telling them that Telemachos was now grown and her marriage was close at hand. In the scene before us the pressure is even greater. The general situation, the danger to her son, and particularly the stranger's unquestionably genuine connection with her hus-band have intensified her pain to the point where she can no longer avoid a decision. There are two ways in which this pain might be lessened. She can decide to believe the signs and predictions of Odysseus's return, in spite of her many disappointments in the past, and wait a few weeks more in hope, or else she can at last accept the fact of his loss and marry a suitor. What particularly recommends the first course is that Odysseus is so much more of a man than any suitor; what recommends the second is that it may save Telemachos's life as well as his property. As we have seen, the option to refuse to marry has been unavailable ever since the assembly of book 2 tacitly permitted the suitors to woo Penelope regardless of her wishes, and in any case it would do little either to lessen the pain or to save the property or Telemachos. Though, as it happens, the first is the right choice, it is also the more gullible, the less painful, the less active, the less Odyssean one.

On reflection, we should be reluctantly glad to see Penelope choose the second if it were not for one thing—her dream of the eagle (19.535–53). In that dream an eagle "coming from the mountain" slaughtered every one of her twenty geese, whom she "delighted to watch" as they ate their corn in her courtyard. She dreamed she wept bitterly at this until the eagle returned and, lighting on the rooftree, told her that her geese were the suitors and he was her husband, come to take his vengeance. Then she awoke and saw her geese "feeding at the trough as before." All this is submitted to the judgment of the stranger, and he replies, as is natural, that it indeed presages Odysseus's immediate return. Even so, Penelope rejects the dream. Her way of telling it suggests two reasons why, one Odyssean and the other the reverse. Her remark that, when she woke up the geese were just as they were before, contrasts dream with reality to the detriment of the former and suggests Odyssean toughness of mind. She may dream about Odysseus, but what she has is suitors. Her fondness for her geese, on the other hand, is a way of showing that, somewhere inside her, she takes comfort in her wooers and would not, even as things now stand, be wholly content to see them killed. There is no doubt that she would prefer, as she says, to see Odysseus return and take revenge, if that were possible; nevertheless, the image of the revenge makes her less able to accept the possibility. Thus book 19 closes with Penelope having made up her mind at last, under the influence of the Man of Pain, both absent and present. For both the right and the wrong reasons, she chooses what is both the correct and the incorrect solution. It is wrong to be squeamish about suitors but right to choose the more likely rather than the pleasanter alternative; it is incorrect to marry a suitor when Odysseus is available, but to do so by means of the trial of Odysseus's bow will mean to marry Odysseus after all.

A "Sweet" Dinner

It has been a long day, and it is not over yet. The suitors are to have their night of love after all, though Homer lets us know it will be their last (20.13). As Odysseus lies awake in the porch "plotting their doom," their sweethearts among the maids troop forth to join them in the town, laughing and sporting together. Odysseus's rage at this would seem uncontrollable except that he controls it. Homer compares it to the ferocity of a bitch standing over her puppies to defend them and even says that Odysseus's heart "barked" as he saw these "evil deeds." His impulse is to spring upon the maids and kill them all. He feels of course something more than a general concern for the purity of womanhood: we must recognize here a strong element of sexual jealousy and plain possessiveness. These are, however, instincts which preserve and protect the family, and we can see why the comparison with the mother-bitch is apt. Furthermore, it is the strongest image of "odysseusing," of meditating pain for, which we have had so far, and it is, at bottom, odysseusing which will bring the poem to its desired and desirable conclusion. Odysseus is defending his own.

The threat he feels is ultimately to his existence and identity, individually and as the leader of a group—in this case, his household. We understand this from his comparing what is happening now to the affair of the Kyklops, where he was leader also. For prudential reasons he cannot act yet, and so he calls on his heart to endure.

> Stand it, my heart; things worse than this you stood before,
> that day the Kyklops, whose force cannot be opposed, ate
> my strong companions; even then you stood it, until my wit
> got you out of that cave, in which you expected to die.
>
> (20.18–21)

As he once watched the Kyklops eat his men one by one, so now too he must look on while the suitors devour his substance and his selfhood, hoping that his wit will find a way to stop it. Realizing that the reasons for his anger are such as these, we will not find it exaggerated that, though his heart stays firm, his body will not keep still but writhes and turns incessantly "as a man turns a blood pudding over a fire" (20.23–27). Though some critics used to find the comparison inelegant, I have no doubt that we are to imagine the look of a turning sausage or haggis, full of boiling, bubbling fat and blood, in order to picture Odysseus's mental agony.

Although so deeply roused, the next thing Odysseus does is to go to sleep. This may well enhance our sense of his greatness. The mind that can resolve such passion as this, we may feel, is a great mind indeed. Homer shows this turn of events as perfectly credible. Athena speaks the words which reason might speak in a case of this kind, convincing words, and we can believe that they would produce the same result without Athena's presence. The relation of god to man is as before: Athena serves to express a natural power and Odysseus's ability to command it, rather than to suggest divine interference with the natural order of events. First, with a sense of almost physical wrenching, she puts things in a different perspective.

> Why now are you awake, saddest of all mankind?
> Here is your house about you, and here is your wife inside it,
> and your child, grown to be what a son should be.
>
> (20.33–35)

Divinities often take this tone in Homer, asking questions which seem to ignore the problem but which are nevertheless effective because of their contrasting point of view. One may think of Thetis in the *Iliad* after the death of Patroklos, asking Achilles why he weeps, since Zeus has done all that he asked; or Eidothea in the *Odyssey*, asking Menelaos whether he is starving on a desert island because he enjoys it (4.372). The tone of these questions, I think, is one we often use in speaking to ourselves when we have reached an impasse. In the present case Athena's words embody a thought which might well occur to a sufficiently strong-minded person at such a crisis, and they change the whole aspect of things. Odysseus tries to argue against this thought, pointing out the near insuperability of what still remains to be done, but Athena waves his objections aside.

> Stubborn man, worse allies have been trusted before now,
> mortal ones, who do not know so many counsels;
> and I am a goddess, one who ceaselessly guards you
> in all your many toils. And this I tell you plainly:

if five times ten companies of such as use human speech
stood about us now, eager to slay us in battle,
their cattle too you would drive off, and their fat sheep.

(20.45–51)

We might have expected Athena to say, "Your cause is just, and I shall aid you"; instead, she gives what Odysseus would consider a firmer ground for confidence: she appeals to what amounts to his sense of his own expertise. She and he together have come handsomely out of situations like this before. The Autolykos-like impudence of the last line is a splendid touch: sharp wits like theirs are what is needed; by using them they will succeed and, what is more, find a grim pleasure in the process. Thus the desirability of the prize almost within his grasp—house, wife, and son—in addition to his sense of what he has done and what he can do combine to bring peace and confidence to Odysseus's mind.

To cap it all, Athena finds an omen in Odysseus's name, a new meaning for it suggesting, for once, an end to pain. She concludes her advice with the words,

So let sleep after all take you: watching is irksome,
waking all the night, and you are about to come through your evils.

(20.52–53)

The word for "you are about to come through" is *hupoduseai*, which, for the sake of the pun, may be misdivided as *hup-oduseai*. Odysseus's name itself means that he will "come through." Even though it is by no means clear as yet how he will solve the tactical problem of killing the suitors, Athena is able to make him see it as solved—and what could be more sleep inducing than that? We end, I think, with an indelible picture of Odysseus's magnificent self-confidence, or rather, confidence in Athena, which is self-confidence tempered with the realization that the gods, not men, ultimately control all outcomes.

Earlier Penelope too found tearful sleep, thinking she had solved her problem by deciding to marry at last (19.603–4), but she is not so fortunate as her husband. We know that her solution (through no fault of her own) is a wrong one, and now reality refutes her, in the shape of a dream of Odysseus. So powerful is his image in her mind. She dreamed that Odysseus lay beside her, and in her joy, thinking it reality, she has awakened; now her disillusion makes her pray the gods a second time for death. (The first occasion was upon awaking from the sleep which preceded her temptation of the suitors, 18.202–5.) It is bearable, she says, to grieve by day if one can sleep at night, but now heaven has sent her this "bad" dream. We see why it is bad: the greater her delight in visions of Odysseus, the more her conviction that he is lost and her consequent decision to marry a suitor torture her. So she prays,

> May the gods, who live on Olympos, banish me from sight,
> or beautifully coiffed Artemis strike me, that with Odysseus's
> image before me I may come beneath the loathed earth,
> before I gladden the thought of any lesser man.
>
> (20.79–82)

So unhappy is Penelope that she wants to be blotted out, the absolute negation of the psukhē preservation which the poem sets as its goal, and even as she wishes this annihilation, Homer makes us feel it to be unbearable through the terms in which she expresses it (20.61–78). She compares it to the story of Pandareos's daughters, orphaned to be sure, but brought up by the goddesses Aphrodite, Hera, Artemis, and Athena, who bestowed upon them every grace. At the same time that Aphrodite was on her way to Zeus to arrange for their marriages, the Harpies, personified storm winds, snatched them away to suffer the ministrations of the Furies. "In just such a way," Penelope says, she would like the gods to snatch her away and "banish [her] from sight [hōs em' aïstōseian]." No doubt she would, but we in the audience cannot allow it. We can see, as she cannot, that for her to give up now would be to change happiness for horror, like the daughters of Pandareos. That she prefers to die with the image of Odysseus still clear before her is the very opposite of her attitude in book 1 and of course the negation of her plan for marriage. Will she still go through with it for Telemachos's sake?

These contrasted scenes leaving Odysseus asleep and Penelope awake prepare the way for the coming day, the day which is to see Odysseus's revenge. As Penelope ends her prayer for death and annihilation, the dawn comes (20.91). It will be a hard-hearted member of Homer's audience indeed who is not ready to see her rescued.

It is important to Homer's conception that Odysseus, even at this late stage, should make sure of the approval of Zeus before he acts against the suitors. We begin with Penelope's weeping, a result of the despair we have just seen. Like most pain in the poem, it is not in vain. It serves to wake Odysseus and to give him a vision of Penelope herself standing at his head "already recognizing him" (20.94). That one phrase suggests everything that Odysseus desires to win. We are reminded of his long and in many ways successful interview with his wife, where the one thing missing was her knowing that it was he, and from the contrast we sense at once how much that one thing means. Yet with all this almost within reach, Odysseus moves deliberately. He stows inside the hall the fleeces and cloak that made his bed, after which he takes his oxhide ground cloth out of doors. There at last, under the sky, he raises his hands to Zeus.

He asks Zeus for a double sign: a *phēmē* from inside the house (that is, a word from someone there which is unconsciously propitious for his purpose), together with a sign from outside. He is given more than he asked: thunder peals at once from a clear sky, and then a *phēmē* occurs which not only calls for the suitors' destruction but is unmistakably sent by the gods to fit his situation. It comes not from one who is just now waking, as Odysseus had asked, but from a woman kept all night at her mill by the suitors' insatiable demands; the woman is herself responding to the thunderpeal and explicitly joins her wish to that of the man for whom the thunder is meant.

> Father Zeus, you who rule over gods and men,
> how you thundered from the star-studded heavens,
> without a cloud in sight! You mean it for some one.
> Mean it for poor me also, as I shall pray:
> may the suitors for their last and final time today
> in the halls of Odysseus enjoy the lovely feast,
> they who with heart-grieving weariness have unstrung my knees
> as I grind their bread. May this be their last dinner.
>
> (20.112–19)

Odysseus also takes encouragement from the double meaning of the word describing the activity in which the slave woman is engaged. Homer emphasizes that she is a grinding woman (*aletris*, 20.105) grinding (*alessan*, 20.109) meal (*aleiata*, 20.108). From this fact Odysseus concludes that he is indeed fated to take vengeance on the transgressors (*aleitas*, 20.121). For Homer, such coincidences reveal the structure of reality itself, as I have already suggested.

We can believe that all or most of this happened or could happen, but we may have trouble believing that it would "really" be significant in the way in which Homer intends. Yet we can and should accept the scene's essential implication: that Odysseus, although under the greatest compulsion to act that we can possibly imagine, still defers to a higher source of approval than his own will or his own judgment. Even Athena's encouragement is not enough: though a great goddess, she is only one among others, and evidently partial to him—perhaps too partial. So, he must find out where all the gods stand in regard to his purpose. The way he asks his question is interesting.

> Zeus-father, if willingly over wet and dry
> you gods brought me home, when you had handled me roughly,
> let someone utter a phēmē. (20.98–100)

Evidently he is not sure whether his preservation from so much peril is significant or not. Only if it is will he feel free to take revenge upon the suitors. Presumably even now, without a sign, he will not go ahead, for fear that he may be defying the gods. Like the omen itself, this may seem to us superstitious and unedifying. What does it mean, after all, for some nonexistent gods to approve of Odysseus's success? Two things: Odysseus is in effect also asking, "If a man is strong, able, and wise enough and can hold out long enough, will he in this world be given the victory?" To this the gods say yes, as they tend to do throughout Greek literature. Even a hero as unfortunate as Sophokles' Oidipus survived and received his reward in full measure. The other question Odysseus is implicitly asking here is, "Will injustice have its way forever?" and to this the gods say no. If we think these answers are correct, we can believe that Odysseus's success accords with the nature of the world as we know it and so has the assent of "the gods." More important even than this, however, is the attitude implied on Odysseus's part: he is conscious that he may be wrong. Homer's Muse may have provided Odysseus with a nonexistent source of approval for what he is about to do, but we can at least admit that one who looks beyond himself and his friends for such approval is less apt to kill the wrong suitors. "Do not try to be Zeus," Pindar advised more than two centuries later. We see that Odysseus is a good example of what he meant.

The more dramatic an episode is, the more we are apt to wish its author to linger over it. Homer does not disappoint us in this respect as we begin what we know will be the poem's day of days. Except for the old grinding woman, Odysseus was the first person awake. Now, the maids assemble and light the fire. Telemachos dresses, enters the hall for a word with Eurykleia, and departs for the agora with his usual insignia—a spear and two dogs. He is to play a big part today. Eurykleia sets the maids to their tasks, not one of which seems to be omitted: sweeping, sprinkling, sponging tables, cleaning pots and cups, and fetching water from the spring. We hear of a special reason for this bustle: today is the feast of Apollo, and the suitors will arrive early. Finally, menservants come in to split the day's wood. All this, we realize almost with a shock, goes on every day in Odysseus's palace.

As usual with Homer, something more than circumstantial detail is involved. We are aware of an unvoiced reason for excitement on Eurykleia's part: she knows that Odysseus is home, and we watch delightedly as Telemachos, who does not know that she knows, asks her what treatment the stranger has received, pretending that he is more interested in his mother's etiquette than in the guest himself. His mother is always so impulsive, he says, for all her wisdom treating the worse man with honor and sending away the better with scant respect (20.129–33). This is calculated to stir us in two ways at once: on the one hand, we have seen how keenly Penelope in fact feels the difference between Odysseus and his lesser rivals; on the other hand, we have also seen her accept the worse man and reject the better in her decision to marry a suitor. This irony increases our delight in the details before us, and so does Eurykleia's reply. Valiantly keeping her secret, she gives the official account of last night's happenings: the stranger was treated with all respect, but when offered a proper bed, he refused on the ground that he was too miserable and ill fated to enjoy it. He preferred to sleep in a heap of fleeces in the porch. "We put a cloak over him," Eurykleia adds with evident concern (20.143). This is the man who ought to be sleeping with Penelope herself.

In the midst of the bustle, together with the hewing of wood and drawing of water, herdsmen begin to come in with the animals which will provide the day's feast: first the good slave Eumaios, then the bad slave Melanthios, and finally the cowherd Philoitios, a new character. Homer's purpose in joining their arrival so closely to the other preparations is no doubt to set off even more sharply the arrival of the suitors, toward which everything is tending. The herdsmen have their own function, however. Eumaios greets the stranger with kind words, whereas Melanthios addresses him with insults. Thus the conflict is emphasized once again in our minds. Philoitios the cowherd, however, is a surprise. At first sight he is very like Eumaios, kindly to the stranger and utterly loyal to Odysseus. What can he add to the scene that Eumaios cannot?

For one thing, he provides a fresh point of view. It is good to know how Odysseus looks on this morning of mornings to a sympathetic outsider. Theoklymenos, because of his second sight, knows too much; Eurykleia has already recognized Odysseus; Eumaios is no longer impartial. Philoitios, on the other hand, can give us an unprejudiced reaction.

To Philoitios, the beggar looks like someone who has been or should be a king; in fact, as he makes clear, like a prime example of the injustice of heaven. Eurykleia too feels the injustice of heaven on meeting the stranger, but she is thinking first and foremost of the Odysseus whom she knew and only secondarily of the man before her. Now even without his name and story and gifts to the gods being known, the stranger inspires the same thought. This is kingliness indeed. Philoitios proceeds to associate the stranger with Odysseus, but not on the basis of physical resemblance, as Eurykleia did; he simply sees the same injustice in both cases. Thus through Philoitios's words Homer applies the problem of evil to the present situation in the most general possible way. Here is what Philoitios says:

> Zeus Father, no other god does us more hurt than you do:
> you have no pity on men from the time you bring them to birth,
> plunging them into evil, and wretchedness and pain.
>
> (20.201–3)

This is the poem's problem in its purest terms. Furthermore, we see that Philoitios, much though he is like Eumaios in his calling and his faithfulness, has come to an opposite judgment of Odysseus's case from the swineherd's. Eumaios reluctantly concludes that Odysseus's misfortunes are the gods' punishment for sacking cities, but Philoitios sees his suffering as evidence that heaven itself is cruel. Happily, both views will be refuted when Odysseus triumphs.

Philoitios differs in another way too: unlike Eumaios, he has actually thought of taking his animals and going off to serve some other master than the suitors. What prevents him is an ineradicable hope that Odysseus may return to punish them (20.224–25). We remember that it was difficult for Odysseus to convince Eumaios that anything like this could happen. Philoitios thus actualizes a whole new set of possibilities for the role of faithful slave, and Homer has apparently brought him in now to heighten, clarify, and confirm what we already know is at stake in the coming conflict; namely, the solution of the problem of evil and the justification of Zeus's ways to man. It will also do no harm to provide Odysseus, Telemachos, and Eumaios with an ally for the coming fight.

When they discovered earlier in the poem that Telemachos had eluded their ambush, the suitors, after some discussion, decided to kill him only "if the decrees of great Zeus should approve it" (16.403–5) and then did nothing, apparently waiting for a sign. Now things have reached such a pass that the suitors again debate this murder, and this time the gods' will is manifested. As they talk, an eagle appears high in the air on their left, holding a dove in his talons. Amphinomos, the same suitor who prevented them before, reads the omen correctly in a technical sense.

> Friends, this plan of ours will not work out in our favor,
> killing Telemachos; instead let us think of our feasting.
>
> (20.245–46)

As before, all are persuaded. The irony here is serious: the very sign which means that the suitors are doomed prevents them from taking the action that might have saved them. All very fine, some readers may say, but rather unrealistic.

The answer, as always, is to consider the spirit rather than the letter. Of course we do not believe in omens, but watching the scene as Homer puts it before us and accepting his premises, we are tempted to say to the suitors, "You fools, seeing the sign which should tell you that you will be killed today, how can you talk of plans not working out in your favor? And how can you think of eating? Can't you ever take anything seriously enough?" The point is that they cannot. If they could, either they would not be engaged at all in this light-minded venture of courting Penelope, or they would have killed Telemachos on the previous day, when Antinoos demonstrated that it was necessary (16.371–86). As it is, the same qualities which induced them to enter upon the crime ensure that they will be punished for it. Evil, by the same sort of poetic logic as the occurrence of the omen embodies, does carry within it the seeds of its own destruction. Thus, however unrealistic the omen may be, it makes vividly a valid point, and we can be glad of its presence.

So the suitors do "think of their feasting" instead of murder, and we watch them troop into the hall, blind to their own destruction. This time they are served by the three herdsmen, and it may occur to us as important that two of the three are hostile.

The rest of the book, some 139 lines, comprises a single, powerful, subtle, and, as Stanford remarks, eerie scene. The suitors become what the Scots call *fey*—disoriented at the approach of their own death, of which they themselves are unaware. This folly, of which we have just seen an example in their response to Zeus's omen, is intensified until, literally hysterical, they are given a foretaste of their own bloody destruction. To our horror, they fail to recognize their own hysteria, accusing the seer Theoklymenos of madness instead. Athena, as the divine embodiment of the strength of wisdom and the weakness of folly, presides, but it is ultimately Telemachos's magnificent defiance of his tormentors which makes them crack. It is perhaps his greatest moment, Odysseus remaining relatively passive throughout the episode.

Appropriately, the background is a scene of feasting. Like Odysseus's crew in the adventure of the cattle of the Sun, the suitors are eating their way to their own death, without paying sufficient attention to what they are doing. In the present case Homer turns the perverted merriment of their feast, as well as the eating, into a figure for what is wrong with them. They make a joke of their pretended role as guests. When Telemachos asserts himself as host and owner of the hall, declaring his intention to protect his beggar-guest come what may, Antinoos responds with what looks like acquiescence: the suitors, he says, will have to take Telemachos's orders, since Zeus has disapproved of their project; otherwise they would have put a stop to his talking. But this is irony. Antinoos is really telling Telemachos to his face that the suitors have been discussing his murder and will go through with it at the first good opportunity. We can tell that this "acquiescence" is really a threat, because Homer adds, "but Telemachos was not affected by his words" (20.275). At the same time we see in Antinoos's attempted irony the suitors' basic error: they do not take the will of Zeus seriously enough. The joke is really on them.

Had they taken Antinoos literally, they might have got through this day at least without offense, but they cannot let well enough alone. Because this failure is crucial, Homer sees it as coming from Athena, who once more, as in the case of Eurymachos previously,

> did not let the suitors
> restrain themselves from soul-grieving insult, that the pain
> might enter yet deeper the heart of Laertes' son, Odysseus.
> $(20.284–86 = 18.346–48)$

Ktesippos is the offender this time, and he tries to carry on the suitors' basic joke. It is absolutely right, he says, that Telemachos's guest have an equal share. He will even give him something extra, so that he too can make presents—to a bath attendant, say—and he throws a cow's hoof from his platter at Odysseus's head. This is the third and last in the progression of missiles, following the stools thrown by Antinoos (17.462) and Eurymachos (18.394–97), and as might be expected, it is the least effective, this time glancing harmlessly off the wall. Telemachos responds with a splendid outburst which for the moment checks the suitors completely: it is lucky that Ktesippos missed; otherwise Telemachos would have run him through; the suitors are now to stop their offensiveness once and for all; he is old enough now to know right from wrong, and if the suitors want to kill him, even that would be better than watching them behave the way they have been doing (20.304–19).

As we see, this is a forceful speech, and we have recognized that the suitors are not without some remaining sense of decency. One of them, Agelaos, even attempts what looks like a sincerely propitiatory answer: Telemachos is right, he says, and the suitors should conduct themselves as proper guests. It was right also for Telemachos and Penelope to resist the wooing as long as they thought Odysseus might return. Now that there is no more hope, however, Telemachos should persuade his mother to marry; then he can possess his house in peace. This is a speech that would be in character for Amphinomos, who dispelled the tension on the previous evening by admitting that Telemachos was right, except that it harps on Telemachos's impasse. To it Telemachos replies with deep exasperation, emphasized by a pun on his adversary's name. "By Zeus and my father's woes [algea], Agelaos [Agelae]," he begins. He says that he does not oppose his mother's marriage; in fact he urges it. But he will not send her away by force against her will. At this point the suitors' hysteria occurs. I think it even relevant that the so-emphasized name of Telemachos's interlocutor suggests in Greek "nonlaughing," with an obvious link to the "woes" of the previous pun. At any rate, what Homer is showing us is clearly hysteria.

> So Telemachos spoke; in the suitors Pallas Athena
> roused unquenchable laughter, and struck their wits awry.
> Already they were laughing from jaws which were not theirs;
> the meat they ate was dabbled with blood. Meanwhile their eyes
> filled with tears, and their hearts felt lamentation.
>
> (20.345–49)

It does not seem that Athena's action is purely arbitrary here. I doubt if her actions ever are. Instead we can see that the suitors' reason for merriment is the same as it always has been: they are not going to do what they say. Agelaos's relenting seems real for a moment, but Telemachos's answer makes them feel how ridiculous it all is. To them Telemachos's predicament and his qualms about his mother are finally merely funny. In spite of what Agelaos has said, there is going to be no new decency in the house, and Telemachos is not going to possess it, ever. Either Penelope will yield and they will give the house to her husband, dividing the rest of the property among themselves (16.383–86), or she will not, and they will continue to feast as before. Telemachos can always be got rid of if he becomes troublesome, as he is doing now. So they laugh—so hard that they become disoriented. This may not be completely scientific, but it is so deeply realized by the poet that our emotions enthusiastically assent. The suitors can no longer tell whether they are laughing or crying; they lose control of their facial muscles, and their food seems—no, is—dabbled with blood; somewhere there is a sound of sobbing. Could anything be more appropriate? They laughed because they thought they knew that their wooing was no wooing but, for Telemachos at least, ruin; so their laughter itself turns in their throats to its opposite, a foretaste of their own death.

I have not yet sufficiently emphasized the disorientation involved in all this.

As Agelaos's speech shows, the suitors are really not quite sure even yet that they are not suitors. I have surmised that, in the beginning, their wooing was sincere, and only gradually, as they hit on the idea of putting pressure on Penelope and became aware of the joys of a permanent feast at others' expense, did their action become what it now is. Now everything has two meanings, and they have indulged themselves by taking whichever one suited them at the time. But this is extremely dangerous. Can they tell any longer where the reality is? For example, is Zeus really protecting Telemachos, as convention would have it, or can they kill him with impunity, as their newfound "realism" suggests? Men living in a world as ambiguous as theirs are fitting victims of a hysteria in which merriment is indistinguishable from horror.

A more effective preparation than this for Theoklymenos's second-sight vision portending the suitors' end could hardly be imagined. In fact their hallucination inspires him.

> Ah, wretches, what is ailing you? Night shrouds
> your heads, and your faces, and your knees beneath you;
> groaning breaks out like fire, your cheeks are wet with tears;
> blood drips down the walls and over the handsome balks,
> the porch is full of ghosts, the court is full as well,
> pushing their way to Erebos beneath the dark.
> The sun is lost from the sky, and a foul mist creeps over.
>
> (20.351–57)

We can well believe him. The suitors, however, fail to realize that anything is wrong. It is Theoklymenos who is mad, they say, and hoot him out of the hall. A vivider picture of doomed folly has perhaps never been painted. They continue to jape, but Telemachos, not replying, looks instead to his father for the signal to begin the battle.

Penelope, Homer now tells us, has overheard the whole scene. As we are wondering what she thinks of marriage with a suitor now, the book closes with one of the poet's rare but magnificent summaries.

> So they made their dinner laughing;
> sweet it was and plenteous, for they had slaughtered largely.
> But a poorer meal than their supper could not be,
> the one a goddess and a strong man were going
> to set them; for they began the wrong. (20.390–94)

Penelope, as she overhears the whole scene, knows, as the suitors do not, that the party is over; she has decided to end the suit by choosing a husband this very day, and she can take pride in her hope to save her son's property and bring to an end his long ordeal. But only we and the Muse know how great a reward awaits her.

Odysseus Strings His Bow

Theoklymenos departs, not to appear again; yet I do not think we have found him superfluous, as some do. The suitors then tease Telemachos about the ill luck he seems to have with his guests, saying that it might be a good idea to sell both Theoklymenos and the beggar into slavery. Ignoring them, Telemachos looks to his father to begin the battle (20.371–86). This is the moment Athena chooses to prompt Penelope to introduce the trial of the bow, and with this prompting, book 21 begins.

Here is one place, at least, where we can be sure that Athena's initiative is not simply her own idea. If it were, there would have been no need for Homer to tell us that Penelope overheard everything (20.387–89). As it is, we may legitimately ask what Penelope has heard to make her (with Athena's help, of course) decide to act. She has heard that the suitors are only waiting for a favorable opportunity to kill her son; she has heard her son not only rise to the defense of the stranger and decency but say that he prefers to die rather than watch any more of the suitors' insolence; and she has heard the suitors, despite vague but bloody warnings from Theoklymenos, finally make a joke of Telemachos's defiance by their comments on his guests. Evidently she feels she must at any cost bring this situation to an end and prevent the coming collision if she can. Without Athena's help she has told Odysseus that today she would select a husband by means of Odysseus's bow game (19.571–81). At that point her reasons seemed to be primarily to help Telemachos and to end her own uncertainty; secondarily, she seemed moved by her dislike of violence, even against the suitors. Now everything she has heard points to violence in the hall, and her decision can only be doubly confirmed. We are not surprised, then, when Athena puts it in her mind at just this moment "to set before the suitors the bow and gray iron/in the halls of Odysseus, the contest, and killing's beginning" (21.3–4). "Killing's beginning," of course, is not Penelope's plan but Athena's.

Something so momentous demands detailed treatment. Accordingly we watch Penelope climb the stairs, take a key from her room, and go with her maids to a storeroom. As she stands on its threshold, the poet evokes the construction of the door (21.43–45) as lovingly as he did when Odysseus entered the palace (17.339–41). Then we watch her untie the bolt strap from the *korōnē*—a hook, ring, or peg on the door near the keyhole (21.46). We see her insert the key and "knock up the door bars, taking careful aim" (21.47–48). At this the doors "bellowed like a bull" (21.48) when they were "struck by the key and opened speedily for her" (21.50). Despite our ignorance about just how this door is opened, we realize that something big is occurring. Penelope is opening the door to "the contest, and killing's beginning." Without knowing it, she is also opening the door to her own happiness. Once inside, she approaches "the high shelf, where the trunks stood" (21.51–52), takes the bow, case and all, from its peg, sits down, and places it on her knees; then she weeps for a time and takes the bow from its case. Finally, she carries the bow and the quiver of arrows downstairs, her maids following with a chest which contains the axheads to be shot through. I think we may agree that there is no chance of our being bored by any of this.

Nor are these details all, for as Penelope mounts the stairs, we are told the story of the bow itself (21.11–41), and this too is important for the poem. As a youth Odysseus was sent to Messenia by "his father and the other elders" to "recover a debt" of three hundred sheep together with their shepherds. On the way, at the same house at Pherai where later Telemachos stopped on his way to and from Sparta, he met Iphitos, archer-son of an archer-father, and they exchanged presents, intending "guest-friendship and mutual regard." Odysseus received the bow carried by Iphitos and his father before him, but their friendship never developed. Iphitos was on a mission like Odysseus's, to recover twelve mares and their mule foals, but his journey did not end so successfully: in the course of it, Herakles entertained him and then "killed him, guest though he was, in his halls," for the sake of his animals.

In this way the bow becomes connected in our minds with a whole complex of appropriate ideas: Odysseus's youthful courage and ability and the evident worth of his friendship; lost property and its attempted recovery; guest-friendship and its violation; and violent murder in the hall. Above all we are aware that men, even Herakles, kill for gain, that protecting one's own is no child's play, and that right by no means always triumphs. It is good for us to know these things as the bow, engine of death, is brought into the hall, where it will soon be put to use.

Penelope's speech to the suitors, in which she consents to marry at last, shows, as we expected, that her chief motive now is to get the suitors out of the house and bring to an end the dangerous situation in the hall.

> Hear me now, proud suitors, who upon this house
> fastened yourselves, to feast, and quaff the wine continually,
> of a man gone from his home this long time, and no other
> cover of speech were you able to frame for what you are doing,
> but your great longing to marry me and make me a wife.
> Good, then, suitors. Come on. Here is a prize for you.
>
> (21.68–73)

The first to react to her proposal is not, as we might suppose, one of the suitors or Telemachos but Eumaios, whom she has asked to set up the axheads. Instead he breaks out weeping and lays the axes on the ground. Philoitios the cowherd, "when he saw the bow of his lord," weeps as well (20.83). This development is a case of what a music critic once called "the unexpected inevitable." That not only the wife weeps at her decision but slaves—and slaves from the outlying parts of the estate, at that—shows that we are witnessing not only the end of a marriage but the dissolution of a great household which meant life itself to many.

Antinoos chides the herdsmen on the ground that their weeping will dampen Penelope's spirits still further (21.84–97), inauspiciously, he no doubt feels, for the present occasion. He also expresses his suspicion that it will not be easy to string the bow and that the contest will be "not without disaster [*aaaton*]," since no one present is anything like the man Odysseus was. All the same, Homer tells us, "his heart within him hoped/to stretch the string and shoot through the iron." We are told, too, how this presumption will receive its fitting reward.

> He, be sure, was the first to learn the taste of an arrow
> sped from the hands of Odysseus, that good man, whom he dishonored
> sitting in Odysseus's halls, and spurred on all his companions.
>
> (21.98–100)

In book 1, we saw Telemachos, with help from Athena, declare his intention to be master in his own hall, and we have seen with what difficulty he has maintained that position since. Now, if ever, will prove to be the moment to assert his authority. He rises splendidly to the challenge, taking charge at once of the contest his mother has proposed. The bitter satisfaction he would have felt in marrying off his mother, if circumstances were as the suitors suppose them, is evidently easy for him to simulate.

> What can this mean except that Zeus has driven me mad?
> My mother, sensible as she is, says she will
> leave this house and go off with another husband,
> and yet I laugh and rejoice in my crazy mind.
> Good, then, suitors. Come on. Here is a prize for you,
> a woman the like of whom lives not in all Achaia,
> not in sacred Pylos, near Argos, nor Mycenae,
> not in Ithaca's self, not on the black mainland.
> You know it all yourselves. Why should I praise my mother?
> Come now, no excuses. Make no more delay
> to string the bow and find the answer.
> I could try this bow myself:
> if I string it and shoot through the iron,
> I'd feel no pain to see my lady-mother leave
> this house to follow another if I'd be left behind
> able by now to handle my father's toys and games.
>
> (21.102–17)

Telemachos is indeed now grown up, in mind at least, whatever his success with the bow may turn out to be.

He begins promisingly by astonishing everyone at how well he sets up the axes, "though he had never seen it done before" (21.123). As it happens, we moderns should be especially impressed with Telemachos's skill because, even after "seeing it done" in Homer's lines, scholars have been unable to agree about what it was he did. As I enter upon this thorny matter, let me plead as usual that it is incumbent on any hearer or reader of the poem to try at least to see something. First, I cannot happily visualize Telemachos digging his trench "and truing it to the line" down the middle of the great hall, moving tables and stepping over the suitors' legs in the process. He must have dug it from the threshold out through the court, thus avoiding the ruin of a good mud floor and the perils of archery in a room containing many more than 108 persons. Such a procedure also explains Antinoos's later remark that it would be safe to leave the axes set up overnight, "for surely no one would come into the palace of Odysseus and steal them" (21.261–62). This sounds more reasonable referring to axes out in the court than to axes within the hall. It is true that the trial is described as one which Odysseus "used to set up in his halls" (*megaroisin*,

19.573–74) and that the word I have translated "palace" above, where the thief might come, is *megaron*; but since *megaron* often means the palace as a whole, I do not think it need force on us all the difficulties I have mentioned.

The trench is the means by which the axes are set up in a straight line, and the earth is tamped around them—this much is clear. But what does the shooter shoot at? It has been put very convincingly by both Stanford (note on 19.572) and Stubbings (Wace and Stubbings, 534) that the arrow is to be shot through the "eyes," or sockets for the handles, in twelve double-bitted axheads. This is a great step forward. Stubbings has even provided a picture of the trench with its mound of earth beside it, the axheads duly aligned along the mound and sticking in it by their bits. The trouble with this is that, judging by the scale of his axheads, their eyes are, at most, ten inches off the ground. Stubbings tacitly admits that this target is somewhat low by saying that it explains why Odysseus shot from his chair; to me it looks as though he would have had to shoot lying on his belly.

I think the answer to the problem lies in Penelope's words describing the arrangement.

> For now I shall set the contest,
> the double-bitted axes which *he* in his halls
> used to set in a row, *like ship's ribs*, twelve in all,
> and *standing* at a distance, would shoot an arrow through them.
>
> (19.572–75)

The only way an ax can look like a ship's rib is when it is complete with handle. The axes stand in a row like a ship's ribs, each with its eye exposed, one bit stuck in the end of its handle. Of course these axes could not be used for anything else until their handles were set in their eyes, and that is why, as we are told, they are kept in a case or box as "the games of that great lord" (21.62).

Now that Telemachos has his axes set up, he tries to string the bow. Three times he makes it tremble; the fourth time he would have strung it, Homer says, but his father signaled to him to desist. The result is that we are satisfied that he is worthy to take his father's place and at the same time spared a too-early success which would detract from his father's when it comes. Desisting, therefore, Telemachos "put the bow from him down on the ground, / leaning it against the joined and polished door boards." Then he "put the sharp arrow in the same place, propping it on the beautiful korōnē" (21.136–38). These details look important, and so we had better try to visualize them too. The door is open, revealing the row of axes in the court and providing light for shooting the suitors later. To judge from the next book, where Odysseus explicitly "stands the bow against the doorpost," Telemachos stands the bow on end, and if this is so, it is most difficult to see how he can prop an arrow against its tip, or why—although this is the preferred explanation. Let us assume that he props the arrow against that part of the door's lock which serves as handle and to which the bolt strap is tied, as we saw above. If the door is open, the handle will be inside the hall, handy for such a purpose. The net result of Telemachos's putting the bow and arrow down in this way is to call attention to the door and its lock; it also calls attention to the arrow. We shall not be surprised when this arrow proves to be important at the end of the book.

Now it is the suitors' turn. Antinoos bids them make their attempts "in order, going around to the right . . . starting from where the wine pourer begins" (21.141–42). This means that the first to try will be one Leodes. Leodes is not a typical suitor. More than any of the others, he is, as we would put it, "in love with Penelope." A gentle soul, he prefers to sit in the innermost recess next to the comforting wine jar, and his father's name, Oinops (Wine Face), reinforces this rather ineffectual impression. He hates the suitors' boisterous insolence and blames them for it. In keeping with his sensitive and apparently contemplative nature, he serves as the suitors' soothsayer, reading the future from the sacrifices that take place daily by looking either at the animals' entrails as they are butchered or at the manner in which the offerings burn. Atypical though he is, he represents the simplest case of a wooer of Penelope: one who wants her for his own, without any ulterior motive. Other suitors can be blamed for insolence, greed, violence, and lawlessness, but not Leodes. It is true he covets another man's wife, but what if that other man is dead? How is Leodes to be judged? Here too we must await the sequel.

As we might expect, Leodes proves too soft to string the bow. His response to his failure is as emotional as we might have guessed it would be, but also as full of insight. He says,

> This bow will take the heart and life
> from many chiefs, since it is better to die
> than to go on living, having failed of that for which
> the suitors assemble each day and live in hope.
>
> (21.153–56)

Leodes' gift for prophecy is greater than he knows, and his words will turn out to be literally true, though not for the reason he suggests. Even more interesting, he goes on to say that, as things are now, a man can hope that he will wed

Penelope, but once he tries the bow and fails, he will have to woo another, while Penelope marries whomever she chooses. The result of this speech is that we suddenly see the bow as the great discriminator between illusion and reality. We realize that Leodes, and no doubt many other suitors, would rather continue to dream than to have matters settled. Furthermore, we now can see that Leodes represents one end of the spectrum of the suitors' characteristics, with Antinoos representing the other. Leodes is the least hostile, least violent, least aggressive, as well as weakest physically, whereas Antinoos is the opposite; but both share the suitors' prime fault, an irresponsible attitude toward reality.

It is no accident that Leodes, the weakest and least offensive suitor, is the first to try the bow. By beginning with him, Homer is able to compress 107 successive failures into 2, separated by a scene of a very different nature— Odysseus's revelation of himself to Eumaios and Philoitios. Antinoos's original remarks have already sketched for us the nature of the contest as a whole: he said that the contest would be "not without disaster" for the suitors, since none of them matched Odysseus, all the while secretly believing that he would string the bow himself. This already set up in our minds the idea of a scale of strength with Antinoos at the top. Now, after Leodes' failure, we get a somewhat different view. On the one hand, Antinoos confirms our sense that Leodes is the weakest, by blaming him for his discouraged words and pointing out that his failure does not mean that all the suitors will fail (21.168–74); but on the other hand, even Antinoos's confidence appears to be somewhat shaken, since he now arranges to have the bow warmed and greased to make it less stiff (21.175–80). In this way our idea of a scale of strength or ability ranging from Leodes to Antinoos has added to it a sense of growing discouragement. We picture to ourselves how, as more suitors try and fail, their desperation will increase, and so the feeling of a serial process takes still firmer hold of our minds.

Homer suggests the long succession of failures in another way as well. Leodes relinquishes the bow in the same striking set of images and in almost the same words as Telemachos did, putting the bow down, propping it on the door leaf, leaning the arrow on the lock, and finally sitting down "in the seat from which he had risen." Because of the repetition we naturally conclude that this is what each suitor will do as he finishes his turn. We are spared hearing the passage repeated 107 times, however. Instead, the warming and greasing of the bow intervenes. Antinoos gives his orders.

> So Antinoos spoke, then ordered the goatherd Melanthios:
> "Up, then; light us a fire here in the hall, Melanthios,

and put a big chair beside it with a sheepskin upon the seat,
and bring out a good-sized round of the fat they keep inside,
so that we young men, warming it and smearing it with grease,
may make our trial of the bow and finish out this contest."
So Antinoos spoke; and Melanthios at once made a fire
and bringing a chair set it down, with a sheepskin upon the seat,
and brought out a good-sized round of the fat they kept inside.
With this the young men warmed it and made their trial, but could not
string the bow; they fell far short of the strength to do it.

(21.175–85)

    This echo, of action ordered by action performed, adds its own weight to the sense of a stereotyped set of movements indefinitely repeated. Therefore the statement at the end of the passage just quoted is really all we need to hear of the next 105 failures after Leodes'. Our illusion of the time which they must occupy is helped by the account of Odysseus's simultaneously revealing himself to the herdsmen. Then all that is needed to finish the contest is for Eurymachos to fail and Antinoos to postpone his own attempt.

    We have for some time been aware of the loyalty of the two slaves Eumaios and Philoitios. While the bow trial continues, Odysseus takes the opportunity to enlist their help, making the opposing sides a little more equal and at the same time giving us the opportunity of witnessing a moving recognition scene, one to which we have been looking forward ever since Eumaios refused to believe in the possibility of Odysseus's return. As it should, the recognition takes place out of sight and hearing of the suitors, not only outside the hall but "outside the court" (21.191), where I assume the axes were set. Once outside, Odysseus asks the two what they would do "if Odysseus were to come from somewhere,/just like that, and some god should bring him home" (21.195–96). We note his emphasis on heaven's hand in the affair, an emphasis which is repeated when he later qualifies his promises to them with the words, "if the gods bring down the noble suitors at my hands" (21.213). As we have seen before, Odysseus is under no illusion that he can do without the gods. Admittedly, the suggestion that they are helping him adds to the persuasiveness of his cause. Great faith will be needed for anybody, no matter how sympathetic, to go to the help of 2 against 108. Nevertheless, because of what has gone before, we know that Odysseus's humility is not just a pose: unlike the suitors, he recognizes the importance and power of something bigger than himself. We remember how earlier in the day he asked for, and got, a sign that his return was with the gods' will. Now he communicates that idea to his supporters.

    The herdsmen too see this as an affair for the gods. They respond to

Odysseus's question about their allegiance just as they did earlier in the day to his oath that Odysseus would soon return, and in similar words. In brief, they pray to the gods. Philoitios cries:

> Zeus father, if you only would grant this wish of mine,
> that that man should come, and heaven should bring him here!
> Then you would know my strength, and what my hands can do.
>
> (21.200–202; cf. 20.236–37)

And Homer adds,

> In the same way Eumaios prayed to all the gods
> for Odysseus rich in wisdom to come back to his home.
>
> (21.203–4 = 20.238–39)

These prayers are not conventional piety but are calculated to make the audience too feel the participation of the gods in the event.

It is noteworthy that Philoitios should be the first to answer Odysseus's appeal, even though Eumaios has a bigger part in the poem. The reason is, I would suggest, that Philoitios is the more active, sanguine, and Odysseus-like of the two. Thus to him the idea of Odysseus's return is more real than it is to Eumaios, who only with great difficulty could be brought to contemplate it at all. So it is fitting that Eumaios's response should be comparatively muted until the actual revelation takes place. When Odysseus does reveal himself, Eumaios is just as strongly affected as the other (21.222–25), and we may assume for him special joy in the recognition because his initial resistance was greater. There now stands before him the living proof that heaven does not, as he once feared, punish the enterprise of a man like Odysseus, but on the contrary is on the way to rewarding it and punishing the suitors.

Another feature of the episode brings up a problem inherent in all such scenes: once his men have proved their staunchness, how does Odysseus go about saying, "Well, then, here I am," without anticlimax? Here are his actual words, as close as I can come to them in English:

> Here I am, then, myself, inside. Through many evils
> I have come home, in the twentieth year, to the land of my fathers.
>
> (21.207–8)

The danger of anticlimax arises from the utter predictability of what Odysseus must say, and this is avoided by that marvelous "inside," which in the Greek is the first word in the sentence: *endon men dē hod autos egō*. Because of it we remember not only the long distance Odysseus has come through space and time but how impregnable Odysseus's palace looked to him and Eumaios as they approached it on the day before this one. "I got inside," Odysseus is saying, and we realize that this is already a remarkable feat. As a matter of fact, *endon eonta* ("being inside") at 16.202 and in book 23 at lines 2, 29, and 71 seems a regular phrase for "being home." Not only has he won a place for himself on the threshold, standing off the challenge of the rival beggar Iros, and then "come nearer the fire" to converse with Penelope, but he now has his own table and chair among the suitors (20.257–59). He has penetrated their innermost defenses, sees everything they do, and hears everything they say, as Antinoos will point out (21.290–92). They are all but in his power. Conveying all this through the one word "inside," Homer has managed to make a surprise of Odysseus's announcement of his presence after all.

As he continues his speech, Odysseus reminds us of Halitherses' prophecy, put before us first in book 2 and recalling that distant day when Odysseus sailed to Troy. At the assembly in which Telemachos denounced the suitors, Halitherses, interpreting the omen of the two eagles, attempted to warn the suitors in the following words:

> And I say that for that man all has come to pass
> as I told him it would when they embarked for Ilion,
> the Argive men, and with them went the wise Odysseus.
> I said that suffering much, losing all his companions,
> not known to any, and in the twentieth year,
> he would come to his home; now all is being accomplished.
>
> (2.171–76)

Since meeting these words, we have been reminded numerous times that it is now the twentieth year and that Odysseus has suffered much. Now, on his own lips, the phrases "through many evils," "in the twentieth year," and "I have come home" make us feel that indeed all that was predicted is being accomplished. Thus what we recognize in this recognition scene is not only that this is Odysseus but that things are working out as they were meant to. This fits well, of course, with the idea both that the gods are on Odysseus's side and that the world is essentially just and ordered. It also, even independently of these ideas, gives us a satisfying sense of the order of Homer's poem.

Homer has found words for Odysseus's announcement adequate to its importance, difficult to do though that appeared. He continues by giving us an

instance of Odysseus's cleverness. He is no man to stop at this point and wait for
the others' disbelief. Instead, he plunges ahead, expressing appreciation for
their loyalty and promising rewards. Then to clinch matters, he bares his scar,
the one the boar gave him on Parnassos. Eumaios and Philoitios are now
convinced, and not only is Odysseus's clever management apparent but so is
the appropriateness of this mark of recognition. It is the mark of a man who
takes life as though it were a boar hunt, deliberately challenging the hostility of
the world. In Odysseus's case the challenge has been successful, at least so far,
and the suffering he has undergone as a result, like the wound which the scar
records, will only serve to make the satisfaction greater in the end.

As a whole, the trial of the bow is a good deal more complicated than its
simple, folktale aspect at first suggests. Of course the basic conception is that it
proves the suitors to be inferior to Odysseus in physical strength, falling short of
him to a degree that no one expected. Penelope offered to marry "whoever
should most easily string the bow and shoot through the iron," and now it turns
out that no one can string the bow at all, let alone make a fancy shot with it.
The obvious way to carry out this conception would be to have everyone try
and fail, which is what we expect will happen as we read; but this entails a
pitfall of which Homer was evidently aware. If all fail, then the suitors must to
some degree at least face the fact of their inferiority to Odysseus. In effect, they
must say to Penelope, "We know none of us is anything like as good as the man
you have lost, but marry one of us anyway." As we saw above, Antinoos has
implied this very thing, accurately stating the case without believing it to be
true of himself. Just as his speech may even have excited our sympathy until we
realized its humility was only pretense, so the humility forced on the suitors by
having them fail to the last man might make them seem less culpable. Their
crime will seem to consist largely in having overestimated their own physical
prowess, a comparatively honorable mistake.

As we have been discovering, however, Homer had something else in mind,
and so he does not do the obvious thing and let everyone fail. Instead, with
Eurymachos, the next-to-last man and the last man to fail, he allows reality
almost to break in upon the suitors, only to have them again turn their backs on
it, following the lead of Antinoos. Eurymachos states the bitter truth.

> What a disaster! Here is shame indeed, for me and for all.
> For the marriage I do not grieve so much, though that, too, rankles—
> there are other Achaian women in plenty, both here
> in sea-girt Ithaca and in many another town—
> but falling so far short in strength and prowess

of godlike Odysseus that we are unable to stretch a string
upon his bow—there's a reproach the future will hear of.

(21.249–55)

Here is something which might eventually lead to facing the facts, but Antinoos contradicts it. There will be no reproach, he says. It is just that they have forgotten that today is the feast of Apollo. Who could string bows on such a day? They need only postpone the contest and try again on the morrow (21.257–68).

Antinoos is the strongest, probably the ablest, and basically the most realistic of the suitors, but here he turns his back on the truth forever. At the beginning he thought he could string the bow himself, though he dissembled his confidence. Now presumably he has seen enough to make him despair. Still, ought he not to make the attempt? He wins Penelope if he succeeds, and if he fails, his feast-of-Apollo explanation will be just as valid as it ever was, if not more so. Evidently, his postponing the contest means that he would rather leave the issue unresolved than take the chance of being seen to be weaker than Odysseus, feast of Apollo or no feast of Apollo. No doubt tomorrow would provide other excuses. Like Leodes, his ultimate choice would be to dream on rather than to face the reality. At the last moment he avoids the painful issue, and that is what is really wrong with the suitors.

We may have suspected a certain flimsiness in Antinoos's explanation of the suitors' lack of success with the bow; if so, this suspicion is greatly strengthened by what happens next: Odysseus asks to try the bow not as part of the contest but rather to see whether his strength "is/what it once was," a pregnant phrase in itself (21.282–83). Has he, by any chance, tried this bow before? The suitors are indignant, and not merely because they hate to see the beggar putting himself on their level; they actually are afraid, Homer says, that he will succeed (21.286). In other words, even though they have accepted Antinoos's suggestion that Apollo will let no one string the bow on this particular day, they are so unsure of their ground that they yield to panic as soon as anyone offers to try to do it, even when it is a man they affect to despise. This is a clear demonstration of the penalties of their playing fast and loose with what is true and what is not. Antinoos's solution turns out to be no solution at all.

Because the suitors neither know nor trouble to find out what the reality of their position is, and in fact owe their very presence in Odysseus's house to the ambiguity of whether he is alive or dead, their efforts are pervaded with irony and tend to turn into their opposites. Antinoos tries to frighten Odysseus by accusing him, as Melantho and Eurymachos have accused him before, of being drunk. He cites the example of the centaur Eurytion, who, because he drank too much, ran amok at Peirithoos's wedding and in consequence was mutilated and thrown out by the other guests (21.293–302). As we listen we realize that in reality the example recoils upon the man who cites it, for it is the suitors, not Odysseus, whose passions rule their judgment and whose behavior disgraces the role of guest. Even more precisely, it is the suitors and not Odysseus who, like Eurytion, have sexual designs on a bride to whom they have no right.

The "bride" herself assists in this reversal of the suitors' position. As Antinoos's words show, the suitors still regard Odysseus as an essentially worthless vagabond, even if they have made him their official beggar.

> Wretched stranger, you have no sense at all.
> Is it not enough that you dine with the likes of us,
> portion for portion, and listen
> to our words as we converse? No other
> beggar-guest hears our conversation. (21.288–92)

Antinoos goes on to threaten to send Odysseus to King Echetos the Mutilator (21.308), as he had once threatened Iros. But Penelope, as we know, now regards Odysseus as an honored and respected guest. Therefore she insists on his right to try the bow, even as she rejects as ridiculous any fear that either she or the stranger are thinking of marriage. Even in a denial, putting Odysseus on a level with the suitors in this way half way reverses the position of the two sides, and Eurymachos's response inspires her to complete the process. When he says that it is not losing the marriage he fears so much as the disgrace of being bested by an inferior, she retorts with the following speech:

> Eurymachos, no men retain their honor
> who, like you, dishonor and devour the house
> of one who was first among us. Where then the disgrace?
> This stranger is big and well built;
> he can claim birth from a good father.
> Give him the fair-polished bow, so we may see.
> I hereby declare and promise
> that, if he strings the bow and Apollo grants him success,
> I'll dress him in good clothes, a cloak and a tunic,
> give him a sharp spear to protect him from dogs and men,
> and a two-edged sword; put sandals upon his feet,
> and send him wherever his heart desires. (21.331–42)

Though there is no question of Penelope marrying the stranger, she can assist in restoring him to the honor he deserves. As for the suitors, though she may be forced to marry one, they have forfeited their honor already by their injustice. They are already the beggar's inferiors because they do not respect Odysseus's house, which means that they do not respect the truth about the Odysseus who went to Troy.

A conflict, we see, has arisen between Penelope and the suitors over whether Odysseus is to get his hands on the bow or not. It is fitting that Telemachos should be the one to resolve this conflict, and it proves not an easy task. We can be glad that he took responsibility for the contest in the first place, since that adds weight to his intervention now. He addresses himself to his mother, though his words are for the suitors (21.344–49): no other Achaian has the right, he declares, to tell him how to dispose of that bow. Thus he makes his point with the utmost firmness, while still avoiding a direct challenge to the suitors. But Penelope too has effectively claimed the right to dispose of the bow, and with some justice, we may feel. Telemachos now opposes her right as well (21.350–53), telling her to go back to her spinning and weaving in her own apartments. He asserts that this and indeed all command in the house is man's business, and we see that, by Homeric standards, he is right, now that he has become a man. Before that, Penelope's claim was justified. We remember that, in book 1, Telemachos told his mother to leave the hall in these very words, except that then the matter of contention was *muthos*, the bard's song, rather than *toxon*, the bow, as it is here; the formula varies in these two words alone, and it is followed in both cases by the identical five-line description of Penelope's astonished withdrawal to her upstairs room to weep for Odysseus until Athena puts her to sleep (1.360–64). We now can see that it was already in book 1, after his interview with Mentes-Athena, that Telemachos took charge of the hall. The difference is that it is clearer now than it was then why that is no job for a woman: in the present case it is vital to get Penelope under cover before the arrows and spears start to fly. Therefore Telemachos for the second time literally renounces his dependency on his mother at the same moment that he asserts before the hostile suitors his right to his position in the world of men.

If Telemachos were now to go and pick up the bow with the idea of handing it to his father, the suitors would probably prevent him physically, but fortunately Odysseus has provided against this. He has foreseen that the suitors would refuse him the bow and has instructed Eumaios to bring it to him as soon as their opposition arises. That opposition, in other words, is to be the signal to begin the battle (21.231–35). Accordingly, as Telemachos ends his speech, not he but Eumaios starts to bring the bow to Odysseus, with the result that, for the suitors, it is now a question not of conflict with an equal, like Telemachos, but of giving orders to a slave. They threaten Eumaios with violent death, adding to their threat the doubly ironic piety, "if Apollo and the other gods show us favor" (21.364–65). Herein they not only call attention to their impiety but allude to their trouble with the bow, implying that, in this case at least, their success is a foregone conclusion, whereas we know better. The din they make, however, is so great and they are so many that Eumaios's nerve fails him, and he puts the bow down halfway, "in the spot where he was" (21.366). So evenly balanced are the scales of power at this point. Then Telemachos coolly counters with his own threat, lighter in tone.

> Come on, old man, bring the bow; you can't obey us all.
> Or, young as I am, I'll chase you out of town
> throwing stones at you. I am stronger than you.
> If I had the same advantage over all who are in these halls—
> over the suitors—in skill of hand and strength to fight,
> I would soon send packing, and in a way they would hate,
> one or two out of our house. For they intend evil only.
>
> (21.369–75)

This speech is the turning point of the poem. The suitors cannot help laughing at the incongruity between Telemachos's power and theirs, committing once more their fatal error of not taking things seriously enough. In a way, their insane laughter of the previous book was a preparation and elucidation for this moment. Here, laughing at Telemachos's supposed plight, they "forget their anger" (21.377), and Eumaios picks up the bow again and brings it to Odysseus. From now on their doom is certain. Could there be a clearer indication than this of the importance the poem gives to the hostile force explicit in Odysseus's name? He and Telemachos do not forget their anger. They can keep their mind on the struggle; they know it is no joke. But the suitors, although their leader is called Antinoos, Hostile Minded, cannot keep their anger; as rivals for Odysseus's wife and position, they have proved to be only bogus Odysseuses.

As we might guess, Homer does not hasten over what happens next. I dare say no reader of the *Odyssey* has forgotten how Odysseus turns the bow over and over in his hands, trying it here and there, "to see if worms had eaten the horn" (21.395). Then he strings it as easily "as a man who understands the art of the lyre and of singing/stretches the string on a new peg" (21.406–7).

Having done so, he tries the bow's tension by pinging the string with his finger. At its sound, "like the note of a swallow," the suitors turn pale, and Zeus sends a thunderclap, causing Odysseus to rejoice.

On this vivid passage there are several comments to be made. The archaeologists, for example, have thrown a good deal of light on Odysseus's bow, particularly Lorimer (277, 292) and Stubbings (Wace and Stubbings, 518–20). If horn is an important part of the bow's construction (and we have seen that it is), it must be a "composite" bow, that is, one made of wood, sinew, and horn compacted together. The horn and sinew act like a steel spring and make the weapon both very powerful and very hard to string. Like Odysseus's, such bows are usually "recurved" (*palintonon*, 21.11, 59): that is, when not under tension their curve is the reverse of what it is when they are strung, permitting a still greater compression of the material and therefore producing still more power. All this is helpful to know in reading the passage, as is the fact that such a bow can be strung only by literally sitting on it, passing it over one thigh and under the other. The archaeologists point out that, when Odysseus comes to shoot, he does so sitting down, and they infer, as is no doubt correct, that he strung the bow while sitting also. But from here on their interpretation is less satisfactory. They argue that the suitors were unable to string the bow, not because they lacked the strength, but because they did not know how it was done: they tried to string the bow standing up. To be sure, Homer does not say this specifically, but they believe he implies it. After all, is not Odysseus the great exemplar of expertise, of *tekhnē*? Should he not overcome through brain, not brawn?

Attractive though this idea may seem, it evidently is not Homer's conception. It must be remembered that Telemachos "made the bow tremble" and "would have strung it" if his father had not prevented him (21.128–29), and Homer gives us no reason to believe that he had any special knowledge which the suitors had not. Again, Odysseus hails his own success as evidence that his "force is still firm" and not broken by old age, as the suitors think (21.426–27). In other words, Homer intends us to regard stringing the bow as a test of strength, and if he really had meant what these archaeologists say he does, he would have had to compose this scene rather differently. Finally, we should be glad that he did not do so. It is essential for our literary satisfaction at this point that Odysseus show himself a better man than the suitors in every way, including physical strength, not just in technical expertise.

Homer's comparing stringing the bow to stringing a lyre (*phormingos*, 21.406) also calls for comment. Odysseus is about to proclaim that it is now time to prepare the suitors' supper, followed by "dancing-song and the lyre [*molpēi kai phormingi*], for those are what grace a feast" (21.430). We first heard that "song and dance" (*molpē t' orkhēstus te*) were "a feast's graces" at

1.152, and somewhat later in the same book that the suitors "turned to dancing and lovely song [*orkhēstun kai himeroessan aoidēn*]" as they "waited for evening to come," to which Homer pregnantly adds, "and black was the evening that came" (1.421–23). We have seen that the identical passage occurs in 18.304–6, referring to the evening previous to this one. That ominous passage in turn was prepared for at the end of book 17, when Homer remarked that the suitors "took their joy of dance and song [*orkhēstui kai aoidēi*], for afternoon was already at hand" (17.605–6). More than all, we have heard already of the grim supper which "a goddess and a strong man were going/to set them" (20.393–94). Thus we have been as solidly prepared as possible for the "lyre" which will inspire the "dancing" on that most special occasion. The lyre is nothing less than the bow of Odysseus.

That the bow's string when plucked should sound "like the note of a swallow" (21.411) seems curious at first, but if the reader will only repeat several times the actual Greek words in which the comparison is made, I think the difficulty dissolves. *Khelidoni eikelē audēn*, when pronounced, renders uncannily closely the sound, or, more accurately, the feeling of the sound, of plucking an extremely tight string.

Two further points concerning this passage remain. At the sound just mentioned, the suitors turn pale. Why do they do so? It has been suggested that they already recognize Odysseus, but this is hardly likely, in view of what happens in the next book. Lines 22.27 and 31–33 prove that the suitors do not know that the stranger is Odysseus until he tells them so at 22.35, and even then they scarcely believe it (22.45). In the scene before us the order of events is as follows: Odysseus tries the string and it sounds like a swallow; "great grief" rises in the suitors, and "their color/changes"; then Zeus makes a great crash of thunder, "showing his signs" (21.412–13). These details combine to give the impression of an utterly significant instant: first, we are given the fact itself, the stringing of the bow and the sound of Odysseus's finger on the string; then the suitors' reaction to it of chagrin and fear. The chagrin we have been prepared for and understand, but the fear is a little puzzling. We know it must be fear because of the formulaic association of color change with that emotion and no other in Homer: "And pale fear seized me" (or "them," or "them all inwardly") is a formula system occurring six times in the *Odyssey*; but still, why are the suitors afraid? Then comes the thunder of Zeus, and all is clear. It shows that the stringing of the bow is a crucial event, the fatefulness of which the suitors instinctively sense even before the thunder sounds. But they never ask themselves what it means. It is their old unwillingness to contemplate the evil that may befall them. Therefore Zeus's thunderclap means nothing more to their minds than the stringing and sound of the bow did, though both affected their emotions. In contrast, Odysseus rejoices in the thunderclap (21.414). He knows what it means because he is "a wanderer expert in life's ills" (21.400), as the suitors have just derisively termed him. The comparatively sheltered suitors, on the other hand, though they turn pale, do not recognize doom when they hear it and feel it.

It remains only for Odysseus to take the "naked arrow," no doubt the same one that we have watched so carefully as each contestant, failing, propped it on the lock of the door, and shoot it through the axes' eyes, "taking careful aim" (21.421). Even in the excitement of the moment, it is legitimate, I think, to be reminded of Penelope's opening the door of the storeroom where the bow lay at the beginning of the book. She too, somewhat more surprisingly, "took careful aim" as she put the key in the lock (21.48), and that too had the aspect of a fateful moment as the door "bellowed like a bull" as she opened it (21.48). The poet has imagined these complementary events in similar terms and made them frame his episode, linking them through the picture of the bow propped on the door with a naked arrow pointing at the door's keyhole. This, I think, is the explanation we have been looking for of that curious image. If I am right, as Odysseus makes his brilliant shot, the moment will be enriched by an awareness somewhere at the back of our minds that he is unlocking the door to the suitors' destruction and his own happiness, and that his wife, providing the bow, has preceded him in this, though she was not fully aware of what she was doing. As far as she could see, her action meant the end of her marriage to Odysseus, not its new beginning; but it was an action in his spirit, a painful taking of arms against the troubles which beset her, and so, with his help, that action now seems likely to prove fruitful beyond all expectation.

The book ends as Odysseus, bow in hand but still sitting in his seat, makes his speech about preparing the suitors' supper with the attendant music.

> Telemachos, my presence here as guest
> has not disgraced you: I did not miss the target,
> nor was I long in stringing the bow; my strength is still firm
> and not as the suitors disdainfully reproached me.
> But now it is time to make the Achaians their supper too,
> while it is light, and afterward entertain them
> with the dancing song and the lyre, for those are what grace a feast.
>
> (21.424–30)

Hereupon Odysseus nods to Telemachos, and Telemachos, buckling on his sword and taking his familiar spear, comes to stand by his father's chair.

Justice

We have reached the climax of the poem. Emerging from his hindering, disguising rags, the true Odysseus leaps to the threshold, bow in hand, and pours out his arrows before his feet, prepared to kill every one of the suitors. With a tremendous concentration of meaning, Homer is about to give us recognition, reversal of fortune, and revenge in a single act. Odysseus never utters his name to the suitors; instead he acts out its meaning by shooting an arrow through Antinoos's neck. The injured one becomes Injurer, and as Odysseus's name continues to unfold in action, justice, with the aid of the gods, begins to take place.

Nothing could be more instructive about the difference between literature and "real" life than this justice. Located within the world of the *Odyssey* as we are, we see Antinoos's death as just for all sorts of reasons. Telemachos, as the poem opened, prayed that the gods might grant "deeds of requital" (*palintita erga*, 1.379), and here they are; it seems just that Antinoos should be removed from the scene by the man whose existence he in effect denied; it seems just that he should be killed in the act of drinking, shot through the gullet, down which so much of Odysseus's wine has already poured, and that, in return as it were, a solid stream of blood should spurt from his nose as he falls; it seems just that his dying foot should, too late, kick away the table for eating at which he is now paying; and it seems just that the food, once so pleasant, should spill to the ground and be fouled. It even seems right that the man who kills him should be called Odysseus, Man of Pain. All these are of course instances of "poetic justice" rather than jurisprudence. With the central justification for Antinoos's death, however, we may seem to be on ground which is more "real." His conduct toward Telemachos and Odysseus has been outrageous, and I think most of us feel that he deserves what he gets in something more than a literary way. Nevertheless, in "real life" we neither believe in retributive justice, nor do we like to see it performed personally by the injured party. If we find the

Odyssey's justice satisfying, it will be because we are temporarily located in the *Odyssey*'s world and not in our own.

The premises of the *Odyssey* are not by any means entirely the ones we would choose, but they hang together, and insofar as they concern this matter of justice, we have already considered them as we looked at books 2, 9, and 17. There we saw that, in the *Odyssey*, a crime is essentially an act or an attitude to which vengeance is the violently desired and utterly appropriate response; so violently desired, in fact, and felt to be so appropriate that gods too are thought of as sharing the feelings which are aroused. This being the conception, we must not object if, in this climactic book of the poem, Odysseus and Telemachos wreak their sense of outrage upon their tormentors to the full. It may even be a very good thing as a psychological cathartic (whatever Aristotle meant by catharsis) if we allow our imaginations to assent to this aggression as wholeheartedly as possible; but catharsis or no catharsis, I am sure that it is the only way to understand the poem.

In the first place, let us note that Odysseus's vengeance is not a sudden outburst of anger; on the contrary, the situation has imposed on him an almost maddening delay. Just as in the Kyklops's cave he had to watch Polyphemos eat six of his men over the course of two days before he could blind him and escape, so against the suitors Odysseus waits through the events of eight books for his revenge to become possible. This is not *mēnis*, "wrath," the subject of the *Iliad*, but *kaka phuteuein*, "planting evils," the translation of Odysseus's name provided by the poem itself. Because of the delay and Odysseus's nature, the revenge is as deliberate, as intellectually and emotionally comprehended, as it is possible for revenge to be, and once we are able to give this revenge our imaginative assent, we can see how greatly its postponement enhances it. What might appear at first cruel and cold-blooded calculation is revealed to be in fact the emotional essence of Homeric justice.

It squares with this studied quality that Odysseus should proclaim the shooting of Antinoos in grimly riddling words beforehand, contrasting it with that other "archery contest" just finished.

> The contest you called "not without disaster" is over.
> A new target now, never yet hit by man,
> I shall see if I can strike and Apollo gives me the glory.
>
> (22.5–7)

Studied too is the formal indictment of the suitors which follows Antinoos's death.

> You dogs! you thought that now I'd never come home again
> from the land of Troy, and so you cropped my house,
> slept with my slave girls by force,
> and courted my wife behind my back while I was alive,
> fearing neither the gods who keep heaven's expanse,
> nor that any wrath of men would follow.
> Now you are tied one and all in the cords of destruction.
>
> (22.35–41)

The monstrous quality of the suitors' crime, one and all, is their impudence in treating a man as though he did not exist. We should notice also that Odysseus puts "wrath of men" on a level with the punishment of the gods. The wrath includes the act of revenge, and together they constitute justice. Any forgiveness that might come between the feeling and the act is not even dreamed of; it would disturb the order of the universe.

Told by Odysseus so forcefully that vengeance is at hand, the suitors at last realize what they have done, and their morale is destroyed. Homer shows this in his characteristically concrete, well-structured fashion. When Antinoos is shot, they at first think it is an accident; they "glance about the walls" (22.24) for the arms which Odysseus and Telemachos have removed, for they mean to kill the beggar for what he has done. After Odysseus's indictment, by contrast, they "glance about" once more (22.43), but this time for a way of escape. The repeated image—it involves the repetition of only one word and therefore cannot be an accident due to the formulaic technique—marks the reversal with absolute precision: they have become not the judges but the judged. Their attendant loss of morale explains the comparative feebleness of their resistance from now on.

The suitors, in a word, feel guilty, for this is justice which we are witnessing, as well as revenge, and the suitors themselves know that they are in the wrong. This is borne out by Eurymachos's offer of an accommodation, when they at last realize what is going on (22.49–59). He admits that they have been behaving outrageously "both in the halls and out" and that Antinoos's aiming at the kingship and leading the attempt to ambush Telemachos are worthy of death. There is no more pretense that what they have been doing is simply ordinary wooing with perhaps a little extra pressure to force Penelope to make up her mind. The suitors admit their guilt; the only question, now that the alleged instigator of their crime lies dead, is whether Odysseus shall "spare his people" (22.54–55), as Eurymachos artfully suggests, and accept a cash payment for the damage that has been done.

Odysseus declares that all the money the suitors might ever hope to have cannot pay for the enormity of their transgression; only the lives of every one of them can do that. Though this may seem excessive, we should remember that Athena from the beginning never had any other thought than the suitors' deaths (1.295–96) and that for Mentor the fact that the suitors were risking their lives even gave them a certain right to what they were doing (2.235–38). To change the rules now would rob them of a certain dignity, and for similar reasons it is good to see Odysseus, deaf to pity, turn down the material gain, which we know he values highly, and choose instead the more difficult and infinitely more dangerous alternative of trying to kill them all.

Odysseus's choice allows both Eurymachos and the "good" suitor Amphinomos to die bravely. Deciding to make a fight of it, each charges Odysseus, sword in hand, hoping to dislodge him from the threshold so that help can be summoned from the town. Eurymachos's death, like Antinoos's, has its appropriateness to his crime: he falls curled about his table, spilling the meat and drink as Antinoos did, and as he lies on his face on the ground, his spasmodically kicking heels shake his chair. Amphinomos, good man that he is, is the only suitor to answer Eurymachos's call for all to charge the threshold. Evidently a concerted effort by all hands would have succeeded, and as it is, Amphinomos got so close to Odysseus that Telemachos, from his position by Odysseus's chair near the door, had to take him in the back with his spear. Amphinomos dies well, and that after all is some consolation for the good qualities which we have seen go to waste in him.

The other suitors are no help to Eurymachos and Amphinomos because their morale has by now completely collapsed. When they heard Odysseus refuse Eurymachos's offer and declare that the choice before them now was to fight or to try to flee, "on the spot their knees went slack and the heart within them" (22.68). This serves not only to set off the courage of Amphinomos and Eurymachos but to demonstrate that right does have certain advantages. As we have seen before, the contrast between the suitors' mood when they thought that Odysseus was the offender and their present mood strongly suggests that conscience rather than congenital cowardice causes 107 men to fail to dislodge 4 from the threshold.

Having established the rationale and mood of the two sides and portrayed the fall of the three most important suitors, Homer means to recount how Odysseus continues to shoot down suitors until his arrows are exhausted and how, having obtained spears, helmets, and shields in the meantime, the four on the threshold then finish the fight. To begin the next phase the poet needs merely to tell how someone went to the storeroom to get arms for Odysseus's party and then to show us the end of the shooting. Instead, before he is through, he makes of this necessity a very subtle scene. First, through Telemachos, he dramatizes the need for armor until we feel it almost physically; then he communicates the pressure of haste under which the armor is brought, so that its arrival and the arming of Telemachos and the herdsmen make a minor climax; then he slows the pace without loss of tension as Odysseus continues to shoot the suitors until at last, his arrows gone, he puts on shield and helmet and takes up his pair of spears. The retardation is very evident: Odysseus takes almost as many lines to put down his bow as Telemachos does to go to the storeroom, get the armor, and return, and he requires twice as many lines to put his armor on as Telemachos, Eumaios, and Philoitios take, all three. This suits the greater, more experienced warrior and brings the scene to a weighty close; it is also specially effective after the excitement which Telemachos's dash to the storeroom has generated.

Homer does not take the time to tell us that Odysseus and his friends need armor; he merely lets us know that Telemachos "leaped back" without retrieving his spear from Amphinomos's body because he

> feared greatly that some Achaian might,
> as he was tugging at the spear, give him a stab
> rushing up with his sword or strike at his head from behind.
>
> (22.96–98)

These lines splendidly communicate Telemachos's feeling of nakedness; furthermore, we know that he is thinking, "I need a shield and helmet" because he at once runs to his father with the following words:

> Father, now I'll bring you a shield and two spears
> and a bronze, temple-fitting helmet,
> and I'll arm myself on the way, and I'll give the swineherd
> and the cowherd arms too; it's better to be armed."
>
> (22.101–4)

He feels the need so vividly that he does not ask permission, he announces, and he has not even had time to combine the three needs into one in his mind; yet he is so aware of his father as the center of the situation that he thinks of his protection first. I find this as good an example as any I have seen of the showing rather than telling, or, in Henry James's terms, the "rendering, not stating," that characterizes the best narrative. As a result of it, we now care intensely about the bringing and putting on of armor, and when at last Odysseus arms himself, as told in the old, deliberate, formulaic phrases, the sense of relief is very strong. The first hurdle on the way to Odysseus's successful revenge is passed.

The relief does not last, however, for the suitors also obtain arms. This serves to create a better final battle, and above all shows how dangerous is the disloyalty of Odysseus's servants, a theme which has been important ever since Eumaios's tale of the faithless slave girl. It is not surprising, after Eurymachos's and Amphinomos's attempt, that no suitors try to come to close quarters with Odysseus's bow as long as the arrows hold out or, when the arrows are gone, make a dash at four men armed with eight throwing spears. In their comparatively unarmed state their one thought is somehow to get someone out of the hall to go to the town for help (22.131–34). We may infer that, if there were no way to do this except through the main door, they might have saved themselves in their desperation either by rushing Odysseus and his friends or by waiting for them to leave the threshold where their backs were protected. But unfortunately for the suitors there is another way: a side door at the back of the hall leads to an alley which in turn leads to the court. What the suitors do not know is that the alley, itself closed by another door, comes out extremely close to the main door. Apparently counting on their making use of this way of escape, Odysseus has assigned Eumaios to watch it (22.129), and if the suitors had actually tried to go that way they would have found themselves trapped, forced to come out the door one by one in easy range of their enemies' spears. As it is, when Agelaos suggests using this side door (22.131–34), the disloyal goatherd Melanthios warns the suitors against it and fetches them arms from the storeroom instead. Thus the stage is set for the final battle with spears.

The seriousness of this unexpected reverse is shown by Odysseus's reaction, which is as grave as the suitors' was earlier. "Then Odysseus's knees went slack, and his heart within him" (22.147). We can sympathize, for spears and shields in the hands of the suitors mean not only terrible danger but treachery. As Odysseus at once recognizes, his own people, Melanthios or the maids, could best warn about the corridor or know where the weapons would have been put away (22.151–52).

To this terrible turn of events, Odysseus's group responds well. There is something startlingly sympathetic about Telemachos as he accepts the whole blame for what has happened, not having shut the storeroom door, and sets about repairing the damage as far as he can by sending Eumaios to shut it. We notice too that, even in their extremity, he feels it important to learn who has betrayed them, asking Eumaios to find this out too. We see, as we have seen before, that punishment matters. Eumaios's courage is revealed as well. Ever since their encounter on the road the morning before, when Melanthios kicked Odysseus, Eumaios has been Melanthios's natural opponent. Now it is he who catches sight of him going for a second armload of weapons and offers to either kill him in the storeroom or bring him back to Odysseus for more condign punishment. Odysseus, as often, has a better plan: on his instructions Eumaios and Philoitios catch Melanthios in the storeroom, tie his hands and feet together behind his back, and then hoist him by his hands and feet to the rafters "so that he may live and feel his pain a while" (22.177). Justice lends strength to the soul. Odysseus, Telemachos, Eumaios, and Philoitios all four, despite their great peril, are high hearted in their determination to punish the transgressor.

A literary actualization of retribution, such as this poem is, shows us what we would otherwise scarcely imagine, the extent to which crime-fitting punishment can create human meaning. I make this observation here because even such an apparently unimportant matter as Eumaios's vaunting over Melanthios brings the point strongly to mind (22.195–99). Part of a herdsman's function is to stay awake at night, protecting his flock, and Melanthios has been performing this function in favor of the suitors rather than of his rightful master. Eumaios pretends he has arranged for him a most comfortable bed which will yet make sure that he neither fall asleep nor miss the sunrise which marks the time to bring in the goats for the suitors' dinner. In other words, he describes Melanthios's punishment as though it were his crime. The crime "meant" the punishment, and now it is the punishment. What Melanthios thought would be good for him has turned out to be bad for him, and that pleases not only Eumaios but all of us, for it both bears out our feelings about treachery and exhibits the symmetry we associate with justice. The facts themselves proclaim that Melanthios was in the wrong and Eumaios in the right. The same denouement provides the force of Odysseus's speeches to the Kyklops and to the suitors, the gist of which is "You thought you could get away with it, and now look! Justice has caught up with you. What you thought was going to be good for you was bad for you, and that is good because what you did was unjust."

For even though this is literature, not life, we are after all dealing with something approaching a moral absolute. Whatever their feelings about retribution, all humans probably detest treachery. Avoiding the question of absolutes, I said earlier that the *Odyssey* defines crime as any act which arouses such indignation that, in the world of the poem, all decent men feel vengeance to be the appropriate response. Aigisthos's murder of Agamemnon and the

Kyklops's treatment of Odysseus and his men are examples. Cattle raiding and city sacking are different: they are such normal occupations for a Homeric male that the first question asked of the newly encountered dead in the underworld can be "Were you shipwrecked, or did strangers (*anarsioi andres*, men to whom you had no recognized ties) kill you as you were cutting out their cattle or fighting them for their city and their women?" (11.399–403; 24.109–13). There is no indignation felt by the questioner here, nor is there any in the famous, "Have you some business, or do you rove on chance/as raiders do on the sea, who rove/risking their lives, bringing trouble to people abroad?" (3.72–74; 9.253–55). We remember Odysseus's statement that a blow sustained in defense of one's property is no grief or pain to the soul (17.470–72). These things are not crimes, but preying on one's own friends is another story. We remember the trouble Antinoos's father got into for joining some Taphian freebooters in a raid on the Thesprotians, who were "in friendly relations" (*arthmioi*; cf. *anarsioi* above) with the Ithacans (16.425–27). Violence to a relative and fellow countryman, like Aigisthos's to Agamemnon, is obviously even worse, and treachery within the same household, such as Klytaimnestra's to her husband or Melanthios's and the maids' to Odysseus and Telemachos, is worst of all. Thus the bite of Eumaios's ironic speech to Melanthios comes not only from the reversal of Melanthios's fortunes but from the fact that he deserves it. There is the satisfaction not only of uniting the opposites, Melanthios's pleasure and Melanthios's pain, but also of seeing a wrong righted.

Melanthios is punished, but twelve of the suitors are now armed. Homer focuses the situation, preparatory to new developments.

> There they stood breathing defiance, one group upon the threshold,
> four of them; opposite, those in the hall were many and able.
>
> (22.203–4)

Athena has promised Odysseus that she will certainly not be unmindful or absent "when we have that work to do" (13.394), and this is the well-chosen moment for her appearance. She comes not in her own form, however, but taking the shape and voice of Mentor, and this has the advantage of permitting both Odysseus and his enemies to show their attitude to their fellow men, particularly their fellow citizens, as well as to the gods. Odysseus calls on Mentor, though he suspects that it is Athena, to help him in the name of their friendship and the benefits he has done him (22.208–10); the suitors by contrast threaten that, if he helps Odysseus, they will not only kill him but take his property and banish his wife and children (22.213–23). In other words, they will do to him what they have been trying to do to Odysseus; namely, obliterate him. This threat of theirs makes us realize that there is no question of their having repented of their ways. Eurymachos's offer to Odysseus of an accommodation was made purely from necessity. Thus Mentor's intervention and the suitors' resulting threat to him clearly reveal that it is the suitors, not Odysseus, in spite of his name, who are fundamentally at odds with their fellow men and so with the gods. Of course it is in Odysseus's interest to appeal to mutual ties and in the suitors' interest to violate them, but even so, in a world which grants as much power to the individual as the *Odyssey*'s does, an attitude like the suitors' cannot be tolerated. Centuries later, Virgil in the *Aeneid* dreams of a world where such people as the suitors might be spared, their power to do ill negated by the benevolent Roman yoke; but for such a dream even to be conceived of as possible Homer's characters were still too free.

Besides demonstrating what is wrong with the suitors, Athena in her disguise as Mentor also makes the connection between Odysseus the city sacker and Odysseus the agent of justice. Threatened by the suitors, she chides not them but rather Odysseus for his lack of spirit (22.226–35): is this the man who fought nine years at Troy to win white-armed, high-born Helen, killed all those men, and took the town by his own stratagem? How can he now, returned to his own house and possessions, be weeping at the idea of showing his strength against the suitors? In a word, Athena with these taunts calls upon the city-sacking spirit as what is most needed when justice is to be done. And she leaves Odysseus's spirit alone to perform it, "testing" him and his son (22.237), no doubt that their credit may be the greater. Although she promises to show "how Mentor, son of Mighty, pays back benefits" (22.234–35), she changes herself into a swallow and flies up to the rooftree instead (22.239–40). The suitors, who never see beyond the surface of things, take comfort from this, thinking Mentor has deserted his friend (22.248–50), but Odysseus, confident of Athena's aid and knowing that he has the gods' approval for what he does, does not lose heart (22.262–65).

Thus this passage of some 115 lines, which recounts the arming of the suitors and the arrival of Athena, punctuates the revenge by separating the shooting with the bow from the spear fight. It seems to heighten the danger to Odysseus at the same time that it increases our sense of the justice of his cause and of the injustice both of the unfaithful members of his household and of the suitors. Furthermore, it unites Odysseus, sacker of cities, and Odysseus, the avenger and agent of justice. My summary of course leaves out much, such as the emotional ups and downs on both sides, the way in which Telemachos and Eumaios each make their own characteristic contribution to Odysseus's cause, and the dramatic aspects of Melanthios's capture and Athena's intervention. All this contributes to a marvelously variegated scene of revenge.

In the spear fight proper, Athena at last rewards Odysseus's confidence in her. She makes all twelve of the spears which Melanthios brought the suitors miss or, at worst, only slightly wound, whereas Odysseus's party kills four men each time they throw. I suppose this is a permissible degree of heightening of the luck which is always an element in such victories. Luck does not always fall on the side of the good, but when it does it seems significant and worthy of poetry. Nor is it entirely luck. The suitors, after all, fight only a gingerly fight. To be sure, Agelaos's plan that they not throw all at once but six at a time, all aiming at Odysseus, makes sense: six spears coming at one man, with six more held in reserve, are no joke. But even so the suitors assist their own destruction. After delivering their first volley and receiving one in return, they retreat to the back of the hall, where there is no chance of their replacing the spears they have thrown. Could they have held their ground and pulled the enemy's spears from their own dead instead of leaving them for Odysseus and his men to retrieve? It is a grim thought, but our being told that Odysseus and his friends retrieved those same spears (22.271) suggests that they might have. As it is, one more volley and they are spearless, as defenseless as before. Odysseus and Telemachos are therefore able to move to close quarters, using their spears now to stab. They kill Agelaos and Leiokritos, and quite naturally the rout begins. Perched among the roof beams in the form of a swallow, Athena raises the aegis, Zeus's magic goatskin which inspires panic, and the fight is over. We need not ask how a swallow can raise an aegis; this is an invisible, if not a metaphorical, event. It is clear that the suitors as a group at no point have fought a very convinced fight, and this fact considerably assists the "luck" of the winners. To us it may well seem "natural," in accord with the nature of things, that the guilt-ridden suitors should undergo panic at this point. If we can accept that in Homer the gods embody the nature of things, we can happily see the victory as primarily Athena's—good luck, bad consciences, panic, and all. Philoitios's vaunt over Ktesippos, the suitor who threw the cow's hoof at the beggar, makes this clear.

> Son of Polytherses, lover of insult, never,
> never yield to folly and speak big words; let the gods
> be the ones to say what will happen; for they are stronger than we are.
>
> (22.287–89)

But at the same time it is clear how necessary Odysseus's own courage and trust in Athena are to achieve the actual result.

The suitors lose the battle for the same reason they got into it: they do not know what strength there is on the side of right. They erroneously suppose that their judgment that Odysseus will not return is infallible and that their combined strength will protect them in what they know is an unjust venture, one which is detested by decent men and presumably by the gods also, one which will provoke revenge as soon as the means are at hand. When it comes to the unexpected showdown, however, they discover that their cause, which is survival, does not fill them with the same will to fight as revenge does Odysseus and Telemachos, who would cheerfully die rather than put up with what the suitors are doing (16.105–11; 20.315–19). Is it so strange that, to Homer and his contemporaries, it should seem that Odysseus and Telemachos were aided by divine power?

All that is left now is rout. Odysseus and his friends,

> rushing on the suitors up and down the hall
> struck at them one after another; they raised a ghastly groaning
> as their heads were smitten, and all the floor ran blood.
>
> (22.307–9)

Comparing the spectacle to the slaughter by "eagles . . . from the mountains" of a flock of birds which cannot escape, Homer invites us to take a kind of pleasure in it, for he says of the slaughter of birds in the simile, "and men rejoice to see them caught" (22.306). We must try to accept the invitation. Compared with most people who have inhabited this earth, we are spoiled by not having to face the fact that eating meat means killing animals. If we assisted personally at the death of every living creature we eat, as people in other ages generally did, our attitudes would be quite different in several respects. In a way we would be less callous; we would better know what our dinners cost. We might even, like Homer's characters, remember the gods every time we killed a steer. On the other hand, we would not repress as something unpleasant and therefore unacceptable the knowledge that most creatures die violent deaths. Were we to behold the eagles wreaking havoc on their natural prey, we would sympathize with the victims, but we would at the same time accept the hunters' success as natural and right. Let me repeat, we shall still sympathize with the victims: Homer's picture of them (pheasants? partridges?), "darting about on the plain as they try to dodge those clouds of death," is too vivid for us not to (22.304), and Penelope's bitter weeping in her dream of the eagle killing her geese shows us that our response is authentically Homeric; but if we really put ourselves in the Homeric situation, we will also identify with the eagles much more than we now tend to do. We will identify with the image of the predation of which the *Odyssey* makes so much. The dog killing the fawn on Odysseus's brooch and Odysseus's boar hunting on Parnassos are but two of its more important examples.

Assuming that we can now at least imagine "rejoicing at the birds' catching," can we take the next step and rejoice to see the suitors killed? As with the birds, so with the suitors. Homer insists that we sympathize with them. As they flee, he compares them, first, to cattle attacked by a gadfly; then, as Odysseus and his men pursue, to the birds whom eagles destroy, already discussed; finally we hear the "ugly" groaning of the men themselves as their heads are struck (22.308). Part of the meaning of doing justice is the ugliness of the punishment, and this ugliness must be given its full value. At the same time, the thirst for vengeance of their executioners is presented as natural and right. In the *Odyssey*'s world, this is the way justice happens. If we can feel that the desire of Odysseus, Telemachos, and the two loyal herdsmen to kill these usurpers is justified, then I think we can imagine rejoicing to see them do so.

The problem of course is to feel that killing the suitors is justified, and Homer faces it squarely. The last suitor to be left alive is the priestly Leodes, who was first to try the bow in the previous book. Though he obviously coveted Penelope, he did not hold with the suitors' insolent, indecent behavior and tried to restrain it. Counting on this, he now flings himself at Odysseus's feet and asks to be spared. Showing no mercy, Odysseus kills him on the spot, for, as he points out, Leodes as priest must have prayed many times that "the goal of sweet return be far from" Odysseus (22.323) and that Penelope become his own wife. This then, and not violent behavior, is clearly Homer's considered definition of what is essential in the suitors' crime. It is not even that they wished Odysseus's death; it is rather that they wished his nonexistence in Ithaca in order that one of them might take his place. In other words, as soon as they thought they had the opportunity, they denied him his place in their world. One is reminded of the distinction Odysseus made to Antinoos: one who comes to drive off your cattle or rob you of your goods or women does not rob you of your place in the world; you have your place as his opponent and he will fight you for your possessions, just as you may fight him for his. Blows sustained in such a broil "are no grief to the soul." But to drive away the beggar whose life depends on charity is to refuse to include him in the world, and this is the unbearable offense which the suitors have committed against Odysseus both as beggar and as himself.

We can see that the crime is worse than wanting Odysseus's death, for if Odysseus were dead he would have to be respected as such. Telemachos would inherit the property and have the disposal of Penelope. But Odysseus's absence has given the suitors the unusual opportunity of treating him as though he were nonexistent. They avail themselves of this opportunity, and that is their crime.

It should now be possible for us to understand why the suitors' crime seemed such a terrible one to Homer. As one of the greatest men of his time and perhaps the best king, Odysseus had every reason to be remembered and respected; his son's position and his wife's freedom should have been utterly secure; instead, after seventeen years of Odysseus's absence, a group of willful men relying on their combined physical force saw fit to ignore all this. Finding his palace convenient and comfortable, they wooed his wife and ate up his stores, not merely without bothering to find out whether he was still alive, but actively trying to prevent Telemachos from finding out; for knowing that Odysseus was alive or that he was dead meant equally that they would have to take some account of him, and that would be the end of their feast. Such unprincipled opportunists are likely to be destructive members of any community, especially one depending as much on mutual respect and as little on centralized authority as this one of Homer's Ithaca; we have seen what the suitors could contemplate doing to Mentor. Nevertheless, in Homer's world that is not the most important point. It is not the community but the individual who counts; and if the individual's right to his selfhood is threatened, Homer considers him justified in asserting it to the utmost upon the aggressors. Because they took no account of Odysseus, Leodes and Amphinomos are basically as guilty as the rest, and we are meant to feel that their punishment is just. This scene of Leodes' supplication is one more remarkable example of Homer's consciousness of the philosophical and moral problems which his narrative raises and of the responsible way in which he deals with them.

Phemios the bard and Medon the herald are of little importance in the *Odyssey's* plot, but they come in most usefully at the end of the fight as a moral contrast to Leodes, bearing out the point we have just been making. Like him, they have been serving professional purposes at the suitors' banquets, but unlike him, they have not wished that Odysseus never return; therefore their lives are spared, even though Telemachos originally listed them as part of the suitors' strength (16.252). That Phemios's attitude toward Odysseus is positive is evident from his having sung for the suitors only under compulsion (1.154; 22.331), but it is even more evident from his enthusiasm at the thought of singing for Odysseus. It is so clear that he and Odysseus each have a place in the other's world that it would be a pity, as Phemios implies, if Odysseus should cut his throat (22.349). Medon, for his part, contrasts with the suitors in his continuing care for Telemachos, a care which Telemachos avows (22.357–58) and which we have seen in Medon's warning Penelope of the plot against her son (4.675–78; 16.409–12). Evidently he wished Odysseus's line to continue, and therefore he is not guilty.

The thought of Phemios and Medon in their comparative noninvolvement serves to relax the tension, even though their fear is real enough. We discover Phemios standing by the side door of the hall holding his lyre, perhaps trying to keep it out of harm's way. As the slaughter comes to an end, he debates whether to go out that tempting door and take shelter at the altar of Zeus in the court. Wise man that he is, he prefers to remind Odysseus of the use he can be to him. Before going up to Odysseus, however, as though bidding it farewell, he sets his instrument down "between the mixing bowl and his silver-studded chair" where it had so often rung out before (22.341). No need, if worst should come to worst, for it to share his destruction. So Phemios is spared, but not before Homer has roused in us a considerable degree of anxiety on his behalf.

The sparing of Medon strikes a more burlesque note. At Telemachos's words recommending that he be saved if he is still alive, he comes out from under a chair where he has hidden himself beneath a new-flayed cowhide. Even so, he is not without dignity as he clasps Telemachos's knees and shows his understanding of the suitors' crime.

> Dear friend here I am. Spare me, and tell your father
> not, in his great strength, to destroy me with the sharp bronze,
> filled as he is with anger because of the suitors who wasted
> his treasure here in the hall and, being fools, slighted your honor.
>
> (22.367–70)

To be expert in propriety is a large part of a herald's profession.

Medon makes Odysseus smile, and in this smiling mood Odysseus tells him that Telemachos saved him in order that he "might know in his own mind, and proclaim it to another as well,/how far superior to evil-doing righteousness is" (22.373–74). This seems to me to give to the simple moral interpretation of what has happened just the right degree of irony. The suitors were indeed killed because they did evil, and Phemios and Medon were spared because their actions were good, but the fact that their lives still hang by a hair suggest that there is more to it than that. Good does not prevail by itself; it needs the assistance of a powerful goddess and of an Odysseus, a Man of Pain.

The action of this book reached a temporary standstill as Odysseus relinquished his bow at last and armed himself. It came to a stop again after the arming of the suitors and the punishment of Melanthios, with the two sides facing one another, one from the threshold and one in the hall. Now for a third time a point of rest is reached as Odysseus, surveying the hall to see if anyone is still alive, finds only heaps of dead suitors, like a haul of fish, Homer says, which fishermen have dragged up on the beach, "and the shining Sun has taken the life from them" (22.388). This possible reminiscence of the fatal irresponsibility which led the Sun to destroy Odysseus's crew may help to make us ready for the fourth and last part of the revenge, the keynote of which has already been given as Odysseus, sending Phemios and Medon out into the court, speaks of "the toil I must perform in the house" (22.377). He uses these painful terms because the last phase of the revenge, though it includes the highest moral expression of the poem, consists essentially of the dirty work of cleaning up, part of which is the hanging of the maids who have slept with the suitors and the mutilation and abandonment to a lingering death of the already-suffering Melanthios. When we come to consider these horrors more closely, we shall discover that Homer likes them no better than we do, or than their location in this part of the revenge indicates; he does, however, consider them right and necessary, and we must try to understand why.

What we have referred to as the highest moral expression of the poem is put before us in the following way. The suitors all being dead, Odysseus calls for Eurykleia, no longer spurning her help as he did when she recognized him. When she comes, the first thing she sees is Odysseus, all spattered with blood and gore, "like a lion, who has just come from feasting on an ox of the field"; then she sees the corpses, and all the blood, and starts to raise the ritual cry of triumph, "for she saw that the deed was a great one" (22.401–8). Perhaps to our surprise, Odysseus stops her with these words:

> Rejoice in your heart, old woman, and check your cry of triumph;
> it is no religion to crow above the slain.
> These the doom of the gods laid low, and their own hard actions;
> for they respected nobody of all who walk the earth,
> of low estate or high, whomever they encountered;
> and so for their own follies they came to an evil ending.
> Come, then, and count off for me the women who serve in the house,
> those who do me dishonor, and those who are unoffending.
>
> (22.411–18)

Victorious Odysseus is like the lion who has killed the ox in that he has proved to be too fierce and strong even for so many enemies as these. Seen that way, his deed calls for simple, uncomplicated exultation, and that is what Eurykleia is expressing. But Odysseus insists that this is more than a lion's kill.

He sees in it, as we should, the triumph of the gods as well as of his own prowess and feels awed in the presence of something bigger and more important than himself. This is the moral perception which raises him above the lion and above the suitors alike. He has the capacity for respect, and they do not. A major indication of this is of course his present restraint, but it is quite clear that he would never treat his fellow man as the suitors do. We cannot imagine him chasing a beggar from his hall, and when posing as a beggar himself, he showed himself willing to share the threshold with Iros. The mildness and impartiality of his government of Ithaca is recognized by everyone in the poem, and he is always scrupulous of others' rights. He tried to treat even the Kyklops as his respected host until Polyphemos made it evident that on him such consideration was wasted.

Odysseus, then, gives both gods and men the respect that is due them. The suitors, by contrast, respect no one, as Odysseus says. We have only to hear these words to realize that this is what is at the bottom of all their nemesis-producing behavior, as seen either in their bullying an old man down on his luck or in their callous treachery to Penelope and the young Telemachos. Most assuredly they deserve the indignation of gods and men, for they have no regard for the selfhood of others. The world which decency desires is one in which each creature is accorded its due respect.

If, in the world which the poem assumes, there is one place where respect is more needed than in another, it is within the household, where a large number of human beings, very large by our standards, must live and function harmoniously together. Odysseus's house has many dependents. Already in book 1, we got the impression of a host of servants and attendants—some slaves, like the maid who pours the hand water, the housekeeper, and the carver; and some free, like the heralds, "squires," and "lads" who serve the suitors; and there are many more. From Eumaios's account of Odysseus's herds in book 14, for example, it is obvious that there are easily fifty herdsmen who serve in the same way as Eumaios himself. For most or all of these, there is no question of setting up a completely independent establishment. When Eumaios receives his wife and farm (14.64), it will be "built near [Odysseus's] house," and his status, still as slave, will be that of "friend and brother of Telemachos" (21.214–16). We can well imagine that this arrangement for living is, in the poem's world, by far the most desirable one for reasons both of defense and economic security. When Telemachos says that he intends to be master of his and Odysseus's house and "of the slaves which Odysseus got for [him] by raiding" (1.398), we can understand not only how accepted piracy is but how large a proportion of the population is, or can become, "slaves." Eurykleia and Eumaios were both bought, Melanthios and Melantho and their brothers were born on Odysseus's estate to Penelope's slave Dolios, and yet in general, Odysseus's slaves were obtained "by raiding": that is, most of them came from other households, like his own but "strangers," on which he descended in the way of piracy. In sum, the impression which the poem gives is that most people were in one way or another dependents of the great houses, or wished that they were (cf. Finley, 57–59).

The poem goes out of its way to suggest what a happy lot it was to be a slave in Odysseus's household. In book 1, Homer tells us that Eurykleia, who gets such evident satisfaction from taking care of Telemachos, received the same respect from Laertes as he accorded his own wife (1.432), and before the poem is finished it is evident that she has almost the status of wife and grandmother. We have already mentioned that Eumaios will be given a wife and farm and treated as "brother of Telemachos," and the same thing is true of Philoitios (21.214–16). Eumaios, in fact, has already implied that Odysseus is more than father and mother to him (14.138–43). Odysseus has almost complete disposal of these people's persons, including the power of life and death, but that is only a recognition of the facts: in a society like the poem's, barons like Odysseus command the physical force to do with their dependents as they will, and there is little or no power to restrain them beyond their own respect for their fellow man. On this respect the members of Odysseus's household seem perfectly able to count. In book 4, Eurykleia can say to Penelope, with complete equality, freedom, and equanimity, that she may cut her down with ruthless bronze or leave her alive in the hall just as she will; she will not hide that she has assisted Telemachos's departure (4.743–74). She accepts Penelope's power of life and death with no fear at all that it might be used unfairly. The general impression is that slaves are little worse off, if at all, than other members of the family. The same kind of affection evidently exists between master and man, or master and woman, as between him and the members of his own family, as the tears and embraces of the servants in Odysseus's recognition scenes show. Clearly it is both the duty and the privilege of all the members of the household to love, honor, and obey its head, whether that head is Odysseus, Penelope, or Telemachos, and most of the members find only satisfaction in such a relationship.

Odysseus and Telemachos enjoy their position partly on sufferance of fate: Eumaios also is a king's son, and had the servants in his household all been faithful, his position would be far different now. Since Zeus has determined otherwise, however, he has embraced his new lot with a will. Though he himself says that Zeus takes away half a man's virtue when "the day of slavery catches him" (17.322–23), he is not referring to himself but to the lazy servants who have neglected the dog Argos. Slackness may be endemic among slaves, but it is not inevitable, as Eumaios's own case shows. According to the *Odyssey*, a slave's lot can be a happy one, and so blows of fate such as befell Eumaios seem the less unjust (15.486–92). If one's master turns out to be bad, one can sometimes, if one is enterprising, seek out another, as Philoitios thinks of doing because of the suitors (20.222–23).

But Odysseus is a good master, and Telemachos will evidently become one. Eumaios takes real delight in the thought that his rightful owner is "godlike" (14.40) and is filled with chagrin at the falling off which the suitors represent. For if Odysseus and Telemachos hold their position partly by luck, they also deserve it more than anyone else does. The trial of the bow is symbolic of this. It shows that these descendants of Laertes are of all men most able to command the respect of such a household, to make it function and to protect it, and so, if there is respect on their side also, to be worthy of its admiration and love. As Theoklymenos in reading the omen of the hawk and the dove put it to Telemachos,

> No family exists more kingly than yours
> in the land of Ithaca; you will always have the greater power.
>
> (15.533–34)

In the position of Odysseus vis-à-vis his dependents in the *Odyssey*, one can see, if one looks at all closely, a relationship that begins with simple physical force and the ability to cause pain (with the victorious bloody lion, in short) and ends with everything that is best in the life of a happy family. It depends on two things: the military potential commanded by the head of the family, and the mutual respect and affection of all concerned.

During Odysseus's absence the suitors took over his house, and because of the force which they represented, all the household, even Eurykleia (20.147–56), had to comply with their wishes. Some went further; namely, certain of the maids and Melanthios the goatherd. Melanthios and Melantho, brother and sister, children of Dolios, show what it means not to respect one's fellow man in the role of man- and maid servant respectively. With a certain contemptible triviality of mind, they both throw in their lot with Eurymachos, both of them being unable to recognize the value of loyalty. They are changing one dependency for another for the sake of a temporary access of power. Melanthios uses his for the purpose of kicking an old man whose visible poverty seems to offer him a chance to show his superiority, while Melantho uses her new "freedom" not only to obtain the pleasure of Eurymachos's irresponsible caresses but for reviling that same old man as well. It is quite evident that, from the point of view of the poem, sexual freedom with outsiders cannot exist in harmony with an institution such as the large Homeric household we have been describing. We have seen how a Phoenician trader corrupted Eumaios's nurse, with the result that Eumaios, a prince, became a slave. Through Melantho, who sleeps with Eurymachos and taunts beggars, and Melanthios, who kicks the down-and-out, Homer is showing us what is lost when respect for Odysseus's position and all it means is abandoned. We have yet to determine, however, why the slaves must be punished so terribly.

To put it somewhat too crudely, respect begins in fear and ends in love. In the first instance, we respect that which, if we do not respect it, can hurt us. Disrespect, on the other hand, engenders in those against whom it is directed indignation and the willingness to do the violence, fear of which would be the beginning of respect. That is why Telemachos's indignation at the suitors expressed itself in the thought of what Odysseus would do to them if he were there (1.158–65), and why Penelope unconsciously echoed the beggar's prayer for the death of Antinoos, who had insulted him (17.492–94; cf. 476). Homer sees this great value—respect—as created first and foremost by the vengeful feelings of the insulted and injured. Therefore to act out these feelings is valuable and right. If we have been content to watch Odysseus act them out against the suitors even in the cases of Amphinomos and Leodes, it should be possible to understand the cases of the maids and Melanthios as well.

There, Odysseus's feelings are even more violent. We remember his terrible wrath and mighty effort to control himself as he watched the maids leave the house for their last assignation with the suitors. The feeling was evidently much what it would have been to see such behavior in his own wife, while the disrespect shown both to Penelope and himself is quite clear. As for Melanthios, we remember the incident at the spring and shrine of the nymphs and how Odysseus had to restrain himself there (17.204–57). In both cases it would be quite legitimate for Odysseus to reflect that these are people who in a sense owe him everything and who have been treated as, and indeed are, a part of his family. Melantho in particular was brought up by Penelope as though she were her own daughter (18.322–23). Above all, there is the revelation of their total treachery in Melanthios's supplying arms to the suitors. All this being so, we must not be surprised at what happens now to Melanthios and the maids.

Twelve maids out of the fifty in the house prove to have "trodden the path of shamelessness,/paying no respect to [Eurykleia] or to Penelope herself" (22.424–25). Therefore it seems just in the Homeric sense (i.e., appropriate to their master's feelings) both that these should be forced to carry out the corpses and clean the hall and that they should then be killed. When Telemachos, evidently adding his and Penelope's feelings of outrage to his father's (22.463–64), improves on his father's instructions by hanging them instead of putting them to the sword, it only shows his worthiness to succeed him. It is a dishonorable death (22.462) and a pitiful one (22.472), and they deserve it.

As almost always in Homer, there is sympathy with the victim, and we may take it that Telemachos feels it too, but it is rightly not enough to override his sense of outrage or stop the course of Homeric justice. The pathos is heightened by a simile comparing the maids to birds, "thrushes or doves," which fly to their roost only to catch their heads in the fowler's net, "and a bitter bed receives them" (22.468–70). This brings out poignantly the folly, the lack of awareness of the danger, coupled with the unthinking yielding to desire, which characterizes all those who go wrong in the *Odyssey*, from Odysseus's men who eat the cattle of the Sun to the Kyklops Polyphemos. The element of pathos causes us to experience the maids' crime from their side, as it were, as well as from that of Odysseus and Telemachos, and while it may seem more understandable from their side, it is evidently no less foolish and fatal.

All this time Melanthios has been hanging by his hands and feet, which are tied behind his back, from the rafters of the storeroom. Odysseus has given no instructions about him at all, but Telemachos, Philoitios, and Eumaios have no hesitation. The whole thing is over in four lines.

> They brought out Melanthios through the vestibule and the court,
> lopped his nose and ears with the pitiless bronze,
> tore out his private parts, to feed raw to the dogs,
> and cut off his hands and feet in their hearts' anger.
>
> (22.474–77)

Then, washing their own hands and feet, they go back inside the house to seek Odysseus, "and the work was finished" (22.479). From the point of view of Homeric justice, it has been a nasty business but necessary if respect is to survive in the world. The women can be excused somewhat for their frailty, but the only feelings which Melanthios inspires are contempt. By his own incapacity to recognize the humanity of others, he forfeits the right to be treated as a human being himself, and he suffers accordingly.

With relief we turn to more agreeable matters. We are glad to see the house, now washed and cleaned, given a final purifying treatment of fire and sulphur. Even before this cleansing, the poem directs our minds to the coming reunion of Odysseus with the rest of his household: Eurykleia's characteristic impatience, first to tell Penelope and then to see Odysseus put on proper clothes, is rebuffed, and we probably applaud Odysseus's refusal to think about presenting himself to his wife until the purification is complete. Now all is ready, and the book ends as Odysseus is reunited with the maidservants who kept their respect intact. It is a scene of great affection, and as the episode ends it is good to see the fruition of the loyalty which Melanthios and the unfaithful maids lacked.

Penelope

When Penelope recognizes Odysseus in book 23, we see at last how thankful she and her husband ought to be both for the Trojan War and for Poseidon's enmity. These "evils" have made possible a happiness as great, perhaps, as any that has ever been celebrated in song.

To regain his wife, Odysseus has gone through much, renouncing even immortality. Finally arrived in Ithaca, with only three men to help him, he has taken on 108 suitors in battle and left not one alive. Now in book 23, he faces the last obstacles of all—the greatness of his achievement and Penelope's love for him. These are obstacles because the more astounding his return and defeat of the suitors, the more difficult it is to believe that any human accomplished so much; and the more Penelope loves him, the harder it will be for her to trust her good fortune and give herself even to this photocopy of the husband who left her to go to Troy twenty years before. These are obstacles, to be sure, but it is clear what happiness the process of overcoming them must produce: before Penelope yields, both she and Odysseus will be made aware of the full extent of their love for each other. Furthermore, and especially delightful for us as members of the audience, Odysseus will meet his match not only in love but in chicanery. Penelope will succeed in making the consummate dissembler give himself away. If she deserves some compensation for the testing to which he has subjected her, this is most certainly it.

The book begins triumphantly. Shouting for joy, Eurykleia goes stumbling upstairs to tell her mistress what has happened, and we in the audience are as eager as she is for Penelope to be told. Nevertheless, as predicted, this proves not to be easy. We watch Penelope, once her initial incredulity has been overcome, embrace Eurykleia in ecstasy, only to doubt again at the magnitude of what Eurykleia's next words convey.

> Now at last our long hope is fulfilled:
> he, alive, has come to his hearth, and found you

with his child still at home; those who wronged him,
the suitors, he punished, all, in his house. (23.54–57)

In Penelope's answer to this we hear not only her sober judgment that only the gods could achieve such a retribution but the disbelief with which she has greeted so many false reports in the past.

Nanny dear, it's too soon to shout and exult.
You know how glad we would be to see him home,
we all would, especially I and the son who was born to us.
But this news is untrue, as you tell it;
no, some god killed the illustrious suitors,
resenting their insolence and evil actions.
For they respected nobody of all who walk the earth,
of low estate or high, whomever they encountered.
So, for their recklessness, they suffered; but Odysseus
lost his homecoming far from Achaia, and is lost himself.
(23.59–68)

Penelope doubts even as, without knowing it, she condemns the suitors in nearly the same words we have heard her husband use so recently (22.414–15). Eurykleia cannot convince her, even by mentioning Odysseus's scar and her own recognition of him; Penelope is too aware of the power of the gods and its inscrutability (23.81–82). She agrees, however, to go downstairs to her son "to see/the dead suitors and who it was who killed them" (23.83–84).

But the news is too compelling for her to maintain this degree of doubt. No sooner are the pair on the stairs than Penelope begins to debate with herself "whether she should keep her distance from her husband and question him/or go up to him, embrace him, and kiss his hands and face" (23.86–87). Should she surrender to the proffered happiness at once, or should she be circumspect? For her to surrender now would violate our conception of her, but it is good to know that she feels the temptation.

Face to face with Odysseus at last, she does neither. The impact of seeing him is too strong for any resolve she might have taken. She sits opposite him instead, silent "in the firelight" (23.89). Shaken she may be, but, as the phrase quoted shows, she makes sure that he can see her. Will he give some sign? No. Odysseus is not in the habit of giving himself away so easily. Instead, he sits "with eyes cast down, waiting to hear/what his brave wife would say when she saw him" (23.91–92). Unlike her, he is not in a hurry to be recognized, and as Penelope looks at him, "sometimes his face seemed the same as the one she

knew,/and sometimes the rags on his body kept her from recognizing him"
(23.94–95).

Telemachos, who is present at this scene with Eurykleia, Eumaios, and the
other faithful servants, is naturally impatient and scolds his mother for her
hard-heartedness. She replies:

> My child, the heart within me is dumbfounded;
> I can't say a word, or ask a question,
> or look him in the face. But if it really is
> Odysseus, and he has come home, be sure that we two
> shall know one another better than now; for we
> have tokens which we two know that are hidden from others.
>
> (23.105–10)

Again Penelope, though shaken, is evidently not at a loss.

From the height of his advantage over his wife in knowledge, Odysseus
smiles and, rightly guessing that it is his disguise which troubles her, advises
Telemachos to let Penelope test him "inside the house" (23.112–16). So
confident is he that all will be well that he turns the talk to another important
matter—what to do about the Ithacans who will surely rise up to avenge their
dead brothers and sons among the suitors. The smile, the phrase "inside the
house," and the implied changing of clothes all suggest that Odysseus is
relishing the intimate implications of Penelope's "tokens" known to husband
and wife alone. In fact he goes as far as to make these implications consonant
with his plan for concealing the death of the suitors: he instructs Telemachos,
Eurykleia, Eumaios, Philoitios, and the other maids and servants to change
their clothes and to sing, dance, and make music as though for a wedding so
that the town will think that Penelope has surrendered to a suitor at last. In
other words, together with the deception, Odysseus is providing the wedding
celebration for the reuniting with Penelope which he so confidently expects to
achieve. We should continue to hear the music of that celebration (23.143–
47) as the next scene unfolds.

As it turns out, Odysseus has set a trap for himself. He is so sure that
restoration of his former looks will win Penelope over that the minute he
returns to her washed and dressed and "looking like a god," thanks to Athena
(23.163), he accuses her of hard-heartedness and pretends to resign himself to
sleeping alone. This is his signal for her to collapse in his arms. To his surprise
and ours, no collapse occurs. Penelope proceeds to test him. Critics and
translators sometimes make the same assumption as Odysseus and therefore
translate Penelope's test as though she were still unsatisfied with his looks,

finding them too unlike those he had when he sailed for Troy; but to judge so is to be disrespectful of Athena's efforts. George Herbert Palmer translates correctly and superbly: "Nay, sir, I am not proud, nor contemptuous of you, nor too much dazed with wonder. I very well remember what you were when you went upon your long-oared ship away from Ithaca. However, Eurycleia, make up his massive bed outside that stately chamber which he himself once built" (23.174–78). This is as much as to say, "I am holding aloof for none of the reasons you suppose. There is no impediment in my feelings toward you, and you look just as you should. Still, I agree with you that you should sleep alone."

No doubt we are pleased to see Penelope behave like this. There should be a test. Things should not, ever, be too easy for Odysseus, and Penelope does deserve something in return for the long scrutiny she has unwittingly undergone. Still, the chief reasons for the test emerge only in the sequel. Penelope's words make Odysseus extremely angry, as well they might. Here is outright sexual rejection, and for no apparent reason. Furthermore, the point of the test is that Odysseus built not only the bedchamber but the bed, using a still-rooted olive trunk for one of its posts. His bed is immovable unless someone has cut the trunk through while he was away. Sexual rejection indeed! Who, he wants to know, has moved his bed?

The answer is, of course, no one, and Penelope can now at last surrender. All during Odysseus's absence she had feared that some man might beguile her as Helen was beguiled. That was not like Helen; there was something uncanny about it, a god must have been involved (23.215–24). So, in her own case, this stranger who seems like Odysseus in all ways may really not be he, but rather some visitation of the gods. Hence her test of the bed.

Superficially, Odysseus has established his credentials by knowing about the olive-trunk bedpost, and no doubt it is not fair to point out that a god might know about that also. Still, Odysseus's self-revelation here has a more inward aspect. The idea that he has lost Penelope's love has jolted him into dropping all calculation, all disguises. What emerges is pure anger that the marriage which he thought he had rooted immovably has been tampered with. And how happy Penelope must be to contemplate such anger! The man before her is not merely a certain set of features with hyacinthine black or yellow hair but the being whom she chose and who chose her so many years ago, and whom she has just tricked into revealing that he feels the same way now, and passionately. The anger of Odysseus, Man of Pain, painful though it would ordinarily be, is the measure of his love for her. And there is also the happiness produced by the pain she has caused Odysseus. She has made him actually experience what he would feel if she had ceased to love him. Could he experience a greater joy than discovering that she has not changed after all? His anger convinces her that it really is he, and so, flinging her arms about his neck and kissing him, "Odysseus, don't be angry [mē moi Odysseu skuzdeu]," she cries through her tears, "for you were always the most understanding of men." Was the sound of his name on his wife's lips ever more welcome to any man?

By this time both have become well acquainted with the good side of pain, Penelope perhaps even more than Odysseus. She speaks of herself as "hard hearted" (apēnea, 23.230) for holding out against her husband, admitting to the quality which she once deplored as earning the hatred of all mankind and of which both Telemachos and Odysseus have recently accused her; she does this even as she and her husband are enjoying the fruits of that hard-heartedness in each other's arms. Odysseus warns her of the "immeasurable toil" still to come, which Teiresias enjoined, in the same speech in which he invites her to come to bed. To his surprise, she asks to hear it in detail, pointing out that she will have to face it some time in any case (23.261–62); this is the woman who in the first book tried to stop the bard from singing of the Achaians' "bitter return" from Troy. On this occasion, by contrast, she takes comfort from the prophecy that, when the "immeasurable toil" is completed, Odysseus will have a prosperous old age and a gentle death (23.286–87). Old age, she implies, is time enough for a permanent "escape from evils." Best of all,

> When the two had had their joy of sweetest love,
> they took their joy of speech, telling one another,
> she, pearl of women, all she endured in the house,
> watching the waste the crowd of suitors made,
> who, in her name, slaughtered so many cows
> and sheep, and drained so much wine from the jars;
> and the scion of Zeus Odysseus told all the woes he inflicted
> on other men, and all he himself bore in anguish;
> all he told, and she delighted to hear, nor did sleep
> fall upon her eyelids until he recounted everything.
>
> (23.300–309)

Not only is this a supreme example of painful experience enjoyed in retrospect, but we cannot fail to respond to the explication in the last four lines of Odysseus's name: the Man of Pain told all the woes he inflicted on others and all that he himself suffered. (For good measure, "bore in anguish," a translation I borrowed from Palmer, is, in the Greek, oïzdusas emogēse.)

Many poets might have stopped their account of Odysseus's and Penelope's recognition and reunion here. Not Homer; the lines I have just quoted introduce a complete recapitulation of Odysseus's adventures, starting with the sack of Ismaros and ending with the Phaeacians bringing him home. This is certainly a good moment in the story to review the hero's accomplishment, and the added implication that the accomplishment is an enactment of the name Odysseus, that the accomplishment *is* the man himself, multiplies the effect of the review many times. As we have seen, Penelope used not to hide her detestation for everything connected with Troy: "Evil-Ilion, the Unspeakable" was her phrase for that city (19.260, 597; 23.19). Now she delights to hear of all the Man of Pain did and suffered during his "bitter return."

When at their recognition Penelope, convinced at last, bursts into tears, throws her arms around Odysseus's neck, kisses him, and asks to be forgiven, he in turn embraces her as follows:

> So she spoke, and made him wish to weep even more,
> and his tears streamed as he held his beloved loyal wife.
> As when land—how welcome!—shows to people in the water,
> whose stout ship Poseidon wrecks on the sea,
> driven by wind and the water's force,
> and few have escaped to shore from the gray salt water,
> swimming, and their skin is caked with brine,
> and in joy they mount the land, escaping evil—
> so welcome to her was her husband as she looked at him,
> never quite loosing her white arms from about his neck.
>
> (23.231–40)

It might seem that the point of view changes here from Odysseus to Penelope with a somewhat disturbing effect, but actually I think we gain thereby. Unlike Odysseus, Penelope has never been literally shipwrecked, and so she is poetically a better candidate for the simile than he is. That *her* happiness should be like a shipwrecked voyager's surprises as well as illuminates. Thus in one way we get a sense of how welcome their reunion is to both of them, and in another we are made to feel how alike, as well as how different, the experience of each has been. It is not to be ignored either that, in the story as well as in the simile, Poseidon's enmity makes the happiness possible.

This indeed has its relevance to the "measureless toil" which still remains for Odysseus. Teiresias has said that he must wander until he reaches

> a people who do not know the sea
> not eat their food mixed with salt;
> who do not even know of red-cheeked ships,
> nor balanced oars, which are a vessel's wings. (23.269–72)

Without braving Poseidon on the sea, there can be no Troy, no Kyklops, no glory. One cannot even get to Ithaca. People who do not know the sea have no savor in their food or their lives. Odysseus is to be a missionary to such people, planting his oar among them and introducing them to Poseidon by the marvelously male sacrifice of bull, boar, and ram (23.278). Then he may go home and sacrifice in gratitude to all the gods for helping him conquer Poseidon.

Something of the quality of that victory is of course suggested in the simile we have just discussed. The land attained by the shipwrecked voyagers is "welcome" (*aspasios*). They feel the same themselves (*aspasioi*) as they mount the shore. In the same way, to Penelope her husband returned from the sea looks "welcome" (*aspastos*). It is fitting, therefore, that Homer crowns Odysseus's and Penelope's happiness in the following words: "Then at last/in joy [*aspasioi*] they reached their old-time bed's firm-foundedness" (23.295–96).

Peace

Odysseus has come home, the poem has reached a most satisfying end or goal in Penelope's arms, but important matters remain. Odysseus lists them for Penelope when they wake (23.350–65): first, Penelope shall see to the household goods, while he undertakes to replenish his flocks and herds, largely by raiding; Odysseus's immediate task, however, is to go to the family's country estate to see his still-grieving father; third, since there will be trouble when the suitors' deaths become known, Penelope must stay upstairs with her maids and see no one. Settling these remaining problems, however, is not all that the poem's last book achieves: it also provides a final answer to Athena's question at the beginning of the poem, the problem of Odysseus's suffering and Zeus's attitude toward him. Here we find at last the definitive pronouncement regarding the problem of evil and the meaning of Odysseus's existence.

Book 24 begins, in fact, by looking at Odysseus in the light of eternity. Hermes conducts the souls of the suitors to the underworld, and there they find Agamemnon and Achilles comparing fates in terms of divine favor and human happiness. Achilles remarks that at Troy Agamemnon seemed dearest to Zeus of all the heroes because of the great army which he led, only to lose all that glory because of the ugly end he came to; far better, he says, for him to have died at Troy (24.24–34). Agamemnon agrees, and then proceeds to portray Achilles' death and funeral at Troy, in contrast to his own death, as the most glorious possible fate. He concludes that it was Achilles who was really dear to the gods.

> Very dear you were to the gods.
> So not even by dying did you lose your name, but always
> among all mankind your fair fame shall live, Achilles.
> (24.92–94)

As Agamemnon finishes, the suitors appear, and one of them, Amphi-medon, tells their sorry tale. As a result Agamemnon finds a new paradigm of happiness in Odysseus, apostrophizing him as follows:

> Happy son of Laertes, ingenious Odysseus,
> truly you won great virtue when you won your wife!
> How good the mind that graced flawless Penelope,
> daughter of Ikarios! How well she remembered Odysseus,
> her own wedded husband! Her fame will never die,
> the fame of her virtue, and the gods will make a song for men
> who live on earth, a lovely song for staunch Penelope—
> not like what Klytaimnestra did
> who killed her wedded husband; hateful her song will be
> throughout the world, and a bad name she will give
> to all the female sex, even to the woman who does well.
>
> (24.192–202)

If Agamemnon's fame was supremely unhappy ("a most lamentable death," 24.34), then Odysseus, having met the opposite fate to his, may turn out to be supremely happy. Though Agamemnon does not quite say so, Odysseus who made his way home from Troy alive seems even happier than Achilles who died there so gloriously, as we have just heard. In this connection it is proper to remember Achilles' preference in book 11 for even the meanest life as compared with the happiness of even the most honored of the dead.

Odysseus too must die, however; in fact, he has chosen to do so. Achilles' name will live forever, and so will Penelope's, as Agamemnon says (24.93, 196). So will Klytaimnestra's, for that matter, although hers will be known for evil, not good. What of Odysseus's name when he comes to die like Agamem-non and Achilles? It can occur to us that the song for Penelope which Agamemnon has just predicted is the one before us, and that in it the most indelible name of all, more so even than Penelope's, is Odysseus's. His is the name and nature that Penelope remembered; he is the one whose happiness Agamemnon has just hailed; he is the one who, more than any other, has "won his ghost," the goal Homer proposed for him in the poem's fifth line. In the terms of this underworld discussion, then, he is not a sufferer but a happy man. The ending changes all, as it did for Agamemnon, though in his case the change was from good to evil; and if anyone's happiness shows him to be "dear to Zeus," Odysseus's does. The answer to Athena's question, therefore, is that what looked like evil even to her was really the preparation for this good, and that her favorite's sagacity and fear of the gods have been rewarded after all. In a word, when Athena asked Zeus why he was so hostile to Odysseus (*ti nu hoi toson ōdusao, Zeu*, 1.62), the question was its own answer: by providing him with the evils which we have seen him overcome, Zeus was indeed "odysseusing" Odysseus, giving him a name which even now still lives. Nor are sagacity and fear of the gods the whole story: for Odysseus's name to be remembered, there had to be also Autolykos's element of enterprise, of the boar hunter and city sacker, which involved him in pain—his own and others'. The suitors' ghosts are evidence enough of this.

The descent of the suitors' ghosts to Hades may serve primarily to emphasize Odysseus's winning of his ghost, but it demonstrates his superiority in another way as well. Homer conveys the suitors' present helplessness and insubstantiality by comparing them, as they flit to Hades compelled by Hermes' wand, to bats in the depths of a cave startled into flight by the involuntary fall of one of them from the cluster in which they cling to the rock (24.1–10). The feeble cries of the ghosts resemble the squeaking of these bats. The squeaking in itself is enough to appall us by its contrast to the suitors' former boisterousness, which once seemed so terrifying, but the bats' action also plays its part because it is involuntary, like the dead suitors' souls' being set in motion by Hermes' irresistible wand. Thus both the actual scene and the manner of the bats' flight in the simile evoke a picture of the soul's involuntary journey to the darkness underground. This is what death is, and we are invited to compare it with the vigorous life of Odysseus and those he loves.

Odysseus's greatness is further heightened because Achilles' end is made to seem so impressive in Agamemnon's account of it. The fifty-six lines of that account attain to something like terribilita, telling as they do of the fighting over Achilles' body, his lying in state, the panic of the Argives at the coming of Thetis with all her nymphs, Achilles' dirge sung by the Muses, his burning on the pyre, his mound by the Hellespont, and his funeral games at which the prizes are donated by the gods. The passage's tone is set by the first few lines.

> Happy son of Peleus, like-to-the-gods Achilles,
> you died at Troy, far from Argos; and over your body
> others died, the noblest sons of Achaians and Trojans,
> fighting over your corpse; and you in the whirling dust cloud
> lay, huge in your greatness, forgetting your charioteering.
>
> (24.36–40)

Under the influence of such words, we must consent to the feeling that all this pain and death and desperate struggle compose a "happiness" of a high order.

What more glorious fate for a man than to be the center and occasion both of such fighting and of such a funeral? By making Odysseus's fate seem better even than this, both now and after he is dead, Homer has brought off a great poetical coup.

We should notice also that Odysseus's greatness is involved with the same sort of pain as Achilles'. For him to have regained homeland, house, family, and the satisfactions of peace would not be nearly enough to surpass Achilles' glory if he had never gone to Troy and were not the object of a painful concern as great as that felt for Achilles. I refer to his family's longing for him, especially Penelope's, and to the suitors' hostility against him and suffering at his hands, now vividly recalled in the scene before us. In this pain which communicates Odysseus's greatness, we find, as we have remarked before, Homer justifying what the world tends to call evil.

Another "beauty" (as Pope would have called it) contributed by the scene in the underworld is Amphimedon's recapitulation of what has happened to the suitors. Simply as a recapitulation it helps to bring the whole poem into focus at its end: it does for the Ithacan struggle what Odysseus's story told to Penelope in bed does for the wanderings; but it is even more satisfactory in that it shows us how the suitors feel about what has happened to them. Even in death they do not win our sympathy, for they think they have been unfairly used, and they take this opportunity to complain of their fate (24.121–90). Their chagrin at being tricked emerges as Amphimedon speaks of the impossibility of recognizing Odysseus in his disguise and of their having abused him with insults and missiles as a result. He implies not that they should have respected the beggar but that, had they known, they might have respected Odysseus. How much that implication is worth, I take it Homer's audience is already aware.

Because of their moral blindness the suitors misconceive the whole situation: they think that Penelope's delays in choosing one of them were a deliberate plot to destroy them and that she offered the trial of the bow in collusion with her husband. They cannot see that she sincerely despaired of his return and that only the strength of her hopeless love for Odysseus made her hold them off with her trick of the weaving; they also cannot see that her offer of the bow trial was sincere, a last desperate attempt to save Telemachos. Because we realize what they do not, our sense of the poignancy of Penelope's case is heightened at the same moment that we note that the suitors are unable to conceive of any motive beyond self-interest. Even when they are right about crucial details, they miss their significance. They see how important it was that Telemachos opposed his single voice to their united clamor in getting Eumaios to put the bow into Odysseus's hands, but Amphimedon's emphasis suggests that they cannot understand how it happened. It does not occur to them that justice might give Telemachos such courage, or that, in Eumaios's mind, loyalty and justice might outweigh the threat of their power. Do they remember now how, instead of preventing Eumaios, they laughed at what they took to be Telemachos's helplessness? In the same way, Amphimedon recognizes that it required a god's presence to turn the battle so soon into a rout (24.182–85), but he seems to have no inkling that the god's presence had anything to do with the suitors' being in the wrong.

Two issues remain to complete the *Odyssey*'s action, as we have noted: Laertes' reunion with his son, and a settlement with those who claim vengeance for the suitors. Into the meeting between son and father, Homer deliberately introduces a problem: Odysseus does not reveal himself immediately, even though there is no longer any practical reason for caution; instead, throughout some eighty lines, Odysseus pretends to be a stranger who has entertained Odysseus abroad. One reason for Homer's presenting the reunion in this way is obvious: it makes a better recognition scene; but in order to make a better recognition scene, its motivation must also be convincing, and Homer manages that too. As we have said, there is no question of testing Laertes' loyalty. Odysseus proposes simply to see whether his father will recognize him after all this time.

> I for my part shall make trial of my father,
> whether he will recognize me and know me by sight,
> or will fail to know me having been gone so long.
>
> (24.216–18)

Accordingly Odysseus sets off to seek his father "in an experimental mood" (24.221). The sight of Laertes, however, strikes such pity into Odysseus as to bring forth tears, and in this state he debates once more whether to reveal himself at once or to wait and see whether his father will recognize him. We are probably glad to see Odysseus hesitate to carry through his original plan, for Laertes' grief is so manifest that it seems heartless to deceive him merely in order to find out whether he now can recognize his son or not. Thus it is all the more astonishing when, instead of revealing himself, Odysseus chooses "to test him first with teasing words" (24.240). The fact cries out for explanation.

Certain things are clear: it is not his own hostility that causes Odysseus's decision, for he is full of pity for his father; and he has no need to test his father's love for him, for that is obvious. What we do see, however, is Odysseus behaving in typical Odyssean fashion: he is resisting an impulse which is clamoring for immediate gratification—how many times have we seen him do this!—and above and beyond that, the impulse in question, to pity, is the one which, according to the meaning of his name, he most characteristically resists. Well and good, but in this case to what end?

The end would appear to be some kind of knowledge, as Odysseus's wish to "make trial of" (*peirēsomai*) and "test" (*peirēthēnai*) his father and his "experimental mood" (*peirētizōn*) suggest. The fictitious name which Odysseus adopts for his father's benefit is *Epēritos* (24.306), close enough to *peirētizōn* in sound, it seems to me, to suggest the meaning "put to the test," and the nature of the name's Greek ending will allow us to take its significance both in the active and passive sense. Like Aithon, this too is not a bad name for Odysseus. We are, then, strongly encouraged to look at Odysseus's meeting with his father as an opportunity for both Odysseus and Laertes to learn something. Furthermore, the language of the passage suggests that, if Odysseus reveals himself, he will learn comparatively little. If he should "kiss and embrace his father and tell him/all, how he had come home and reached the land of his fathers" (24.236–37), there would be less for his father to do or say. He would rejoice, and that would be that. Already then, we have an inkling of what Odysseus is up to. He wants to experience more of his father than simply revealing himself is likely to produce.

The "teasing words" are called forth by Laertes' appearance, which is in fact most remarkable. As he stands there, head down, hoeing his well-kept garden, he is wearing a dirty, patched tunic, patched leather gaiters "to protect him against scratches," gauntlets "for the brambles," and a goatskin hat; and in wearing this costume, he is said to be "making his grief greater" (24.227–31). As we have been told (1.189–92; 11.187–96), Laertes, since long before the arrival of the suitors in the palace, has been showing his grief at the loss of Odysseus by adopting the life of a farm slave. He never comes to town, has one old woman to tend him, and sleeps in winter in the ashes with the slaves, in summer in piles of leaves in his garden. "Increasing his grief" (11.195; 24.231) thus seems to be largely a matter of covering himself up, a withdrawal from pain into the arms of Kalypso—and this of course is a paradox. In any case, the way in which he "makes his sorrow greater" both for himself and for others in the present case is by wearing clothes which are as expressive as possible of misery. Odysseus, rather than reveal himself to his father, deliberately chooses to call attention to Laertes' miserable appearance, and these are the "teasing words" to which the passage refers. He pretends to take his father for a slave, though remarking that in size and shape he appears kingly, like one who, if he were fed and washed, might well "sleep soft, for that is what old men do"

(24.255). By his "teasing words" he accepts and carries through to its end the meaning of what Laertes is trying to express, giving it its full value by contrasting it with the fortunate, kingly old age which belongs to Laertes by right. In other words, instead of avoiding or seeking to obviate his father's pain from a mistaken tenderness, he indulges it to the full.

Incidentally, the emphasis on "sleeping soft" as the way of the old suggests that there is no blame attached to Laertes' withdrawal. It suggests rather the reason for it: the weakness of age. He has reached the time of life for rest, and it is, as we suspected, a question only of the manner of this rest. By his squalor he is suggesting that, without his son, kingly life is nothing to him. Odysseus's teasing words in effect test that claim, and Laertes triumphantly vindicates it. To being mistaken for a slave he makes no protest at all; his whole thought is concentrated on the loss of his son. Thus Odysseus, by accepting the pain inherent in the situation instead of avoiding it, is giving his father a chance to play out his role and be himself. We cannot imagine Odysseus saying all this to himself as he makes his choice, but we do know that he is by nature wise enough to distrust his own pity and brave enough to prefer to have the experience rather than to avoid it, even if it means pain for himself and others. This is the Odysseus of the boar hunt, and of Troy.

For the experience in question is a mutual one, involving not only Laertes' grief for his son's loss but Odysseus's grief for his father's grief. Though at the moment there is no longer any reason for this grief, there has been reason for it for twenty years, and it would be a pity if twenty years of grief should not find their expression. Nor is it a thing which can be accomplished in a moment. Odysseus, unseen, weeps as soon as he sees his father's misery (24.234), and Laertes weeps at his son's speech in which he pretends to have played host to the absent Odysseus (24.280). Their grief then reaches a further stage. As the two converse, the image of Odysseus develops from cherished guest to son lost somewhere on land or sea, devoured by beasts and vultures or eaten by fishes, with no chance for his parents to dress and mourn him or for his wife to close his eyes (24.289–96). Finally, at his "host's" picture of him five years past, departing happy, with good omens, in expectation of further meeting, it is the joyful image that by its contrast pushes grief to the uttermost (24.309–14). Laertes pours dust upon his head, whereat Odysseus feels a surge of pain in his own nostrils. Here, it would seem, Homer has felt the need to go beyond the conventional as he expresses in this way, apparently unique for the heroic style, the extremity of pity which Odysseus is feeling. Now at last the experience has reached its limit, and revelation and recognition can commence. I think we can see that the delay, the deception, and the pain were necessary. A large part of the recognition will be to recognize that this particular great grief has ended, and for that it is necessary first to recognize the grief, a process for which time and suffering are necessary.

After the grief comes the recognition, which itself shows certain remarkable features. First, though the knowledge of his son's return makes Laertes faint away for joy, he refuses to faint until he is sure that what he has received is indeed knowledge. In his son's very embrace he demands proof and gets it, and only then does he collapse. So important in the poem are Odyssean mistrust, caution, and presence of mind.

Second, the means of proof bring into focus another side of Odysseus's nature as well as reiterating the familiar one. He first shows his boar-inflicted scar and names Autolykos but then identifies a large number of fruit trees in the garden in which they stand, which Laertes gave to him as a child and taught him about (24.331–44). At once we see in the old man and his continued care for his garden, despondent though he is, the productive, creative passion which causes his sorrow for the loss of his son. We also see that Odysseus, even as a child, inherited that fruitful urge. Taken together with the boar scar, these trees add new meaning to the phrase "planting evils" and to his name, Odysseus, which the phrase translates. Odysseus was born to be a planter of evils, but a gardener like his father nevertheless. In this very scene we witness the good fruit which the evils he has planted bear.

Coming to, Laertes exclaims, "Father Zeus, surely you gods are still on Olympos" (24.351), recognizing that divine justice has been vindicated by Odysseus's return and the defeat of the suitors and answering the complaints of Eurykleia (19.363–69) and Philoitios (20.201–3) that Zeus is unjust. With this thought of justice and the end of the suitors, Laertes begins to regain his kingly pride. Triumph does for him what it did for his son, and when he is washed and dressed and ready for the feast, Athena makes him look a new man, as she did Odysseus earlier. It is not long until he finds himself wishing that he had been young enough to take part in yesterday's battle, and before we are done, we actually see him hurl his spear and kill Antinoos's father, the leader of the suitors' kinsmen. So powerful is the effect of the joyful recognition which it has been his lot to experience, an effect which would have been less without Odysseus's decision "to test him with teasing words."

One more recognition occurs as Laertes, Odysseus, Telemachos, and the herdsmen are joined at the farmhouse by Dolios and his sons, the farm slaves. One purpose of this development is to add to the forces about to be arrayed against the suitors' kinsmen, but another purpose is served as well. Dolios, who is Penelope's personal slave (4.736), quite naturally asks whether Penelope has been told yet, to which Odysseus replies with emphasis that he need not worry about that (24.407). This simple, brief exchange reminds us that, powerful as the scene with Laertes has been, there has been another more powerful still which preceded it, the recognition of Odysseus and Penelope. As a result these scenes range themselves in descending order of intensity, and as we near the end, we sense the shape of the poem as a whole.

One task remains, to deal with the suitors' kinsmen. Predictably, they assemble and call for vengeance upon the slayers of their sons and brothers, but it is something of a surprise that they blame Odysseus for the deaths of those who were lost during the homecoming as well. As members of the poem's audience we are not used to thinking of Odysseus in these terms, and it is good for us to face the possibility of his guilt so that, by refuting it, we may become quite sure that he is not at fault. We know that his own ship's crew perished through their folly in eating the cattle of the Sun. Those lost to Skylla and the Kyklops were victims of the hazards of the heroic life, hazards to which Odysseus was as exposed as they were. As for the eleven ships lost to the Laistrygonians, there too Homer suggested that it was the victims' own fault, at least in part, for anchoring inside the too-snug harbor. These reflections are not irrelevant to the case of the suitors, who also perished, as we are aware, through their own fault. Like Odysseus's crew on the island of the Sun, they slaughtered and ate cattle they should not have slaughtered, pursuing a course which they were told, and should have known, would be fatal. From this point of view, then, Odysseus is not to be blamed for the deaths either of the men of his fleet or of the suitors. To persuade their kinsmen of this, however, proves to be another matter.

On the one hand, there is the justice of Odysseus's punishment of the suitors; on the other, the terrible pain and anger of the fathers and brothers of the dead. How can these two claims ever be reconciled? The assembly of the suitors' kinsmen itself suggests two methods, and these are ultimately one and the same: recognition of the will of the gods, and recognition that the dead deserved to die—in other words, that justice takes precedence over vengeance. These points of view are introduced by Medon the herald and Phemios the bard, eyewitnesses to the battle in the hall who, to the astonishment of all, join the meeting, and by the prophet Halitherses. Medon speaks for the witnesses. He makes the point that "not without the gods' will/did Odysseus do what he did"; he, Medon himself, saw "an immortal god, who stood by Odysseus/and looked like Mentor in every way." "An immortal god was also evident," Medon reports, "cheering him on from in front and rushing through the hall/putting the suitors to flight" (24.443–49). These are the words of a "wise herald," who by virtue of his office is supposed to know about such things, and they agree with what we have heard of Athena's participation in the battle. If in the previous account she put the suitors to flight by raising the aegis, having earlier taken the form of a swallow and flown up to the rooftree, that is because the Muse knows exactly what happened, whereas what Medon saw was different. As we implied in our comment on the earlier passage, from the human point of view the divine intervention is not strictly visible but rather to be inferred from its results. I take it that Medon saw Athena in the guise of Mentor and, for the rest, herald and diplomat that he is, improved on what he actually saw in order to make the right prevail.

Halitherses, the soothsayer who interpreted the omen of the eagles at the assembly in book 2, rises now to blame not only the suitors but the very men before him. Were they not warned in that earlier assembly by Mentor and himself to stop the suitors' dangerous behavior before it was too late? The kinsmen have brought this disaster upon themselves by their own cowardice (*kakotēti*, 23.455), and if they continue to seek revenge they may merely be inviting further disaster. Halitherses thus adds the element of right and wrong to Medon's identification of the will of the gods by bringing into the argument against vengeance the responsibility of the suitors and their kinsmen for what has happened. To the extent that the kinsmen caused the deaths in question, Odysseus is exonerated. The suitors and their kin are alike responsible in that they engaged in or assented to behavior which, by common consent, was justly punishable. They merely thought that they were secure in this particular case because the man to punish them would not return. What the suitors did was "reckless behavior" (24.458) because they violated the respect due to the property and wife of "a man of note" (24.460). They should have known that their lives were at stake, as Mentor pointed out in book 2. Because Halitherses puts so much stress on punishment as well as on the crime, it is perhaps misleading to call his point a moral one. Nevertheless, we have seen that "wrong" itself is perhaps best defined as behavior that makes others want to kill you. In any case, Halitherses' argument is that, since the suitors' kin brought the disaster on themselves by countenancing their sons' and brothers' dangerous behavior, they have no right to vengeance and may well get hurt if they attempt it. Obviously it is intended that we in the audience should be convinced by this, as indeed are some of the suitors' fathers and brothers. Nevertheless, more than half of those present opt for revenge.

Conflict is about to break out once more in Ithaca: will it go on indefinitely, or will it be settled? The answer is obviously up to the gods, and so the scene is transferred to Olympos, where Athena asks Zeus the question which we have just proposed. He refuses to dictate; Athena, having herself been the architect of the revenge, may do as she pleases; he will simply tell her what would be suitable: that the humans swear to a compact under which Odysseus rules forever, while the gods cause the killing of sons and brothers to be forgotten, a solution resulting in peace and plenty for all (24.472–86). Let us observe first the part in the reconciliation assigned to the gods. Whatever the rights of the case, reconciliation cannot take place in actuality until the bitterness of the kinsmen is to some extent dimmed. To Homer it seems natural that only the gods can bring this about. Second, and this is a related matter, could anything convey more clearly than Zeus's words here that "the suitable" by no means always happens? It is suggested that other things (we have mentioned bitterness) often interfere with what is right and that Zeus by no means always cares to prevent them. Nevertheless, there it is: there does exist a suitable solution for men and gods to avail themselves of if they will—a moral right, as it were, opposed to wrong.

A large body of kinsmen are not yet ready to accept the right, however, and as we view the ensuing battle, we may well find Athena's role in bringing about the reconciliation peculiar. Her function at first seems to be to rouse the fighting spirit of Odysseus and his family to invincible heights, only for it to be curbed later so that the affair may end in reconciliation rather than massacre. Was all this necessary? The result suggests that it was: the angry kinsmen who have been unable to see reason in the recent assembly are thoroughly beaten and cowed, and then at last it is possible to arrange a permanent reconciliation between them and the party of Odysseus. We see further that Odysseus, being more reasonable than they, can restrain himself even in the midst of his battle fury and that, if it were not so, what seems suitable to Zeus could not be brought to pass. The reconciliation depends both on the reestablishment of respect in those who are to be ruled and on the ruler's demonstration that he is worthy of that respect.

On the battlefield Athena appears as Mentor throughout, and it is not clear that the humans know whether the goddess is present or not. This is appropriate because for them to recognize the mere possibility of her presence is sufficient to make events work out as they do. In inspiring Odysseus and his family, for example, she might as well be Mentor himself. We are told that, at the sight of her in the shape of Mentor, Odysseus rejoiced (24.504). Did he suspect her presence under her disguise, as he did in the battle in the hall (22.210)? It would not be strange if he were expecting her, in view of her earlier promises of help (13.393; 20.45–51), and yet it may be simply that he is glad to see another human ally. Homer does not tell us. Instead he sees Odysseus as turning straight to Telemachos and urging him not to disgrace the proven valor of his forebears in the present conflict (24.506–9). Evidently there is a connection between the presence of Mentor-Athena and Odysseus's exhortation, and I think it is to be found in Odysseus's memory of Athena's appearance as Mentor in the battle in the hall. There she urged Odysseus on with "sharp taunts" (22.225), and so now, without waiting for these, Odysseus is stimulated to make his boast. It does not matter whether Mentor this time is perceived as divine or human; the memory of the taunts would have the same effect. The mood in both cases is one of a certain angry excitement. This is borne out when Odysseus's boast leads to Telemachos's spirited reply that his father need not worry about *him* in his present mood, and finally to Laertes' delight at seeing his son and grandson "quarreling about which is the braver" (24.515), a moment which is one of the most famous in the *Odyssey*. Once more we have been invited to contemplate the positive aspect of hostility in one of its many guises.

To complete the process of inspiring Odysseus's party, Mentor now invites Laertes to pray to Athena and hurl his spear (24.517–19). This results in the crucial event of the battle, for the old man actually kills Antinoos's father, Eupeithes, the leader of the other side. There is a temptation here to exalt the power of Athena at Laertes' expense by thinking that only a very powerful goddess could bring such a success to a man so old; but I am sure Homer saw it rather differently. It does not seem impossible for an old and despondent man to be incited to undreamed of heights of valor: one thinks of Lear's "I killed the slave that was a-hanging thee." Inspired by the undreamed of felicity of the occasion, Laertes accomplishes the utterly unexpected and himself surely attributes his feat to the goddess he prayed to at Mentor's suggestion. Nevertheless, as Odysseus and Telemachos now fall upon the enemy, all these events have enough human truth behind them to keep the supernatural from stealing the scene.

What happens next requires some explanation. We hear that "now [Odysseus's party] would have killed them all" (24.528) if Athena had not shouted to the kinsmen to "stop fighting/and be reconciled without bloodshed" (24.531–32). At these words, uttered by Mentor, so far as they can actually see, whatever they may believe, the kinsmen drop their weapons and run for their lives; Odysseus, with a terrible cry, swoops after them "like an eagle." Something seems to have gone wrong. Both Mentor's cry and the kinsmen's response are appropriate. With Odysseus's party putting up so brave and successful a show and with Eupeithes dead, the gods are clearly on Odysseus's side; consequently, the kinsmen are ready to hear a voice counseling peace and reconciliation rather than continued peril. But what is Odysseus doing, preparing to slaughter unarmed men? Antony's old soldier in Shakespeare's play has said it: " 'Tis sport to maul a runner"; Odysseus is both enacting his name and showing the true heroic temper. This is a quality over which Athena presides as happily as she does over sagacity; but it is not the way people are reconciled.

We might now expect Athena to restrain her protégé, but this does not happen. Although she came down from Olympos eager for the peace (24.487) and though as Mentor she has suggested reconciliation to the kinsmen but a moment past, her own heroic soul evidently has now forgotten all that as she watches her human counterpart make his magnificent charge. Therefore Zeus must take a hand. He drops a thunderbolt not before Odysseus's feet but before hers, confirming our hypothesis that it is she who needs reminding. What we must visualize, of course, is the bolt falling before the apparent Mentor, who only then is inspired to cry,

> Zeus-sprung son of Laertes, ingenious Odysseus,
> stop; cease this strife of leveling war,
> or far-seeing Zeus, Kronos's son, will be angry with you.
>
> (24.542–44)

These are wise words, befitting the goddess's more reasonable aspect; but it required Zeus to get them uttered. They do show, however, that she has understood the answer to her question about Odysseus in book 1: Zeus has "odysseused" Odysseus, but Zeus has not been angry with him; by planting evils for him, Zeus has made Odysseus's name eternal. To our satisfaction and approval, Odysseus now not only obeys Athena's words, he rejoices to do so (24.545); he is, after all, her human counterpart. And so at last the poem ends as, by the grace of Zeus, she

> made a sworn treaty for all the future between both sides,
> Pallas Athena, daughter of Zeus who bears the aegis,
> likening herself to Mentor in both form and speech.
>
> (24.546–48)

It makes one wish gods still took human shape.

Works Cited

Austin, N. *Archery at the Dark of the Moon: Poetic Problems in Homer's Odyssey.* Berkeley and Los Angeles, 1975.

Burkert, W. *Greek Religion.* Translated by J. Raffan. Cambridge, Mass., 1985.

Butler, S. *The Humor of Homer and Other Essays.* Books for Libraries Press, Freeport, 1967.

Detienne, M. *Les maîtres de vérité dans la Grèce archaïque.* François Maspero, Paris 1981, original edition, 1967.

Dimock, G. E. "From Homer to Novi Pazar and Back." *Arion* 2, no. 4 (1963): 40–57.

Eastman, M. *The Sense of Humor.* New York, 1921.

Finley, M. I. *The World of Odysseus.* Rev. ed. New York, 1978.

Finnegan, R. *Oral Poetry: Its Nature, Significance, and Social Context.* Cambridge, 1977.

Gantar, K. "Zu Aristoteles' *Poetik* 8, 1451a 23–25." *Ziva Antika* 11 (1962): 294.

Glenn, J. "The Polyphemus Folktale and Homer's *Kyklopeia*." *Transactions of the American Philological Association* 102 (1971):133–81.

Knox, B. M. W. *Oedipus at Thebes.* New Haven and London, 1957.

Lattimore, R., trans. *The Odyssey of Homer.* New York, Evanston, and London, 1965.

Lord, A. B. *The Singer of Tales.* Cambridge, Mass., 1960.

Lorimer, H. L. *Homer and the Monuments.* London, 1950.

Nagy, G. *The Best of the Achaeans: Concepts of the Hero in Archaic Greek Poetry.* Baltimore and London, 1979.

Palmer, G. H., trans. *The Odyssey: Homer.* Bantam, New York, 1962.

Rieu, E. V., trans. *Homer: The Odyssey.* Penguin, Baltimore, 1946.

de Romilly, J. *Perspectives actuelles sur l'épopée homérique, ou comment la recherche peut renouveler la lecture des textes.* Paris, 1983.

Rose, H. J. *A Handbook of Greek Mythology.* New York, 1959.

Shakespeare, W. *King Lear* V, iii, 276; *Antony and Cleopatra* IV, vii, 14.

Stanford, W. B., ed. *The Odyssey of Homer.* London, 1965.

Vermeule, E. *Aspects of Death in Early Greek Art and Poetry.* Berkeley, 1979.

Wace, A. J. B., and Stubbings, F. H. *A Companion to Homer.* London, 1963.

Woodhouse, W. J. *The Composition of Homer's Odyssey.* Oxford, 1930.

<h1 style="text-align:center">Index</h1>

Note: Homer, Odysseus, Penelope, Telemachos, Athena, and Zeus occurred too frequently and variously to be worth indexing in their entirety. I have also left Nestor, Menelaos, and Eumaios unlisted as extremely frequent in their respective sections of the book.

Acheron, 135

Achilles, 5, 265; contest for armor of, 148; dream of Patroklos, 136, 142–44, 151; quarrel of Odysseus and, 95–96, 100; in the underworld, 157–60, 323–26

Aegis, 304

Aeschylus, 65, 257; *Odyssey* as source for, 157, 212

Agamemnon, 95, 110, 112, 113; disagreement with Menelaos, 38–44, 200; murder of, 13, 47, 53, 56, 65, 150, 187, 301, 302; in the underworld, 148, 156–60, 163, 323, 324; vengeance for, 54–55

Agelaos, 273, 275, 300, 304

Aiaia, 122, 131, 162, 163

Aias, son of Oïleus, 56, 58, 65, 110

Aias, son of Telamon, 148–49, 157–60

Aidōs, 41, 98, 102

Aigisthos, 27; example of recklessness, 13–14, 28, 44, 63, 70, 159, 174, 234; murder of Agamemnon, 41–43, 56, 150, 301–2; vengeance on, 53–54

Aiolos, 119–24, 126, 130, 155

Alkinoos, 76, 83–90, 92–96, 99–103, 105–8, 155–56, 175–77, 179–81, 221, 258

Allegory, 75

Amphiaraos, 138

Amphimedon, 324, 326

Amphinomos, 213–14, 234–36, 244–45, 249, 271, 274, 298–300, 307

Amphitrite, 74, 168

Antigone, 32

Antikleia, 134, 147, 149–51, 153–55, 204–5

Antilochos, 157–58

Antinoos, 23, 34–35, 58, 213–14, 225–30, 232–34, 236–38, 244–45, 249, 251, 272–73, 279–80, 282–84, 287–89, 291, 295–97, 302

Antiphates, 122

Apeiraia, 83

Aphrodite, 26, 100–101, 104, 217, 248, 267

Apollo, 28, 43, 52, 79, 92, 153, 221, 229, 269, 288–89, 291, 296

Ares, 100–101, 104, 194

Arete, 81, 83–93, 102–3, 107, 110, 119, 154–56, 165, 180–81

Argos (the dog), 223–24

Aristophanes, 133

Aristotle, 3–4, 209, 260, 296

Artemis, 48, 78–80, 267

Athena, anger of, 13–14, 26, 38–45, 56, 65–66, 184–85

Athens, 86

Atlas, 14–15

Austin, 120

Autolykos, 256–60, 266, 325, 330

Belly, the, 77, 90, 203, 222, 227

Bergson, 100

Boar hunt on Parnassos, 3–4, 258, 306, 329

Burkert, 7, 78
Butler, 102

Cape Lithinion, 43
Cattle lifting and false swearing, 256–57
Cattle of the sun, 163, 164, 170–72, 272, 331
Colonization, age of, 70, 118
Conrad, 70
Councils of the gods, 63–64

Deiphobos, 49–50, 104
Delphic oracle, 95
Demodokos, 95–96, 100–101, 103, 107–8, 165, 176
Detienne, 6
Dimock, 7
Diomedes, 39–40, 49
Dolios, 312, 330

Eastman, 100–101
Echeneos, 88
Eidothea, 52–53, 55, 265
Elpenor, 132, 134, 136, 140–41, 143–47, 151, 163, 175, 181
Elysion, 54, 88, 151
Erebos, 136, 139, 148–49, 167
Erechtheus, 86
Euboia, 88
Eupeithes, 334
Euripides, 65, 78, 168
Euryalos, 97–98, 101–2, 159
Eurykleia, 4, 24, 36–37, 40, 60–61, 218, 247, 255–57, 259–61, 269–70, 309, 311–12, 316–17, 330
Eurylochos, 125–26, 129–30, 170–72
Eurymachos, 16, 23, 33, 35, 201, 206, 215, 221, 238–39, 243–44, 247, 249, 273, 284, 287–89, 297–98, 300, 303, 312
Eurymedon, king of the giants, 85
Eurynome, the housekeeper, 237
Eurytion, the centaur, 289
Eurytos, 99
Evil, problem of, 14, 20, 22, 57, 61–62, 64, 66–70, 74, 125, 132, 144, 146, 154, 159–60, 165, 200, 204, 215, 217, 223, 248, 260, 271, 320, 323–26, 334

Finnegan, 3

Folktale, 116–18, 287
Furies, 25, 152, 202, 227, 257, 267

Gaia, 109
Gantar, 4
Genesis, book of, 69
Glenn, 116
Gods (heaven, divine agency), 5, 13–14, 16–20, 25–34, 38–45, 58, 69, 72, 74–75, 85, 88, 98, 100, 104–5, 113, 121–23, 126, 132, 137, 144–47, 171, 174, 182–84, 186, 193, 196, 200–201, 210–11, 226, 235, 243, 265–67, 269–71, 284–85, 295–96, 302–5, 309–10, 317, 319, 322, 325, 330–31, 333–34
Good, the, 233
Gorgon's head, 149

Halitherses, 30, 32, 35, 286, 331–32
Harpies, 267
Hektor, 141–43
Helen, 47–51, 54–55, 67, 100, 104–5, 152–53, 200, 202, 210, 303, 319
Helios, the sun, 8–11, 66, 122, 129, 134, 138, 144, 163, 171–74, 254, 309, 331
Hephaistos, 87, 100–101, 104
Hera, 5, 56, 103, 167, 267
Herakles, 99, 149, 151–52, 159–61, 278
Hermes, 13, 28, 63–67, 101, 126–28, 160, 174, 256–57, 323, 325
Hermione, 47
Herodotos, 6, 141
Heroines, list of, 151–55, 157
Hesiod, 6
Human advancement, 113–16
Hymn to Hermes, 256

Idea of the world, 8, 63, 286
Identity, 68, 74, 90–91, 99, 127–29, 146, 149, 154, 156, 175, 194, 210, 216, 218, 220, 224, 228–29, 232, 248, 258, 260, 264, 321
Idomeneus, 195, 251–52
Iliad, 3, 5–7, 10, 25–26, 85, 95–96, 124, 126, 128, 134, 136–37, 141–44, 152, 156, 173, 214, 227, 234, 250, 265, 296
Ino-Leukothea, 71–74, 257
Intentional fallacy, 3
Invocation of the Muse, 8–12, 24, 170–71
Iphitos, 256, 278
Ipthime, 61–62

Iris, 232
Iros, 232–34, 238, 286, 289, 310
Ismaros, 110, 321
Ithaca, 15, 21, 32, 55, 57, 62–63, 66, 70, 76, 103, 109, 111, 120–21, 124, 126, 129–31, 133, 145–47, 156, 174–75, 177, 179, 183–84, 186, 194, 200, 307, 322
Ithacans, 31, 33, 35, 37, 40, 60, 213, 318

James, 299
Jason and the Argo, 167–68
Joyce's *Ulysses*, 240
Justice, 13–14, 19–20, 23, 25–26, 28, 33, 35–36, 54, 58, 67, 113–15, 117, 159, 193, 195–96, 213, 216, 232–33, 235, 245, 247, 251, 256, 270, 275, 286, 295–97, 303, 305–6, 314, 327, 330–33

Kalypso, 12–15, 21, 23–24, 28, 52, 54, 55, 62–63, 65–74, 77, 91, 97, 100, 109, 115, 117, 135, 140–41, 161, 165, 170, 178, 181, 217, 221, 223–24, 328
Kassandra, 56, 157
Kastor and Polydeukes, 152–53
Kikones, 110
Kimmerians, 134, 138
King Echetos, 233, 289
Kirke, 68, 102, 107, 109, 119, 121–41, 146, 155, 160, 162–71, 178, 240, 261
Kleos, 20–21, 24, 80, 238–40, 249–51, 254–55, 260
Klytaimnestra, 13, 28, 42, 53–54, 152–53, 157, 302, 324
Knox, 28
Kokytos, 135, 138
Kreon, 32
Ktesippos, 273, 304
Ktimene, 204–5
Kyklops (Polyphemos), Kyklopes, 14, 76–77, 85–86, 89, 99, 111–19, 122–23, 127, 129, 144, 159, 163–64, 166, 170, 177, 185, 213, 216, 227–28, 259, 264, 296, 301–2, 310, 322, 331

Laertes, 24, 37, 60, 67, 109, 204, 208, 209, 251, 312, 323–24, 327–30, 334
Laistrygonians, 119–25, 130, 155, 177, 331
Laodamas, 96, 98, 101
Leiokritos, 35, 304
Leodes, 282–83, 288, 306–7

Leopold Bloom, 240
Leto, 79, 88, 159
Lord, 12
Lotus-eaters, 110–11, 123–24

Magic, 71
Majority, 35
Marathon, 86
Marriage, 79
Mediterranean, 135, 179
Medon, the herald, 58, 60, 64, 307–8, 331–32
Megapenthes, 47
Melampus, 202
Melanthios, 220–21, 225, 233, 249, 270, 283, 300–302, 304, 309, 312–15
Melantho, 242, 244, 249, 255, 288, 312–13
Menos, 16, 21, 24, 26, 30, 33–34, 51
Mentes, 16–18, 20–21, 26, 30–31, 34, 40, 58–59, 290
Mentor, 28–31, 33–36, 38–42, 44–46, 58, 60, 64, 202, 302–3, 331–35
Mētis, 30, 112, 124
Minos, 149, 159, 252
Motto, Stoic, 74
Muses, 5–8, 28, 118, 325

Nagy, 95
Nausikaa, 77–81, 83–86, 88–89, 91–92, 99, 102–3, 109, 154, 165–66, 176, 180–81, 210, 239
Nausithoos, 76, 85–86
Neleus, 152, 202
Nemesis, 25–26, 29–31, 33, 35
Neoptolemos, 47, 158
Neriton, 186
Noemon, 33–34, 57, 71

Odysseus: aliases of, 111–12, 253, 328; household of, 300, 310–15; mildness of, 27, 64, 215, 310; name of, 4, 13, 25–27, 39, 48, 61, 67–68, 71, 73, 105, 108, 111–13, 124, 141, 154, 168, 177, 193–94, 196, 200, 208, 218, 225, 230, 238, 244, 248, 252, 255, 257–60, 264, 266, 295–96, 319–20, 325, 330, 335; scar of, 256–60, 287, 330; wealth of, 189, 196
Oidipus, 152, 157, 269
Olive (thicket, wood, tree) as associated with Odysseus, 116, 177, 186, 319

Olympos, 77
Opening of the poem, 12–15
Oral technique, 11, 240, 297, 329
Orestes, 13, 27–28, 40, 43, 54, 158, 257
Orion, 149, 159
Otos and Ephialtes, 153

Pallas Athena, 17, 26, 62, 65, 82, 182, 274, 335
Palmer, 319–20
Pandareos's daughters, 267
Paris, 47, 49–50
Parry, 11
Patroklos, 10, 128, 136–37, 142–43, 151, 157–58, 265
Peira, 83, 85, 87–89, 92, 96–100, 104–5, 303, 316, 318–19, 327–30
Peirithoos's wedding, 289
Peisistratos, 46–47, 49, 52, 57, 105, 199, 200, 206
Peleus, 158
Penelope's marriage, 15–16, 18, 21–22, 36–37, 58–60, 240–41, 251, 255, 262–63, 267, 274–75, 278–80, 289–90, 294
Perse, 122
Persephone, 122, 132, 135, 137–38, 149–50, 159
Phaeacians, 64, 74, 76–78, 80–81, 83–92, 94–102, 105, 107, 109–12, 118–20, 125, 146, 154, 156, 165–66, 170, 173, 175–76, 178–84, 206, 232, 321
Phemios, 7–8, 22, 38, 65, 307–8, 331
Pherai, 201, 278
Philoctetes, 98–99
Philoitios, 212, 270–71, 279, 283–85, 287, 301, 304, 311, 318
Philomeleides, 52
Phorkys, 177, 179, 186
Phrontis Onetorides, 43
Pindar, 73, 168, 269
Planktai, 163, 166–69
Planting evils, death and doom, etc., 26, 71, 73, 194–95, 200, 210, 218–19, 249, 296, 330, 335
Plato, 8, 233
Polis, 76
Polites, 126
Pope, 326
Porter, 18
Poseidon, 13–14, 22, 38, 45, 63, 69–75, 81, 85, 88, 105–6, 113, 115, 117–18,
120, 145–46, 151, 166, 173, 176, 179–82, 184, 260, 316, 321–22
Priam, 143, 227
Prophecies and omens, 13, 17, 26, 28, 30, 31–33, 44, 58, 113, 145, 150, 200, 202, 206, 210, 219, 229, 236–37, 261–63, 268, 271–72, 275, 282, 286, 320
Proteus, 51, 53–56, 65–66, 119, 219
Psukhē (ghost), 10, 112, 117–18, 121, 131, 133–34, 139–40, 142, 146, 147–51, 156, 161, 163, 169, 172, 175, 260, 267, 324–25
Puns, 73, 97, 125, 164, 211, 214, 221, 254
Pyriphlegethon, 135, 138

Recklessness, 9–10, 12, 13–14, 24, 29–30, 32–33, 38, 42, 44, 98, 115, 129, 174, 196, 234–35, 309, 314, 317, 331–32
Recognition scenes, 182–83, 186, 203, 207–12, 223–24, 254, 256, 259–61, 284–87, 295, 314–22, 327–31
Removal of the arms, 212, 246, 297
Rhadamanthys, 88, 92
Rhexenor, 86, 89
Rieu, 165
de Romilly, 3
Rumor, 5–6

Scherie, 74–76, 86, 88, 91, 93–94, 103, 109, 171, 176–77, 179, 185
Sirens, 163–66, 170
Sisyphos, 159
Skylla and Charybdis, 163, 166–70, 172, 174, 176, 331
Slavery, 190–92, 223, 310–12
Solon, 30
Sophokles, 31–32, 42, 141, 149, 157, 269
Sound (of Homer's poetry), 8–12, 14–15, 293
Spinners, 87
Stanford, 168, 180, 191, 272, 281
Stesichoros, 8
Stubbings, 281
Styx, 135

Tantalos, 159
Teiresias, 32, 131–33, 137–38, 140, 144–47, 158–59, 161, 171, 181, 187, 320–21
Telemachos, coming of age of, 21

Themis, 159
Theoklymenos, 201–3, 206, 208, 217–19, 229, 236, 262, 270, 272, 275, 277, 312
Thersites, 141
Thetis, 265, 325
Thucydides, 112
Tityos, 88, 92, 159
Trojan War, 39, 47–48, 65, 91, 95–96, 103–5, 107, 109–12, 115, 153, 163, 165, 167, 190, 194–95, 234, 254–55, 259, 316, 321–22, 329

Utopia, 83

Vermeule, 134
Virgil, 133, 303
Virtue, 30

Woodhouse, 14